CONTINENTS OF EXILE

REMEMBERING

MR. SHAWN'S

NEW YORKER

William Shawn. New York. 1968

VED MEHTA

CONTINENTS OF EXILE

REMEMBERING

MR. SHAWN'S

NEW YORKER

THE INVISIBLE ART
OF EDITING

The Overlook Press
WOODSTOCK & NEW YORK

First published in the United States in 1998 by
The Overlook Press, Peter Mayer Publishers, Inc.
Lewis Hollow Road
Woodstock, New York 12498

An excerpt from this book first appeared in *The Atlantic Monthly*.

Library of Congress Cataloging-in-Publication Date

Mehta, Ved.
Remembering Mr. Shawn's New Yorker:
the invisible art of editing/ Ved Mehta.
p. cm. — (Continents of exile)
The author's 8th autobiographical work.
1. Shawn, William. 2. Editors—United States—Biography.
3. Periodical editors—United States—Biography.
4. New Yorker (New York, N.Y. : 1925) 5. Mehta, Ved.
6. Authors, American—20th century—Biography.
7. Blind authors—United States—Biography.
I. Title.   II. Series: Mehta, Ved, Continents of exile.
PN149.9.S53Z77   1998   808'.027'09—dc21 [B] 98-10022

Manufactured in the United States of America

ISBN 0-87951-876-6
First Edition
1 3 5 7 9 8 6 4 2

To John and Patricia Grigg

FOREWORD

A friend who read this book in manuscript writes:

Your book is an unabashed work of veneration, and I imagine that your decision to retain the title "Mr." before "Shawn," which you always use when you refer to him in conversation, is a deliberate decision to distance yourself from him. Yet, because this is a book that concerns a man who is no longer alive and who was such a very close friend of yours for so many years, it strikes me as something of an affectation to call him "Mr. Shawn." I am sure you have thought long and hard about this, and my discomfort may be due to no more than that hero worship is out of fashion and unfamiliar nowadays. I can only say that for myself I would feel more comfortable if you were to call him simply "Shawn."

Maybe so. Indeed, writing of William Shawn, who died in 1992, at the age of eighty-five, as Mr. Shawn throughout this book may strike some not only as an affectation but also as an oddity. Certainly in his lifetime it was a source of amusement for some people who did not know him that not just I but many of his colleagues who were older than he was generally addressed him as and spoke of him as Mr. Shawn. He himself, however, addressed many of his colleagues, and his assistants and secretaries as well, with the same formality. Moreover, in speaking about even those colleagues of his whom he had known for a long time and with whom he was on a first-name basis, he referred to them with their formal title. (Frequently, he also referred to

Harold Ross, *The New Yorker's* founder and his immediate predecessor, who had died in 1951, as Mr. Ross.) His colleagues, therefore, by calling him Mr. Shawn, were doing no more than returning his gesture of deference and respect. Whatever the origins of
the convention—his shyness, his punctilio, his inbred courtesy—
its effect was to sustain a certain formality, calm, and order in the
editorial process of bringing out a weekly magazine; after all, as
an editor he had to deal constantly with writers and artists, who
often had big egos, often led turbulent lives, and were often
seething with emotions. The little formality of address drew an
invisible line between him and us, making clear that when it
came to upholding his professional standards he would be inflexible, although he would be completely flexible when it came to
helping writers and artists with personal matters. In any event,
the spouses and children of his colleagues and the people he knew
socially were under no such constraint, and they usually called
him Bill. And there was something of the plain Bill about him—
simplicity of habits and lack of pretension, right down to his
dress. Finally, as my friend suggests, I did venerate him as I
would a hero, but so did most of my colleagues. A. J. Liebling,
who was not normally given to hero worship, once compared
Mr. Shawn—in his own particular domain—to Mahatma Gandhi
and also to Winston Churchill. Like the rest of us, Joe was nothing if not irreverent: irreverence was our stock in trade. We also
realized that in this democratic age, when all of us are supposed
to be equal, and in these psychologically sophisticated times,
when all of us are supposed to act only from motives of self-
interest, the whole notion of anyone's being a hero was anachro-
nistic, if not absurd. No doubt, if we had been living in the Old
World, which honored its citizens of "degree and quality" with
titles, he might have been Sir William, or something higher. But
in the essentially middle-class New World, which abhorred titles
and honorifics as monarchist, "Mr." became a part of Shawn's
name—a little like "Lord" in the name of Joseph Conrad's

protagonist Lord Jim, or, from a different perspective, "the Venerable" in the name of the medieval historian and theologian the Venerable Bede.

Although this book is based largely on research into the public record, on conversations and correspondence with my *New Yorker* colleagues, and, above all, on my memories and my close reading of *The New Yorker* for thirty-five years (from 1959 to 1994), during which I was first a contributor to and then a staff writer on the magazine, I could not have undertaken to write it without gaining the consent and the coöperation of Mr. Shawn, who edited almost everything I wrote and was also my mentor. He was an intensely private—even a secretive—man, and ordinarily didn't want anything written about him. Indeed, it suited his temperament that all his work as editor in chief of *The New Yorker* was anonymous and was carried on behind the scenes—that his role, in its way as imaginative and creative as the roles of his writers and artists, was as invisible as theirs were visible. In my case, he made an exception to his rule of silence only because the book was to be part of my ongoing autobiographical series, Continents of Exile, which he had edited and had published in *The New Yorker* over the years. My thanks to him are unbounded.

I also want to express my gratitude to Mr. Shawn's widow, Cecille, and their sons, Wallace and Allen, for they have all given me unsparing help, so personal that there is no way of acknowledging it in a note like this; to Marisa Kantor, Deborah McLauchlan, Nina Nowak, and Elizabeth Wagner, who at various times were my amanuenses, and whose responses in the course of the work immeasurably enriched this book; to Gwyneth Cravens, Charles McGrath, Hilary Rubinstein, Jonathan Schell, and William Whitworth, who read and generously commented upon drafts of the manuscript; to Eleanor Gould Packard, for her inimitable editorial work on the book; and to my wife, Linn, for everything. It goes without saying that none of them bear any responsibility for what appears in the text: the responsibility is all mine. Finally, I wish to express my thanks again to Cecille Shawn, this time for her permission to quote material from the Shawn papers, and to The New Yorker Magazine, Inc., for permission to reprint a substantial part of his Comment (copyright 1985); my thanks to Sir Isaiah Berlin (1909-1997), Jasper Griffin, Elizabeth Hardwick, Ruth Jhabvala, William Maxwell, Dom Moraes, and Lillian Ross, for their permission to quote from or reproduce their letters; my thanks also to Eleanor Cousins for her permission to quote letters of Norman Cousins (1912-1990), to Joel White (1931-1997) for his permission to quote a letter of E. B. White (1899-1985), and to McMaster University Library for its permission to quote a letter of Bertrand Russell (1872-1970). The frontispiece and an early portrait of Mr. Shawn are reproduced with the permission of Fairchild Syndication and Hilde Hubbick, respectively. Under another heading, I wish to express my gratitude to S. I. Newhouse, Jr., for continuing *The New Yorker's* long-standing agreement to provide me with an office and an amanuensis on the magazine's premises; and to the Freedom Forum Media Studies Center, which by selecting me as a senior fellow, 1996-1997, helped me complete this book.

V.M.

New York
December, 1997

CONTENTS

PHOTOGRAPHS

William Shawn. New York. 1968 / frontispiece

CONTINENTS OF EXILE

REMEMBERING

MR. SHAWN'S

NEW YORKER

I

A STORY IN THE NEW YORKER

WHEN I WAS THINKING OF SETTLING IN INDIA AFTER graduating from Oxford—by then I'd been away in the West for ten years—I had written to Norman Cousins, the editor of *The Saturday Review*, who was a friend of my father's, for his advice on how to go about it. He had written back:

4 September 1959

Dear Ved:

You want to know what the best way is of finding your way back to India. I should have supposed that the question should go the other way around. You will have no trouble in metabolizing your way into your homeland. Your country, on the other hand, may have some trouble in getting to know the new man that is you and giving you a place commensurate with your stature and capabilities. . . .

You are only now at the beginning. You have the responsibility, therefore, to do those things that will best contribute to your own continued development. In doing this, you also serve your country and, in a more basic sense, the cause of people everywhere who want to believe in the limitless possibilities of the human mixture.

Norman could be embarrassingly extravagant—even rhapsodic—in his enthusiasms, and this particular enthusiasm of his had the effect of making me feel uneasy. At Oxford, I'd become so sensitive to people's style that I was put off by his writing; many of the observations in his letter struck me as well-meaning rather than accurate. Still, my father, who had met him about a decade earlier, when Norman spent some time in New Delhi interviewing Prime Minister Nehru for his book "Talks with Nehru," set great store by his opinion, and I—in part, no doubt, because I had become blind shortly before I reached the age of four—set great store by my father's opinion. Moreover, Norman had written a high-flown, emotional review of my young autobiography, "Face to Face," which I'd finished just before going up to Balliol College, Oxford, as a freshman, three years earlier, at the age of twenty-two, and he had also put a drawing of me on the cover of his magazine. Although I was touched by that generous gesture, I felt that I could never measure up to his grandiose expectations of me. Yet my father, perhaps because of his upbringing in British India, seemed to think that doing well in life often depended on having friends in high places. As children, my brothers and sisters and I had all rebelled against this view of the world and had wanted to make our own way. Still, in some corner of my mind, without knowing it, I must have grown up to be my father's son.

I had just spent two turbulent months in India—months that led me to postpone the decision of where I should live—and now I was on a plane taking me to New York so I could go to Harvard, where I had a prize fellowship to do a Ph.D. in history. I suddenly remembered Norman, and felt the need to explain to him and to others how India had affected me and why I had chosen to postpone my decision about settling there. In fact, I suddenly felt the need to write a sort of postscript to "Face to Face," to bring it up to date.

The plane made a stop at London's Heathrow Airport, and I called Kingsley Martin, the longtime editor of the British weekly *The New Statesman and Nation,* and asked if he would be interested in my Indian article. I had come to know Kingsley, a man of shrewd, independent judgment, through "Face to Face." After it was published in England, he had written to me, "I have been reading your book over the week-end with very great pleasure. It is a book to keep and reread." Some time later, I had sent him a little article I'd written about my experiences at Oxford. He had rejected it, but with a very pleasant letter, saying, "My guess is that the time has come for you to work very hard on improving your writing. Not that it is bad in any way, but that you might be able to make it far better with pruning, compressing, and sharpening. However, we will talk about this when we meet." During my Oxford years, we became fast friends, and later he put me up for his club, the Savile.

Now, when I got him on the telephone from the airport, he said, "We could always use a political article on India by you. But the article you have in mind sounds personal and impressionistic. That would not be suitable for our readers. What about trying your idea on David Astor?"

I felt nervous about ringing Astor, the editor of the London *Observer.* Although I had several friends on the paper and had visited its offices, I knew Astor only by his reputation, and some of my reporter friends referred to him as God. In any event, I didn't think that my writing was up to his paper's standard. I was so much in awe of the *Observer* (as it then was) that whenever I could I read practically every word of it—even Katharine Whitehorn's column for women, on, say, "Tips to Mothers," for the sheer pleasure of her style. The paper had taught me a lot about England and the world, about the revolutions taking place in theatre and music in the late fifties, and about letters and politics generally. But now I decided that I would try Astor. His paper had published an extremely favorable review of "Face to Face." Moreover, he was a Balliol man and was known to be hospitable to people from his college.

I got Astor on the line just as my flight was called. He's going to ask me to describe my idea for the article in two minutes, and I will be unhinged, I thought. Instead, he asked, "How long will your screed be?" His manner, at once grand and pointed, took me aback. Reaching for a figure out of thin air, I said, "Oh, thirteen thousand words."

"The most we could do would be fifteen hundred," he said. "The American magazines like long, boring things. You might try one of them."

Back on the plane, I told myself that since his paper ran to only fourteen pages he couldn't possibly use the kind of long article I had in mind. Still, his response, together with Kingsley's, left me feeling limp and discouraged.

Almost as soon as I got to Harvard, I started making trips to New York and peddling the idea of the postscript to various newspapers and magazines. I had no trouble seeing editors. Some of them lorded it over me; Philip Horton, the executive editor of *The Reporter,* for instance, asked me how I thought I could aspire to appear in the company of luminaries like Arthur M. Schlesinger, Jr., who regularly graced its pages. Others—among them Carmel Snow, the chairman (as she was then called) of the editorial board of *Harper's Bazaar*; Irita Van Doren, the editor of the New York *Herald Tribune Book Review*; and John Fischer, the editor of *Harper's Magazine*—took me to lunch at expensive restaurants, like Château Henri IV, and listened to me with half an ear. A mere mention of the idea of a postscript, however, seemed to cast a pall over our meetings. After all, I was reminded, the book had been out for more than two years. If there was some additional material, it surely belonged in a new edition. Anyway, a magazine should not be expected to publish what seemed like an appendix to a book. For my part, I wondered how writers survived on nothing but lunches. I wished I could tell the basically discouraging, if hospitable, editors what I thought of them; but that, I felt, was a luxury granted only to those with private means and no fear of consequences. My series of dead-end conversations with editors should have made it clear to me that there was something wrong with my idea, but I kept pressing on, as if dogged determination were all I needed in order to succeed.

Stopping in at Norman Cousins's office, I brought up the subject of the postscript with him.

"Did you suggest it to Ted Weeks?" he asked. Aside from Norman himself, Edward A. Weeks, the editor of The *Atlantic Monthly* Press, who had edited and published "Face to Face," was my only real friend in the American writing establishment. The two men had so little in common that it was hard to think of them as working in the same field. Weeks was sedate and literary, his talk full of contemporary writers like Hemingway and of country pursuits like fishing. Norman was brisk and political, and what he enjoyed most was talking about world statesmen and big causes. In a voice that was as warm and rough as his handshake, Norman added, "I'm sure Ted would jump at the idea."

"Weeks was the first of many editors to whom I've mentioned the idea, but he, like all the others, wants something short," I said. "He has all the good will in the world, but he's hemmed in by the constraints of space in his magazine."

As we talked, Norman kept jumping up and taking from a bookshelf one or another of a group of primitive African artifacts he had collected on his travels, and handing it to me, then wait-ing expectantly to see whether I could tell what it was and per-haps whether I could admire it with my fingers as he did with his eyes. It seemed like a second- or third-grade test at a school for the blind. Even as I correctly identified the artifacts, I squirmed, feeling guilty at not being able to live up to his kind, outgoing nature.

"What's this?"

"A giraffe."

"Why don't you do a thousand-word teaser for the S.R.?" he suggested. *Atlantic* articles finished just as one got really inter-ested, but the ones in *The Saturday Review*—or *S.R.*, as he called his magazine—were like little introductions to articles that might be written for *The Atlantic* one day.

"I couldn't possibly," I said. "There is too much to say. But thank you all the same."

"And this?"

"A zebra."

"How many words would it take, then?"

"About thirteen thousand words, I think."

"This?"

"A rhinoceros."

"I know what," he said abruptly. He opened his office door, stepped out, said something to his secretary, and came back in, almost in one swoop. He was restless and fast-moving, and seemed to be happiest when he was doing something active.

Soon he was describing me and my project in lavish terms to someone on the phone, as if I were not in the room.

At one point, I tried to step out, but he handed me the tele-phone, saying, "Talk to William Shawn, the editor of *The New Yorker*."

I had not heard of Mr. Shawn and was scarcely familiar with the magazine. But I was aware of its great reputation and its mys-tique—qualities that made me think it would be the last place to welcome a personal article by a struggling twenty-five-year-old graduate student. Yet I recalled that the magazine had published a brief review of my book and, in it, had described my character in one unsettling word, which when I read it gave me a shock of recognition. The word was "truculence."

I now found myself speaking to a person whose voice was hard to make out. At first, I thought this person must be a very youthful man who worked for William Shawn. In my Oxford setting, voices had tended to be forceful. This one was quiet and gentle, and even seemed on the verge of a quaver, although it hardly ever actually quavered. It was very clear and friendly. Above all, it had not a hint of the self-importance or condescension I had come to associate with editors. But I soon found out that I was indeed speaking with William Shawn.

"How long are you going to be in New York?" he asked.

"Only a day or two," I said. Actually, I had planned to return to Harvard that evening and had made no provision for an overnight stay, and I had no money.

"Would it be convenient for you to drop by today for a cup of tea?"

I remember thinking how ironic it was that the editor of such a supposedly sophisticated magazine should sound natural. I was bowled over. "Yes, please," I said eagerly.

"What time would suit you?" he asked.

"What time would suit *you*?" I asked.

He was reluctant to propose a time, and, although normally I would have taken the initiative, his courtesy was so disarming that I couldn't find my tongue. It took some negotiating in the manner of "After you" before we settled upon four o'clock.

❧

AT THE APPOINTED time, I went to the *New Yorker* offices, at 25 West Forty-third Street. On the nineteenth floor, I gave my name to the receptionist, and Mr. Shawn himself came out and shook my hand. (At other magazines, a secretary had invariably come out to greet me and usher me into the office of the editor.) I was interested to discover that his voice was as small as on the telephone, and also that he was a couple of inches shorter than I. I eventually learned that he stood five feet five and a half inches tall, had rosy cheeks and blue eyes, wore horn-rimmed glasses, and was dressed in a dark-blue suit, a white oxford button-down shirt, and black shoes. (I will explain in due course how I gather visual impressions.) The few editors-in-chief I had met tended to be tall, with big voices and big handshakes, as if having a domineering presence went with their august job. When I met with such editors, I had tried to adopt their bold, almost aggressive manner, feeling that if I did not deal with them on their own terms I would not be taken seriously. But Mr. Shawn's manner was so soft and guileless that I was caught off guard, and I found myself saying, "I'm so sorry I'm shaking so much, but I am very nervous."

He laughed warmly, and that made me feel at ease. I noticed that he had a faint smell of witch-hazel after-shave, which I associated with my father.

I followed Mr. Shawn along a couple of corridors, which had the hush of Sleepy Hollow and made me wonder how a weekly magazine was put out from those premises. We walked into his office. It was a large, cheerful corner room. On the walls were caricatures and drawings, one of them signed in a child's hand "Wallace." The desk had ranged across it neat piles of manuscripts and proofs, along with jars of pencils.

Mr. Shawn offered me the end of a sofa near his desk. Most of the sofa was stacked with large manila envelopes, no doubt containing more manuscripts and proofs. Mr. Shawn sat down in an upholstered swivel desk chair—beside which were a typewriter and a telephone, and behind which was a stand holding the Second Edition of Webster's New International Dictionary—and turned to me.

After his secretary, Pat Broun, brought us each a cup of tea, I suddenly realized I had his full attention, as if he had set aside all his concerns and interests and kept a completely open mind for what I had to say. The experience was so heady that my words poured out of me, and I found I was thinking and saying things about my project and about myself which were so honest that they almost invited rejection.

"I am not a real writer," I said. "I just want to get a few things off my chest about Oxford and India—to update my autobiography, as it were, most of which I wrote when I was twenty."

He said that he knew about the autobiography.

I went on to say that at Oxford many of my literati friends had written for various undergraduate publications, but that I hadn't. "Many of them led a bohemian existence and engineered a coup in this or that publication, whereas I had a dark-suit persona and was so apolitical that I didn't even know the names of editors who decided which undergraduate writers got the limelight and which ones were snubbed," I explained. "Like many of my scholarly friends, I had mostly contempt for undergraduate publications and thought of them as 'rags.' Compared with the abiding values of scholarship and academic life, the posturing and self-advertisement of the literati seemed fleeting. At the same time, many of my close friends were literati, but they were both writers and scholars—were able, as it were, to run with the hare and hunt with the hounds—and I secretly wished I could be one of them."

"Would you like to write about your literati Oxford friends?" he asked.

"Oh, no," I said, realizing that I had gone off at a tangent. "I was just saying all that to tell you I am not a writer. I don't know why I am here taking up so much of your time."

"You are not taking up my time," he said. "I am enjoying our conversation."

"What I meant to say was that my time at Balliol College, Oxford, had a deep effect on me and changed the way I felt about

India," I explained, and I told him that I had just spent two months in the country after ten years' absence, and had discovered that the India I'd carried in my head bore no relation to the real place—that my memory of that India might have been exceptionally sharp and vivid because I had been abruptly cut off from it when I was fifteen, and that my impression of it had become petrified because I had not been able to revise and reinterpret my childhood experience of it. My return had taught me that there was no way I could hold on to my romantic notions of the country while I was seeking to accommodate myself to the day-to-day demands of the real India. I went on to say that I'd had trouble coping with the combined excitement and disappointment of my return—with my relatives' treatment of me as if I hadn't changed at all, with their total incomprehension of the eruptions and landslides that had reshaped my soul in the West. Even though I tried to slow down my pulse rate to the, as it were, thin-blooded Indian level, I said, I found myself homesick for the West. In some part of my mind, I knew that I would not be in India long, so I avoided pressing any disagreements and didn't make any real effort to fit in. Indeed, I met up with an Indian friend from Oxford, the poet Dom Moraes, in New Delhi, and we travelled and bummed around like two spoiled Oxford brats, spending some time with extremely flirtatious but essentially innocent teen-age girls, whom we called the "pinks"; staying with a Nepalese prince who was reputed to have a flock of concubines and to fret about losing them in a revolution; indulging in spirited high jinks; appearing extravagant in a poor country; and adopting arrogant personae. The impulse behind much of what we did was self-protection, but whenever I stopped to think about our conduct I felt demoralized and guilt-ridden.

Here I ceased speaking, for I felt that I had been blathering about all kinds of things that were perhaps only tangentially relevant to my Indian article.

I thought that the reason I'd said so much might be that I had never before had anyone in my life listen to me at as deep a level as he was doing, with no wish to judge—with only boundless interest and curiosity. He seemed to listen with childlike wonder, his gaze so steady and penetrating that I felt he was looking straight into my soul. Most people in conversation tried to impress you, hurried you along, had their own preconceptions or agendas, or were distracted by their own worries or cares. In contrast, he seemed to absorb words as a musician absorbs music.

"Is it your homecoming that you would like to write about, then?"

"Yes, homecoming," I said, and I thought, "Homecoming" is much better than "postscript." His mere use of the word gives a form to all the flotsam and jetsam that have been knocking around in my head.

"Did you meet people in India whom you admired?" he asked.

"I wish I could respond to life with the idealism of Prime Minister Nehru, whom I got to know a little—I had lunch with him," I said. "He seemed so at peace with himself. He did not seem to be at all conscious of the power he had—in fact, seemed hardly aware of his gifts."

"He sounds wonderful. You might find a way to write about him."

I felt like saying that he and Nehru were kindred spirits, but I checked myself, because I had become aware that as I was talking almost confessionally he had listened to me with the formality of a priest, and that to say anything personal about him would be to overstep the bounds of propriety.

"Do you think it's an article that *The New Yorker* might be interested in?" I asked abruptly. I had talked for almost an hour without getting to the point.

After a moment, he said, "I don't think that your article sounds like a *New Yorker* piece—although I don't know what that

13

is. But if you write it, and want to send it to me, I would be glad to read it and help you revise it. I would also try to think of a magazine that might be interested in publishing it."

I felt a little disheartened. In some part of my mind, I had thought that his listening to me with complete attention meant that he would accept the article. I wanted to ask how I could go about writing an article for *The New Yorker*—for him. But I realized that if I did I would come off sounding like a child who was asking his father to do his homework.

Instead, I said, "How long do you think the piece should be?" Not knowing what to say, I was trying to sound professional by asking him the question that editors had asked me, and for which I'd had no satisfactory answer.

"You should not worry about that. You should simply write it to its natural length—whatever that is," he said.

The simplicity of his answer dazzled me. I came away feeling that everything about Mr. Shawn and *The New Yorker's* offices was magical. How modest and unpretentious they were, compared with, say, the club-like atmosphere of the London *Observer* and its socially prominent editor.

The next day, when I sat down to write Mr. Shawn a note to thank him for seeing me, I found myself comparing *The New Yorker's* offices to a sanitarium. I wasn't sure what, precisely, had given me that impression. Perhaps it was Mr. Shawn's profound silence and his attention to every nuance of my thought and feeling. Or perhaps it had to do with the fact that I longed for a sanctuary from what I felt was the anonymity and coldness of Harvard graduate school. Or perhaps it was simply that I just happened then to be reading F. Scott Fitzgerald's "Tender Is the Night."

As soon as I had posted the letter, I began to worry that Mr. Shawn would consider me mad for comparing the midtown offices of a magazine to a mental hospital. I thought of calling him and telling him not to read my letter, but then, I feared that that would only compound my mistake.

I FOUND MY meeting with Mr. Shawn so inspiring that I wrote a piece within three weeks. I called it "Indian Summer," in part because my summer in India as an Oxford graduate seemed to mark a change in my writing from pedestrian and earnest to stylized and playful, with a corresponding change in my persona. (Friends who later read "Indian Summer" accused me of consciously trying to model my prose to fit the mold of *The New Yorker*, but in fact I became a *New Yorker* reader only after finishing my piece.) Coincidentally, the piece turned out to be fifty pages—or just about thirteen thousand words—long.

The moment after I sent it off, I began rewriting and editing it in my head. Is the title a foolish play on words—should I have changed it? Is the tone too self-indulgent—should I have put more starch in it? Mr. Shawn won't like the "me" in the piece—I should have made myself nicer.

I sent the piece off on a Thursday, and didn't expect to hear anything from Mr. Shawn for a month or two, since Weeks and Cousins, with whom I had some experience, had taken months to get back to me. I thought that, at most, I would get a quick note of acknowledgment from his secretary. But the following Thursday the telephone in my rooms in Eliot House, where I was a resident fellow, rang at about nine o'clock in the evening, and the caller was Mr. Shawn.

"Am I calling you at an inconvenient time?" he asked. There was a little quaver in his voice, as if he had been lost in a manuscript and might be just coming back to the real world.

I was so unnerved that I immediately started telling him what I thought was wrong with the piece, as if to have an alibi for his pending rejection.

At the first pause in my apology, he said, "Thank you for letting me read your India piece. It is funny and marvellous. It will require some editing, and if the finished piece is agreeable to you we would like to publish it in *The New Yorker*." (The "if" concerning editing was not pro forma, I was soon to learn. A writer always had the right to withdraw his piece from the magazine if he did not agree with the editing, and he would still be paid for it.)

The telephone almost dropped from my hand. I felt that his acceptance was the greatest thing that had ever happened to me—and, indeed, that first call from him was to transfigure my life.

❧

A WEEK OR so after that first call, Mr. Shawn telephoned again, also in the evening. He asked if it was convenient for me to go over some queries he had on my manuscript, and when I said yes he began going over them.

At one point, he said, "In the fifth sentence of the third paragraph of your piece, when you are comparing Moraes to Dylan Thomas, you mention Thomas three times. Each time, you refer to him as 'Dylan.' That sounds as if you were being familiar with him—something I don't think you'd want to do. Also, a sort of cult has grown up around Thomas's memory, and you wouldn't want to sound as if you were a part of it. Would it be all right with you if we used his full name at the first mention and thereafter called him 'Thomas'?"

"But at Oxford when people were comparing Dom—I mean Moraes—to . . ." I hesitated, because I now didn't know whether to say "Dylan" or "Thomas," or, whether I should even say "Dom." (I later realized that this was probably the beginning of a protracted period of self-consciousness about my talk, in which I tended to edit my speech almost as if it were a piece of writing that would be scrutinized by Mr. Shawn.) "Well, they just said 'Dylan.'"

"But then when they were talking about Sir Isaiah Berlin they also probably just said 'Isaiah,'" Mr. Shawn observed.

"People at Oxford probably assumed a certain familiarity with one another because they thought of themselves as members of an Oxford family."

"But wouldn't calling him 'Thomas' change the informal tone of the piece?" My question was in the spirit of a student wanting to learn—not in that of one seeking to challenge his teacher's judgment.

There was an audible silence on the telephone; I could almost hear Mr. Shawn studying the sentence. "I don't think you lose anything by calling him 'Thomas,'" he said, and he read out the amended sentence: "He wrote like Dylan Thomas, he was lovable like Thomas, and, like Thomas, he was a ladies' man."

As he read, I immediately saw that his change had made an improvement. "It sounds better," I said, feeling happy in a surge.

"Should I then call Dom 'Moraes'?" I asked, catching myself thinking about the text as he did, and raising a kind of question I thought he would raise.

"Oh, no," he said. "The two of you are friends, travelling in India. In the fifth paragraph—" He started reading.

"That won't be necessary," I broke in. "I know the manuscript almost by heart. I am worried about taking up so much of your time and running up a big telephone bill."

"You shouldn't worry about any of that—it's just part of the routine of getting out the magazine," he said reassuringly.

"Still, this must be so laborious for you. Wouldn't it be easier just to mark up the manuscript and send it to me?"

"We'll handle proofs by mail. But I would like to get the piece into type, so that we can perhaps get it into the magazine in the next few weeks, when we have more columns for editorial matter, because of the Christmas issues coming up." He resumed, going back to the text, "In the fifth paragraph, in your sentence 'Dom who has come to New Delhi with his father has spent some weeks in Bombay doing much the same thing I have been doing,' is it all right to enclose the 'who' clause in commas?"

"Why do we need the commas?"

"Without them it sounds as if there were more than one Dom, and one of them had come to New Delhi with his father."

I was about to say that that seemed far-fetched—that it was a rather Jesuitical distinction—but I found I agreed that his change would make the sentence clearer.

There was a pause, and I could hear him flipping pages back and forth rapidly.

"I'd like to plant the word 'bummy' in the first sentence of the lead," he said. "And then repeat the word, or 'bumming,' in these sentences in the paragraph." He read out the proposed sentences: "'Before spending a bummy month together in India, Dom Moraes and I were great friends at Oxford. . . . I am not quite sure what friendship means elsewhere, but at Oxford it means being able to spend a whole day together—that is, from breakfast to bedtime—and being able to roam from room to room, sometimes bumming drinks, sometimes taking along hip flasks and sharing drinks with other friends. . . . At Oxford, we worked frightfully hard perhaps for five or six days, five or six weeks, and after this intensive period we took a physical and spiritual holiday, bumming and being amiable, visiting and being visited. These bummy days were an Oxford specialty.'"

"By my count, that makes no less than—" I broke off, realizing that I should have said "no fewer than," and quickly corrected myself. "That makes no fewer than four 'bummy' words in a paragraph of about thirty lines. Doesn't that seem a little heavy?"

He paused, apparently studying the sentences, and then said, "I don't think so. I think 'bummy' helps to establish that the way you conducted yourself in India was out of character—that you are not normally as rakish and irresponsible as you appear in this piece. The repetition would set the tone of your high-spirited Oxford holiday in India. But when you get the proof you can look at it and we can consider the question again."

It soon became clear that Mr. Shawn would not change a word or a punctuation mark without first consulting me. Yet I was twenty-five and inexperienced, with a foreigner's shaky grasp of English, and with only one simply written book to my credit. I wrote mostly by the way things sounded. For example, I had so little understanding of the use of a comma that I put it in anywhere I thought I needed a pause in a sentence, without understanding the rationale for it. But I was wary of exposing my ignorance of such matters to Mr. Shawn. At the same time, I didn't think that there was any point in trying to bluff him. Not only did I imagine that he had X-ray perception and could see directly into my brain but I wanted to be as honest with him as he was with me. I decided that I would be like the English and somehow muddle through.

As our conversation continued, I was sometimes able to guess his explanations before the words were out of his mouth. There were many more times, however, when I was stumped by the reasons for his changes, and he then carefully explained them to me. In any event, his suggestions for changes were always offered as "fixes." And if there was a lacuna in a thought, and it required an addition, he would offer me a "dummy" phrase or a "dummy" sentence, and ask me to put it in my own words. I would have to think on the spot and stumble through my emendations. He would take them down like a scribe and edit them there and then. Having him go over my text was like being back in an Oxford tutorial and having my tutor go over my essay, word by word. It was an education in itself. But sometimes, even if I agreed with Mr. Shawn that my version was grammatically infelicitous, I would not adopt his suggestion, because I was attached to the way I had put something. Then, in order to be as considerate of him as he was of me, I would laboriously give my reasons, such as they were. He would retreat at the first sign of resistance, for he seemed never to lose sight of the fact that it was my piece and should be improved only if I wanted it to be.

Mr. Shawn grasped my objections or modifications so fast that I got the impression that he had the entire piece in his mind, as if it were out of time—as if it were a painting. And not once did he make me feel that he was the dictatorial editor and I was a supplicant writer. There was not so much as a hint of coercion or condescension in his style. His only concern seemed to be the artistic perfection of the piece, his only aim to make it accurate to the experience and courteous to the reader, irrespective of its complexity or its length. His fixes, however, were never designed to write down to the reader. Quite the contrary. Since he didn't know who the reader might be, he worked as if he and I were the ideal readers: he assumed that if we liked something the readers would like it, too. Under his inspired guidance, I was learning that a writer and an editor had a higher calling than self-glorification— that they were partners in a search for truth. I fell completely under the spell of his manner—kind, courtly, respectful, and patient. The editing process was arduous and time-consuming, since there was hardly a paragraph that was not touched. Yet he made our work, which could so easily have degenerated into a power play, intensely pleasurable. All the while, I felt that he was sensitizing me to the force and the importance of each word—to its weight, tone, and texture—and was teaching me new ways not only of writing but also of thinking, feeling, and speaking.

How different was Mr. Shawn's process from that of Mr. Weeks—as I was now thinking of him, though I had ventured not long before to address him as Ted. Mr. Weeks had published a couple of extracts from my book in *The Atlantic*. Any editing of those sections of the manuscript had been done without reference to me. He had just sent me proofs of the articles and asked me to look them over. To avoid expense, I was to make only changes that were absolutely necessary, he had told me. More often than not, his own changes had seemed to me to be directed at enhancing the articles' readability and commercial value. When I made some substantial changes on the magazine proofs, he had telephoned me; the bottom line of the call was to tell me in a gentlemanly, good-natured way to keep down the printer's bill.

Mr. Shawn's call went on for about two hours. As I was thanking him and saying goodbye, I remarked that the piece belonged as much to him as to me.

"No, it belongs to you—I just made it more yours," he said.

❦

A BIG MANILA envelope, about twice the size of the magazine, arrived from *The New Yorker*. It was so large that it couldn't fit into my mailbox and was left on the table under it. My heart jumped. I ripped the envelope open. In it was a sheaf of proofs with a single column of print in the center, leaving huge margins for writing and rewriting. Attached to the proofs was a note from Mr. Shawn saying that I should feel free to change anything I didn't like. I read through the piece fast. It seemed perfect, and at first I was afraid to put a mark on it, in case I might mess up Mr. Shawn's editing. Indeed, when I did change a word or a clause it seemed to throw the sentence out of kilter, requiring me to make other changes. By the end, I seemed to be changing practically every sentence, only to be horrified at the extent of my changes. I remember crossing out slews of commas throughout, because they seemed to impede the flow.

I returned the proofs to Mr. Shawn and immediately got a call from him. He said, "The changes look good, but I'm afraid that we are going to have comma trouble."

When I gave my reasons for deleting the commas, he explained to me that the commas were put in the text not for pauses but for meaning, and he seemed to be getting ready to go over the explanation for each comma I had crossed out.

"I honestly don't understand much about commas, but I am sure that your instincts are right," I said.

"It is not a matter of instincts but a matter of meaning," he said gently.

I told him that I took his word for it, and he said that he would send me a new "revise."

"One more thing," I said. My mouth suddenly went dry. Toward the end of the piece, I had described driving through one of Calcutta's red-light districts with Dom and spurning the girls who came up to the taxi importuning us. We had only been teasing them as a diversion from our frustration at being in India. At one point, a pimp had jumped halfway through the front window beside the taxi-driver and his partner. (Taxi-drivers there went in pairs for self-protection.) I had written:

He straddles the door—an ugly, bony face peering at us with bloodshot eyes, a hand holding a ridiculous little penknife. The unoccupied taxi-driver and the man on the window fight. The other driver accelerates the car and rushes through the street like a madman. The front door, which the man is straddling, opens and sags with the burden, but he clings on. He wraps his hands around the back door, and both Dom and I get down on the floor. Then there is the most terrifying scream, which rings through the streets like a death gong. The taxi man who is not driving has the figure by his testicles, and before Dom and I can get any words out of our throats the figure is dropped on the street and left.

Mr. Shawn had changed "testicles" to "thigh." I didn't know quite how to bring up the subject with him. But I now said, in a small voice, "There is one change, to 'thigh,' that I don't think works."

"I knew you'd feel that way," he said. "But in this piece any clinical word would stick out. I would feel differently if the whole piece were on a clinical matter."

There was something in his voice that made me realize I shouldn't press my point, and I quickly dropped the subject.

"All your other sexual references, such as to concubines, are fine," he said, as if to reassure me. "They'll go in just as they are."

I said that I worried not only about the cost of my alterations but also about taking up so much of his time. Any other editor would have considered what amounted to copy editing beneath him, I thought, and would have left it to an underling. But I'm sure that he himself will be involved until the last full stop is in its place.

"I enjoy my work," he said. "You should treat each set of proofs merely as a draft—that is simply the way we do things here."

When the revise arrived, as I read it I discovered that just the act of doing so made me want to take a pencil to it, as if I were catching on to the joys of rewriting, editing, and revising. But no sooner had I returned my marked-up proof than a new, clean proof arrived. I reread my piece in proof for the third time and thought of a hundred more ways of improving it.

All told, I received four revises, each completely reset—and in those days the magazine was set by linotype. Along with the revises, I got more telephone calls from Mr. Shawn, at odd hours of the day or evening.

"Is this a convenient time to go over some questions?" he would ask, or "Have I got you at a bad time?"

He invariably had "queries" about new ambiguities that had crept into the piece because of my changes. In the later stages of our work, he began to preface his queries with "Someone asks" or "Someone wants to know." Eventually, I caught on to the fact that there were many "someone"s at the *New Yorker* offices, each of whom had read the piece with an eye to its logic, its grammar, its factual content, or its legal ramifications and had handed in a proof to Mr. Shawn, and that he had sifted through their queries, had disposed of most of them, and was referring to me those few which only I could answer. Part of his job as the editor of the piece was to serve as the mediating intelligence between the *New Yorker* editorial query people and me. "Someone" was just his way of protecting their identity; after all, writers—even more than other people—do not like to have their mistakes pointed out.

I recalled that while I was in India I had written some quick feature pieces about America for *The Statesman*, then the most deeply respected English-language daily in the country. I had been travelling around the country and had typed out the articles whenever I could get my hands on a typewriter. Being without experience in newspaper journalism, I had had no idea of how fast a piece of writing might get into print, without the author's having a chance even to check and correct the copy. I hadn't worried much about the quality of the pieces, however, dismissing them as ephemera, which would be tossed out with yesterday's newspaper. I had simply basked in my new-found prominence. People I scarcely knew would ask me to parties and would listen to me as if I were a person of consequence, giving me the illusion that through the printed word I could free myself of some of the burdens of blindness—of being patronized and discounted.

Soon after I reached Harvard, my newspaper persona received a rude shock: I got a withering three-page scolding for one of my *Statesman* articles about American education. It came from William Olson, a former professor of mine at Pomona College, in California, where I had taken my American undergraduate degree before going on for an English undergraduate degree from Oxford. Without explaining how an article published so far away had come to his notice, he wrote:

I was surprised to read your views about Pomona as you expressed them in your article on "Democratic Education." . . . There are a number of things I feel impelled to say to you about it, more in sorrow than in anger, but I must confess with a bit of that too. . . . You cite "ten thousand colleges and universities which were dotted all over the [American] map." There may be as many as 1,800, but the figure is probably closer to 1,300, a fact of which I, as an American, am very proud, but which you, as an Indian, may not find praiseworthy. I also doubt that there are ten million undergraduates in America; no doubt someone . . . has been pulling your leg.

I had never thought highly of Olson, but his letter was dev-astatingly accurate. To add to my embarrassment, he noted that he had sent a clipping of my article and a copy of his chastising letter to the president of Pomona, E. Wilson Lyon. Instead of admitting my mistakes, and explaining that the newspaper had not sent me proofs and that the article had been written in India, where I didn't have books or papers to refer to or an amanuensis or a reader to help me, I tried to cover up my blunders in a blustery letter to Olson, with a copy sent to Lyon. The whole experience was mortifying. Now, though, I trusted that my forth-coming *New Yorker* piece could have the effect of sweeping away all the inaccurate, ill-judged pieces I had written in *The Statesman*, whether from India or from America. (During my first months at Harvard, I continued to write some pieces for *The Statesman*; they appeared in a column headed "Letter from America.")

I began sitting anxiously by the phone waiting for Mr. Shawn's call, as if I were in love. I started saying to myself com-pulsively, "I wish Mr. Shawn would ring," at the oddest times of day or night—when my mind wandered from a badly written book I was reading in my office in Widener Library, or when I was eating alone in the Eliot House dining room, or when I was taking a shower, or when I was trying to get to sleep. Why his telephone calls had such an effect on me I can scarcely analyze even now. Was it that his kindness stimulated some childish hunger for love, long unsatisfied because I had been sent away from home before my fifth birthday and then, on my return, some three years later, had found I was still missing out, because my father was always gone half the night playing poker at his clubs? Was it that I was looking to my piece to give me the attention I had luxuriated in at Oxford but had not received at Harvard? Was it that I had suddenly started thinking of my writing as a way out of various emotional problems I was being faced with at Harvard? Or was it that I was mesmerized by Mr. Shawn's magic in turning a sow's ear into a silk purse? I had no doubt that in

Mr. Shawn I had found a literary guardian of impeccable taste, the soul of kindness and generosity. I was filled with reverence for him. But I kept asking myself what kind of person Mr. Shawn was, and how it was that he would treat me as if I were a writer of consequence writing a piece of great literature; that he would devote so much thought to something that was, after all, to appear over my signature; that he would feed my vanity at the expense of his own; and that he would put at my disposal his inexhaustible storehouse of energy. Was he married? Did he have a family? Did he sleep?

I was now reading *The New Yorker* with new respect. Its copy was so clean and concise that I began having trouble reading my history books, because as soon as I read a paragraph I would start mentally editing it the way I imagined Mr. Shawn would edit it, and I would find the text full of holes, ambiguities, inconsistencies, and sloppy thinking.

❦

ONE DAY AROUND the middle of November, when Mr. Shawn and I had finished working by telephone, he said, "Would a payment of eighteen hundred dollars for your piece be O.K. with you, Mr. Mehta?"

I was flabbergasted. "Eighteen hundred dollars for one piece!" I exclaimed. "That's six times what I was paid for an *Atlantic* piece, and almost twice the advance on my book."

He laughed. Though he was an extremely serious man, his laughter had an amazing lightness and freedom. "Perhaps I should mention that our rates are the same for all our contributors, whether they are just starting out with us or have been around for years," he said.

"You mean I get the same rate as Salinger?" I asked. In the public mind, Salinger's name was linked with *The New Yorker.*

Mr. Shawn became audibly uncomfortable. "At *The New Yorker,* there is no system of seniority," he said. "All writers are treated equally."

I grasped the point—that it would be indiscreet of him to disclose what any particular writer was paid for his pieces—and yet, because I was still under the influence of the rigid Indian and English systems of seniority, I persisted, saying, "But surely a writer with seniority must earn more."

"All writers are paid the same for pieces of similar length," he said, "although we reserve the right to make an extra payment in the case of a piece we especially want. Rates may also vary according to where a piece appears in the magazine."

It was my turn to be uncomfortable. It seemed obscene to be discussing money—a violation of the sacred editing process into which he had initiated me. I shouldn't have drawn him into a discussion of money, I thought. I should have just thanked him and left it at that. That is what he would have done had he been in my place. I now quickly changed the subject, asking him if the heading he had put on the piece, "Our Far-Flung Correspondents," was necessary. "'Far-Flung Correspondents' may make readers think that I was in India for the express purpose of writing a piece for *The New Yorker*, when in fact I went home to see my family," I said.

There was a pause, as if he were considering my query, and then he said, "I don't know what other heading we could run it under."

"Why do we need any heading?" I asked. My acquaintance with the magazine was so new that I didn't realize that every factual piece had to appear under a heading.

"Let me read the piece again with your query in mind," he said.

Then, around the time when I was expecting a copy of *The New Yorker* with my piece in it, a new proof arrived, with this note from Mr. Shawn.

December 10, 1959

Dear Mr. Mehta:

Your proof. Please disregard typographical and other technical errors, such as all those mixed tenses in the right-hand column of the first page. Too bad we missed out this week, but, as I believe you know by now, we seriously intend to publish your piece.

Best regards,
William Shawn

My heart sank. For some days now, I had been waking up from a recurrent nightmare that my piece had been killed because of the outbreak of the Third World War. Moreover, the new proof had fewer pages, and that made me think that it had been cut for reasons of space. I later learned the explanation. Mr. Shawn had taken my chance query about the heading to mean that I would prefer my piece to run as a "casual"—an intramural term for fiction and all other kinds of imaginative writing. His surmise was understandable, since my piece was constructed like a short story, even to the point of my having adopted a sort of fictional "bummy" persona. My piece had been scheduled to run in the issue of December 12th, but the slots for fiction in that issue had already been taken by John Cheever and Penelope Mortimer, and, for logistical and other reasons, those pieces couldn't be pulled. He had therefore had to replace my piece with another factual piece and have mine reset in what was loosely called fiction format, which meant that most pages would carry three columns of text, as opposed to a fact format, which, by and large, meant that there would be only one column of text on a page, between two columns of advertisements.

I consoled myself with the thought that Mr. Shawn was the kind of person who would get the piece in the magazine at the first opportunity, and that, although in the new format my piece might take up fewer pages of the magazine, readers would not be distracted by surrounding advertisements.

The piece appeared in the issue dated January 2, 1960, about two and a half months after I met Mr. Shawn. As I picked up a copy of the magazine a couple of days earlier from a newsstand in Harvard Square, I was in a daze. I had expected to be elated, but instead I felt sad and confused. I resented the fact that Mr. Shawn had insinuated his values of clarity, courtesy, and harmony into my generally muddled, rude, and dissonant consciousness, imperceptibly altering my thinking. There was already a subtle shift in the way I thought of my piece and of myself as its author. On one level, I felt it to be my offspring that had gone out into the world; on another, I couldn't claim it to be solely mine, for at every turn I saw Mr. Shawn's invisible hand. I felt that his editing had laid the groundwork for a permanent dependence on him—that I would never be able to write a sentence again without feeling the need of his judgment. Perhaps because gratitude is one of the strongest human emotions, it is human nature to deny it—by not acknowledging help, by not giving credit where it is due. So I kept telling myself that his changes had not changed the character of my piece. But then I felt the pangs of a guilty conscience: I knew that without his editing and publishing of the piece it would not exist.

On the first day of January, 1960, Mr. Shawn called to wish me a Happy New Year and to say that he thought the magazine should pay some of the expenses that I must have incurred in writing the piece. Does the man ever sleep or take a holiday, I wondered. How does he have time to remember me on New Year's when he has to put out a weekly magazine and must have two or three hundred writers to take care of? "What do you think those expenses should be?" he asked.

I was always in need of money. Everything I did required a reader or an amanuensis. But, thanks to Mr. Shawn, I had got it fixed in my head that writing should be done for its own sake, without a thought for its rewards. I told him that I had already been paid plenty, and thanked him, and hung up quickly. A few days later, I received a check for four hundred dollars with a note from him. In India, such a matter would be handled by the most junior clerk, I thought, but Mr. Shawn seems to do everything himself.

❧

AFTER THE PUBLICATION of the piece, compliments poured in from all the people who had turned down the idea of the postscript—Carmel Snow, Irita Van Doren, John Fischer, Philip Horton. Friends like the historian Paul Noyes wrote, "I see you have attained the high point of human fame," and the critic Dwight Macdonald, whom I had met through some London literary friends, sent these lines:

I've just read Indian Summer with much delight. You've added a new word to the language—bummy. (Too bad you couldn't have called it In the Good Old Bummytime.) Even after the New Yorker's bowdlerizations, it remains essentially lowclass and picaresque, in short—bummy. I also like the under played style, though perhaps at times it is TOO underplayed, I mean you ought to rise to occasions a little more. Thus, most frustrating sentence in a long time for me was "First stop, Agra—the Taj Mahal seen through the haze from two thousand feet." Would it have been naïve to have a LITTLE more on Agra and/or the T.M.? But it's a fine piece and I congratulate you. Now you must do the same thing for Cambridge (Mass.).

. . . I'll be up [in Cambridge] in the next few months and let's be bummy for at least one evening. I also like the new definition of revolution, when you lose your concubines.

But when I had scarcely begun to enjoy my new-found fame a flood broke over my head. My family and their friends took my "bummy" persona literally: they didn't understand that I had adopted it in order to write lightly about a sombre subject. My father felt that I had disgraced my family and my name, had portrayed myself as an immoral, dissolute fellow, had held my country up to ridicule, and had forfeited forever any chance of holding an official post there. Mrs. B. K. Nehru, the wife of the Minister in the Indian Embassy in Washington, was very close to our family, and she telephoned to say, "What is this word 'bum-bum-bummy'? I've never hated a piece of writing more." Oxford friends scolded me for not portraying either myself or Oxford accurately. For instance, my closest friend there, the classicist Jasper Griffin, wrote:

I enjoyed your story very much, but I thought the part at the beginning, about Oxford, was not as successful as the main parts, about India. What is this awful word "bummy" with which you make so free? I never heard it from you—or indeed from anyone—in Oxford. Nor were you really as dissolute and irresponsible as you try to make out; though you won't thank me for reminding you of the fact, you were actually a pillar of respectability and straight living—even to your daily dark suit. You are an old fraud, and I have a mind to denounce you to the great American public as the moral man you are.

And then there was this letter from Mrs. Ethel Clyde, a rich American friend of the family, whose good opinion was very important to my father, because he worked for her off and on as a personal doctor:

Before telling you of my reaction to your article "Indian Summer" let me report that Bill Wynkoop, who, as perhaps you know, teaches English at Rutgers, telephoned me with enthusiasm after reading it and said it was "terrific," which I understand, in modern parlance, is high praise. . . .

Knowing so many members of your family and through them having a personal interest in India, I regret the embarrassment that "Indian Summer" may cause them and am sorry that, after your first trip home in ten years, you chose to present India to the world as seen "through whiskey-colored glasses."

Perhaps you know that I cannot "take" India, but I believe that in spite of the extreme poverty, etc., there is far more beauty, dignity and decency there than your article would indicate.

The New Yorker certainly paid well for your article, but I cannot help wishing that it had not been written by you about you and India. Another thing—it is my feeling that while accepting hospitality one should not subject one's host to embarrassment or ridicule. I am referring to the concubine incident in Nepal.

I much hope that you will accept this letter in the spirit of friendly concern for you and yours in which it is written. I am conscious of the fact that times and customs have changed and that more than half a century divides us. However we can try to understand and, if we are frank with each other, perhaps we will succeed and even be helpful to each other because of that great difference.

Mr. Shawn and I, in our readings and rereadings of the piece, had anticipated and discussed many of the criticisms that were now being levelled at it. Indeed, we had edited it with possible criticisms in mind. The truth was that a number of the people who wrote to me had read it quickly, perhaps even cursorily, and got out of it only as much as they brought to it.

❦

I SENT A copy of the piece to the girls in New Delhi whom we had called the "pinks," with a note saying that I hoped they would not be offended by my writing about them, and reassuring them that their anonymity had been preserved.

Early in April, I received a four-page letter from a firm of solicitors in New Delhi, informing me that they were acting for a daughter of a foreign diplomat in India. The letter referred to my article and said:

On page twenty-seven of the magazine you describe how you and a friend, Dom Moraes, met two girls whom thereafter in the article you refer to as the "pink girls" or the "pinks." The third column on page twenty-eight of the article contains the following sentences. . . :

The sisters begin talking about their friends.

"Have you heard of Gigi?" the younger pink says.

"Who's Gigi?" I ask.

"She's the most wonderful person in the world," she replies enthusiastically. "She has slept with many, many, men, and she's experienced. She's only fifteen, but she's writing a book, 'Nuns and Champagne', and even Ruffles has kissed her."

"Who's Ruffles?" Dom asks.

"You know, the prince in the president's bodyguard," says the younger pink.

The older pink says he is silly and stupid.

The solicitors contended that Gigi was a "well-known figure in Delhi society and elsewhere," was "universally known by the nickname Gigi," and was known by her friends to be contemplating a novel called "Nuns and Champagne." The letter asserted:

The disgraceful and totally unfounded allegation that our Client has led an immoral life, which through publication in *The New Yorker* has been given the widest circulation amongst her family, friends, and to the world at large, has occasioned intense distress and mental suffering to our Client and is calculated to prejudice seriously her chances of successful marriage and future happiness. . . . We are therefore instructed to call upon you, as we hereby do, to write to our Client care of ourselves, within 14 days from the date hereof, in terms of the draft letter enclosed herewith, retracting the libel and offering an unconditional apology to our Client. Please note that our Client reserves the right to cause a copy of such letter, or details of its contents or effect, to be reproduced in *The New Yorker* and in any newspaper or other organ, whether in India or elsewhere.

We are also instructed to call upon you, as we hereby do, to pay to our Client, by way of damages for defamation, the sum of $100,000.00 (one hundred thousand dollars).

The draft letter to Gigi had me state, among other things, "I am completely satisfied that the allegation I made against you is totally unfounded, and I ask you to accept my unconditional apologies for the malicious and offensive remarks I made about you, which must have caused you, and must continue to cause you, considerable distress."

"Gigi" was the title of a film very popular at the time, and I had assumed that the Gigi of the "pinks" was an alter ego modelled on the heroine of the film. If I had thought that their Gigi was a real person, I would have changed her name. But then I had read somewhere that all libels are unconscious slips. Moreover, I was in such a vulnerable state of mind about my piece that the solicitors' letter persuaded me of my guilt. (It didn't occur to me that the solicitors' letter might be a hoax.)

I was sure that a copy of the letter had been sent to *The New Yorker* and that I would never be able to write for the magazine again. I thought Mr. Shawn would type me as a troublemaker and as accident-prone, even as a sort of vampire-writer, who had drained him of his time and energy only to land his magazine in an expensive transcontinental lawsuit, with the prospect of huge damages. I called Mr. Shawn's office to explain and apologize, but he was at home with a cold, and I wasn't able to reach him.

The more I thought about the letter without having a chance to talk with him, the more I felt that he would be much pained at having caused intense mental anguish to an innocent victim, not to mention compromising her chances of successful marriage and future happiness. Even though he would wash his hands of me, I thought, I would in some measure redeem myself in his eyes by wasting no time in signing the draft letter and so apologizing to the young girl and making a clean breast of my mistake. I could never lay claim to the high moral ground that I imagined he occupied, but I could at least show him that I was beginning my climb.

I signed and dated the draft letter, and set out to post it. On the way, I met John Finley, the Master of Eliot House.

"You look green," he said.

I didn't know where to begin, but I blurted out something about being sued and signing a "mea culpa" letter.

"Is that the letter in your hand?" he asked.

I nodded.

He snatched the letter from my hand and tore it in two. "You don't want to convict yourself before there is even a case," he said. "Get yourself a lawyer."

I burst into tears. He could have no idea of the kind of man Mr. Shawn was, nor could he realize that by his impetuous action he had sealed my coffin as a writer. Having nothing better to do, I telephoned Mr. R. H. Davison, a lawyer in Boston who had helped me a few years earlier with the problem of my receiving book royalties in America while I was resident in England. To my surprise, he said, "Thank your stars that you didn't send the draft letter. The Gigi business might amount to nothing. But send me and Mr. Shawn a copy of the solicitors' letter."

I was far from reassured, and wrote to Mr. Shawn, "Enclosed is a rather frightening letter. I really did not know 'Gigi' was a real person. I am asking Mr. Davison of Haussermann, Davison & Shattuck, 15 State Street, Boston, to look into it for me. Could you let me know what your lawyers think about it? Forgive me for being such a terrible nuisance."

I didn't know what kind of response I would get from Mr. Shawn—an explosion couched in the gentlest terms, a funereal goodbye, an Olympian silence. My head was full of images of things I had always feared—being expelled from school, being banished from home, being shunned by my family. I felt suicidal. Yet all that night and the next day I kept repeating compulsively, "I wish Mr. Shawn would ring, I wish Mr. Shawn would ring," as if an impulse other than fear were at work—as if in some part of my mind I felt sure that he would save me.

❧

ON THE MORNING of the second day, the telephone rang. It was Mr. Shawn.

"How are you?" he asked.

I couldn't find my tongue for even a formulaic answer.

"Thank you for your note. We have received an almost identical letter from the Indian solicitors. I don't think that there is very much to worry about. But I think that you should come down to New York and talk it over with our lawyer."

I barely got out, "Yes, I'll get on a plane right away."

"Would four o'clock today be convenient?"

"Yes," I said.

"When you come to *The New Yorker,* I will introduce you to our lawyer."

In answer to a question I asked him about retaining Mr. Davison, he told me that he didn't think it was necessary for me to go to that expense.

Only after we hung up did I realize that our conversation had been concerned almost entirely with the mechanics of the situation—that it had left me no wiser about the pending lawsuit seeking damages of a hundred thousand dollars. Every time I thought of the suit, I started shaking with fright. Since I didn't know what Mr. Shawn was really thinking or feeling, my imagination took over. He can't bear to think of me, but he can't dismiss me from his mind, either, until this law business is settled, I told myself. But then every writer in the world must be trying to write for his magazine, so why would he give me a second thought? He is not the kind of man who would drop me at the first hint of trouble, though. Still, he must put the interests of his magazine before those of any individual writer. He said that there was not very much to worry about, but that is what he would say as the editor. After all, his magazine and I are in the same boat.

❦

I ARRIVED ON the nineteenth floor trembling. The handshake with Mr. Shawn steadied me a bit.

"How are you?" he asked.

"O.K."

"Any news?"

"Not really."

No one can be more receptive than he, I thought. I can tell him anything. But how dare I take up his time with trivialities? He has a weekly magazine to put out. His quiet ways seemed so superior to my usual volubility that I couldn't think of anything to say that would be worthy enough for him to hear. And yet how I would have liked to unburden myself—to tell him why I had thought Gigi was not a real person, how Mr. Finley had rescued me just in time, how I feared that the solicitors would freeze my bank account, why I was convinced that I was finished as a writer.

We walked upstairs to the twentieth floor, and into an office where Mr. Shawn introduced me to not one but two lawyers— Milton Greenstein, the house counsel, and Alexander Lindey, *The New Yorker's* outside counsel. The presence of the two lawyers stunned me. The suit must be even graver than I had suspected.

Greenstein, who had a strong New York accent, was a guarded man with a twinkle in his eye, as if he knew something he wasn't letting on. Lindey seemed like a Dickensian character: he repeated everything at least three times.

"When you wrote your story, had you seen the film 'Gigi,' Mr. Mehta?" Lindey asked me at one point. "Had you heard of it? Were you aware of the film 'Gigi'? Did you know about it? Had

37

you been thinking about 'Gigi' the film? Was it in your mind when you wrote your story?"

I felt that I was already in court, and Lindey was the counsel for the plaintiff. I was afraid to answer any of his questions in case I incriminated myself.

"Alex, all that you need to establish is that Mr. Mehta knew about the film," Greenstein said.

"Now, wait a minute, Milton," Lindey said, and he started repeating his questions. "Was the film playing in Delhi?" he asked me.

"I was certainly aware of the film, but I can't honestly say that the 'pinks' knew about the film," I finally said.

I must have been in Greenstein's office for about half an hour. At the end of the meeting, I asked the lawyers whether there was a chance that Gigi was a real person, and, if so, could prosecute me.

They both said that there was no way of telling, but that if there was to be a case it would have to be argued in a New York court.

"Do you mean that the 'pinks,' Gigi, and the solicitors would have to fly here?"

"Not the solicitors, but certainly the 'pinks' if they were going to appear as witnesses," Greenstein said.

The thought of the "pinks" in New York made me laugh out loud, and also feel a little relieved. The possibility of the whole lot of them getting into a plane in pursuit of *The New Yorker* and me suddenly seemed remote.

A day or so later, Lindey sent me a copy of his reply to the solicitors rebutting each of their allegations in masterly fashion. We heard nothing more from them for many months, then received a duplicate of the original letter, complete with the draft letter to Gigi. Lindey sent them a copy of his reply. That turned out to be the end of the matter.

❧

A COUPLE OF months before my meeting with the lawyers, both of my parents happened to be in New York. My father, a doctor and a retired public-health official, was in the city because he had just concluded a three-month American lecture tour on subjects like "Longer Lives Through Modern Medicine," and had decided to splurge by flying my mother to New York from Delhi. They were making the trip on a shoestring, and I had arranged for them to stay with a friend in the East Nineties. My mother was so ill prepared for America that she had arrived with only one sweater to keep her warm. Mrs. Clyde, on whom she had immediately paid a call, had noticed her shivering and had taken her to Saks the next morning and bought her a warm coat.

"Your dear mother is already England-returned," my father said to me as we were idling along Fifth Avenue. "Now she will be America-returned." He went on, "I must thank Mr. Shawn for everything he's done for you. This may be your mother's only trip to America, and she may never get another opportunity to meet your Mr. Shawn."

Unlike Mrs. Clyde and a number of Indian friends, who still took strong exception to "Indian Summer," my father had long since reconciled himself to the article, was proud of what Mr. Shawn had paid me for it, and rationalized that it would be overshadowed in due course by other pieces and books he thought I would write. Indeed, he had even come to laugh over the word "bummy," as if it were a declaration of poetic license in contrast to my real persona, which he thought was correctly portrayed in "Face to Face."

"Mr. Shawn is busy day and night putting out the most deeply respected magazine in the world," I told them. "He scarcely has time to breathe. He reads and writes all day long. Please don't even think of taking up his time with a social call. Please don't think of troubling him."

"We'll just stop in and say hello—nothing more," my father said.

Knowing that there was no way of dissuading him, I stopped trying.

A few days later, I got a note in Cambridge from Mr. Shawn that made me realize that my impression of him, however exalted, had left a lot out of consideration. He thanked me for a manuscript I had sent him, and then wrote, "Your mother and father visited me at the office yesterday, and I was both touched and enchanted. What wonderful people they are! I was quickly drawn to them, and was sad when they had to leave." I couldn't get over the fact that in the middle of so much pressure he had found time not only to see my parents but also to write me such a wonderful note, so direct and straightforward.

Some weeks later, on May 11th (I remember the day because eleven was my mother's lucky number), as I was walking away from Eliot House along Dunster Street with Peter Stansky, a fellow graduate student in history, a taxi pulled up, and I heard Mr. Shawn call softly, "Mr. Mehta."

It was startling to hear his quiet, gentle voice there at Harvard, and I was embarrassed to be seen in the company of someone who couldn't have been more unlike him. Stansky was loud and flamboyant. He was born and bred on Manhattan's Upper West Side, but had spent two years at King's College, Cambridge, and had been so deeply affected by his English experience that if one didn't know and like him one would think he was doing a transparent and rather ludicrous imitation of a sophisticated Englishman. When I was with Mr. Shawn or was talking to him, I unconsciously adopted what I imagined were his values, and tried to appear as saintly and quiet as he was, even disguising my Oxford mannerisms. The attempt was absurd, since, of course, my writing persona in the piece that Mr. Shawn had edited was full of wildness. And in my Harvard life I was behaving like a dangerous madman—a social anarchist, who might say or do anything. I wanted to keep this side of myself hidden from Mr. Shawn, thinking that if he discovered it he would abandon me—just as I had been assuming that Stansky might if I showed him the way I felt when I was by myself, which was lonely and subdued.

In what seemed to me a very uncharacteristic action, Mr. Shawn leaped out of the taxi, followed by three other people, and, with unconcealed enthusiasm, introduced me to Mrs. Shawn and their two sons—Wallace, sixteen, and Allen, eleven. I remember thinking that Mr. Shawn could have ridden right past me and I would never have known anything about it.

I stumbled through an introduction of Stansky to the family, shifting awkwardly between what I imagined were my Stansky Harvard and my Shawn *New Yorker* personae. Stansky, who was a rising Harvard star, took one look at the Shawn family, all of them short and small; greeted them with a certain amount of condescension, as if they were four country mice who had wandered into the big city; and strode away. I should have told him that Mr. Shawn was the editor of *The New Yorker*, I thought. But then I realized that he would have stayed around and taken over the Shawns.

"What are you doing here, Mr. Shawn?" I asked, and immediately felt mortified at asking such a bold, un-Shawn-like question. I should have asked, "How is it that you all happen to be here?" I could picture him only in his office or on the telephone.

"We are showing Wallace around Harvard," Mrs. Shawn said. "He's thinking of applying here."

I thought of warning him about the place, but then told myself that it was not Harvard that was at fault but I, with my English snobbery, so I bit my tongue, as Bhabiji, my paternal grandmother, used to tell us grandchildren to do when we were tempted to say something indiscreet.

"Would you like to come up and see my rooms?" I asked, and stupidly invited them up to my rooms for tea, as if they were friends at Oxford. Then I realized, with a start, that, unlike Oxford, Eliot House made no provisions for serving guests tea or coffee—

had no junior common room to send up tea—and that I had just a wretched old refrigerator (abandoned by previous tenants), which could only make ice. And I realized, further, that actually I was lucky even to have furniture, since I had had to buy some hastily when I discovered that Harvard rooms came unfurnished.

To my relief, Mrs. Shawn said that they couldn't stop for tea but they would love to see my rooms.

I thought that Mr. Shawn would dismiss the taxi, and perhaps I could show Wallace around Harvard Yard, but Mr. Shawn told the taxi-driver to wait. I was astonished by that extravagance. The ticking of the meter kept drumming in my head as I led the family through the Eliot House quadrangle and up the stairs to my rooms, embarrassed that I had nothing to offer them. They didn't sit down but looked around the living room and were full of praise for the accommodations at Harvard, which, now that I saw them through their eyes, suddenly seemed rather ample, and even grand. In fact, Wallace and Allen were so observant and enthusiastically admiring of everything—right down to a Harvard desk chair I had bought, which had the Harvard seal, with "Ve-ri-tas," painted on its back—that I felt I had missed out by not having been brought up a Shawn child. Wallace and Allen embrace life wholeheartedly and I approach it warily, I thought.

I accompanied the family downstairs with the taxi meter still running in my head, yet all the Shawns seemed reluctant to leave so soon.

I asked them if they might be coming up to Harvard again, and Mrs. Shawn told me in a simple, direct way that they would, because Allen had a twin sister, Mary, who was retarded and attended a special school in the area and was learning to play the piano. Then they got in the taxi and were gone. I thought that what Mr. Shawn had written to me about my parents could well apply to all of them.

II

THE SIGHTED
BOOK

"I NDIAN SUMMER" WAS ONLY HALF OF THE POSTSCRIPT I had set out to write. Moreover, I had so glamorized Dom and so belittled myself when I was writing the piece that I had fallen into the role of a clownish Sancho Panza to Dom's Don Quixote, or of a dense Dr. Watson to his quick-witted Sherlock Holmes. While that approach gave "Indian Summer" a certain light and playful tone, I felt that it didn't really portray me correctly—or, rather, that it portrayed only one part of me, which most of the time was kept under wraps, like the mischievous side of a good child. Even before the piece was paid for, I asked Mr. Shawn if I might try my hand at a sequel, explaining that the travels with Dom were only a very small part of the experience of my Indian return, and that the tone of the piece had not lent itself to writing about such serious

43

matters as my getting reacquainted with my family, and my meeting with politicians and statesmen like Nehru. Another editor might have said that I had already done the homecoming in "Indian Summer," and at the time my state of mind was so fragile that I would have squelched the idea—and that would have been the end of my relationship with *The New Yorker.* All the magazines I was familiar with were perpetually trying to leaven their regular columns and departments with new kinds of pieces by new writers, to give their publications an up-to-the-minute and varied look. But Mr. Shawn immediately welcomed my proposal. I then said, "I've just started reading *The New Yorker.* I don't know how to go about writing for it. I wonder if you could suggest some pieces that I could model my sequel on."

"Every *New Yorker* piece is different," he said. "You should feel free to write any way you want to."

"Still, could you direct me to a few pieces about homecoming in *The New Yorker?*"

He said he would—no doubt to allay my anxieties.

A few days later, he sent a package to me at Eliot House containing tearsheets of perhaps a dozen pieces about various kinds of homecomings which had appeared in the magazine over twenty years. One piece, a two-part article by Joseph Wechsberg about his return to war-ravaged Czechoslovakia in 1945, was so moving that I had tears in my eyes as I finished it. In fact, the writing of all the pieces was so vivid and sharp, and the observations of the writers were so precise and clear, that I felt I would need eyes in both the front and the back of my head to come up to their standard. The fact that Mr. Shawn took "Indian Summer" is a fluke, I thought. I should leave well enough alone, and not push my luck again.

I voiced more of my anxieties to Mr. Shawn during one of his telephone calls, and he said, "I'm sure you can write a sequel for *The New Yorker.*" His confidence took my breath away. He doesn't realize how hard it is for me to write, I thought. What I wrote last time worked because, without knowing it, I had absorbed Dom's impressions. Set against my feelings of inadequacy was Mr. Shawn's utter receptiveness. I imagined that if he believed I could fly I would be able to do it.

Around the time that "Indian Summer" was to make its début, I started working on the sequel, and I finished it in a few feverish weeks. As I read it over, the piece struck me as a little too earnest. Certainly it lacked the gaiety that Dom's presence might have given it. But then "Homecoming," which is what I entitled it, seemed to me to portray a person more like the real me. This person was truthful, prudent, even reverent—characteristics I was lately cultivating because I associated them with Mr. Shawn.

No sooner had I posted "Homecoming" to Mr. Shawn than I started having nightmares. The piece was no good. It was backtracking to a summer already covered and disposed of. Anyway, it should have preceded "Indian Summer." It was devoid of irony. It was sentimental. I imagined the worst. I was scarcely able to eat or sleep, and fell into a state of deep gloom.

A few days later, Mr. Shawn called. "'Homecoming' is very moving," he said. "It is beautifully written."

"No!" I exclaimed, and I started enumerating my reservations.

He listened with his usual complete attention, and then said, "It is, of course, very different from 'Indian Summer,' but good in its own way."

"Hooray!" I shouted to my empty room as soon as I hung up. "I've brought off another *New Yorker* piece!" His acceptance made my spirits soar. It was as if I were only as good as Mr. Shawn thought I was, as if my self-worth required his validation.

Around the time that "Indian Summer" appeared, editorial work on "Homecoming" began. Perhaps because I had assimilated many of Mr. Shawn's editorial principles, his telephone calls were less frequent and our editorial conversations were shorter. I felt sad, and wished that I were still a first-piece writer, so that Mr. Shawn would have to talk to me more.

As with "Indian Summer," however, "Homecoming," by my count, received no fewer than sixteen readings by different people. Each time Mr. Shawn started on a new proof turned in by "someone," I feared that it would bring up an unforeseen checking, legal, or editorial query that I wouldn't be able to handle satisfactorily, and then the piece would have to be killed. I simply couldn't believe that a second piece of mine could survive all those readings. At the same time, both his telephone calls and the fact that there were fewer of them were reassuring, in that they were an indication that the piece was clearing the editorial hurdles and moving toward publication.

❧

"YOU USE 'SELF-MORTIFICATION' in the lead of the new piece," Mr. Shawn said during one of his calls, "and then you repeat it." I could hear him shuffling pages of the proof. He mentioned a page and a paragraph.

"The instances are so far apart I don't think anybody would notice the repetition," I said.

"But 'self-mortification,' like 'bummy,' is a striking word, and someone here wonders what the reason for the repetition is."

"What is a 'striking word'?" I asked. "I've never come across the phrase before."

"Oh, it just means a colorful word that is different from, for example, a working word, like 'laugh' or 'say.'"

"Oh," I said, and I racked my brain for a synonym for self-mortification, wishing that I had a thesaurus at hand.

But Mr. Shawn was offering me synonyms from the other end of the line. None of them were satisfactory. In the end, we recast the sentence with "brooded" and "shortcomings" to take care of problem.

As we continued to work on the text, it dawned on me that Mr. Shawn and his helpers seemed to treat a piece of writing like a musical composition—that they had developed such a keen ear for the overtones of words that the least discordant note, like the repetition of a colorful word without good reason or the use of slang in the middle of a periodic sentence, seemed to jar them. Later, Mr. Shawn said something that made me realize that "someone" had read "Indian Summer" alongside the proof of "Homecoming" to make sure that there were no inconsistencies or conflicts in the two texts—that, for instance, not even a character or a word appropriate for the first had, by oversight, slipped into the second.

To lavish such attention on ephemera—and that in a magazine that people perhaps mostly browsed for its cartoons and advertisements—seemed like a kind of fanaticism. But as soon as I hung up I myself started reading the two pieces together, treating them as an organic whole. I divided "Homecoming" into two parts and sandwiched "Indian Summer" between them. Later, I found myself refashioning them—cutting them up and stitching them together, and seeing places where this or that section could be expanded to advantage. Then I realized in a flash that what I was making was a little book. The thought was thrilling: it was as if I had crashed the barrier of a one-book writer.

When I had barely got used to the idea of a second book, I received this letter from Dom, which was, as usual, not dated:

as from- 6A Phene Street
London S.W. 3

Moon of my delight,

By the time you get this I shall be back in England. After you left I went to Sikkim, to the Tibetan border, and since then into Tibet a little way. The book is written—Little, Brown are doing it in the States.

I have written about Nepal—what one might call a garnished version of our wanderings. I hear the New Yorker are publishing you. Inexplicable, I call it. You lucky bastard. They pay well.

Though garnished, my Nepal chapters are moderately true. Am sending you copy.

Write and say how all things are. . . .

Love,
Dom

I greeted the news of his book with mixed emotions. One book on a short Indian trip by a recent Oxford graduate seemed to be already tempting the fates, but two, and on the same trip, and by such close Oxford friends, seemed really to be asking for trouble. Indeed, if I had known that Dom was intending to write a book I might never have written my *New Yorker* pieces. To complicate matters further, "Face to Face" had also been published by Little, Brown. I suspected that that might have been the reason Dom's book was submitted to that house in the first place.

I immediately got hold of proofs of Dom's book, and discovered that what he called "a garnished version of our wanderings" was, by and large, fiction. I therefore told myself that the two books were not as similar as, say, the "Rashomon" versions of truth—that, in fact, they were not really about the same trip, and so there could be no conflict between them. We could both publish our books.

When I submitted my book to Weeks, he read Dom's along with it, then took me to lunch at the Ritz in Boston and said, "You may be right that Dom's version is not all true, but it's a good read. Anyway, it's longer, fuller, and more like a book than your brief account. I feel that if Little, Brown were to bring out the two books they would both suffer, since they would undercut each other's sales. Therefore, my advice to you, dear boy, is to suppress your book—forgo it—and concentrate on the next book. That will be a happier outcome all around. Little, Brown will be happy because they will have only one book to sell; Dom will be happy because you will not be undermining his sales; and you should be happy because you will be putting your friendship with him above a mere book."

"But forgo a book! I may never write another one."

"You will, dear boy. Anyway, your *New Yorker* pieces will have been widely read and enjoyed. The publication of them in book form would be only icing on the cake."

He was talking like a publisher, I realized, while I was thinking like a writer.

❧

SOME TIME AFTER the publication of "Face to Face," Norman Cousins had helped me acquire an agent—Elizabeth Otis, of McIntosh & Otis—but I hadn't depended on her to place *New Yorker* pieces, because I felt I should get established before I started leaning on her. I now asked her to submit my book to Knopf, despite the emotional wrench that would be involved in leaving Mr. Weeks, for whose help and friendship I felt boundless gratitude. Henry Robbins, the executive editor of Knopf, made a good offer for the book. When I called Weeks and told him that I was going there, he seemed much hurt. He immediately changed his tack and matched Robbins's offer.

"I thought you said Little, Brown couldn't possibly bring out both books," I observed.

"It's true that the sales force will be the same, but technically your book will be published by Atlantic–Little, Brown and Dom's book by Little, Brown," Weeks explained. "As your *Atlantic* editor, I will be pushing your book, and Dom's Little, Brown editor will be pushing his book. Who knows? The two books may even help each other."

Weeks's use of the word "will" made me realize that I actually had no choice but to stay with him. When I informed Robbins of my—or, rather, Weeks's—decision, and apologized to him, he wrote back:

15 February 1960

Dear Ved Mehta:

Thank you for your letter of February 8th. I'm certainly willing to accept your gracious apology, and I assure you that I had always assumed that your action was due to naiveté about publishing practice, rather than a desire to have two publishers competing for your book. Certainly publishers do bid against each other under certain circumstances, but only when they are aware that they are doing so. If you had not assured me that Little, Brown was out of the picture, I would not have taken the trouble to read . . . and discuss the manuscript here, and certainly I would not have dreamed of bidding against Ted Weeks. Well, since you are surely going to be writing and publishing many more books, I hope a lesson has been learned, and I do want to wish you good luck with the book.

❦

MY BOOK, ENTITLED "Walking the Indian Streets," was to be published in July. As the time approached, a lot of excitement arose. The publicity woman at Little, Brown rang to say that the editor of the *Times Book Review*—whose name, as it happened, was Francis Brown—had called her himself to say that the *Times* was sending a photographer to Cambridge to take pictures of me at Eliot House. "The scuttlebutt is that the *Times Book Review* is going to do a big picture spread about you with a big review of the book," she said. "We couldn't have asked for a better break. Perhaps they'll follow it up with an article on both your book and Dom's." (The two books were to be published at about the same time.) The photographer, accompanied by the publicity woman, spent the better part of an afternoon with me at Harvard. I started dreaming about pictures of me in the *Times Book Review* and about fame in Harvard Square.

A fortnight or so later, Weeks called to say that the idea of the big picture spread had been shelved. "We smell a rat," he said.

When a copy of the review came, I knew why. The review, by Herbert L. Matthews, was so devastating that I wanted to go to bed and never get up. Matthews wrote:

Ved Mehta plays an extraordinary trick on his prospective readers and on anyone who does not know about him or has not read his previous book, "Face to Face." Mr. Mehta, a Punjabi Hindu, now 25 years old, has been completely blind since the age of 3. He has written this book about his return to India after ten years' absence as if he had normal vision.

His publishers carefully play the game, saying nothing on the jacket blurb to indicate that the author is blind. . . .

Mr. Mehta is doing in this book what he does in life. He asks no quarter and he lives, in so far as it is humanly possible, as if he could see. Knowing he is blind, we can only regard this work as an astonishing tour de force.

Mr. Mehta has learned to minimize his handicap amazingly, but it naturally remains a severe handicap. The author has tried to do the impossible.

Anyone reading the book simply as an account of India today by a young Hindu in possession of all his faculties will get an entertaining and touching work with flashes of deep insight. . . . Here are a few examples to show how the author confuses the reader:

"I find the newspapers and magazines too grim," he writes after getting to Delhi, "and search them for theater criticism."

Or this at the end of the book: "I open my journal and begin thumbing through my impressions of the summer in India." . . .

Knowing that Mr. Mehta is blind, one presumes that someone read the newspapers to him, that he has some method of keeping a journal he can read back. . . . The reader who does not know is simply—although harmlessly, to be sure—fooled.

The point of all this is that Ved Mehta handicaps himself doubly in "Walking the Indian Streets." He cannot help his blindness and has, indeed, turned it by a miracle of will power and courage into something resembling an asset, but he could not hope to write a book about India as if he were not blind.

He has done so, and it would be unfair to say that, even taken at its face value, this book is a failure.

Matthews had, perhaps unwittingly, tried to take the bread from my mouth. He seemed to be condemning me to be a blind writer, in which case I could write only about blindness, and that field, as far as I was concerned, was as barren as the Gobi Desert. I wanted to compete on equal terms with writers who could see, but the *Times Book Review* was such a powerful influence in publishing generally that I feared that, if I continued to write as though I could see, no publisher, and certainly no magazine, would publish me. Letters of commiseration about the review poured in, confirming my drastic interpretation. One of the letters was from Norman Cousins:

August 31, 1960

My dear Ved:

I bled when I first read the Matthews review, for it represented the essential defeat of everything you have been trying to do in life. In a curious sense, Matthews resented the fact that you were not asking for a privileged review which you could have had shamelessly by skillful exploitation of your blindness.

The shame, of course, is that Matthews doesn't know you personally. For then he would know that you live without handicap and that to claim one would be to feign one. Your achievement in life is that you have freed other people from their obligation to you. They can love you or despise you because of your goodness or your venality; they don't have to see you through special perspectives. And you are the same toward them.

It would be fatuous of me to tell you that you shouldn't feel hurt. A man would have to be an armadillo not to be hurt by it. But what I can do is to emphasize the fact that Matthews was not reviewing the book; he was reviewing philosophical factors that basically were apart from the book. In this sense, he was unwittingly paying tribute to it, for readers will be intrigued rather than offended by the point Matthews lamely tries to make.

If all goes well I hope to see you next week.

Affectionately,
Norman

❧

MATTHEWS'S MAIN POINT was: How dare a blind person write as if he could see? Isn't writing in that way dishonest? That was a matter that had preoccupied me for years. I had discussed the subject with Frederick Mulhauser and W. T., or Will, Jones, two professors at Pomona whom I respected and to whom I was close.

Mulhauser had happened to be in London once while I was at Oxford, and I had gone to see him over tea at a flat he was renting there. He was thoughtful and wise, and was physically well put together. He generally favored a tweed jacket with leather patches on the elbows and shirts with narrow stripes, and in the setting of Southern California he came across as the archetypal English professor. He was one of the best-loved teachers at the college.

"What plans do you have for writing more books?" he asked, pouring me a cup of tea. He had read a first, incomplete draft of "Face to Face," and eventually his wife, Margaret, had read the proofs of the book.

"I have not given the subject much thought," I said, and I added, as a conversational gambit, a little in the manner of a child who wants to get the attention of a beloved elder, "But if wishes were horses I would write many books in many genres—autobiographical books, journalistic books, fictional books, and travel books, besides scholarly history." Though I said this half-mischievously, I went on, in a tone so serious that I myself was surprised by it, "But I don't want to write like a blind writer. I feel I have written everything I know about blindness in 'Face to Face.' I feel I have done with the subject. I want to be free to write—to put it boldly—as if I could see."

Mulhauser stood up and started pacing vigorously, as he used to do when I was having a conference with him and had said something dumb and he was trying to work out how to set me straight without saying something crushing. An extremely energetic man, he had a touch of the athlete about him. Now he stopped and stared out of the window. "You talk differently from the way you used to talk at Pomona," he said, twiddling the string on the windowshade.

"I know," I said. "Oxford has strange effects on people."

"Shades of 'Zuleika Dobson' and 'Brideshead Revisited,'" he said. He himself had never gone to Oxford—he had attended Wooster College, in Ohio, and then Yale—but I got the impression that he wished he had. For some time, he had been working on the correspondence of the poet Arthur Hugh Clough, who had been a Scholar at Balliol. I'd always thought that there was a mismatch between the professor and the poet, for Mulhauser was optimistic, an amiable man who was perfectly at peace in the pleasant climate and amiable surroundings of Pomona, while Clough had continually been bedevilled by spiritual agitation and religious doubts, had generally had a dark outlook, and had died at forty-two. As for me, outwardly I was cheerful, like Mulhauser, but inwardly I identified with Clough.

I then pursued the subject of blindness, rather like a gambler who has put a substantial amount in the ante and can't draw back from the gaming table; at the same time, I felt that I had never been more cautious. "The fact is that I don't want to write as a handicapped writer," I told Mulhauser. "I feel that I am no more a blind writer than, at the risk of using exalted examples, Milton was a blind poet or Beethoven was a deaf composer. I want my work, however scanty or indifferent, to be judged purely on what is written, rather as I respond to 'Paradise Lost' or the Ninth Symphony. Nor do I want to write like an Indian writer. I feel that I am no more Indian than Conrad was Polish, or Nabokov is Russian, or Beckett is Irish. This is not to say that I don't feel sad about not belonging to a national tradition. Indeed, I am sure that, except for a few notable exceptions, all the really great writers do belong to one. Dante, Shakespeare, Voltaire, Tolstoy, Goethe, Melville, Yeats—all of them are inseparable from their national traditions. But, of course, as an Indian living in England and America and writing in English—my fourth language—there is no way I can lay claim to any national tradition."

Mulhauser returned to his chair and picked up his cup of tea.

"I would, of course, have to pass muster as an expatriate writer," I went on. "But I feel that my doing so will depend on my command of the English tongue and, of course, on my talent. In any case, it will have nothing to do with my blindness."

" 'The Wound and the Bow,' " he said, abstractedly.

I didn't quite catch the literary reference, but I thought that he was saying something complimentary. I felt a rush of love for him. Without exactly realizing it, I made every teacher I loved into my father—into an almost god-like figure. Teachers I didn't like I hated passionately, as though they belonged to the Devil's party. For me, as for most people with romantic temperaments, there was no middle ground. I said, almost to myself, "But how am I to write as if I could see—convincingly, honestly, and naturally? To be blind and to want to do that is rather like trying to square the circle." The image was a favorite of one of my Oxford tutors.

"I sympathize with the impulse, but I think it is highly impractical," Mulhauser said thoughtfully.

I was taken aback. It was one thing for me to have reservations, quite another thing for my college professor to have them. Though I couldn't forget that Mulhauser was one of the most benevolent people I had ever met, I now told myself that perhaps he was not the best judge of my "impulse." He had settled for a comfortable life in a small college town when, given his considerable abilities, he might have aspired to something more adventurous and challenging.

"Maybe so," I said. "But I'm determined to try."

"How do you plan to go about it?" he asked kindly.

"Just the way I go about the business of living," I said, metaphorically thinking on my feet. "I live among the sighted. I dress, I eat, I walk with the sensibilities of the sighted in mind. I hear the talk of the sighted from morning to night. My whole inner life is made up of visual assumptions. My unconscious must contain a whole reservoir of visual images and references. After all, I could see until I was almost four."

"I can understand that in fiction you can invent visual details, but in other kinds of writing you will have to describe the actual way people look and what they wear," he said. "How will you do that?"

I was stumped, and felt so frustrated that I almost had a murderous impulse against my beloved professor for throwing a realistic difficulty in my path.

"There are so many visual details about how things look that I just pick up by diligent use of my four senses," I finally said. "How could it be otherwise, when people are constantly talking in images—'It's a bright day,' 'What a pretty blue dress she has on' . . ."

I broke off. I felt tired.

"The subject of what visual images you have in your head and how you assimilate them from one day to the next would be worthy of a book in itself," Mulhauser said. "And perhaps only you could write it. Writers do best when they exploit their special gifts, and your special gift may be to explore the universe of the blind."

"As I've told you, I feel I have done that in 'Face to Face.'"

"That's what you think now. But as you develop as a writer you will also develop as a person, and you'll find you have more to say about the subject and greater skills with which to say it."

The English tea, I had been brought up to think, was an occasion for chit-chat, not for talking about unpleasant or embarrassing matters. Among the reserved English, I had become as reticent as they were, and would certainly never have dreamed of getting into such a personal conversation, especially over tea. Mulhauser had brought out my confiding, American self, I realized, yet I wondered how I had come to bring up the subject. The only books I had ever hoped to write were scholarly ones. The fact that I was blind might be relevant to the method of my research but not to its results. I recalled that I had recently attended some lectures by Richard Pares, a historian I greatly admired. He was so enfeebled by paralysis that someone had to stand next to him and turn the pages of his lecture scripts, yet when people discussed his lectures after they were collected in book form, or wrote about his other books, it no more occurred to them to mention his physical infirmities than to mention, for instance, the youthful looks of Hugh Trevor-Roper when they were discussing his works.

"But I wish to be free of blindness—free of all the baggage that goes with it!" I cried.

Mulhauser apparently sensed the rising tide of my frustration, for he made no reply.

❧

SOME MONTHS AFTER my tea with Mulhauser, and while I was still at Oxford, Will Jones, who had been my philosophy professor at Pomona, turned up in London. He was a stout man who laughed easily, often seeing the humorous side of things. As a philosopher, he had Voltaire's faith in reason. As a professor, he was not just interested in but gleefully excited by our conceptions of whatever we were studying in class. Indeed, he took great pleasure in the variety of ideas in the history of philosophy and treated our ideas almost as respectfully as the texts we were studying.

Like Mulhauser, Jones asked me what plans I had for writing more books, and observed that I could easily combine writing with teaching. I became expansive on what was by now an obsession—my determination to write as if I could see.

I had assumed that he would dismiss the idea as a fairyland fantasy, but instead he said enthusiastically, "What a marvellous idea! You must do it. If you can do it successfully, you may earn a place in the history of letters."

I found myself saying, "What I want to do is really what a historian routinely does—describe and re-create people he's never actually seen."

"That's right," Jones said. "You could describe me the way I might describe Socrates or Kant."

"Writing like that will be only an experiment," I said, feeling humbled by the task I was setting for myself.

"No one has done it before," he said.

"That is true. There are no guidelines."

"Then you'll be a trail-blazer," he said. "Everybody gives lip service to originality, but it is seldom, if ever, attained. You have a chance to do something really original."

I told him what Mulhauser had said about writers' exploiting their gifts.

"Maybe you can experiment with the kind of writing you say you want to do and later on in life also explore the internal universe of the blind, as Mulhauser would have you do."

I certainly hadn't expected him to get as fired up about my idea as he did. His approach had always been light-hearted and somewhat distant; he often treated ideas as mere reflections of the biases of the people who held them. But he left me with the impression that he thought my so-called experiment was the most important thing I could do with my life.

☙

AFTER THE SHOCK of Matthews's review had worn off, I told myself that his was a cranky, if not a cliché, response, and that I should rise above it, and struggle on with my original idea about writing. Still, I wondered how I could guard against having to take the Matthews kind of beating in the future. I gathered my forces and tried to put my defense in a letter to the *Times Book Review*, and the letter was published a month after Matthews's review appeared:

TO THE EDITOR:

In a favorable review of my new book, "Walking the Indian Streets," Herbert L. Matthews raises an interesting point: how far an author must feel morally committed to transfer his personal handicaps to his writings.

Now when Mr. Matthews accuses me of "playing a trick on my prospective readers," and chastises my publishers for also "playing the game," and says about me, "He has tried to do the impossible" by attempting "to write a book about India as if he were not blind," he seems to subscribe to the idea that any disabilities of the writer as a person must inevitably find their way into the pages of his work, not merely apparently in the cases of bad writers, but in the instances of good ones also.

This idea is an insidious one: it almost would have prevented Beethoven from composing after he went deaf, Milton from evoking the past through the eyes of his daughters, and me from piecing together a world of five senses by the diligent use of four.

The notion is treacherous, because it wishes to put art into a straitjacket and to clip the wings of the imagination, fixing it to the ground and time of the artist.

VED MEHTA

Friends in the literary and journalistic world with whom I had discussed my letter rallied around me. They felt, indeed, that to forestall further criticism such as I'd received in the *Times Book Review* required some kind of public announcement beyond a letter. I decided to make the announcement in the form of a short preface to the English edition of "Walking the Indian Streets," which was soon to be published by Faber & Faber, and I wrote about that decision to John Douglas Pringle, a friend and the deputy editor of the London *Observer*. He replied, "I am rather glad you have decided on a preface to the English edition of your book, as I had come to the same conclusion that this was right and meant to write and give you the same advice. I think that you should write it and make it so clear and definite that you would never have to explain, apologize or argue about the subject again." It turned out, however, that I was so emotionally wrought up over the subject that I couldn't write a short preface myself, and in the end I left it to Charles Monteith, my editor at Faber & Faber. He had several goes at a draft and eventually came up with the following, which appeared as a publisher's note in the London edition:

As readers of his autobiography, Face to Face, will know, Ved Mehta has been totally blind since the age of three; and they may be surprised to find no reference to his blindness in this book. This is entirely deliberate. By the diligent use of four senses Mr. Mehta is able to piece together the world of five; and when he describes what he "sees" he is in fact describing what he sees through the eyes of other people. In recreating the visual world for himself in this fashion, he finds that he is helped most by the chance and spontaneous remarks of friends and strangers.

By profession Mr. Mehta is an author and journalist and he is anxious that no special allowance should be made for his work on the grounds of his disability. Indeed, he feels this so strongly that no note such as this will appear in any of his future books. It appears here only because some reviewers of the American edition seemed puzzled by the lack of any explanation.

❧

I THOUGHT THAT after Matthews's review *The New Yorker* would never publish me again, but, characteristically, Mr. Shawn cabled me in England, where I was spending my summer vacation, and the cable said, "THE REVIEWS OF YOUR BOOK HAVE ALL BEEN EXTREMELY FAVORABLE THOUGH OF COURSE EYE FEEL THAT WHATEVER IS EXPRESSED IS INADEQUATE PERIOD."

In 1988, when Mr. Shawn was no longer at *The New Yorker,* I asked him during one of our lunches if he had ever had any second thoughts about my writing as if I could see. While he was the editor, he had published my articles in that vein for twenty-seven years.

"No, I didn't," he said without a moment's hesitation. "Your writing seemed totally convincing and natural to me."

"How did you feel when people said that it was totally dishonest?"

"I didn't worry about it, since it worked."

To complicate matters, after I had written in that vein for more than twenty years I started writing like the blind person that I was. I brought up that subject and asked him how he had felt when, as it were, I switched horses in midstream. "I don't think that any other editor would have allowed me to write in both ways," I remarked.

"That was O.K.," he said. "The writing, whichever way you did it, was completely convincing. I felt that whatever you wanted to do, as long as it worked, was O.K."

The simplicity of his answer was stunning. In my years as a writer, I had seen many editors of books and magazines come and go. Each one had typed me as a blind writer or an Indian writer, for instance, and had been interested in my writing on only one or the other of those subjects. In contrast, Mr. Shawn, without having been given a word of preparation or explanation, had jumped in with me in my writing projects, each more outlandish and improbable than the last, as if he were my Siamese twin, who would have to accompany me wherever I went, even to the ends of the earth.

I thought at that moment that I had an inkling of how I had been able to overcome reviews such as Matthews's—reviews that even by 1988 had, mercifully, appeared only two or three times in my writing life—and thus had been able to go on to publish piece after piece in *The New Yorker* despite always fearing that my latest piece was my last. In my own small way, I identified with Mr. Shawn so much that, just as he was the invisible presence in every issue of the magazine published under his stewardship, I became the invisible presence in my pieces and books, in the manner of an actor who assumes a different voice and a different personality for each play but still remains independent of the part.

Some writers of my acquaintance have fulfilled their calling by becoming more visible—publishing books with titles like "Advertisements for Myself," and parading around like celebrities. But many of my *New Yorker* colleagues and I, in the manner of Mr. Shawn, always let our work speak for itself, and were satisfied as persons to fade into the woodwork.

III

FROM ELIOT HOUSE TO THE PICASSO

I N APRIL, 1960, WHEN "HOMECOMING" WAS ALL BUT closed, I began casting about for an idea for a new piece I could submit to *The New Yorker*. I wanted to talk to Mr. Shawn, and I rang up his office. I was immediately put through.

"I can't bear the thought that I won't have any more *New Yorker* proofs to go over—that I won't be working with you," I said.

"Why should you think that?" he asked, sounding genuinely astonished.

"I have nothing more to write. I have written everything I could."

He laughed in a fatherly way, as if I had said something simple-hearted, and asked if we might have lunch to talk about a new piece when I next came to New York.

"I am free today," I said, and then, remembering that I was in Cambridge and it was almost lunchtime, corrected myself. "I mean I could have lunch tomorrow."

I thought that he would need to consult his diary or check with his secretary, but he said, as if, like me, he carried everything in his head, "Would one o'clock tomorrow be convenient?"

"Yes, of course," I said. "Where shall we meet?"

I was afraid that he would suggest a restaurant and I would have to walk into a strange place by myself and be guided to his table by a gauche waiter or, alternatively, would have to wait at a table for him, straining to look alert, so that when he turned up I wouldn't appear stony-faced, as I imagined that blind people generally did when they were not talking with someone. Instead, he asked, "Would you like to meet in my office?"

"Sure," I said, with relief.

After we hung up, I couldn't stop wondering where he went for lunch and what kind of things he ate. There was something so private and ascetic about him that I sometimes had trouble imagining him in a restaurant or in any other public place—or, indeed, eating at all. Even after I met his wife and children—evidence that he was firmly rooted in the world—he still seemed to me otherworldly, and I could picture him only as a monk, perhaps the abbot of a monastery. The most I could imagine was that he ordered a sandwich sent in and ate it sitting at his desk, with proofs spread out in front of him and with pencil in hand, but that only got me wondering what kind of sandwich he ate. I fancied that it would be something delicate and austere, which he would eat almost invisibly, and in silence. I wondered what I should eat in his presence. I thought that I should order something bland, which I, too, could eat invisibly. My staple sandwich—ham and Swiss cheese on rye, with lettuce and French mustard—didn't seem at all the appropriate thing to eat in his office; the rye bread seemed too pungent and the act of eating lettuce too noisy. But then every sandwich I could think of seemed either too rich or too strong. I decided I would wait for him to order first and follow his lead. But what if he insisted that I order first? Well, I would order just a milkshake.

I am aware that I sound as if I had fallen in love with Mr. Shawn. And, indeed, I had had such fantasies when I was in love—when I had lost my sense of self and, like a slave, had subordinated my wishes, my desires, and my very thoughts to a woman I loved. Such love is considered a form of sickness, and is certainly not associated with a writer and his editor. Ironically, however, I considered my love for Mr. Shawn a sign of health: his kindness and generosity, his lack of preconceptions and of condescension, and his publication of my writing as if I were a typical writer rather than a blind or an Indian writer made me believe that I was not losing myself to him but, rather, discovering my true self—that, for once, I was, as it were, speaking not in an Indian-American voice or an English voice but in my own. That was, in a sense, an illusion, though, since under Mr. Shawn's influence I was developing a writing style—a new voice—that was a fusion of my various selves.

❦

ON THE RED-LETTER day, as I thought of it, I flew to New York and arrived at the nineteenth-floor reception desk.

Mr. Shawn came down the hall wearing his coat and carrying his hat, and suggested that we go to lunch at the Algonquin.

I had never heard of the hotel or of its association with the magazine. While other *New Yorker* writers, ranging from its early days right up to the present, had all frequented it and had all read such *New Yorker* stalwarts as E. B. White and James Thurber, either I was not yet born or I was poring over the monumental volumes of S. R. Gardiner and Charles H. Firth on seventeenth-century English history. My only association with the word "Algonquin" was that it was the name of a tribe of American Indians. Now, trying to say something bright à la Oxford, I observed, "Isn't it remarkable that there isn't one state in the entire country which belongs to the American Indians?"

Mr. Shawn was quiet for a moment, as if he were puzzled by why I had chosen that particular conversational gambit, and then said, with surprise in his voice, "It really is."

Later, when I learned about the mystique of the hotel and its connection with *The New Yorker*, I was chagrined, and thought that anyone else would have laughed at my remark or squashed it. Instead, he had made me feel that I'd said something interesting.

"So America had its own form of imperialism in its back yard," I said.

He replied, "I hadn't thought of that, but it's an interesting idea."

Eager to please and to appear as independent as anyone who could see, I bounded to the elevator bank and pushed the "Down" button. The doors of an automatic elevator opened immediately. I would have stepped into it except that I was determined that Mr. Shawn should go first.

"If you don't mind, I'd like to wait for the hand-driven elevator," he said, inserting a key in a lock near the "Up" and "Down" buttons.

Having a special key was a sign of privilege that did not square with my view of him as someone who put on no airs. Later, I learned that he needed a key because he was afraid of heights and enclosed spaces, and therefore of elevators—that, in fact, he had such a fear of riding in an elevator that he required an attendant to operate it manually, and so when the office-building elevators were automated, some years earlier, one hand-operated car had been preserved for his use. Mr. Shawn provided so little occasion for gossip that a great deal was made of his few phobias; they were never as extreme as people contended, and they got exaggerated with each retelling. One writer once told me that Mr. Shawn carried a hatchet in his briefcase so he could hack his way out of an elevator if it got stuck.

Now, as we were waiting for the hand-operated elevator, he asked, "How are you?" People ask that question all the time in a rather pro-forma, mechanical way, but he asked it as if he really cared and wanted to know.

His question went right through me, but all I said was "O.K." Perhaps because he seemed so protective of me, the last thing I wanted to do was to add to his burdens by telling him about my growing unhappiness at Harvard.

"Any news?" he asked encouragingly.

I couldn't hold back any longer, and started telling him about how I didn't like the coldness of certain Harvard professors, but I quickly caught myself and broke off. I thought of asking him how *he* was and if *he* had any news. But, for some reason, I felt that that would be rather like a patient with a fever asking after his doctor's health, so I said nothing.

The hand-driven elevator arrived. The gate was so wide that we were able to walk in together, almost in step. Except for us and the operator, the car was empty, and we rode straight down, without stopping.

We walked side by side, mostly in silence, through the crowded lobby and out onto noisy, congested West Forty-fourth Street, as if we had always walked together, with the sleeves of our coats occasionally touching. Someone else might have offered me an elbow or a hand, but he seemed to grasp intuitively my need to appear independent and to be treated as absolutely normal, and so left me to manage everything—even crossing the street—myself.

The Algonquin Hotel seemed to me like a little piece of the Raj in the middle of New York. The public lobby was cozy, with guests sitting in small groups on sofas and in armchairs around individual tables, and occasionally ringing bells to summon wait-ers, much as people did at my father's clubs in India. At the entrance to a panelled restaurant—the Rose Room—the head-waiter greeted Mr. Shawn as if he were the first citizen of the place, and showed us to a big, semicircular booth in a nearby corner, just steps away from the lobby, as if to shield Mr. Shawn from having to walk past a lot of tables and, at the same time, to provide him with a quick exit in case of an emergency. This meant, though, that, besides a general hubbub, we were subjected to the intrusive ringing of the headwaiter's telephone at the entrance and to the opening and closing of elevator and telephone-booth doors in the lobby, but Mr. Shawn seemed oblivious of the clatter.

The bar waiter came up and asked if we would like anything to drink.

As a rule, I never drank at lunch, but, feeling that this was an unusual occasion, thought of ordering a Campari, because of its festive color and Old World aura, but settled on a *Punt e Mes* on ice—a light, spicy drink that I was barely acquainted with. I had simply read somewhere that it was a favorite apéritif of sophisticated writers when they were lunching with their editors. I should have known better, but I thought that Mr. Shawn would also order an apéritif. Editors who were under much less pressure than I supposed him to be seemed scarcely able to get through the day without drinking and smoking. But Mr. Shawn ordered a glass of freshly squeezed orange juice.

Despite my reticence in his presence, I found myself asking, "Do you ever drink? I mean, wine and such?"

"No."

I blundered ahead. "Do you smoke?"

"No."

"In Arkansas, where I went to high school, kids in my class used to chew tobacco." I realized that my remark was a non sequitur, and felt suddenly shy.

He sat silent, as if he had all the time in the world, and waited for me to speak. I talk out of nervous habit, I thought—fill my conversation with idle chatter, witticisms, or accounts of my own little successes—but he seems to be free of any such need. I wished I could be like him. He was a shadowy presence in my life, yet was already a stronger presence than anyone had ever been before.

"You wanted to talk about doing the next piece," he said, coming to my rescue.

"Yes." And I couldn't think of anything else to say.

"Do you have any ideas?"

I recalled that my second piece was running under the department head "A Reporter at Large," and asked if that meant that I could write something as a reporter for *The New Yorker*. "I mean not recount a reminiscence or tell a story but learn about something new and write about it," I said.

"Sure," he said. "Do you have an idea in mind?"

"I don't," I said. "Do you?"

"After your call, I was thinking about it and wondering if there was something at Oxford that might interest you—that you might like to write about."

I felt a surge of happiness: he seemed to have sensed that Oxford was the driving force of my life at the time. "You mean write something like the history of the university?"

"That would be worth doing, but I was thinking more about something going on there now."

"Like what?" I had the odd sensation that I was sounding like an editor and was putting him in the role of a writer.

"I have been reading a book about Oxford philosophy. What they are doing over there with philosophy sounds fascinating. Would something like that interest you?"

The idea was more than interesting; it was exciting. I asked myself, a little egotistically, why I hadn't thought of it. Indeed, at that time Oxford philosophy was a revolutionary movement and was making waves in philosophy departments everywhere. I was astonished not only that Mr. Shawn knew about it but that he wanted a piece on it. At the time, I associated magazines with travel, current affairs, fashion, and perhaps criticism, but certainly not with little-known philosophers. The idea of doing a piece on Oxford philosophy for *The New Yorker* seemed nothing less than fantastic. Moreover, I rationalized that if I went along with Mr. Shawn's idea I could get back to Oxford, and not as an undergraduate who had failed his promise, by failing his viva for a First, but in the guise of a *New Yorker* reporter.

In replying to Mr. Shawn's suggestions, however, I couldn't help dissembling my real reasons for wanting to do the piece, and so I said, "It's a marvellous subject, but you want somebody like one of my friends—Jasper Griffin or Alasdair Clayre—to write the article. Or, better still, perhaps Isaiah Berlin would agree to write it." I was under the influence of the English system, in which one got an expert to describe the intellectual currents of the day for the general reader.

"I had in mind a writer talking to the philosophers and finding out what they're thinking, what they're getting at—not a summary written by a philosopher, the kind that appears in English journals and newspapers, " Mr. Shawn said, as if reading my mind.

I was startled. He seemed to be saying that he would prefer a piece on Oxford philosophy by me to one by Isaiah Berlin. I also had a glimmering of what he might have in mind—writing about philosophers the way one might write about a place or a tribe. As I pondered tackling the piece, however, I had a sinking feeling. I imagined that such an article would take me a year or two to write. There would be so many philosophers to talk to, so many philosophical works to read—it would be like starting a whole new career.

But then, I thought, a lot of my Oxford friends had done philosophy. I could turn to them as sources. I myself had done philosophy at Oxford for a time, and had gone to the lectures of some of its luminaries. In a sense, the topic seemed tailor-made for me, in that I was capable of picking up a philosophy book and reading it. But that was a private activity. Talking to philosophers for an article—well, that was another matter. I could interview them neither as a fellow-philosopher nor as an innocent reporter who had just stumbled on the subject. How, then, was I to go about my work? The mere thought of interviewing, say, Bertrand Russell was terrifying.

"Can you suggest any models?" I asked, trying to get used to the idea of my writing such a *New Yorker* piece.

"I don't think there are any," he said. "People haven't reported on intellectual movements in the way I was thinking of."

By this time, I had finished my *Punt e Mes,* which I'd found very pleasing. The waiter came up to the table and asked if I would like to know what was on the menu. I feared that he might start reading it—or, worse, that Mr. Shawn might be put to the trouble of doing that—so I asked the waiter hurriedly if there were any specials.

"We always have roast beef on the menu. It's very popular," he said.

To get the whole business over with quickly, I ordered it, without telling the waiter that I liked my meat well done, or even inquiring whether it was hot or cold or how it would be served. I felt that my time with Mr. Shawn was so precious that it should not be taken up with trivialities.

Mr. Shawn, for his part, ordered a piece of toasted pound cake and a cup of coffee.

My first impulse was to blurt out, "No, that's not all you're going to have!" I wanted to ask him if he ordinarily had a late breakfast, what time he began his work, what he did when he didn't have lunch, how late he stayed at the office. My second impulse was to restrain myself from asking such obvious questions, as he seemed to restrain himself in talking to me. I even suppressed the urge to ask after Mrs. Shawn and their sons, because I didn't want to be presumptuous—didn't want him to think that I was trying to put our essentially professional relationship on some other basis. Certainly in England, and possibly in America, it was bad form to ask personal questions. In any event, his manner was so formal that to bring up a subject he hadn't introduced, I thought, would seem almost like an invasion. (I later learned that Mrs. Shawn regularly gave him a big breakfast.)

The waiter brought me my lunch. I was mortified by the size of the plate, by the size of the piece of meat, by the big serving of potato salad and various garnishes—pickles, lettuce, tomatoes, and the like. Moreover, the meat was almost raw, making every bone in my Hindu body rebel at the mere thought of taking a bite. I ate a few bits of the potato salad in a gingerly fashion.

The headwaiter came over and said, "Oh, Mr. Shawn, I'm sorry. They didn't toast the pound cake well. Let me take it back."

"It's O.K.," Mr. Shawn said after a moment's hesitation, as if he would have liked to have it toasted well but didn't want to give the kitchen the trouble.

When the headwaiter had left, I said, "I think Oxford philosophy is a wonderful idea. I could read the books here, but I would need to go over to England to talk to the philosophers. Maybe I could spend my Harvard summer vacation in England. That would, of course, be expensive." I then asked if he was commissioning me to do the piece, and if he would allow some expenses for it. The subject of money made me uncomfortable yet simultaneously emboldened me.

It seemed to have a similar effect on him. He told me in a slightly raised voice that, unlike other magazines, *The New Yorker* never commissioned pieces.

"Why not?" I asked.

"That would take a lot of explanation," he said. "But it happens to be the magazine's tradition." He went on to say that *The New Yorker* had grown up as a writers' and artists' magazine, allowing contributors the freedom to write and draw what they liked, and that one trouble with commissioning, he supposed, was that it turned contributors into employees. He had adroitly ducked my question about expenses. Perhaps he thought that being concerned with money was corrupting to the sanctity of a writing project, and that the matter should be left out until the project was brought to fruition.

Later, I could explain to myself only in negative the powerful impression made on me by the meeting we were having: that not once had Mr. Shawn tried to impress me: that he had revealed not a touch of self-importance or any hint of the importance of the magazine he edited (rather, he spoke of it almost as if it were a little thing he happened to be involved with); that he had let me do all the talking, almost as if he had nothing to say; that he had in no way tried to prescribe the length of the proposed article or the manner in which I might write it, or to influence me in deciding the kind of article I might write; and that he never suggested, as another editor might have, that he would like copy on Russell and Berlin, because they were well known to the American public.

I now asked him, "What if I can't get interviews with Russell and Berlin?"

That wouldn't matter, he said. I could read them. What was important was not whom I got to see but what I made of the people I did get to see.

"When I write to philosophers, can I tell them that I am hoping to publish the piece in *The New Yorker*?" I asked.

"Oh, sure," he said.

"What if, in the end, I couldn't write it? That would be very embarrassing for *The New Yorker*," I said.

"No, I don't think so," he said. "But I'm sure you'll write it very well."

His assurance was infectious, and I walked out of the Algonquin hungry but with a new lightness in my step and a new future. I began mentally going over the people I would write to as soon as I was back in Eliot House—Bertrand Russell and Isaiah Berlin, A. J. Ayer and Stuart Hampshire, Iris Murdoch and Elizabeth Anscombe. I would merely ask to see them. I had never formally interviewed anybody, had no idea how one went about it. I thought I would adopt Mr. Shawn's style—just turn up without any questions or preconceptions, and keep silent and listen with close attention. But then I started fretting. Keeping silent would take a lot of self-confidence. Talking was often my way of proving to people that I was worth talking to. I felt that, lacking eye contact, I had a blank facial expression, which was off-putting. Still, I couldn't come up with any other technique.

When I got back to Harvard, I immediately took out of Widener Library "An Inquiry Into Meaning and Truth," by Bertrand Russell; "Tractatus" and "Philosophical Investigations," by Ludwig Wittgenstein; "Language, Truth and Logic" and "The Problem of Knowledge," by Ayer; "Thought and Action," by Hampshire; and "Two Concepts of Liberty," by Berlin. Reading them along with my history books, for Harvard, meant that I was scheduling readers from early in the morning until late at night, but the work was so exhilarating that I never felt tired.

❦

IN THE MIDDLE of June, I took a cheap charter flight to London for Harvard professors and students who wanted to spend the summer abroad. I decided to settle down in London, which was within easy access not only of Oxford but also of Cambridge, where Oxford philosophy was said to have originated, and, with the assistance of a friend, I rented digs—a pleasantly furnished room, with a shared bathroom—at Brooks Mansions, 32 Hans Road, in the shadow of Harrods. Then, through an advertisement in the "agony" columns of the London *Times*, I found several readers and an amanuensis. Although I was soon so engrossed in philosophy and history books that I cancelled a walking tour in Wales I had planned with an old Oxford friend, I felt somewhat at a loss. I had never lived in a metropolis on my own, and without the amenities of college life, like a dining hall across the grass, I didn't know what to do with myself on my free evenings.

Then my mother and father stopped in London on their way back to India from America, and took a bedsitter in Earl's Court Road by the week. They set up house there, my father doing the shopping and other errands, and my mother doing the cooking, on a gas range in the hallway just outside their door, and washing pots and pans, and doing the laundry, in a little sink in the room. The room was more spacious than most of the other bedsitters in the house, but that was partly because it was sparsely furnished, with twin beds, a ratty armchair, a few straight chairs, and a rickety table. They wanted me to move in with them, and enjoy "Indian home comforts in London." I explained to them that I needed to live in a room of my own, where I could work with my readers. My father immediately understood. My mother, however, was unable to grasp why I couldn't have my readers come there.

"I'm sure your readers would enjoy some good Indian food," she said.

I couldn't tell her that I would be embarrassed to have my English readers work with me in what was essentially a bedroom filled with the smells of Indian cooking and an appearance of Indian disorder. (Clothes, suitcases, and old newspapers were lying about.) So I gave her an excuse that I thought would make sense to her. "I couldn't work with you going in and out of the room all day, and Daddy having to take naps," I said.

I now started living a sort of split life—my English life in Brooks Mansions, where I received my readers, read books in English, and corresponded with Oxford philosophers to arrange interviews with them, and my Indian life in Earl's Court Road, where I saw my parents, ate curry sitting on a bed, and discussed family matters in Punjabi. In addition, I had drinks with my English friends in pubs, or met them in elegant restaurants or in their homes, presenting myself as an Oxford man and a writer from exotic parts.

Strains of my split life began to tell on me when my parents once visited me. After they left, my landlady told me she didn't want any woman who was not wearing a frock or a skirt to come to the house. "My mother was beautifully dressed in a sari," I protested, and she replied, "Those are not fit clothes for an English establishment." I wanted to throttle her, but I had paid the rent in advance, so I stuck it out.

❧

AFTER THE ACCEPTANCE of "Indian Summer," I had show-ered Mr. Shawn with old manuscripts from my desk drawer. Then I didn't hear anything from him for a couple of weeks, and I thought the worst, imagining that, like great masters who didn't want to discourage their pupils by giving them bad news, he pre-ferred silence to rejection and worked through a sort of sign lan-guage, which in time I would learn to interpret. The story that I entertained the most hope for was entitled "Sunset," and con-cerned a teen-age Indian boy coming to terms with a lie that the adult members of his family tell his grandmother about the death of her son at the hands of the Japanese in the Second World War. I would wake up in the middle of the night bedevilled with all kinds of fears about "Sunset." What if it had got buried under a pile of manuscripts? What if he had read it but was waiting to get back to me with some ideas for revision? What if he had already written to me and the letter either had not been sent or had got lost in the mail? All the next day, I would resist the temptation to call his office, but by evening it would get the bet-ter of me and I would be on the telephone to his secretary, Miss Broun, asking her about "Sunset."

Her answer was always the same: "Mr. Shawn has it. I will tell him that you were asking about it. Would you like him to call you?"

"Oh, no," I would say, quickly retreating. "In fact, don't bother to tell him that I telephoned."

"I'll do what you tell me," she would say, dutifully, and I would hang up in a sweat, and no wiser.

Many months went by, and then, in London, I received this cablegram from Mr. Shawn: "SORRY TO SAY AFTER HOLDING YOUR STORY SUNSET ALL THIS TIME THAT WE DECIDED FINALLY WE DID NOT THINK IT COULD BE WORKED OUT FOR US PERIOD MUCH OF IT IS LOVE-LY BUT SOMEHOW OR OTHER THE STORY AS A WHOLE DID NOT SEEM QUITE STRONG ENOUGH AS IT NOW STANDS PERIOD EYE KEPT HOPING THAT SOMEONE HERE WOULD HAVE PRACTICAL SUGGESTIONS TO MAKE FOR REVISION BUT SADLY NOBODY HAS BEEN ABLE TO DO THAT PERIOD EYE WILL TALK TO YOU ABOUT IT IN MORE DETAIL WHEN YOU RETURN PERIOD."

I was so touched and elated that the story had all along been under consideration that I did a little jig in my room in Brooks Mansion. I wasn't the slightest bit disappointed at its rejection. On the contrary, I was grateful to Mr. Shawn for suppressing the publication of a weak story. And I found his response especially overwhelming because of little journalistic experiences I was having away from his magazine.

After some badgering from me for a book to review, Francis Brown, the editor of the New York *Times Book Review*, had sent me, of all things, an autobiography of a blind person. I had hoped for a book about India or the British Empire, and it seemed to me that his choice was so narrow-minded as to be almost patronizing. Then the book, written by a Dane, turned out to be a work that was alternately sentimental, melodramatic, and pathetic. I sent in an essentially unfavorable review, only to get a chastening call from Brown. He said that Americans did not have the tradition of publishing harsh reviews—thereby implying that I was better suited to writing for an English paper—and that the book's publisher, Alfred Knopf, was very unhappy about mine. "The book came garlanded with quotations from European reviewers," Brown said. "Alfred expected a big selling review from us. He thinks you spoiled the party." Brown's implication was that I wouldn't be getting many more books to review.

My experience with other papers was chastening in a different way. In response to some soliciting from me, Arthur Crook, the editor of the London *Times Literary Supplement,* sent me a couple of books on India to review. The review, as was the custom at the *T.L.S.* then, was published anonymously, and I was paid three pounds ten for it—a sum that hardly covered the cost of a reader's reading to me just a part of one of the books.

Soon, however, I was particularly honored to land a review of "The Lotus and the Robot," by Arthur Koestler—a cultural Pooh-Bah in England—from Terry Kilmartin, the literary editor of the London *Observer.* Not only did the paper pay at a considerably higher rate than did the *T.L.S.* but, more important, all my friends in those days were London *Observer* readers. And no sooner did my review appear than I got this postcard from Dwight Macdonald: "Ved! A masterly review in the *Observer* of Koestler's Philistine obtusification of Yoga and Zen. Much better than C. Connolly in the *Times.* I was proud of you." Terry, though, scarcely ever sent another book my way. He had his own stable of English reviewers, and only occasionally opened his book pages to an outsider. On the whole, all the editors I met were glad to have an occasional piece from me but actively avoided any long-term arrangement, as if they were afraid I would become dependent on them. Mr. Shawn was the exception, insofar as I could read his sign language. He seemed to be committed both to my writing and to me.

❧

SEVERAL ACADEMIC PROBLEMS I encountered as I tried to settle back in at Harvard in the autumn of 1960 were put in perspective for me by a letter from an American friend, part of whose stay at Oxford had coincided with mine. He had since been doing graduate work in history at Yale for two years. In other words, he was well along on the road that I was just setting out on. He wrote:

> You know how the intellectual aristocracy of Oxford looks down upon the Ph.D. route as the *via dolorosa* of second-class minds. The thought of our brilliant English contemporaries putting up with the drudgery of dissertating boggles the mind. The Isaiah Berlins, John Sparrows, and Hugh Trevor-Ropers may have encouraged all kinds of research among their mostly American graduate students, but these intellectual patricians have no intention of ever soiling their hands with Germanic-American *archiv-arbeit*.

After I received this letter, the idea of a Ph.D. as a *via dolorosa* got fixed in my mind, and, although I stuck it out at Harvard for another semester, I didn't feel I belonged there. Anyway, in December I finished my philosophy piece, and I showed it to my old Balliol friend Jasper Griffin, who was at Harvard on a fellowship for the year to do research in classics. He read it within a day, and told me, "You've really put the cat among the professional pigeons. Leaving aside your ironical style, what's impressive is that you've got it right." Since he was a friend, I disregarded his compliment, even as I was flattered by it. I told him that, for a start, my working title, "Words, Words, Words," seemed forced, and asked if he could suggest a better one. Thinking faster than most people snap their fingers, Jasper said, "Alms-Basket of Words," and he quoted this exchange from two pedants in "Love's Labour's Lost":

Moth: They have been at a great feast of languages, and stolen the scraps.
Costard: O! They have lived long on the alms-basket of words.

"Smashing," I said. But I quickly had second thoughts. The title would mean little without the Shakespeare quote, and I could see no way of fitting that in. Anyway, I was assailed by doubts about the manuscript itself. The piece, which was constructed around Ludwig Wittgenstein and half a dozen preëminent Oxford philosophers—their works and my interviews with them—highlighted what they thought about one another's ideas and characters, so it was neither strictly scholarly nor strictly literary. Moreover, the philosophical arguments were so subtle, so dependent on nuances, and so interwoven that I couldn't imagine any editor in the world having the patience to plow through the piece, let alone publish it. I imagined that if I sent it to Mr. Shawn he might decide that I was suited only for scholarship. But I told myself that, having gone this far, I had little to lose, and I posted the piece to him—without, however, giving an address or a telephone number where he could reach me during the Christmas holidays, as if to signal to him that I didn't really expect an answer. That done, I left Harvard for New York.

❧

DURING VISITS TO New York while I was at Harvard, I always faced the problem of where to stay. At first, I dossed down on a hammock in an apartment shared by a group of Oxford friends, but the hammock had only a bearskin for a mattress, and I would wake up in the morning feeling as if I'd been mauled. Then I stayed with Allen Ginsberg, who was one of the few Americans I knew in the city; he had visited Oxford when I was there, and I'd helped to show him around. But the novelty of staying at Allen's quickly wore thin. His friends, all male, seemed to be always huddling under blankets on bare mattresses on the floor and lighting up marijuana joints, and I would wake up in the middle of the night thinking that the apartment was on fire. One night, there actually was a fire, but in the building next door. The fire gave off so much smoke that we all had to get out of Allen's apartment and stand around on the street for an hour or so while firemen battled the flames, and during that interval Allen and his friend Peter Orlovsky composed a poem in praise of the salamander. Soon after the fire, I moved to a very cheap hotel on the Lower East Side. There I would drop off to sleep hearing in my overactive imagination things scurrying in the corners, and have nightmares of cockroaches crawling up my legs. Still, I told myself that the fear of onanism—if that's what it was—was better than the fear of Sodom and Gomorrah.

A couple of times, I went up to New Canaan and stayed with Norman Cousins, who had given me an open invitation, but his house had the crazy atmosphere of a train station. He had four daughters who were all still in school, and they and their friends were constantly racing in and out; the television was always on; the telephone was always ringing; and the blender seemed to be always whirring as his wife, Ellen, prepared various healthy concoctions. Norman would start a game of chess with me, and while I was pondering a move he would rush off to the television to watch part of a football game, or to his study to type out a thought for his next editorial, or upstairs to change for a game of golf or tennis. I would come away with our chess game unfinished but, maddeningly, with Norman winning.

After I had my début in *The New Yorker,* I sometimes found myself thrust into one or another corner of the New York intellectual world. In early 1960, for instance, I attended a cocktail party given by Dwight Macdonald which was full of intimidating people, like Mary McCarthy, Hannah Arendt, and Harold Rosenberg. I felt out of place there until I fell into conversation with a British couple almost twice my age, Arthur and Mary Hillis.

Arthur was an adviser from Her Majesty's Treasury to his country's Permanent Mission to the United Nations, but, unlike the conventional Treasury men, who are generally pleased with themselves for being the crème de la crème of the civil service, he was shy and retiring. Mary seemed to complement Arthur perfectly. She, too, was shy, but her kind of shyness came across as warmth: she talked almost without stopping to take a breath. "When I was a young girl, I wanted to be a dancer," she said as we chatted. "But, as it turned out, I had bad feet—bad feet even as a young girl." After a pause, she added, "If I'd had a stage career, I couldn't have married Arthur. I've made my career at the BBC, doing research on how our foreign-language broadcasts are received overseas. I feel more at home with writers and artists than I do with Arthur's diplomats." It was unusual for someone British to be so confiding at a first meeting. Both Mary and Arthur struck a sympathetic chord in me, for, despite their shyness, they threw themselves into life with great energy and verve.

❦

NOW, AT CHRISTMASTIME, on the train bound from Boston to New York, I felt I could never return to Harvard—I had almost willfully botched an important examination for my Ph.D.—but had no idea where I would end up. I recalled something that the poet Robert Lowell (or Cal, as he liked to be called), who had become a friend, had said to me earlier that month: "You know life only in institutions. They haven't prepared you to live in New York City as a writer. Outside the protective fold, you'll kill yourself." He and his wife, the writer Elizabeth Hardwick, were then living in Boston, and they and a couple of their Harvard literati friends had almost adopted me as a literary mascot. Now his words reverberated in my head with the force of a doomsday bell. But then I thought of the Hillises. I had encountered them several times since our first meeting, and they had repeatedly invited me to stay with them in their apartment, a furnished sublet on Sutton Place South. "You can have a room of your own with us," Mary had said. In my present mood,

I felt I needed friends like the Hillises, who could serve as an anchor to my wanderings.

As soon as my train pulled into Grand Central, I got Mary on the telephone, but then I was overcome with hesitation. "I can't imagine you wanting guests during the Christmas holidays, but I'm looking for a place to kip," I said, trying to sound offhand.

"It would be lovely to have you," she said. "We're staying put in New York. We'll be here all through the holidays."

So it was that I took a taxi to the Hillises'.

Mary put me up in her sewing room, which doubled as her guest room, and I was surrounded by sewing paraphernalia—an electric sewing machine, curtains in the making, and swatches of material. It all underlined my feeling of transition, as if a new life were mysteriously being readied for me. I stayed with the Hillises for a few days, hanging around the apartment and debating with them which offered a better life—remaining at Harvard and eventually teaching or coming at once to New York and writing full time for *The New Yorker*. I knew that the debate was a sham, though, since my pride would never let me go back to Harvard and my philosophy piece would almost certainly put an end to any chance I'd ever had at *The New Yorker*. I secretly dreaded everything to do with the outside world, and mentally battened down the hatches for a storm I sensed gathering around me; I had an unsettling feeling that I was a coward, not facing up to the fact that I would be leaving something unfinished for the first time. But, because I admired the Hillises for their stiff upper lip, I somehow instinctively fell into handling my situation as I supposed Arthur would—with humor and stoicism.

The day before New Year's, prepared to hear the worst, I called Mr. Shawn. "Oh, I've been trying to reach you for days now, Mr. Mehta," he said. He came straight to the point. "I think your piece is brilliant."

To repeat his remark now sounds self-congratulatory, but I can't forget how that single sentence affected me: it simultaneously uplifted me and humbled me. "You can't mean it," I said. "Don't you think the introduction is terrible? But tell me, what did you like about it?"

❧

IF THE PAYMENT for the philosophy piece turned out to be anything like that for "Homecoming," which was twelve hundred dollars more than I'd been paid for "Indian Summer," it would be enough to keep me afloat for months. The life of a writer was no doubt full of risks, I reflected, but it had its rewards, and maybe I was better suited to it temperamentally than to the safe harbor of college teaching. The thought even occurred to me that the reason I hadn't flourished at Harvard was that everything there was smugly secure. But at the moment I didn't have much time to think. The Hillises were about to take me to a New Year's Eve party—given not by diplomats, as I'd expected, but by a folksinger, Cynthia Gooding, who lived on East Thirty-eighth Street, in what Mary described as the "artsy part of the city."

In the taxi, Arthur and Mary told me a little about Cynthia. She was thirty-six, was divorced from a Turkish economist, had two daughters, and lived a bohemian life. When we arrived at her apartment, the ground floor of a brownstone, she turned out to be a combination of gypsy and well-brought-up hostess. She was tall and statuesque, had a deep, husky voice, and wore a billowy skirt and oversized, flamboyant jewelry. As she navigated us deftly around the room, which was already crowded, I was awestruck to discover that two of the writers I'd lately been reading in back issues of *The New Yorker*—A. J. Liebling and Joseph Mitchell— were there, along with folk singers, gospel singers, and people in the news, among them Josh White, Jean Richie, and Alger Hiss. The guests all mingled without any aura of self-importance or condescension. How different Cynthia's party was from parties at either Oxford or Harvard, where class consciousness and university rank were palpable!

I remember that when Cynthia introduced me to Liebling I automatically came to attention and "sir"ed him.

"Joe," he corrected me, and he mumbled something under his breath.

I was flustered. From the finish and the clarity of his prose, I had expected Liebling to be a great conversationalist, but he scarcely seemed to want to make any effort to talk. Moreover, from the lightness and agility of his writing, I had imagined him as a sort of Ariel, but he turned out to be a man of such amplitude that I was acutely aware of the amount of floor space he was occupying in the crowded room. I was so much in awe of his writing that I felt inferior to him, but I comforted myself with the thought that perhaps I was socially more adept. That illusion was dispelled a bit later, though, when, in an attempt to impress the writer Jean Stafford, I mentioned my friendship with Cal.

She turned on me, saying, "I hate him."

"You can't mean that," I said stupidly.

"Why can't I? I had the bad luck to be his wife."

Joe shuffled across to us. "You giving my wife a hard time?"

Joe and Cal were so different that it boggled my mind to think that the same woman could have been married to both of them. I didn't know what to say.

Midnight came and went without the kissing and fuss that customarily accompany the ushering out of the old year and the ringing in of the new. A large man, who had long since fallen asleep in the biggest armchair in the room, didn't wake up to greet the new year. (I later learned that he was Rogers E. M. Whitaker, a longtime fact editor at *The New Yorker*.) After the crowd had thinned out, however, the Hillises, their usual stalwart selves, tried to lead the remaining guests in "Auld Lang Syne," and a few discordant voices did join in.

Not long afterward, the Hillises and I made our way out onto Thirty-eighth Street and hailed a taxi. Some of my mother's superstition must have rubbed off on me, for I felt that my happy New Year's Eve was surely a good omen for 1961.

❧

A DAY OR two after the party, I went to see Mr. Shawn. He said that my philosophy piece would need a new introduction, and that when he'd had a chance to reread it he would have some suggestions for me. He added, "I hear from Mr. Liebling and Mr. Mitchell that they met you at a party." He is so close to his writers that he even knows whom they meet at parties, I thought. "Are you enjoying getting around the city?" he inquired.

"Very much," I said, and, seeing an opening, I rushed in headlong, asking, "Do you think I could move to the city and write for *The New Yorker*?"

We had not previously discussed the subject, although I had once mentioned that I was unhappy at Harvard. He had replied, in his usual understated way, "Harvard isn't what you'd expected?" The question had threatened to open the sluice gates of my dammed-up feelings. I had almost told him that Harvard and *The New Yorker* exemplified two widely different Americas—one big and worldly, the other small and idealistic—and that I had no doubt about which I really belonged to, but I had restrained myself. Now I found something intoxicating about the idea of making a life for myself writing for *The New Yorker,* yet, upon asking my question, I felt a pang of apprehension.

Without a moment's hesitation, he said, "Yes, of course."

That response brought a surge of elation, but then I realized that I had no idea what writing for the magazine would entail. I hesitantly asked him how many articles one had to write during a year in order to make a living. Usually, four long articles, he said. I couldn't think of a subject for a single article, so I pressed ahead with my other preoccupation. "Where could I live?" I asked. "I feel I should be out of Eliot House before the new term begins, so that someone else can have my rooms."

"Would you like me to look for an apartment for you?" he asked in reply.

I was flabbergasted to think that someone with his responsibilities and pressures could have either the time for or the interest in apartment-hunting for one would-be writer. "I wouldn't dream of putting you to such trouble," I said, "but maybe you have someone in your office who could tell me how to go about it."

"We don't have anyone in the office for this kind of project," he said. "Apartments are very personal things, so people really have to see them for themselves. But your situation is a little unusual." He gave a slight laugh, as he often did when he was talking about the office or the magazine, and added, "Although I don't know what a usual situation around here is." He went on to say, "What I could do is see a few apartments for you and describe them to you on the telephone. If one of them sounded appealing, you could come down and look it over for yourself."

The truth was that I was afraid to look at apartments, for fear of having to meet their landlords. I was sure that once a landlord saw that I was blind he would refuse to rent to me—that had been my experience with summer rentals—and then Mr. Shawn himself might have second thoughts about letting me write for *The New Yorker*. But I didn't voice any of this to him. "Thank you," I brought out instead.

❧

IT SEEMED ODD to return to my rooms at Eliot House. I already felt like an exile from Harvard. Going through the rooms, I surveyed my accumulation of possessions. I would have happily left everything behind, except my books and records, but decided that the few pieces of simple furniture I had bought while I was there could help to deaden the echoes of loneliness in my new place, if I actually got one.

I started hanging around the telephone, waiting for word from Mr. Shawn. Then, on the next Saturday evening—the time of the week when my spirits were usually at their lowest, because I was usually alone, and felt excluded from the American institution of the "Saturday night out"—he called. He said that the few apartments he had seen didn't seem exactly right to him, but he was ready to describe them to me, in case I wanted to look at them myself.

"If you don't think they're right, then I'm sure they're not," I said, cutting him short without intending to.

In the middle of the week, I had a second call from him. He said he had found an apartment that might be appropriate.

"How exciting!" I exclaimed, and immediately realized that my enthusiasm was a bit premature.

"It is in a fairly new building on Fifty-eighth Street, off Third Avenue, called the Picasso," he said. "The apartment is light, pleasant, and well kept." He went on to tell me that it consisted of a spacious kitchen, a bathroom, and an L-shaped room with a Japanese-style screen separating the sleeping alcove from the living room. Two girls had been living in it, he said, and they were going to leave the screen behind but wanted fifty dollars for the carpeting and the curtains, which were a nice neutral beige. He thought that it would be worth my while to come down and look it over.

I said, "I'll take it, curtains and all."

"I think you should see it first and be sure that you like it," he said, and he gave me the girls' telephone number.

I got in touch with them, made an appointment, and took the train to New York.

The building was somewhat flashy and modern for my taste. There were framed reproductions of Picassos along the halls—apparently an attempt to give it some character. The apartment itself had the compactness of a railway car, and to me it hardly felt lived in. I immediately missed the customary bustle of students walking, talking, and horsing around in corridors and courtyards. But I could see why Mr. Shawn liked it. It was open and airy, and would be convenient to manage. The building had twenty-four-hour doorman service, and was in a good section of the city and not too far from the *New Yorker* offices.

One of the tenants was there, and she offered to throw in her bed along with the carpeting and the curtains for an additional thirty dollars.

"I'll take them," I said, and I offered to get her the eighty dollars by evening.

"You'd better see if you can get your application approved first," she suggested. "A lot of buildings are restricted, which means that the renting agents don't accept some people. You're an Indian, and, besides, in your case they might worry that you would fall, and sue them."

I rushed to Mr. Shawn's office. He had someone with him, but he came out, and we talked in his secretary's little alcove. "The apartment is perfect," I said, and stumbled through an account of what the tenant had told me.

He knew, he said, that I would have to be personally interviewed by a renting agent, and he offered to have Joe Anthony, who looked after the *New Yorker* offices, accompany me.

As he escorted me to Joe Anthony's office, he said, "I should have mentioned that the rent is a hundred and eighty-five dollars a month. That seems a lot, but it includes utilities." The annual rent alone would be almost as much as my yearly tuition and all my expenses at Harvard, but I told myself that I would rent the apartment by the month, and if I couldn't make a go of writing I could always return to doing a Ph.D. Even before I'd got used to the idea of the rent, he added, "The lease for the apartment will be for two years."

I stopped dead in the hall. "I couldn't possibly sign such a lease," I said.

He seemed to grasp my anxiety immediately. "If you couldn't pay the rent at any time, *The New Yorker* would take over the lease," he said.

I was filled with relief and gratitude.

❧

JOE ANTHONY PROVED to be, if anything, more nervous than I was. He spoke of my being approved for the apartment as being a little like his getting his daughters—he had four of them—into college. "It's not unusual for it to take a year to find the right apartment and be approved for it," he said.

The renting agent kept us waiting for half an hour, but as soon as he saw from my application blank that I was connected to *The New Yorker* he approved me. After taking the checks for a month's security and the first month's rent, he asked me what color I would like the apartment repainted.

"Gray, light gray," I said, choosing the most unpretentious color I could think of, to counteract the Picasso décor.

Then we were out on the street. Although the whole interview hadn't lasted more than a few minutes, I was shaking as if I had just taken a difficult examination.

Once the apartment business was settled, Mr. Shawn asked me if I would need an office to work in.

"You mean an office at *The New Yorker*?" I exclaimed. I had such an exalted notion of the magazine that I couldn't believe I was being offered an office there. The idea of sitting in the Picasso and trying to write had already struck me as daunting, and I told him that an office would be wonderful.

He explained that, although many *New Yorker* writers preferred to work at home, an informal system of giving writers offices had grown up over the years, along with a method of giving them advances against future pieces, called drawing accounts. He would like to propose to me a drawing account of seven hundred dollars a month and offer me a *New Yorker* agreement. He was quick to add, however, that neither the office nor the drawing account was guaranteed for more than a year, because both depended on the continued financial health of the magazine.

"Is the magazine not doing well?" I asked, growing alarmed.

"It's doing very well," he assured me. "All this is a mere technicality, and you shouldn't worry about it."

Seven hundred dollars was three times what I was receiving per month at Harvard, and a little more than three times the Picasso's monthly rent. I said that it seemed like a princely sum.

IV

EMBARKING ON A DANGEROUS PROFESSION

I RETURNED TO HARVARD, NOTIFIED THE GRADUATE school that I was leaving, arranged for the movers, said my goodbyes, and within a day was back in New York at the Hillises'.

Mary and I made the rounds of the Salvation Army and some thrift shops, picking out a small round table for eating, a couple of straight chairs, some dishes, and a standing lamp. Members of the Cousins family, as soon as they heard that I was setting up housekeeping, dropped off old sheets and towels and a few more chairs. From the Door Store, which advertised that it could make any piece of furniture cheaply from doors, I got a clunky-looking bar cabinet and some glasses, and I visited a lumberyard for planks and a hardware store for brackets in order to fashion a hanging bookcase. With the arrival of my Eliot House possessions, the apartment was nearly furnished.

I still recall vividly the odd sensation of sleeping there for the first time. The whole place smelled of fresh paint. It had a feeling of newness that was exciting and also a little scary.

In the morning, a package arrived from Mr. Shawn, with a note, beginning "Dear Ved." (At the last interview, I had insisted that he call me by my first name. He said that then I could call him Bill, but any such move was blocked by a heap of inhibitions I could never surmount.) The note read, "I hope that life will go serenely for you on East Fifty-eighth Street. With affection, William Shawn." In the package were jars of jam, different kinds of pâté, and round tins of thin cheese crackers. I became so addicted to the crackers that for years afterward I ordered them for snacks.

❧

NO SOONER HAD I settled in than I began to worry that I had no place to put up my Oxford friends, who might come to stay with me while they were studying or travelling in this country. I picked up a divan bed from the Salvation Army, but the mattress and the bolsters were so stained that I felt I couldn't live with them even for a day unless I could give them covers. I did cover them with sheets and blankets, but the stains continued to loom large in my mind. I became obsessed by them, as if their presence soiled what was otherwise a spotless apartment.

Mary, who was in Mexico on vacation, happened to telephone, and I told her about my problem. The next thing I knew, she'd flown back a day or two before her scheduled return, bought a nubby purple material, and sewn covers for the bed and the bolsters. I suspected that they were not in keeping with the neutral colors in the apartment, but I could feel nothing but gratitude to her for taking such a motherly interest in me and sacrificing part of her vacation to relieve my anxiety.

Everything in the apartment had a temporary, makeshift quality, it seemed to me, as if I were about to pull up stakes and leave at a moment's notice. The only things in my new life with a hint of permanence about them were my relationship with Mr. Shawn and the manner of an elderly man who came to my apartment from *The New Yorker* a day or so after I moved in. His name, sadly, I've forgotten, but I recall that he had been with the magazine for years, and he spoke of it as if it were an ancient order. He had brought a copy of the agreement for my signature, and greeted me as the magazine's latest inductee, giving me the sense that I was embarking on a lifelong undertaking. The agreement, in the form of a letter dated February 16, 1961, was scarcely a page long, and I went over it quickly. It said that in the course of a year the magazine would pay me a thousand dollars for each Reporter at Large article that was accepted, would pay me an additional twenty-five per cent if I wrote six or more articles, and would make a cost-of-living adjustment "if it so wishes and in its absolute discretion." The text was silent on all my principal concerns: how long the articles had to be; when, or if, *The New Yorker* would publish those it accepted; what would happen if I couldn't write anything "acceptable"; and, in that case, how long I could have to pay back the money advanced to me. In fact, it was essentially an empty agreement: there was no mention of my having a drawing account or an office or of my writing pieces other than Reporter articles and short stories—or, for that matter, of *The New Yorker*'s taking over my lease. But, having felt all along that my informal arrangements with Mr. Shawn were tokens of emotional bonds that needed no formal confirmation, I signed the agreement as eagerly as if it were my pass to an enchanted kingdom.

❧

THE NEXT MORNING, I called Miss Broun to find out where my office would be. I didn't want to trouble Mr. Shawn with such a routine real-estate matter, but he came on the line and said that if I could stop by he would like to show it to me.

When I arrived, he took me down a flight of stairs and opened the door to a small, bare corner room on the eighteenth floor, containing only a metal desk, an old, beaten-up typewriter on a typewriter table, and a chair. It was a cubicle the size of a large closet, but it had a window that looked out to the west, with a view of the rooftops of the Times Square buildings and a sliver of New Jersey. Before he left, he offered to point out the men's room and the fire stairs, saying they were just around the corner from my office. Because I wanted to appear above such concerns, however, I brushed him aside, and he delicately retreated. It wasn't until some time later that I learned which door was which.

In my office, I sat down at the typewriter, inserted a sheet of paper, and was seized by terror of the blank page. Although I often typed rough notes on what I was reading, I generally dictated my papers and essays, because they required, among other things, reading over and polishing. At college, I had relied on a variety of part-time student helpers wanting to supplement their incomes, but now I felt I would need a full-time assistant, and could scarcely imagine the expense that that would involve. I hadn't said anything to Mr. Shawn, because until then the problem hadn't occurred to me; no doubt I had unconsciously been afraid of derailing the arrangements he was making for me. Now I sat there for an hour or so in a daze, wondering how I would write.

There was a knock—four gentle taps—and Mr. Shawn came in. "I should have mentioned that if you need assistance you can call Miss Terry," he said. "She's in charge of our typing pool, and I've told her about you." He's a mind reader, I thought.

As soon as he left, I made my way to the twentieth floor and sought out Miss Daise Terry. An elderly woman, she turned out to be less interested in talking to me about my problem than in talking about about her memories of Truman Capote when he worked as a messenger at the magazine. It was some time before I could get her to focus on what I'd come for. Then she said she would be glad to send someone down to me for an hour or two whenever I called her.

"But I think I will need somebody full time," I said.

She grasped my situation so quickly that I felt I had underestimated her. "I have Adrianne Driben here," she said. "She doesn't fit into my department. Just yesterday, I dropped a pencil and asked her to pick it up, and her skirt rode up her leg in a most unladylike way." Later, I learned that the typing pool was the one corner of Mr. Shawn's *New Yorker* where, thanks to Miss Terry, strict rules of behavior were enforced. "You can walk out with her right now," she added.

The expression gave me pause. It conjured up a picture of my taking Miss Terry's misfit out for an ice-cream soda rather than just down to my office. But I said only, "Shouldn't we check first with Mr. Shawn?"

"He's already told me to give you whatever help you need. Anyway, if you'd been at *The New Yorker* as long as I've been, young man, you'd know that when it comes to facilitating his writers' work Mr. Shawn will stop at nothing."

Perhaps I should note that, because of my special circumstances, I was the only writer at *The New Yorker* to be given a full-time assistant, for the magazine was very proud of its tradition of treating all writers equally, and requiring them to do their own research and writing.

Within a few minutes, Adrianne Driben, as no-nonsense as her name, had walked down with me, and we had secured a second chair and pushed the typewriter aside. In those days, I could not dictate to a typewriter; I was so sensitive to noise when I was trying to write that even the sound of dangling earrings on an amanuensis, to say nothing of the tapping of typewriter keys, would interfere with my concentration.

Pencil poised, Adrianne asked impatiently, "So which article do you want to write today?"

I decided that I would write a story based on a ne'er-do-well uncle of mine in India, but every time I dictated a sentence to her and then started to amend it, she laughed, though not unkindly. I've got myself a full-time witness to my incompetence, I thought, and, perversely, I missed being alone with the typewriter, but I doggedly dictated a page of gibberish. It soon became clear that Adrianne was no happier with the new arrangement than I was. She didn't enjoy being yanked out of the typing pool, where the young women often had time for reading popular novels as they waited to retype a writer's manuscript for editing or to pinch hit at the reception desk. She certainly hadn't counted on being plunked down with a writer to wrestle with words all day. All the same, we stuck it out and gradually adapted to each other, like two shipmates setting out to sea.

❦

ALL MY ADULT life, I had lived in the institutional setting of a school, a college, or a university, and had never had to fend for myself in such matters as preparing meals and doing laundry. I had imagined before I moved to the city that I would be able to pay someone to come in for an hour a day and cook for me, but the doorman quickly disabused me of that idea. "No one in New York will come for such a short time," he said. "What many people in the building have is a cleaning woman for four hours once a week. She cleans and does the laundry. We have a washing machine for tenants."

I arranged with him for a cleaning woman, and realized that I would have to get my own meals. But, aside from making coffee and toast, I was helpless in a kitchen. I scarcely knew how to wash a plate. Merely to accomplish that, I tried to do what my father used to do when he was living without my mother in Los Angeles—put a cake of soap on the end of a fork and apply it to cups and saucers. But the method was not very successful. Either the cake of soap kept falling off the fork or I couldn't manage to rinse the soap off the cup, no matter how hard I tried.

Dinner in restaurants was hardly a solution. It was not only expensive but embarrassing. At several restaurants I tried out, I would wait in a long line, and when my turn came the host would shout out, "All alone today?" I would be seated, only to have the waiters neglect me in favor of the bigger tables, from which they could expect bigger tips. Thinking that everyone was looking at me and feeling sorry for me, I wished that, like other people, I could hide behind a book.

❦

BACK IN THE winter of 1959, almost a year and a half before I joined *The New Yorker*, my telephone in Eliot House had rung, and when I picked it up I had been hypnotized by the voice at the other end. It was a female voice, light and innocent, yet also hard-edged and tough. "Is this Mr. Mehta I'm talking to?"

"Who wants to speak to him?" I had asked, automatically putting up my guard.

"This is Lillian Ross. I am a writer for *The New Yorker*."

I immediately relaxed. Although I had not read any pieces by her, just the thought that someone connected with *The New Yorker* was calling me had a softening effect.

"I need your help," she went on, and added, as matter-of-factly as if she were asking me for a telephone number, "Do you think you could help me adopt a baby?"

The request was so bizarre, and I was so unprepared for it, that I hedged, merely replying that I had no experience in such things. "I wonder why you thought of me in this connection," I said.

She didn't offer an explanation but went on, "I want my baby to have a Burmese or an Ajanta look."

It took a me minute to follow her train of thought. The Burmese were, of course, a distinctive racial type, while Ajanta was a village known mainly for its twenty-two-hundred-year-old Buddhist monastic caves with frescoes depicting scenes from Buddha's life.

"I saw a picture of a small, Buddha-like man with a soft, gentle face and delicate features, a little like Mr. Shawn," she said. "That's exactly the kind of baby I want. I thought because you're from that part of the world you could help me." She added, "I hope it's all right to call you. Mr. Shawn thought it would be."

"Of course," I said. "There are millions of unwanted babies in India. What could be better than for one to be adopted and brought to this country? I have some friends in the consulate and the Embassy in America, and also in volunteer agencies in India. I will get in touch with them and get back to you."

"I can't tell you what it would mean to me."

"Please don't mention it," I said, then realized I was speaking in a slightly English way.

After I hung up, I started thinking. I didn't know a thing about Lillian Ross. Whom was she married to? Did she have any other children? Why did she want to go all the way to Southeast Asia to adopt a baby? These were a few of many questions I felt I wouldn't be able to ask her directly, so I did the next best thing— went to the library and took out a couple of her books. Once I started reading them, I couldn't stop. She had an unerring eye and ear, as if she were a walking camera and a walking tape recorder, and she seemed to be able to unmask the people she was writing about: despite their social carapaces, they clearly delivered themselves unsuspectingly into her hands.

Her call and her writing exerted a mysterious influence on me, and I took a train down to New York specifically to meet her. I remember walking into her *New Yorker* office, on the twentieth floor, and feeling very self-conscious around her. She had an ingenuous, almost gushing manner, very much at odds with her writing. In fact, she was so disarmingly folksy that I felt she was seeing through me, and, although I had nothing to hide, I was sure that what she found was totally inadequate—all the more so since there was also a touch of the bully in her.

At one point, she mentioned that she was single.

I'd never heard of a single woman adopting a child, and the idea was an arresting one. She's very brave, I thought. She'll have to be both mother and father. That wouldn't be easy even if she weren't in the uncertain trade of a writer.

Back in Cambridge, I made many calls and wrote many letters to Indian officials in America and India, keeping Lillian Ross abreast of what I was doing, so that she could follow up my leads. The oddest facet of my involvement with her quest was that soon she was treating me as if I were a seasoned expert on adoption, rather than a twenty-five-year-old Harvard graduate student. She wrote to me at Harvard, "I seriously think of you as my adviser on all the official aspects of this adoption."

Although I wrote to Prime Minister Jawaharlal Nehru himself about the possibility of adoption, the bureaucratic hurdles of arranging for a single, forty-one-year-old American woman to adopt an Indian child proved insurmountable. (She eventually adopted a Norwegian child.) But, as a result of her getting in touch with me, we became good friends.

Soon after I moved into my office at *The New Yorker*, she dropped in to see me.

"You are amazing. You're wonderful how you manage everything," she said.

The compliment was totally wide of the mark, and I blurted out, "I'm not managing at all with my meals." Before

I knew it, I had told her all about my eating problem.

She said that the solution was TV dinners, and added that Stouffer's, among other outfits, was coming out with dinners that were so good that even gourmets ate them. "They're as simple to make as toast," Lillian said.

When I went home to the Picasso that night, I found she had dropped off some ready-made dinners in plastic bags and trays.

The next day, I missed my lunch, and decided when I got home that I would have the most delicious-sounding of the dinners—bœuf bourguignonne. Lillian had told me it needed only a few minutes' immersion in boiling water, and then I could open the bag with scissors, and serve it. I put on the kettle. I didn't know how to tell exactly when water boiled, but now I waited until the kettle started gurgling and the lid began to rattle, and then lifted the lid with a dish towel and dropped the bag in, splashing my cheek with scalding water. Next time, I'll lower it gently, with tongs or a ladle, I thought. As I was standing over the stove, wondering how I would wash the plate after I finished—I was afraid I would clog the sink if I hadn't scraped the plate properly—there was an explosion. The top of the kettle flew off, and before I knew it bœuf bourguignonne from the burst bag was raining down on my head.

My telephone was in the bedroom alcove, but I was afraid that if I walked out of the kitchen I would track the French sauce onto the parquet floor and the carpet. I carefully took off my shoes, cleaned my shirt and trousers as best I could, and tiptoed into the alcove. It never occurred to me to call Lillian. Perhaps because she wielded her pen like a scalpel, I was afraid of her. Instead, I automatically dialled Mary's number and asked if she could come over immediately.

"What have you done? Have you set something on fire?"

"No, no. Just please come."

"I have some guests here from the mission. Can it wait till morning?" I became aware of a rumble of voices in the background, fading in and out.

"Of course," I said, and hung up.

I tiptoed back into the kitchen and called the doorman on the intercom.

"I can't leave the door, sir."

"I'll give you five dollars for two minutes' work."

He came up, took one look at the mess, and backed out, saying that it was a job for the cleaning woman.

There was no help for it. I closed the pair of kitchen doors, which were really little more than frames holding wooden slats, and went to bed. All night, I was tortured by dreams of grease-covered bugs crawling through the slats and onto my pillow—a variation on a recurrent nightmare that had haunted me since I was small. Perhaps it had to do with the fact that as a child in India I'd been bitten often by bugs I couldn't identify. Or perhaps it was a general fear of things I couldn't see, whether they were bugs, stains, or even spilled ink on a typewritten page—part of an obsessive wish to have perfect order around me.

Thanks to the cleaning woman, when I returned from the office the next day the kitchen was spick-and-span.

A couple of days later, I ran into Lillian in a crowded elevator. "How are you doing with your TV dinners?" she asked me. I avoided answering her until we got out, and then told her about my experience. "Clearly, you have trouble boiling water," she said. "You'll have to get an electric grill and cook steaks."

She told me where to get the grill, stopped by with an individual steak, and showed me how to tell with a fork when it was done. I tried her method, but had so much trouble even taking the tinfoil off the pan without spilling the grease that I decided steak was not an answer to my problem. Besides, I immediately realized that there was no way I could sit down to a big piece of meat by myself. Because I grew up in a large family, eating had always been for me a communal activity. Lillian, however, kept encouraging me, as in this note:

Dear Ved:

I telephoned Mr. Bloom this morning at The Venice Market—BU 8-2880—and you now have a charge account there. I told him you would probably want steaks a little smaller than the one last night. But each steak will be enough for ONE PERSON only. (Man-sized steak.) I forgot to tell you that although Venice Market carries the staples—fruits, vegetables, beer, sodas, cans, etc.—it does not carry the small (one-or-two-person-man-sized) cans of tomato juice, petit pois. If you should want to order these cans or other items geared to single living, a good place in your neighborhood that carries the stuff is Food-O-Mart—the branch nearest you—UNiversity 1-7009. They will be happy to open a charge account for you and to deliver.

Suggestion: Down with TV dinners!

Best,
Lillian

The Samuel Katz-Venice Market was probably the most expensive market in New York, but I quickly got hooked on it, not because of its steaks but because I could order by telephone everything I needed and have it delivered, without ever having to go into a grocery store. Mostly, I ordered things that required no cooking and that I could eat or drink standing up, sometimes in the middle of the night, or in midmorning—brioche, juice, jars of peanuts with their skins, and apples. The loneliness of single living was inescapable. I began to understand more clearly than I ever had through letters or conversations why Lillian wanted to adopt a baby.

❧

FOR LUNCH, *NEW YORKER* staff members patronized a couple of restaurants. The Algonquin was too expensive for most of us. Generally, Mr. Shawn went there when he had a guest; otherwise, he ate either at his desk in the office or at a counter in Fritzl's, a modest but clean and tidy Swiss place near the office. Whitaker, the editor who had slept through Cynthia's New Year's Eve party, once said, in his acerbic way, "I don't know why anybody ever goes to the Algonquin. I once asked the waiter for a Dry Fly sherry, and he brought me a sherry with a fly floating in it." No doubt this was fantasy, but we all enjoyed it, because it enhanced our touch of sour grapes. By contrast, the complaint of *The New Yorker's* Paris correspondent, Janet Flanner, that as soon as she sat down she was charged for bread when in fact she didn't have any bread was very much to the point. Staff members who were heavy drinkers tended to gravitate to the Cortile, a couple of doors west of the office, where drinks were generous and food was cheap. Others frequented the Lobster, Oyster, and Chop House, on Forty-fifth Street between Sixth and Seventh Avenues. Joe Mitchell, the office authority on fish and everything to do with fish, thought that the Lobster, as it was generally known, was one of the top fish houses in the city, and Joe Liebling, the office gourmet, patronized it regularly. In fact, he was the first one of my office colleagues to ask me to lunch in my early days, and that is where he took me.

When we walked into the restaurant—as unpretentious as our offices—Joe was greeted by the manager as if he were a dignitary, and we were shown to a big table in the back of the main dining room. No sooner had we settled down than the manager said, "I'm very sorry, Mr. Liebling, but I just can't come up with five dozen oysters today. Would four dozen do?"

I had put an oyster in my mouth only once, and then had been unable to swallow it. The thought that something was slithering almost alive in my mouth had been too much for me.

"Could you please try again?" Joe asked the manager. "I'm counting on them."

I mentally prepared myself to spend the rest of the afternoon in the restaurant while Joe worked on his oysters, and, as a protest, ordered a hamburger. But, like many epicures, Joe seemed to be preoccupied with his own pleasure, and my protest scarcely registered. Finally, I said, "I've never heard of anybody sitting down to a lunch of sixty oysters."

He laughed heartily. It turned out that he had ordered the oysters as a takeout for a dinner party he was giving that evening.

Later that day, he came into my office. He had just received some flattering reviews of one of his books. I thought he would leave them with me to read, but he was so bucked up that he sat down and read them aloud to me, in his usual mumble, and even reread his favorite bits. A big man, he had something babyish about him. I loved his writing and was delighted to see him in such good spirits, especially since his books never got the attention or the sales they deserved.

Joe and his wife, Jean Stafford, and Joe Mitchell and his wife, Thérèse, were about the first guests I had over to my apartment at the Picasso for dinner—a dinner that was cooked and served by a Finnish woman I had hired through an employment agency. When I was first furnishing my apartment, Joe Mitchell—who was known for writing mostly about eccentric, bohemian, down-and-out characters and about businesses in New York that particularly attracted him, such as the Fulton Fish Market and McSorley's Saloon—had come along with me to a Salvation Army store and had spotted a serviceable armchair there for me. I had bought it and taken it to my apartment in a taxi, and the taxi fare had exceeded the cost of the chair, which had been exactly a dollar and a half. When I told Joe about it the next day, he laughed and said, "I know it," which was his way of saying that he really didn't know it but that life was full of such ironic surprises.

At one point during the dinner, talk about James Joyce and Ernest Hemingway—Mitchell had made himself an expert on one and Liebling on the other—got so heady, and the drinks were flowing so fast, that Mitchell and his wife started dancing to a succession of Gershwin tunes streaming out of my phonograph.

The floor space was so small that one could barely turn around, but that seemed to make no difference to them. Their dancing suddenly made me feel that the apartment was a little palace, in which I could comfortably entertain, and I think it was because of their dancing that afterward I never felt the slightest bit self-conscious about asking anyone or everyone, no matter how grand, around for dinner at the Picasso.

In time, my difficulty with cooking for myself was solved when I discovered a wonderful French restaurant, called L'Escargot, just across Fifty-eighth Street and up the block on Third Avenue. It was run by a French couple, Henri and Rose, who, as it happened, also lived in a one-room apartment in the Picasso, and there was a certain camaraderie between us. They were in America to make enough money so they could retire in Brittany, where their children were in school.

Once I had established myself as a regular patron of L'Escargot, Henri always saved a table for me, no matter how long the line. He would take my order and see to it that I was served right away. I had almost the same thing every night: a glass of Chablis, which Rose, who worked in the bar and at the cash register, would bring me; œufs à la russe (boiled eggs with caviar); filet of sole amandine; and coupe de fruits. Rose kept track of how much I owed and sent me a bill at the end of the month. The waiters, all of whom were French, would come and talk to me whenever they had a moment to spare, making me feel that I was a writer in a bistro on the Left Bank who had chosen to eat alone.

I would walk home from the restaurant whistling to myself.

As I began to feel at home in the Picasso, I invited friends from abroad to visit. I was often amused at their reactions to how I lived. Many of them seemed to think that because I was writing for *The New Yorker* I would be ensconced in a grand apartment. One day, I got a letter from an Oxford friend, William Oxmantown, who was a lord, saying "Could I really descend on you for a few days in New York, as you very kindly suggested in your last exclusive letter-cable? Do please send me another, saying 'No, all couches occupied' or 'Yes, double bed at your disposal,' whichever may be the case." I told him to come. He had grown up in a castle with a hundred rooms, and when he saw my apartment he was taken aback, but he was very sporting about it. The first day of his visit, he asked me if he could have an evening alone there, because he wanted to take up an introduction he had to the daughter of an Irish Minister. I came back late that night to find my door chained from the inside, and was obliged to spend half the night in a restaurant, waiting to repossess my apartment.

❦

WHEN VISITORS CAME from abroad and wanted to see New York life, I would take them to Off Broadway plays, to night clubs like Baby Doll, in Harlem, or to parties. I remember taking one friend to a party given by a New York woman who liked to entertain a lot of literati. At one point, the writer Norman Mailer and his girlfriend (later his third wife), Lady Jeanne Campbell, arrived. Mailer was riding high, and Lady Jeanne, although she came across as a commoner, was the daughter of the Duke of Argyll and the granddaughter of Lord Beaverbrook, the British press magnate.

The hostess brought Mailer and Lady Jeanne around, and introduced my friend to them. "You must have read Mr. Mailer's famous book 'The Naked and the Dead,'" she said.

I expected Mailer to lash out. I knew he got angry if only his first book was mentioned, as if to imply that his later books were not as good. Also, he seemed the kind of writer who thought his name alone was sufficient introduction. But he put on a gallant face.

"I'm very happy to meet you, sir," my friend said. "I've not read your book, but now that I've met you I most certainly will."

Mailer simply turned away abruptly.

I, however, was leery of Mailer still, and rightly so, for later on, without any provocation, he came back to me, thrust a fist in my face, and called me an impostor. "You are faking being blind," he said. I thought he was referring to the visual elements in my writing, but then realized from something he said that he was talking about the way I got around. I tried to move away, but he challenged me to a boxing match outside. "If you don't come out and fight with me, you will show yourself to be a coward," he said. Luckily for me, Lady Jeanne intervened.

❧

ONE DAY, FRANK MORAES, the leading Indian journalist and the father of my Oxford friend Dom, arrived in New York. He rang me and asked if I could bring Mr. Shawn around to his hotel for a drink so he could meet him.

I said that that was out of the question. Among other things, Mr. Shawn didn't drink.

"I've never heard of an editor who doesn't drink," Frank said. "What does he do—smoke cigarettes and sip coffee all day long?"

"He doesn't smoke and drinks very little coffee."

"Blimey!" he said. "He must be a bore."

I said, "Quite the contrary. He is wonderful company and a genius."

"Could I take him to lunch?"

I said that, as far as I knew, Mr. Shawn didn't have many social lunches, and that perhaps the best thing would be for me to ask him if he, Frank, might stop by and see him in his office.

"What a strange bird he must be," he said.

My affection for Frank was boundless, and I asked Mr. Shawn if I might bring him around. He said that, having edited "Indian Summer," he was eager to meet Dom's father.

That afternoon, I took Frank in, introduced him to Mr. Shawn, and started to leave, but Frank, who seemed to be at a loss without the social crutch of a drink or a meal, asked me to stay. Then, before I realized what was happening—and possibly out of nervousness as much as anything—he launched into a full-scale attack on *The New Yorker*. Because he was ordinarily very gracious and polite, I could later justify his conduct only by assuming that, like quite a few people, he had become unhinged in Mr. Shawn's presence.

"The *New Yorker* pieces are too long and boring," Frank said. He was speaking like the newspaperman he was, and I expected Mr. Shawn to offer a defense, but he listened quietly, curious only to know why Frank thought that. So after a while I said that, while opinion pieces could be short, re-creating an experience, as many *New Yorker* pieces did, required a lot of space.

"You mean to say Americans are just long-winded," Frank said. "I prefer the English."

"That's not what I said at all," I said. "Are you thinking of any particular piece?"

They all looked boring, Frank said, and The Talk of the Town was pretentious and pointless. The critical pieces were social essays, and one had a hard time telling which movie, play, or book was being reviewed. "It seems to me no one here does any editing," he said. The irony of that statement made me wince.

As Frank's outburst continued, I had a sad sense that a gulf was opening between him and me, between his kind of journalism and *The New Yorker's* kind of writing, and even between England and America—that, of course, we would continue to be good friends, but our channels for significant conversation were closing down.

Frank's attack went on for more than half an hour, and Mr. Shawn mostly just continued to listen. In time, I learned that, while Mr. Shawn was a tiger when it came to fighting for his writers, he was a total pacifist when the subject was himself or his editing. I now recall how, month after month, magazines that were envious of *The New Yorker's* success attacked it. The charges were ludicrous—such as that *The New Yorker* never published any first-rate fiction—and we writers felt that they could easily be refuted. We often urged Mr. Shawn to reply in the magazine's pages, or, at least, not to dissuade us from sending in letters to it ourselves. But, although every attack pained him, he wouldn't be provoked into answering, and invariably discouraged us from taking up the cudgels.

Frank got up to leave. As I was walking to the elevator with him, I avoided chastising him, and merely asked what he made of Mr. Shawn.

"Is he really the editor-in-chief of *The New Yorker*?"

"Yes."

"I would have taken him for a messenger."

"Is that why you spoke to him so disrespectfully?" I asked.

"No, no," he protested, a little too vehemently, and then said, "I was very moved by his gentleness. He reminds me of a character in a novel."

"Which one?" I asked, with keen interest.

"I can't say. It's been so long since I've had the luxury of reading novels. Which character does he remind you of?"

Until that moment, I hadn't posed any such question to myself, but I immediately said, "Alyosha in 'The Brothers Karamazov,' or possibly even Myshkin in 'The Idiot.'" I added that, like Myshkin, Mr. Shawn was so seemingly innocent and vulnerable that one felt he must be protected.

"Exactly," Frank said, in his most worldly manner. "That's exactly what I was going to say."

❧

THE NEW YORKER had an air of complete privacy. The offices of editors, writers, artists, and other people connected with it were all mixed together, and there was no way of telling who was to be found where. None of the offices had names on them. Most were little more than cubicles, each with an individual window and outfitted with a desk, a chair, a typewriter, and, in some cases, a divan bed, which would always be piled high with books, manuscripts, and old newspapers. The monotony of the halls of cubicles was somewhat relieved by two large, cheerful rooms: one housed the checking department, where the copy was vetted for factual accuracy, and the other held the makeup department, where the issues were designed. Still, dusty hallways and dingy walls gave the place a bleak atmosphere, as though *The New Yorker* were making a conscious statement that writers and artists should be above worrying about their surroundings. I gathered that not much had been changed since the magazine moved into the building, more than a quarter of a century earlier. Mr. Shawn once said, "*The New Yorker* has a longstanding tradition of squalor with which I am loath to interfere." And, indeed, in time one became fond of the place the way it was. It seemed somehow cozy, compared with other offices in the city, which might be highly decorated but had an impersonal air. We savored the irony of an elegant, immaculate magazine being put together in an inelegant, un-dressed-up shop. In fact, *The New Yorker* didn't have any of the trappings generally associated with publishing. There was no reception room on any floor. There were no memos, no general conferences, no general editorial meetings—no hierarchy or bureaucracy of any kind. (Even the weekly art meeting was a bilateral affair between Mr. Shawn and the art editor.) There were not even introductions, as if such things were considered invasions of people's privacy. I met only such people as I needed to meet, as in the case of Miss Terry.

Though it seemed that everything was set up to prevent distractions and allow people to concentrate on their work, I felt as I sat in my new office that I couldn't get started until Mr. Shawn had edited my philosophy piece, so that I could learn where I might have gone off the track with the introduction and could guard against such pitfalls in the future. Adrianne, however, who liked to rile me, if in a good-natured way, told me that my piece might not get attended to for years, if at all—that every week Mr. Shawn accepted manuscripts hundreds of pages long and sent them up to be retyped, and that they were then put in the bank to await publication. The bank was so large, she said, that if all the writers dropped dead in some catastrophe the magazine could continue coming out for at least five years without any of its readers being the wiser.

I asked Mr. Shawn about my piece, but all he would say was "We hope to get it in soon."

Afraid of letting my drawing-account debt mount, I sent him one note after another proposing ideas for additional pieces: a report on Moral Rearmament, a quasi-religious movement that was in the news because it was recruiting many celebrities; one on marriage bureaus in London which had recently started up to help people find mates in an increasingly impersonal metropolis; and Profiles of certain English literary figures. Each time he turned a proposal down, he said that the idea wasn't quite right for the magazine. The first suggestion was polemical, he said, and there were so many good subjects around that he didn't believe in giving the pages of the magazine over to attacks unless something was pernicious or dangerous. The second was commercial, and the magazine always tried to do pieces that were off the beaten path. The third was simply too close to home: writing about writers was a little bit like writing about ourselves. In desperation, I asked him to think of an idea for me. He said that generally writers did their best work when they became impassioned about a subject, but he would try to come up with something.

Late one afternoon, he dropped by and suggested three ideas: the first was the World Bank, and I dismissed it as too gray and institutional; the second was the International Monetary Fund, and I objected to that for the same reason; and the third was something I'd never heard of—the United Nations' Technical Assistance.

"What is it?" I asked.

"I understand that it's a program the United Nations has for teaching skills to people in poor countries to improve their standard of living," he told me. "I was reading last night that the U.N. had sent an Australian expert on sheep shearing all the way to a country in South America to show shearers there how to cut the wool off a sheep in one swift motion."

At first, I found this subject, too, somewhat gray, and I asked him if I might make it more lively by reporting from one of the countries being helped. He said that, as he saw it, it was really a New York piece. The program administrators were in New York, and no doubt the experts came to them to get instructions and to report on their work, so there was no need to incur expenses by going abroad.

I thought this idea over for a night and persuaded myself that it could be an exciting one. It would help me to understand what was being done for poor countries like India, and give me a chance to test my descriptive abilities by writing about something I would never witness.

Miss Broun kept records for Mr. Shawn of the ideas that writers were working on or had reserved with his approval. I told her that I would be doing the U.N. piece, and immediately started making daily trips to the U.N. headquarters, interviewing administrators and experts and consulting documents in the library. The experience was chastening. The administrators, who talked in a lofty way about bringing the light of industrial society to the poor so they could join the "human family," regularly snubbed their own staff members. Moreover, they spoke as if they would provide every person with "everything necessary to the Modern Man,/ A phonograph, a radio, a car and a Frigidaire"— to quote lines I recalled from a poem by W. H. Auden. (One of the top administrators was an alumnus of the Ford Motor Company.)

After several months of unremitting work, I had a long two-part piece entitled "A Phonograph, a Radio, a Car, and a Frigid-aire," highlighting the contradiction between the highfalutin talk of the propagandists and the real concerns of the people they were supposedly dedicated to serving.

Within a day of my turning it in, Mr. Shawn had read it. He came down and said, "It's a good, strong piece of writing."

I was thrilled. Counting the two India pieces and the philosophy piece, I had four pieces accepted. I ventured to ask him when he might run it.

"After the philosophy piece," he said.

My spirits sank. Since I still had no idea when the philosophy piece would run, it could be years before I would see proofs of the Technical Assistance piece. And how I longed for the parade of proofs, the excitement of rewriting and perfecting, the hum of the editorial process, the tension that mounted as the date of publication approached. Moreover, so much of my time and energy—indeed, even of my dreams—had lately been taken up by the Technical Assistance article that without it on my anvil I felt empty and at a loss. I wanted to start something else immediately but again didn't have a single idea.

Later that day, I hung around Miss Broun's office until Mr. Shawn was free. I wanted only to stick my head in for a quick word, but he invited me to sit down.

He had a way of making one feel that he had all the time in the world. I asked him if he had another idea for me to work on. Since those early days, I've never been short of ideas. On the contrary, my head is usually teeming with them, so I become desperate that I won't get to all of them in my lifetime. But back then the sheer anxiety of earning my livelihood through writing paralyzed me.

Mr. Shawn said he'd been thinking about something in President Kennedy's Inaugural Address. Kennedy had named as two of his goals to "tap the ocean depths" and to "explore the stars." Although the idea of space exploration had captured press headlines, in the long run converting seawater into fresh water might turn out to be much more practical, Mr. Shawn felt. He asked me, "What would you think of doing a piece on desalinization?"

I had just read somewhere that malnutrition was causing tens of millions of children in poor countries to grow up every year with brain damage. If the deserts can be made to bloom, maybe the problems of famine and malnutrition can be solved, I thought, embracing the idea.

❧

BEGINNING A NEW piece was rather like beginning a new career. Within a day of accepting the desalinization idea, I got to work on it. I borrowed books on the subject from the library. I went to Washington and talked to President Kennedy's Secretary of the Interior, Stewart Udall. He treated me to a lecture on the great technological advances being made in converting salt water to fresh water, and one of his assistants, Walter Pozen, wanted me to look at conversion plants on the island of Aruba and at some former deserts in Israel where people were living exclusively on converted water. I asked if there was a plant closer to hand, and he directed me to Freeport, Texas. I went down there, and learned that, despite all the advances, the basic technology still involved boiling the seawater, and that it cost two dollars to produce a thousand gallons of fresh water. (Most people, I was told, used a hundred gallons just for a shower.) It was clear that unless the expense could be brought down drastically conversion had no practical application in agriculture, say, and, in fact, was practical only in places that had no fresh water at all. After reading books about water-conversion experiments from ancient to modern times, I wrote what I thought was an impressive two-part piece, taking special satisfaction in my description of the Texas plant, which had a complicated network of pipes that had cost me considerable effort to visualize and master. I called the piece "The Gin-Clear Water"—the Texas engineers' term for the pure converted seawater—and handed it in.

The next day, Mr. Shawn came down to my office and said that since the process was so expensive he could see no justification for running a piece on it. Kennedy's remark, which had sent us on a wild-goose chase, might have been simply a rhetorical flourish, or, more likely, an emotional reaction to the fact that during the war he had been marooned for six days on a desert island after his PT boat was sunk.

With any other editor, I would have tried to argue, but not with Mr. Shawn. Instead, after I recovered from the shock, I simply asked him if he thought there was any way I could rewrite the piece to save it. It was one of the first of hundreds of conversations I had with him about suggested pieces or pieces in progress. Each time, I was astonished at how clearly and succinctly he was able to put into words what was right or wrong with them and to come up with solutions to any problems that arose. When he was accepting a piece, he was very quick. He never felt the need to prove that he had read the piece and mastered the material, and he always had an exact word or phrase to express what he felt about it. When he was rejecting a piece, however, he was apt to spend a long time explaining what didn't work, and he seemed to feel as sad about the rejection as the writer did. In the instance of "The Gin-Clear Water," however, he simply said that he could see no way of redeeming the piece: since the procedure could have little practical application, there was no real story.

I immediately realized that he was right, and that, without acknowledging it to myself, I had come to the same conclusion in the course of writing the piece, but, loath to abandon the project, had forced a story out of the material. I now felt that the expenses I had been allowed for the piece, which enabled me to fly to Washington and stay at the Hay-Adams, Washington's best hotel, and then fly on to Texas, were to blame for my pressing on when good sense should have made me abandon the whole idea. (After the desalinization piece, for reasons best known to Mr. Shawn, I was never given an open-ended expense account on any project. Instead, I had an expense allowance of three hundred dollars, eventually raised to five hundred, per five thousand words of any article published. The allowance seldom covered more than a small fraction of my expenses, and thus made sure that I kept a tight rein on them. For instance, to cross the Atlantic I took Icelandic Airlines, the cheapest way to do so; I stayed in bed-and-breakfast places rather than in hotels; and I seldom offered drinks or lunches to the people I interviewed. It gave my research a certain spartan, puritan quality, which colleagues on other magazines, who had big expense budgets, sometimes commented on. Mr. Shawn did give writers expense accounts when they were doing pieces, like covering the Olympic games, that *The New Yorker* really needed, but I think he generally considered them corrupting, in contrast to the expense-allowance system, which, in keeping with *The New Yorker's* principles, rewarded only good work.)

It was all I could do to hold back tears at the new disappointment of the rejection, since both the philosophy and the Technical Assistance pieces were still in limbo, which is to say in manuscript. Generally, pieces were paid for only after they were set up in proofs, because compensation was calculated by length, and Mr. Shawn couldn't know until a manuscript was edited how much of it would actually be used.

Mr. Shawn kindly left me alone, and Adrianne immediately walked in. (Whenever Mr. Shawn came, she stepped out. Mr. Shawn, who was so discreet that he liked all conversations to be kept private, was always constrained in the presence of a third party.)

"When are they going to publish your 'Gin-Clear Water'?" she asked.

"They're not," I said.

"I always thought the subject was boring," she said. "What article do you want to do now?"

To myself, I said, "Writing is going to be like beating my head against the wall. Adrianne is right. If I want to prevail, I have to start another piece right away."

That same week, Mr. Shawn gave me good news—that *The New Yorker* would be buying a short story about a profligate character which I had started on during my first day in the office and had entitled "Delinquent Chacha, Esq." I had become so used to bad news that at first I didn't fully take it in. When I did, I cheered up, since it meant that I was now considered both a fact writer and a fiction writer at the magazine—something quite rare around the office.

❧

ONE EVENING LATE in the spring of 1961, I got a surprise call from the Indian fiction writer R. K. Narayan, who was in the city for the publication of his novel "The Man-Eater of Malgudi." (Malgudi was an imaginary pastoral town.) I identified with him to some extent, because, although he wrote in English, he was able to portray Indians in India authentically—something I was trying to do in my short stories. I proposed writing a Profile on him. Since the piece would be about a writer, Mr. Shawn was reluctant to approve the idea, but I made a case that I wanted to write about Narayan in order to explain how an Indian writer wrote about Indians—something that, as an expatriate, I had had difficulty doing.

I had a wonderful time tagging along after Narayan in New York. He went around the city as if he were a character miraculously transplanted from Malgudi. My piece about him almost wrote itself, and Mr. Shawn liked it. Because it was short, he thought he could get it into the magazine quickly, and he put it in type before either of my other pieces. While we were editing it, we had some good laughs at scrapes that the innocent Narayan had got himself into in the alien, commercial world of New York, like missing a dinner party given in his honor because he didn't know how to work the buzzer in the apartment building. But when the piece was all ready to go, its every hair in place, it was continually put on the schedule only to be taken off again, rather like a man dressed up for a party that is repeatedly postponed. One Friday afternoon, it appeared on the short schedule as going to run in B issue—that is, the issue following the one being worked on, which was A issue. Both Narayan and I told our friends to look for it, but by Monday afternoon, when the revised short schedule was distributed, it had mysteriously disappeared. I consulted the updated weekly long schedule—posted inside the door of the checking department—which listed pieces months before they were due to run, so that the checkers would have plenty of opportunity to verify their factual content, but the Profile was not even on that. Narayan and I were left with the embarrassing task of calling our friends again and telling them that the Profile would not be coming out after all.

The piece appeared and disappeared on the schedules no fewer than thirteen times, and I wondered if it would ever run. There was never any explanation of why it was put off, and my imagination went wild. Was it because Mr. Shawn's doubts about running a piece on a writer had resurfaced, or was it because a scene with the occasional *New Yorker* writer Santha Rama Rau was a worry to him (she had not come off well in it), or was it only a casualty of some technical conflict? I knew that any last-minute minor glitch could knock something out of the magazine. (Once, a drawing that showed policemen chasing a malefactor down the street was pulled because a review of a movie about policemen appeared on the same page. Another time, an article I had written about Indian music was nearly held over because in the same issue Winthrop Sargeant, the music critic, had a Profile of the conductor Zubin Mehta, who presented the added complication of sharing my surname. I was so upset that Mr. Shawn ran both pieces, saying, "We'll just have an Indian-music issue this week." He put a note in Sargeant's Profile stating that Zubin Mehta and I were not related.) I hated to ask Mr. Shawn directly about the Narayan Profile, because I didn't want to put him on the spot and force him to give me an explanation, but whenever I ran across him in the hall I would ask him if there was any news of its publication. He would say he hoped to get it in soon, and would then hurry away, as if he preferred not to talk about it. But "soon" in his language could mean anything from tomorrow to five years from tomorrow. In due course, I caught on to the scheduling problem that Mr. Shawn wrestled with every day as he tried to create an organic mixture of material about the city, the country, and the world—he treated each issue as a work of art—and, at the same time, keep his writers and artists happy. He was like a good farmer in that his crop never failed, but the result was that the crop was sometimes overabundant: it ranged anywhere from one hundred to two hundred long fact pieces on the bank, and writers were always breathing down his neck to get him to publish their pieces, because the pieces were topical, or because the material in them was becoming dated, or because they were imminently coming out in book form. For all of us, publication in *The New Yorker* was the main validation of our writing life, and some writers and artists actually went around the bend waiting for their work to appear.

The Narayan Profile ran about a year after it was bought.

❦

WHEN I WAS working on a long piece, I could have been in a cubicle in a library in Kalamazoo or Timbuktu. No one telephoned, no one dropped in to see me, and no one except Adrianne, Mr. Shawn, and Miss Broun knew whether I was working, let alone what my subject might be. Indeed, nobody seemed to care whether I lived or died. The whole idea of a cubicle was to protect one from interruptions, but sometimes it felt like such a cocoon that one longed for people to drop by. The community aspect I had taken for granted at school and college was totally absent in the individualistic, retiring atmosphere of *The New Yorker*. It was as if all of us on the eighteenth floor, which was where most of the writers and artists were quartered, took our cue from Charles Addams, who came and went like a dapper apparition. I was lucky in having Adrianne to add a certain social element to my work.

In some part of my mind, I must have always known that the fate of long pieces was uncertain, because I was continually doing short ones in the hope of keeping a place for myself in the magazine. I kept trying to come up with ideas for Comment pieces, Talk stories, or Books leads—the intramural terms for Notes and Comment, The Talk of the Town, and the long book reviews. No one explained to me how ideas for such pieces were proposed, and I was too shy to ask Mr. Shawn. Since I couldn't believe that he would deal personally with all my harebrained ideas, I decided to bounce them off someone else before investing time and effort in putting them on paper. But I quickly discovered that he had no intermediaries—he did everything himself. I thereupon started bombarding him with ideas. An idea for a Talk story, I found, went through a regular system. If Mr. Shawn approved it, he sent it to the office of Eugene Kinkead, the Talk idea man, to be checked against past stories in the magazine and against records of ideas assigned and pending. If there was no conflict, an outline of the idea was typed up and sent to me as a formal assignment, marked in the upper right-hand corner "O.K. S.K." ("S" and "K" were the initials of Shawn and Kinkead.) If there was a conflict, or if Mr. Shawn just didn't like the idea, my suggestion was returned with a remark such as "We've already done a similar story" or "Not for us, thank you for sending it along." The system, however, was frequently short-circuited. Mr. Shawn's own memory of what had appeared in *The New Yorker* was so long and so accurate that sometimes when he received a note of mine suggesting a story he would either pick up the telephone and call me or send my note back to me with a handwritten response like "Yes, looks promising." This most often happened if a piece was timely—if, for instance, it concerned a person who was going to be in town only briefly. An idea for such a story would be returned with a pink slip clipped to it on which were printed "For use only with rush messages or material" and a giant "T," meaning "timely," in a circle, to indicate that it was not part of the message. Hundreds of such slips flew around all the *New Yorker* offices every day.

With experience, I was often able to guess which Talk ideas would get the green light. Although Mr. Shawn evaluated each idea on its own merits, and didn't really worry about where it came from, he generally didn't like stories about people who were in the current news or were being hyped by press agents. The best ideas were those which came into being through a chance happening or encounter, and, of course, the more they had to do with the city the better. It was O.K. to write about a Nepalese diplomat living in New York, say, but not about one living in Washington. Mr. Shawn believed that Talk was the one part of the magazine that should stay close to home. With time, the department did acquire something of a world flavor, but most of the stories were still to be found someplace just around the corner, since, after all, this *was* The Talk of the Town.

I wrote a number of Talk stories, and also a Books lead, that immediately got into the magazine. Comment, however, always seemed to trip me up.

Mr. Shawn and I would discuss my idea for a Comment piece over the telephone, even deciding what tack I should take. I would write one and send it up and hear no more about it. In this way, at least half a dozen of my Comment pieces vanished into oblivion. I imagined that Mr. Shawn had a cubbyhole under his desk where he deposited all the pieces he didn't like or couldn't use, in the hope that he would someday find time to discuss them with their authors.

In those days, Comment was the closest *The New Yorker* came to offering an official opinion on any subject, and the writing presented a special challenge, because it had to be in a voice that Mr. Shawn would approve. Moreover, it seemed to have a form that, in its own way, was as set as that of a sonnet or a haiku. Out of desperation, I called Mr. Shawn one day and asked him if he could explain the form to me.

"Would you like to come up now?" he said. As a rule, he saw writers in their own offices, but at that moment he apparently wanted to be sure he could be easily reached by telephone.

As ill luck would have it, no sooner had I sat down in his office than a fire alarm went off. The building was trying out a new alarm system, and since he knew the alarm to be merely a drill we decided to ignore it. Although the *New Yorker* offices were in a building right next to a firehouse, and I had learned to tolerate the coming and going of fire engines, with their sirens screaming, all day long, this particular alarm was so loud that I had trouble concentrating on what Mr. Shawn was saying.

"E. B. White more or less invented the form, and you might want to look at some of his Comment pieces," he said. "Insofar as they can be described, they are ironic, funny, and elliptical."

"I don't understand what you mean by 'elliptical,'" I said. "I thought that was a geometric term."

"I mean something elusive—hard to get hold of."

His description of a Comment piece could be equally applied to him, I thought.

I wondered aloud if the fact that I was not born in America meant that I couldn't get the voice of a Comment piece quite right.

"I don't think so," he said. "Talk is also written in a certain voice, and you have no trouble with that. Writing a Talk story or a Comment piece is really a knack. Some young reporters who come to the magazine catch on to it right away, and there are established writers who are not able to do it at all. From what I've read of your Comment pieces so far, I'm sure you'll soon be writing some that will get into the magazine."

I had a childish fantasy about Mr. Shawn: I thought him almost omniscient. If he felt I could do something, I believed I really could—and, sure enough, in due course I was able to turn out a number of Comment pieces. My batting average for them was never very high, though. A Comment piece could succeed as a piece of writing and yet not get in, because Mr. Shawn didn't want the magazine to express that particular opinion, even if he himself happened to agree with it. I remember one such case, which had to do with the Cuban missile crisis. Everyone seemed to be praising President Kennedy for facing down Khrushchev, but I felt that he had run a frightening risk, which might have brought what he himself called the sword of Damocles down on our heads. Mr. Shawn agreed, and even called me to say he liked my Comment very much, but he never put it into type. I gathered that he felt that the magazine should not come out against Kennedy's action just then.

Whether I had a Comment piece or a Talk story in mind, I would send up the idea on Monday or Tuesday, and if it was approved, I would hand in the piece by five or six o'clock on Thursday. Mr. Shawn would read it right away, since Thursday evening was when he decided which Comment piece and which Talk stories were to run in the A issue, and in what order. I would come in the following morning eager to see if what I'd written had made it into the page proofs. Once a piece was in the page proofs, checkers, a proofreader, and, ultimately, the final reader, called the O.K.er, would get to work on it. Their queries would go to Mr. Shawn, and over the weekend, working at home, he would review the material with the changes and put through revised page proofs, so that they would be on everyone's desk on Monday morning. Although he and Eleanor Gould, an indefatigable query editor, gave the various weekly Talk proofs at least five readings, consultation with the writers was minimal—there was very little time—but in the matter of a Comment piece, whatever the pressures, it was not unusual for the writer to get many calls from Mr. Shawn. Although the magazine went to press at two o'clock on Monday, Comment was held open for last-minute changes, which could be telephoned to the printing plant as late as six. At any stage, a Comment piece could be pulled, whether because it was overtaken by a breaking news story, because a writer could not successfully dispose of the queries, or because Mr. Shawn had second thoughts after studying the queries himself. No writer could ever be sure a piece was running until it actually appeared in the finished magazine. Sometimes a piece that didn't make it into the page proofs would be held in galleys and not run for months, then might be rushed in to replace one that had to be pulled. In October, 1961, I sent this note to Mr. Shawn: "There has been only one Notes and Comment piece on the United Nations garden—I believe it was a mood piece—but the peacocks were never mentioned. Could one do a piece about them, their origins, and their caretakers?" Mr. Shawn called me and said that it was O.K. to do the story. I wrote the piece, pegging it to the arrival of autumn. It was set up in galleys, and I was credited with a payment against my drawing account. After that, every week, when the page proofs came out, I looked for my story, but when autumn passed and I saw no sign of it I gave it up for dead. Then, in March, I got the magazine in London, and there was my Comment piece, slightly touched up, heralding spring.

At *The New Yorker,* any piece that was thought good and was paid for was almost certain to be used sooner or later. The idea was that good writing could never date, and could be read or reread at any time. People used to joke that one piece by John Updike was on the setup sheet eleven years before it was used.

Mr. Shawn's personal involvement in every detail of the editorial process not only provided a potent stimulus for working on a piece—short or long—but also became an occasion for talking to him, either on the telephone or in person. I looked forward to being in touch with him, in one way or the other, at least two or three times a week, and when I was stuck I would walk the halls in the hope of encountering him. Unlike other people in the office, who passed by me without a word or a nod, he always greeted me and asked how a piece was coming along. Because he was non-judgmental and knew more than anyone else about my working life, I often ended up saying more in reply than I'd intended to. In fact, I felt free around him in a way I never felt around anyone else.

❧

EARLY IN NOVEMBER of 1961, when I'd been at the magazine about eight months and was debating what sort of long piece I dared take on after the debacle of "The Gin-Clear Water" and the continuing on-and-off status of the Narayan Profile, Mr. Shawn came into my office and told me in a sad voice that he had reread my Technical Assistance piece in preparation for editing it and had reluctantly concluded that he could not run it.

"But I thought you liked it," I said, trying to master my welter of feelings.

"I did, and I still do," he replied. "But the national climate has changed since Hammarskjöld's death." A couple of months earlier, Dag Hammarskjöld had died in a plane crash in what was then Rhodesia. "If we had been able to get it in when he was around, it would have been fine. But now the U.N. is in a weakened state. Also, there is such a tide of anti-U.N. sentiment that if we were to publish your strong but critical article we would seem to have become part of it."

I thought he was ignoring my interests and the possible literary value of my piece because of some vague perception of the political climate. Disloyally, I even thought that perhaps he was holding back from me his real reason for killing the piece. But I found myself unable to put any of these thoughts into words without exposing the rising anger I felt against him.

"I can imagine you must feel angry and frustrated," he said. "I want you to know that I have the interests of your article at heart, but I also have to think of the interests of the magazine and the country." I realize, quoting this remark now, that it was uncharacteristically immodest for Mr. Shawn, but, even in my agitated state, I understood that he was only trying to comfort me by giving me an explanation. After all, if he hadn't been concerned for me he could have simply sent down a word or a note and so spared himself the ordeal of confronting my anger and anguish. Still, I was far from pacified. I felt that sometimes *The New Yorker* treated its writers like children, and I resented that. I wanted to sweep away all the delicate formalities and constraints, and talk to Mr. Shawn—as I thought of it—man to man.

But I swallowed hard and said, "The piece represents months of work. Could it be published sometime in the future, when the U.N. is having better days?"

"I wish I could say yes, but the people you've written about would have all moved on by then, and the piece would be irrelevant."

"But I thought a *New Yorker* piece is never dated. Couldn't I turn it into a historical piece?" I was clutching at straws.

"Unfortunately, it's written in a journalistic style, and there's really no way to do that. I'm awfully sorry." He stood up to leave.

I am eating and paying rent but earning nothing, I thought. How long can Mr. Shawn indulge me? Even if he is prepared to keep me on the drawing account for some time, I don't want to accept his charity. But what else am I fit to do? I have to sit here and try to write.

Just as he was at the door, I asked him abruptly, dropping any attempt at courtesy, if he planned to pay me for the piece.

He said, "In cases like this, we always pay 'breakage,' since the piece is being dropped as a result of forces beyond anyone's control."

I reread the piece that night and battled with him again the next day. I told him that he was treating the U.N. as though it were sacred, but that, like any institution, it had its ups and downs, and no piece could wound it mortally. He remained immovable. At the time, I thought he was wrong, but in later years I came to see his wisdom. I was concerned only with my piece, he with the honor of the magazine. Our interests had temporarily diverged, but in the long run they were one and the same.

❦

A MONTH BEFORE the fateful Technical Assistance conversation, Mr. Shawn had taken me to lunch at the Algonquin and told me that he had reread my philosophy piece, along with a new introduction I had written and sent up to him, and that the two seemed to work fine. He felt, however, that the ending still needed a little work.

I asked him if I should write another ending, but he said I should wait until I had the galleys and saw his edited version.

The piece was twenty-seven thousand words long; in fact, it turned out that at the time it was second in length only to John Hersey's "Hiroshima," which had run to some thirty-one thousand words and had taken up the entire issue of August 31, 1946. Another editor might have required me to cut it, with the injunction that, after all, I was writing for a magazine; and, even in Mr. Shawn's *New Yorker*, in the ordinary course of things it would have run in two or three parts, in successive issues. But Mr. Shawn could see no way of either cutting it or splitting it up. The only issues large enough to accommodate the entire piece were the autumn ones, which got always got fatter with advertisements as Christmas approached, and thus had more columns for editorial content.

However, we were now well into November, and there was no sign that my piece was still alive. Then, on November 13th, less than three weeks before the last fat December issue was to go to press, my door opened without a knock—a signal that there was a delivery by messenger—and two sets of galleys of the philosophy piece were dropped on my desk. They smelled fresh, as if they'd just come down from the printers, and each set was as thick as a small paperback book. Suddenly, I felt that the piece had an existence—that I had an existence. With the manuscript in galleys, there would be a big payment, and a surplus in my *New Yorker* account at the end of the year.

I studied the slug—a line running across the top of each galley. There was "8-S," which meant that the piece would be the first major fact piece in the magazine and would be handled by Mr. Shawn himself, rather than by one of the fact editors. There was also "MG SOON" (Must Go Soon), which indicated that it was not certain when the piece would run.

I began reading the proofs. I had submitted the piece almost exactly a year earlier and hadn't looked at it since, except for the introduction. I was so far removed from it that it seemed to have been written by someone else. Although most of the editorial changes were imperceptible, some stuck out—most notably a new title, "The Philosopher's Stone," and a concluding sentence that Mr. Shawn had put in.

I called Mr. Shawn and said I didn't like, among other things, either the title or the ending.

"They're just dummy changes I made, so I could get the piece moving, knowing full well that you would be able to improve upon them," he said. "I hope to get the piece in before Christmas."

That was all I needed to hear, and I set to work revising and rewriting.

Until the philosophy piece, all of Mr. Shawn's editing had been done on the telephone, but now whenever he could make a slot of time free he would call down and I would go up and sit at the end of his sofa, hunched forward, my stomach tightening, my fingers twisting and untwisting. He would look at my proof, with my changes, and then go over with me the changes on his proof and on proofs that had come in from the other readers. Those proofs were covered with queries. Many of the queries had to do with punctuation, and he dealt with them on his own. Others were more substantial, and we would talk them over. When he and I agreed with a query, he would cross out the question mark that followed it. When we didn't, he would cross out the query. He seemed to be happiest when he was editing. He sat on the edge of his chair, sounding as if he were about to jump up at any moment in his enthusiasm. He went through proof after proof so fast that I wondered how he had time to absorb the queries, but then I realized that he already knew the piece better than I did.

Throughout, I tried to come up with appropriate fixes for the queries raised in the various proofs. Some fixes were easy. For instance, a striking word used early in the piece had been repeated later, and an alternative was needed. I would propose synonyms, and when I hit on the right one Mr. Shawn's voice would become high with excitement. Other fixes were much more complicated. I had to think up a sentence, modify a description, or clarify an idea on the spot.

Ordinarily, when I was writing in my office I would often dictate a tentative, very rough draft and then rewrite it—revising and refining it. I couldn't subject Mr. Shawn to such incoherent attempts, and yet I was no more capable of coming out with a well-formed sentence on demand than I was of sitting in his chair. I would struggle and wrestle with my thoughts until I had something passable. Then I would dictate it to him, and he would write it on his proof, suggesting improvements as he went along.

While we worked, I could hear the telephone ringing continually in his outer office. Occasionally, the door would open and someone would come in with proofs of drawings or of other pieces that were going into the A issue. Mr. Shawn would study a revised caption for a cartoon, for instance, and then either laugh out loud or exclaim, "Oh, no, we can't have that!" Then he would scribble something on the proof. He seemed to be able to switch effortlessly from my piece to whatever else came down the pike. I worried that I was taking up too much of his time, that I was being too slow. But Mr. Shawn was calm. There was scarcely an issue for which he didn't handle a major piece. Although he seemed completely relaxed in the face of deadlines, I got the impression that he welcomed interruptions, as providing a diversion from his intense concentration. He once told me that while he was going over proofs at home he even watched television, in order to get a sense of what was going on in the country. Apparently, he often watched programs with a lot of activity—people doing their thing, whatever it was. (Allen has described him as sitting in front of some banal television show and looking off into space with his pencil held in the air, no doubt wondering whether the word chosen in the proof was the right word or whether there was a lacuna in the thought which required a phrase or a sentence from the writer.)

One afternoon, Mr. Shawn came down to my office and said that it would be a wonderful idea if Saul Steinberg would agree to illustrate my piece, and he added, with a laugh, "He doesn't like the word 'illustration.' He thinks of a piece as illustrating his drawing. If Steinberg can't do it, is there another artist whose work you like and whom you would want me to try?"

It is characteristic of him to indulge me in my fantasy that I can see drawings, I thought. Aloud, I thanked him and said that I would leave everything up to him, but that it would be marvellous if Steinberg would do it.

As it turned out, Steinberg did do the drawing, and Mr.

Shawn brought down the rough sketch and described it to me with such care and precision that I thought I could almost visualize it. Subsequently, every time a piece of mine was going to run, he would talk over with me who would be the best artist. Since drawings were his prerogative, and I had no competence in the matter, I was puzzled at first by his taking such pains, but I came to realize that he thought of the piece and the drawing accompanying it as organic, and would no more have thought of foisting an artist on me who in spirit was unsuited to the piece than he would have injected a paragraph of his own into my prose.

❦

PEOPLE WHO PICKED up the magazine and read a piece had no idea of the magazine's Byzantine labyrinth; and the writers themselves, many of them egomaniacs, even denied that any such labyrinth existed. They seemed to think that the magazine came out like ice from an ice machine: they took the editorial process for granted, much as the editors working on the nineteenth and twentieth floors took the printing process for granted. I myself, when I first occupied my office, knew the people who got the magazine out week after week only as "someone"s. Soon I began snooping around to find out how the magazine was put together. Partly, this was to satisfy my natural curiosity, and partly it was because in those days whenever I couldn't think of anything to write I would wander the halls, introducing myself to people, in a very un-*New Yorker* fashion, and asking them what they did. I came to think of the editorial process as part of the mystique of *The New Yorker*.

The route of submissions for long fact pieces was as tedious as it was formidable. Whereas manuscripts that were developed from ideas discussed with Mr. Shawn went directly to him, unsolicited manuscripts were culled for him by readers, and any that looked at all promising were sent to his apartment. He read the manuscripts over the weekend and brought them back on Monday. The ones he accepted would be sent up to the typing pool, and it would prepare triple-spaced copies with big margins for editing. The typed manuscripts would be read aloud and checked against the authors' originals, then sent back to Mr. Shawn, and he would put them in his own pile for editing or eventually assign them separately to one of the four or five fact editors. He would generally tell the editor how long a manuscript should be and whether it should be edited to run in one issue or in several issues. If it was to run in several issues, the editor was required not only to re-identify in the later parts every person and event mentioned in the earlier ones but also to do so in a way that would orient readers picking up the series in the middle but would not irritate those who had read it from the beginning. This basic editing was generally done without consultation with the author. Then the edited manuscript was sent on to the copy desk, which was restricted to making routine corrections in spelling and punctuation. From there it travelled to the makeup department and on to the printing plant, to be set up in galleys. The galleys got at least three readings besides those of the author, the assigned editor, and Mr. Shawn. They were read by Greenstein, who went over the piece for legal problems; by a checker, who made certain that every fact was correct; and by Eleanor Gould, who read them for grammar, sense, clarity, and consistency, and whose queries and notes on a galley were sometimes almost as long as the text. The galleys, once the editor handling the piece had dealt with the queries, were sent on to the collating department, and there all the changes were consolidated and transferred to what was known as the reader's proof. During that process, conflicts among various changes were resolved by the editor of the piece. The reader's proof then went to the makeup department and on to the printing plant to be put into page. The page proofs were read not only by the checker, who would make any late fixes needed to keep up with current events, and by Mr. Shawn, who tried to reread everything before it ran, but also by a proofreader and an O.K.er, both of whom were seeing the piece for the first time. The new changes were consolidated on a new reader's proof and were read through again by the O.K.er to iron out any new conflicts. The checker and the editor got one last look. If there were revised pages, as there often were, the whole process was repeated. (At one time, a single O.K.er had worked on fact and fiction, but over the years the size of the issues had increased, and eventually fiction got its own O.K.er.)

In part because *The New Yorker* had an arrangement with the printing plant which allowed for unlimited alterations, everyone worked on the proofs as if they were typed manuscripts, rather than texts set in molten type, and, because at each stage the writer and the editor had to reread the piece, new changes were constantly being generated and passages rewritten. The miracle was that the piece never lost the individual style of the writer, and the explanation of the miracle was that once the piece was in galleys nothing was changed without his or her approval.

The last stage in the whole process was the foundries—proofs of the final plates, from which the magazine was printed, complete with advertisements and artwork. Even at that stage, changes were allowed, whether to correct mistakes or only for literary value, although changes at that stage incurred great expense for the magazine.

The fulcrum of the whole editorial process was the makeup department. Makeup calculated the columns available in a particular issue, using a complex formula to determine the ratio between editorial and advertising material. Mr. Shawn then decided what to run, adding editorial columns if he thought it necessary. The pieces almost always ran in the same order: major fiction pieces came before fact, Theatre before Cinema, a Profile before a Reporter at Large, and so on, with book reviews coming last. The rationale for the order was to strike a balance between short and long pieces and between imaginative and factual writing. The order not only gave the magazine a distinctive character but also allowed it to accommodate drastic changes and still retain a sense of familiarity.

Six men worked in the makeup department. Except for the checkers and the young women in the typing pool, the people in makeup were the only ones at *The New Yorker* who constituted any semblance of a community. These men, all of them Catholic, worked together at long tables, and, unlike any other *New Yorker* group, nearly always went out to lunch together. They were cheerful and friendly, and were not above horsing around, in contrast to most staff members, who tended to be solitary and preoccupied, or even to appear dour. In the course of a day, many writers, becoming desperate in their struggle with words, would look into the makeup department in search of distraction.

❧

EACH TIME MR. SHAWN and I finished a set of proofs of my philosophy piece, Mr. Shawn attached one of *The New Yorker's* pink slips to it and sent it along to Ed Stringham, in the collating department. Stringham was known for being able to decipher the illegible scrawls of editors and of hundreds of writers, and he would copy the changes onto the reader's proof in a neat, clear hand. Like many of the people involved in getting *The New Yorker* out from week to week, he had a mostly solitary job. Except in notes from Mr. Shawn, he received little appreciation, and he had little contact with writers. In fact, we writers scarcely knew where his office was, let alone where he lived, whether he was married, or what kind of life he had outside the magazine. He did have one assistant, not because he necessarily needed one—he preferred to do everything himself—but because *The New Yorker* had a policy of having a double for every person required to get the magazine out, in case someone got sick or dropped dead.

It used to be said that R. Hawley Truax, a lawyer who had been connected with *The New Yorker* since its earliest days and eventually became treasurer and vice-president of the company, stayed awake nights worrying about how *The New Yorker* could come out without interruption in case of accident, flood, or, indeed, atomic war. People laughed at him, but his worry was not wholly unfounded. Once, the messenger who took the final *New Yorker* proofs of fact pieces by train every Thursday night to the printers, in Greenwich, Connecticut, had a heart attack en route. The conductor knew him and his routine so well that after calling an ambulance he rushed the proofs to the plant himself. The magazine came out without missing a beat, but to Truax the episode was an example of what could go wrong.

And once Stringham, sitting in an armchair in his department late at night, waiting for some proofs with last-minute changes to reach him, fell asleep while smoking a cigarette. He must have dropped it, because it started a small fire. He woke up in time to save himself and the office, but this was yet another episode underlining the fragility of the process.

❧

NOW AND AGAIN during the editing of the philosophy piece, Mr. Shawn and I would hit a problem for which neither of us could think of even a stopgap solution, and the matter would hang over us from day to day. One such problem was what title to give the piece. My latest suggestion for a title was "Fly and the Fly-Bottle," from Ludwig Wittgenstein's statement in his "Philosophical Investigations" that the aim of philosophy was "to show the fly the way out of the fly-bottle." The title came from my text and seemed to sum up in one image what the piece was about. But early in the week that it was going to press Bill Mangold, the A-issue man, came in to say that there were two "flies" in the issue's titles. It turned out that one of the fiction editors, Robert Henderson, had written a story with the title "The Dürer and the Dragonfly" which was running in the issue, and the title was integral to the story and couldn't be changed. The decision was therefore made that my title would have to go.

"It's a bad break, but maybe you can use the title for a book in which you publish the philosophy piece," Mr. Shawn said.

We both had trouble thinking of a substitute. As Monday, Tuesday, and Wednesday went by, I came up with more and more ludicrous titles, partly because my anxiety was mounting, and partly because I found Mr. Shawn's inability to think of a title unnerving. At one point, I said, "What about calling it 'The Magic Flute'?"—because the piece contained a passing reference to the opera and in my overactive imagination the philosophers sometimes reminded me of the characters in it. He laughed. Sobering up, I finally suggested using as the title another Wittgenstein line quoted in my piece: "A Battle Against the Bewitchment of Our Intelligence." But I thought it was too long, and said, "Maybe we can abbreviate it."

Mr. Shawn repeated it a couple of times, then declared, "That's a wonderful line, and it's just right. We should use all of it."

"But no one will ever remember it," I said.

"That doesn't matter," he said. "What's important is that it fits the piece."

Most editors go in for short, snappy titles, I thought, because they imagine that such titles are what readers like, but Mr. Shawn makes no concessions, and I hope he's right. Indeed, he was proved right. Twenty or thirty years after the piece went to press, I would meet people who had read it, and they would refer to it by its full title.

On Thursday, Mr. Shawn called me around one o'clock and suggested that we get together over lunch in his office to finish up the latest proofs, so that the checker and the O.K.er would have the maximum time to review them.

As soon as I sat down, he said he was sending out for sandwiches from Chock Full O' Nuts, and, turning to his typewriter, asked me what I would like. After several lunches with him at the Algonquin, I had finally found a dish I liked that was easy to eat in his presence—corned-beef hash. But I had no idea what sandwich to have, so I was determined not to order before he did. I asked him what he was going to have.

"Cream cheese on date-nut bread, and some coffee," he said.

"I'll have the same," I said, wondering what date-nut bread could be.

"Anything to go with it?" he asked after typing our order.

"No," I said, and he typed, "No garnishes."

He rang for Miss Broun and gave her the typed sheet for the messenger, as if typing out a lunch order were a routine affair. I later learned that it was by no means unusual.

I was surprised at how much work was still left to be done on "A Battle Against the Bewitchment of Our Intelligence" and also at how relaxed I felt, even though we were now working against the Thursday-night deadline. His calm had at last begun to have a soothing effect on me.

We scarcely paused while we lunched, but I remember thinking that my sandwich, in its sweetness and its texture, was almost like cake. By four o'clock, we'd finished with everything, and Mr. Shawn said that he would call me if the checker or the O.K.er had any new queries.

For the rest of the afternoon, I wandered around the office, feeling lost. People in the messengers' room were playing cards and listening to Elvis Presley on the radio. The messengers were mostly children of *New Yorker* writers or recent college graduates who wanted to try their hand at writing or drawing, and who therefore hung around the office—under the eye of Mr. Monsees, an ex-policeman—hoping for a break. Messengers frequently submitted copy to Mr. Shawn or drawings to the art department, and there was great excitement on the eighteenth floor when a piece of their handiwork got into the magazine.

In makeup that afternoon, people were sitting around waiting for the reader's proof on my piece and for the Talk order. "It looks like a late night," Carmine Peppe, who had been head of the department since 1932, said to me. "The O.K.er hasn't got through even half of the reader's proof yet. She's finding it hard going."

"Who is the O.K.er?" I asked.

"Thelma Sargent, and—boy!—you should see the notes she's taking," he said.

"You mean on the proof?" I asked, in some alarm.

"No," he said. "She jots down things like which nouns are capitalized and where they are in the piece."

"What's the latest you've ever been here?"

"Four or five or six in the morning, but I try not to remember that, or I wouldn't be able to get up every day and come to work."

The checking department was empty except for the checker who was working on my piece. The other checkers were free until the next morning, when the Talk proofs would hit their desks.

At six o'clock, Adrianne went home. At seven o'clock, Mr. Shawn called to say that I should go out to dinner but perhaps leave the telephone number of the restaurant with him.

"What will you do for dinner?" I asked.

"I'll get something when I go home," he said.

I went out and came back. Mr. Shawn's secretary had gone home. He was in his office reading manuscripts.

"Any news?" I asked, appropriating the question with which he generally greeted me.

"Not yet," he said. "I don't think there will be any until ten-thirty or eleven."

I went down to my office and tried to read, but I had trouble concentrating. I was shepherding only one piece to Mr. Shawn's dozen or more, yet I felt totally spent. I feared that there would be a score of additional queries to be disposed of before I could leave.

Many of them would never have come up if certain changes hadn't been made along the way, and many of those changes would never have been made if someone hadn't raised other queries in the first place. Every day, we seemed to spawn queries, as if that were our raison d'être, and I suspected that a reader could have happily read my original manuscript without being aware of any problems at all. So what, exactly, was the point of the whole process, which turned us all into neurotics about minutiae, as if we were producing great literature instead of writing a magazine article? And even most great literature, if it were to be scrutinized the way *New Yorker* proofs were, would be found full of holes. Yet I told myself that in the end clarity was its own justification.

At two o'clock in the morning, I was still touching up my concluding sentence. Soon after that, Miss Sargent signed the reader's proof and handed it in to makeup.

I rushed to the elevator, hardly saying goodbye to Mr. Shawn, who I thought must have seen enough of me. But while I was waiting for the elevator he caught up with me.

"Do all the long pieces require this much work?" I asked him.

"It's not unusual, but the kind of thinking that went on in your piece did present some special difficulties," he said.

"I don't think I've been so tired since I took my finals at Oxford," I said. "How do you bear it?"

"I'm used to it," he said, and then he asked me if I was going home and if he could give me a ride.

"Wouldn't you rather be alone?" I asked.

He was genuinely taken by surprise by my question, and said no, he would enjoy having me along.

It was the kind of late-November night so bitterly cold that even the doormen, hatted and gloved, could stay on the street for only a few minutes at a time. I assumed that Mr. Shawn, like the English editors I knew, would have a chauffeur-driven car waiting for him, with its engine running and the heat on, and we would jump right in. Instead, he stepped off the curb and hailed a taxi. I realized that he instinctively didn't do things that would set him apart from his writers and artists.

The taxi whizzed up Fifth Avenue, which was then two-way. I was so exhausted that I could barely find my tongue, but after a while I said stupidly, "I hope someone will read the piece."

"I'll be happy if twelve people in the country read it," he said.

"You can't mean that," I said. "How could the magazine keep going if people didn't read it?"

"I want any piece to be read by its natural readers—people who will understand and enjoy it."

He went on to say that he edited the magazine as if we were the ideal readers, and assumed that if we liked a piece the readers would.

It seemed such a utopian notion that I could scarcely believe he could hold it. But in subsequent years I learned that that was just one of a number of utopian ideas that he held and was somehow able to indulge while still turning out an extremely financially successful magazine.

As the taxi was about to turn onto Fifty-eighth Street, I said he could drop me off at the corner and I could walk the few blocks to my building, but he insisted on taking me to my door.

Once I was in my apartment, I couldn't get to sleep for a long time. In the morning, I was awakened by the telephone ringing around nine-thirty. It was Mr. Shawn. He said he had just read the foundry proofs, and wondered if we were correct in describing Ayer as a "left-wing intellectual."

I said I'd check on that and call him right back. As I hung up the phone, I recalled that I had once written a review of James Baldwin's "The Fire Next Time" for the London *Observer,* and that its literary editor, Terry Kilmartin, had refused to correct two glaring typos because they would cost the paper something. But apparently Mr. Shawn gave no thought to the expense of making a correction even now that the piece had gone to press. No wonder *New Yorker* writers soon found that they could write for no other publication, that the only sacred text was their *New Yorker* copy. Many writers would tell me to read their pieces in *The New Yorker* rather than in the books in which they were collected, because the books had been printed before the pieces had finished going through the magazine's editorial process.

❦

AT NOON ON Tuesday, I received my copy of the issue, which was stamped "Rough Copy." Although I was long familiar with the label, which was *The New Yorker's* way of tagging the first run of the issue, so that if someone at the office noticed a blooper it could still be corrected in the rest of the run, this time it gave me a turn. Was anything ever done with at *The New Yorker*? The magazine would be out at special newsstands in the city the next day and at all the newsstands the day following. By Friday, it would be in subscribers' mailboxes throughout the country.

I sat waiting in my office for colleagues to drop by and say something about the piece. For days afterward, I walked the halls, still expecting someone to say something about it, if only something as simple as "I saw your piece, it looks good." Of course, that wouldn't mean that anyone had read it, but at least its existence would have been noted. Hardly anyone at the office commented on its publication, however, as if the magazine did indeed come out of an ice machine. (This was not an uncommon experience among us writers, perhaps because each of us was so deeply engaged in his or her own work.)

The world outside was another matter. *Newsweek* and the New York *Post*, among other publications, wanted to interview me. I asked Mr. Shawn for his advice. He said he was in favor of writers' doing occasional interviews for the press but was opposed to interviews for radio or television. "You can say something of substance in a paper or a magazine, but radio and television interviews do little more than cater to the vanity of the writer," he said. I followed his advice and gave only a few interviews, and those only to print journalists.

Early the next month, while I was still savoring the publication of my piece, Mr. Shawn came by and handed me a five-page letter from Ernest Gellner, one of the philosophers I had written about. "As you will see, Gellner is very angry," he said. "He tried to stop the distribution of the magazine in England, and is now threatening a libel suit against us. Could you let me know what you think of his letter? Don't be too upset by it."

"Oh, God, not again," I said to myself. "The lawyers are going to cut me off at the knees before I've even found my legs as a writer." Aloud, I said, "But my account of Gellner is true, Mr. Shawn."

"I'm sure that's so," he replied, "but Mr. Greenstein tells me that the law of libel is much stricter in England—that truth is not a defense against libel."

Quaking, I read the letter. It was as polemical as Gellner's book on Oxford philosophy, "Words and Things," which I had made the starting point of my piece, but I dealt with it point by point in a letter of my own to Mr. Shawn.

He then wrote a long and detailed reply to Gellner, but Greenstein advised us against sending it, on the ground that it could only serve to complicate the legal situation. In the end, Gellner's threat was not carried out, possibly because there was little basis for it.

In the middle of the fuss over Gellner, an older *New Yorker* colleague of mine, St. Clair McKelway, walked into my office. "Sam Behrman wants to meet you," he said.

"Why?" I asked. The playwright S. N. Behrman, who had written a stunning seven-part Profile of Max Beerbohm for *The New Yorker* and was known to be close to Mr. Shawn, was such a distinguished figure that I thought McKelway—or Mac, as he was called—was playing a practical joke on me. Mac was a manic-depressive, and when he was in his manic phase he was apt to come into my office and say that President Kennedy wanted me on the telephone.

On this occasion he said, "Sam wants to look you over. Freddy Ayer has been bad-mouthing you to him, and he wants to see for himself the whippersnapper who has got this great Oxford philosopher so worked up."

"Ayer is one of the vainest people I know," I said. "I'd be happy to tell that to Mr. Behrman."

"He wants to take you to lunch at Sardi's."

So it was that I found myself lunching with Mac and Mr. Behrman at what was then still the watering hole of the Broadway celebrities. People kept stopping at our table to greet Behrman, who was at the height of his Broadway fame, and he clearly basked in the attention. He was a wonderful talker. Listening to him was a little bit like being plied with champagne. We didn't ever talk directly about Ayer or my philosophy piece. But then Behrman was apparently more interested in looking me over as if I were a horse than in hearing about any particular race I had run.

Back at the office, Mac slipped a piece of paper into my hand and disappeared. It was the bill from Sardi's, which Behrman had settled. On the back he had written in pencil, "Fuck Ayer, this is the boy for me."

Once Ayer had cooled down, he thought better of the piece—and, indeed, publicly praised it. In later years, we saw something of each other.

❧

IN DUE COURSE, I got hundreds of letters about my philosophy piece from dons and professors all over the English-speaking world. Most of them were complimentary. Those I forgot as soon as I had acknowledged them. The ones that loomed large in my consciousness were barbed, and I labored long over my replies to them. I had written "Face to Face" in six months and "Walking the Indian Streets" in less than half that time, but now that I was at *The New Yorker* I seemed to be incapable of writing even a letter off the top of my head. As soon as I put down a sentence, I saw problems with it and started over. By the end of the day, I often didn't have even one sentence that I liked, and answering a handful of letters sometimes took me most of a week. In the meantime, I could get no other work done, and felt like a taxi-driver going up and down the avenue with his meter running but without a fare.

What took up the most time was answering letters from the philosophers I had written about. Some of them offered their congratulations, others expressed indignation, and still others first congratulated me and then, after talking to their colleagues and rereading the piece, grew indignant. Although Hampshire wrote to me, "Indignation is an emotion that very quickly dissolves," I didn't like the thought of some of the people I admired most having a bad opinion of me, however fleetingly.

Bertrand Russell, who in an initial letter had attested to the authenticity of the piece, later talked to Gellner and wrote me a second letter, saying that the tearsheets of it "had been sent to me in a disorderly form with separate sheets which were not consecutive, and I regret to say that I did not read it as carefully as I ought to have done." He added, "I find now that there are things in your report of me which do not seem to me to be accurate."

Similarly, Isaiah Berlin first wrote, "Altogether I congratulate you on your long and splendid piece. . . . I had no idea it was possible for a non-philosopher to convey so much and so justly." A couple of weeks later, he wrote another letter, in which he seemed to have had a change of heart. Yet he changed his tack from sentence to sentence, as if he weren't quite sure what he felt. He wrote:

You ask me what the reactions of my colleagues are to your piece on Oxford Philosophy . . . those to whom I have spoken are in various degrees outraged and indignant. This I will not attempt to conceal from you. And I understand most of them quite well: if one is engaged on a serious and extremely difficult vocation, such as that of philosophy, it is, to say the least, irritating to be represented as believing and saying things that certainly do not exactly correspond to what one is attempting to think out and explain very precisely and painfully. *The New Yorker* is a satirical magazine, and I assume from the start that a satire was intended and not an accurate representation of the truth. In any case, only a serious student of philosophy could attempt to do that. . . . Moreover, I thought it was a remarkable feat for a non-philosopher to have given a picture—however ironical—of this most complex phenomenon, and anyone reading it would, I think, at any rate obtain as much of a notion of Oxford philosophy as perhaps a Westerner reading an anthropologist's account of native beliefs and rites would obtain of that kind of remote and alien society, with a large degree of caricature, intended and unintended, due to the remoteness of the author from the civilisation he is describing. . . . I cannot deny, when I am invited to consider it by my colleagues, that the readers of *The New Yorker* will certainly not glean a just picture of what people here are thinking and teaching—but neither, I assume, were they intended to. Satire, as I said before, is the purpose of *The New Yorker* and as a gay and disrespectful account, sometimes cruel, sometimes amiable, it is of a piece with other escapades made by the writers for that very intelligent magazine. But do not let me be taken as certifying the piece as a serious analysis or reliable impressionist picture of a major philosophical movement. . . . I think the piece is a genuine success in a Toulouse Lautrec sort of way, rather like Tolstoy's accounts of German theorising with which he does not sympathise, or Voltaire's (and Russell's) reflections on, say, the schoolmen of the Middle Ages. But I fully understand the feelings of such of my colleagues as must feel about your piece what Christians would feel about Gibbon when they have been caricatured to make *The New Yorker's* holiday. Still parody is your right. . . . Meanwhile, I personally hope, out of my great regard for you, that you are faring well in the dangerous occupation which you have embraced.

The letter ended with this postscript:

I have no recollection of what I said to you in my first letter, but what I have just written to you—quite apart from gathering that it was not too well received by my colleagues . . .—represents what I felt on first reading.

There were many points I wanted to make in response to Berlin's letter: that the kind of writing I was doing was as serious and precise in its way as he said philosophy was; that, although *The New Yorker* published satirical and humorous articles, it was an extremely serious magazine, and everyone who worked on it was a fanatic about accuracy and truth; that the task I had undertaken in the piece was not beyond the abilities of an amateur philosopher, which was how I thought of myself, nor, indeed, were the "beliefs and rites" of Oxford philosophers as inaccessible as those in Berlin's "alien society"; that many people who didn't know *The New Yorker* patronized it, as perhaps he did (as in "*The New Yorker's* holiday"), because their impressions were based on advertisements and cartoons, rather than on the text; and so on. But such a response was not in keeping with the groping, well-meaning spirit of his letter. Anyway, I had come to adopt Mr. Shawn's point of view that, although we might clear up confusion in *The New Yorker* copy, there was no way of clearing up the confusion that persisted in people's minds. So I wrote Berlin a respectful letter, making one or two of these points but leaving the rest unsaid. I thought that that would be the end of our correspondence, especially since I was going to be in England and we were planning to meet. But within ten days I received yet another epistolary critique, this one six pages long, which read, in part:

. . . I suddenly realised that all those personalities about the philosophers, their appearances, their physical characteristics, their opinions of each other, the anecdotes, the estimates of their relative importance or whether or not they were likely to be productive in the future, etc., all this did combine into something much more like the regular *New Yorker* "Profile"—of which the victims, as you know, sometimes take to their beds with mortification and shame—than a sober assessment of a philosophical school and its doctrines and its importance. . . . [Philosophy] needs, as I need not tell you, immense sensibility, the most delicate and irritable nervous civilisation, and purity of character to attain to the heights of that profession, apart from intellectual power and the peculiar organisation which makes one interested in and capable of doing philosophy at all—does create a fine and vulnerable human texture which the fun you make from time to time would quite naturally upset. . . . Imagine what would have been the reactions of Kant or Hegel and their colleagues if their personal quirks, the clothes they wore, the remarks they casually made, what was said about them by the citizens of Königsberg or Jena, etc., had been exposed to public view during their lifetime. . . . It will no doubt one day all blow over, but if you wish to describe living individuals in a manner likely to make them interesting to the readers of *The New Yorker,* you must expect indignation and resentful feelings. . . . [T]he whole modern art of showing people's faces, warts and all, may suit Cromwell or the business tycoons of whom you speak, because their whole view of life rests on the assumption that in life one eats or is eaten, beats or is beaten, together with a contempt for self-protective seekers of private existence, and those who believe that personal relationships are everything—but I need not go on, you understand all this perfectly, I am sure.

This time, there was this interesting postscript:

I suppose what it all boils down to is the degree to which it is right and decent to penetrate into and give publicity to private lives. Tycoons and politicians are obviously public property. Professors and Dons do lecture in public and are accountable for their acts academically, and some by constantly appearing on television let us say and generally playing a public part as politicians or otherwise, may have forfeited their right to be treated as wholly private individuals, with their lives protected from the rude public gaze. . . . In general it is obviously very bad to destroy privacy, tear down walls and expose private relationships to public view, even if it is not done with a certain degree of irony. Where does the frontier between public and private lie? You rightly do not speak about my colleagues' personal relationships with their wives or children or their marital affairs, or which of them are divorced and which are not; you would surely think it terrible to publicise facts like that or attribute views to calamities in private life, by which they may well have been influenced in fact. What is allowed and what is not allowed? That, I suppose, is in the end the issue between you and Ayer, Hampshire, Ryle, etc. There are no rules about this, but those of conscience, ideals, taste. When you come I shall be happy to talk to you about this for it is a very real subject in any case.

His letter served only as an impetus to renew my mental rebuttal. Which subjects of Profiles had taken to their beds? Most of the subjects I knew, like Narayan, had loved their Profiles. In fact, one change in *The New Yorker* under Mr. Shawn, for which he was much criticized, was that he generally published admiring Profiles of people he thought were doing something worthwhile, instead of publishing pieces that dissected or made fun of their subjects, as the magazine had sometimes done under Ross. Then, too, Berlin seemed to think that only philosophers had delicate nervous temperaments, were pure of heart, and were vulnerable. I could point to many of my colleagues—not to mention Mr. Shawn—who fitted that description to a T. Anyway, weren't those characteristics common to many serious people engaged in intellectual pursuits? And would Kant and Hegel have really been as put out as Berlin claimed? Many people have biographies and memoirs written about them while they are still alive. (Indeed, a biography of Berlin himself was published in 1995.) Furthermore, writing descriptions of people which included "warts and all" was not characteristic of Mr. Shawn's *New Yorker,* which was always at pains to protect people's feelings. But the most important point that Berlin made in his letter concerned the demarcation between public and private life. No one was more preoccupied with not invading people's privacy than Mr. Shawn, perhaps because he himself and, taking their cues from him, most of *The New Yorker* people were extremely private. Mr. Shawn hardly ever gave an interview, and on the few occasions that he did so it was because he deemed it necessary for the economic health of the magazine. In any event, he had an iron-clad rule that we should never write about anyone who did not wish to be written about. Before setting out on my quest, I had written to many philosophers, telling them formally that I was preparing a long piece on Oxford philosophy and would like to come and talk to them, and that my interviews with them would be on record. I never pursued those who—like Gilbert Ryle and Elizabeth Anscombe, for instance—didn't respond; I didn't badger those who, like Marcus Dick, said they would prefer not to be interviewed; and I respected the wishes of those who, like Berlin, gave me interviews but later had second thoughts and asked me not to print them. Except for quoting published work, I wrote only about those philosophers who had responded enthusiastically to the idea of being part of my piece. Some of them, like Ayer, regularly appeared on television and otherwise conducted themselves like public men. Even so, by Berlin's own admission, I had not written anything about their personal lives—only about their professional relationships.

In general, the reactions of the philosophers were so diverse and so contradictory that sometimes I felt they couldn't all be writing about the same piece. While Berlin condemned me for being ironic, other philosophers scolded me for writing flatly, putting down everything straight. I wondered if the trouble might lie in *The New Yorker's* reportorial form of writing, in which the points were made implicitly, allowing the reader to draw his own conclusions. Or might it lie in the fact that I had written about intellectuals in terms of both their ideas and their persons—something they were perhaps not used to? (Hampshire was so innocent of journalistic practice that he was indignant upon finding I had quoted him directly.)

All the letters that I received I shared with Mr. Shawn, confident that his opinion of me and of the piece would not be swayed by attacks on me, even though they came from some of the most illustrious people in the intellectual establishment. I thought he might want to publish some of the letters in the magazine, even though *The New Yorker* had no regular letters column. Such columns in other magazines, with their arrays of contradictory facts and opinions, seemed only to sow confusion, and, since *The New Yorker* was not an opinion magazine, and its copy was rigorously checked, what we had instead was a Department of Amplification or, alternatively, a Department of Correction, which appeared whenever it was necessary. But it was clear to both Mr. Shawn and me that the philosophy piece might require a departure from normal practice, since we might seem to have crossed into the territory of opinion, and perhaps it was only fair that the philosophers be given an opportunity to state their points of view publicly.

We spent considerable time going over the letters together, but realized that much of the thinking in them was so loose and the ideas were so convoluted and contradictory that printing them would serve only to show the philosophers in an unflattering light. At one point, I myself did a draft of an Amplification, quoting the most interesting material from the letters, but with no better results. Mr. Shawn and I finally reached the conclusion that since I was planning to publish the piece in a book one day I could take account of their criticism at that time and modify certain passages of my text accordingly—and they, of course, would be free to publish reviews. (When the book was eventually published, in 1963, I was terrified that it would be panned, especially in England: How dare an Indian write about the British for an American magazine? In reality, it got very long, favorable reviews. Some of the critics, however, missed the point and wrote that it provided proof of the decline of British culture.)

The last word on the whole problem with interviewing may belong to Bertrand Russell. He wrote in his letter to me, "I have always found that interviewing is a very difficult matter and that the impression conveyed is often not that intended." Not long after the publication of my piece, I felt the full impact of that observation. I myself was so unused to being interviewed that when Beverly Gary came to do a "Closeup" piece on me for the *Post* I couldn't stop shivering, out of nervousness. I thereupon put on two sweaters, only to read in the paper later, "His face is large, his body somewhat thick."

V

ELEVEN-FIFTY

I N THE SPRING OF 1961, SOME NINE MONTHS BEFORE the philosophy piece ran, Mr. Shawn's older son, Wallace, surprised me with a visit to my office. He said he was a senior at Putney, a school in Vermont, and was organizing a school conference on "The United Nations and the Underdeveloped World" for an upcoming weekend, and he asked me if I could help him find an Indian diplomat for the conference.

I said that S. K. Roy, the Consul General of India in New York, was a friend, and that I could approach him.

"Actually, the real reason I came here—" He broke off. He spoke hesitantly, with a lot of "um"s and "ah"s, and apparently wanted to avoid asking a direct question. Instead, he seemed to back into a subject, as if he thought that it was courteous to feel out people's reactions before making a request. "I mean, um, I came to ask you, ah, if you would possibly consider coming to the school and talking yourself—being a part of the conference, you know. You see, your Indian pieces had a great effect on me—

although, um, of course, I'm only a high-school student, and why should you care about my opinion?" He laughed a little devilishly, and added, "Dad would disapprove of my asking you, but he doesn't know."

I was excited at the thought of doing something for a member of Mr. Shawn's family and immediately accepted the invitation.

Wallace left, after shaking my hand in the manner of the aristocrats I knew in England—holding his hand out above my hand, as if he were giving it to me rather than taking mine. He's much more worldly than his father, I thought.

Hardly had he left my office, it seemed, when there came four gentle taps on the door, and Mr. Shawn walked in. "I hear that Wallace was in to see you," he said. How he heard I never knew, but I realized that nothing remained a secret from him for long. "I understand that he's asked you to speak at his conference. But you shouldn't agree just because he's my son."

"Of course I wouldn't," I said, feeling like a hypocrite. "I've already agreed, because I would enjoy being part of the conference."

Mr. Shawn was gone so quickly that I thought I had dreamed his visit.

❦

DWIGHT MACDONALD'S WIFE, Gloria, and Daphne Hellman, the ex-wife of a colleague of mine, Geoffrey Hellman, were parents of children at Putney, and they offered me a ride to the school in a pickup truck that Daphne, a jazz harpist, used for transporting her harp. The truck had only two seats, and I was put in the back, on the floor, next to the harp. It was a long trip. I could scarcely ever stay awake in a moving vehicle, but this time whenever I fell asleep I hit my head on the harp and woke up to the jangle of harp strings.

When, hours later, I arrived at Putney, frazzled and battered, I was taken in hand by a sixteen-year-old classmate of Wallace's named Eve Cary, who was to be my "hostess." After I had been settled in a guest house, Eve took me on a tour of the school, which included a memorable stop in a barn with a lot of cows and an overpowering smell. "The cows are part of the curriculum," she said, over music of Bach that was coming from a nearby window. "All the students here have chores. Right now, Wallace and his roommates have to wake up early in the morning, when it's still dark, and shovel the manure."

"Shouldn't they be hitting their books instead of shovelling manure?" I asked, and added, somewhat scathingly, "Putney doesn't seem to be very rigorous academically."

During the tour and later, I kept up some rather condescending banter with Eve, Wallace, and Wallace's two roommates—Turner Brooks, who could easily have been mistaken for the actor Charlton Heston, and Jonathan Schell, who was almost as handsome as Turner and easily as enthusiastic as Wallace. I expected to be challenged and given my due in return, as would have happened in an English school, but instead they all just laughed in a knowing way, as if they were humoring an enfant terrible or an unreconstructed reactionary.

❧

ON THE FIRST day, the conference was broken up into small groups, and several of us speakers addressed them at the same time. Wallace was not in my group, but I was horrified to discover that Mr. and Mrs. Shawn were, along with their younger son, Allen. It hadn't occurred to me that they might show up at the school, let alone in my audience. I was speaking extemporaneously, and the thought of subjecting Mr. Shawn to my off-the-cuff ramblings was mortifying. But there was no help for it.

I had been asked to talk about Mahatma Gandhi and poverty, and, thinking that I would be talking only to a group of teenagers, I had made some mental notes of a few provocative points, and I now ran through them quickly. In the course of my speech, I got wound up and let fly some barbs at schools that, in the manner of Gandhi, were more interested in enabling their students to live self-sufficient lives—by shovelling manure, for instance—than in teaching them Greek and Latin.

As soon as I finished, I felt guilty for patronizing Putney, and possibly Gandhi—all the more so because Mr. Shawn was never patronizing. I felt that in secretly trying to please him by doing something for his son I had surely forfeited his good opinion.

"That was a good, strong talk," Mr. Shawn said, immediately coming up. "There was so much about Gandhi I never knew." His words were so generous that I could scarcely find my tongue, even to thank him.

Mrs. Shawn, who was effusive in her praise (I was soon to learn that she was demonstrative in everything), asked me if I was free to have supper with them at the Chanticleer, in Brattleboro. I accepted her invitation with alacrity.

Later, sitting around a table at the Chanticleer with Mr. and Mrs. Shawn, Wallace, and Allen, I couldn't stop marvelling at the sensitivity and attention with which they listened to one another and at how the children participated as equals with their parents in a wide-ranging conversation that roamed from politics to art and on to education.

At one point, Allen, who was thirteen, said that he wanted to be a composer.

"That's a very hard life," I said. "A much harder way to earn one's keep than by writing."

"That's true," he said. "Charles Ives sold insurance."

I blanched at the very idea that a Shawn child might end up selling insurance.

"Everybody has to earn a living," Mrs. Shawn said.

They seemed like an ideal family. Indeed, they approached

everything with such open minds, rather than with the dismissive, judgmental prejudice I associated with more traditional schooling, that I found myself reëvaluating my opinion of Putney. It now seemed like a good school, combining learning with a healthy outdoor life. After that evening at the Chanticleer, when I imagined that I was taken into the family fold as a fifth member, I never stopped comparing myself and my family unfavorably with the Shawns, perhaps because, as my friends like to say, I have a romantic nature and tend to invest things—especially when they're things I don't have—with a rosy glow, even to the point of unconsciously attributing magical powers to anyone who can see.

❦

AFTER THE PUTNEY conference ended, I didn't hear anything from Wallace until November, when, out of the blue, he called me on the phone and invited me to his eighteenth-birthday party, in his parents' apartment, at 1150 Fifth Avenue, a few days later. I found something childlike in the idea of his having a birthday party—an event I associated with characters in English novels. At home, our parents had marked the birthdays of each of us seven children merely with their wishes for many happy returns and with a new ten-rupee note to be spent for anything we liked. After coming to the West, I had usually commemorated my birthday alone, keeping it a secret, as if there were something embarrassing about the day and about drawing attention to myself by mentioning it.

"Are you sure it's all right for me to come?" I asked Wallace. "Will it be all right with your parents?" Although Mr. Shawn never treated any of his writers as employees, he was still my boss, and I didn't want to do anything that might appear to be out of line. Anyway, I was eight years older than Wallace, and wasn't sure I would fit in with his school friends.

"Yes, of course. Mother and Dad are excited at the idea of your coming," Wallace said. His voice became whispery and confidential. "You know, it's not something I would tell people—I mean, at the office." He laughed in his devilish way. "Maybe you could just keep it to yourself. You know what I mean."

Wallace's injunction was superfluous, but it lent my going to the Shawns' something of a clandestine air.

❧

WALLACE, NO DOUBT understanding that I wanted to be treated exactly like everyone else, hadn't told me that the entrance to his building was on the side street, so on the appointed evening I kept going up and down Fifth Avenue between Ninety-sixth and Ninety-seventh Streets, searching for it, and spurning the thought of asking anyone's help. I finally figured out where it was, and got to the Shawns' apartment, on the second floor.

I was greeted at the door by Wallace and Allen and then by Mrs. Shawn, who hugged me with such spontaneous affection that I stiffened and immediately remonstrated with myself for not being as warm as she was.

"Everyone is here except Father, who's held up at the office," Mrs. Shawn said. Her reference to Mr. Shawn as "Father" gave me a curious shock. I think it was the first time I had consciously thought of the whole *New Yorker* staff as a family.

Everywhere in the apartment there were books, records, family photographs, family mementos. Everything in the place seemed to have a personal meaning, in contrast to many other New York apartments, which were filled with antiques or decorator items and seemed to belong to people other than the ones who lived in them.

To my great astonishment, the Shawns' living room held more grown people than young ones. Many of them were middle-aged colleagues of mine. They all seemed to be talking at the same time, and so noisily that it could have been a gathering of my crazy aunts and uncles. There was the late Edith Oliver, the magazine's Off Broadway critic, smoking up a storm with her childhood friend Joan Kahn, who was perhaps the leading New York editor of detective novels. Edith and Joan and Joan's younger sister, Olivia, a distinguished artist, who was also there, formed a sort of eccentric family of their own, and were affectionately known around town as "the three weird sisters." (The brother of Joan and Olivia was Jack, a colleague of mine known to *New Yorker* readers as E. J. Kahn, Jr.) Also among the guests were Bruce Bliven, Jr., and his wife, Naomi, and Philip and Edith Hamburger with their two sons—Jay, who was fourteen, and Richard, who was ten. Bruce, Naomi, and Philip were all *New Yorker* writers. Allen and Wallace and Wallace's two roommates, Jonathan and Turner, along with Eve Cary, completed the party, and they were mixing and talking with the older crowd as if it consisted entirely of contemporaries.

I heard the turning of the lock on the front door. "Father has come!" Mrs. Shawn cried, rushing out into the entrance hall, with Wallace, Allen, Jonathan, and Eve close behind. I followed.

Mr. Shawn walked in, hat in hand, and dressed in his characteristic navy-blue suit and waistcoat—a kind of uniform that seemed to belie his artistic temperament. He was weighed down with a huge stack of familiar manuscript-size *New Yorker* envelopes and with a briefcase. Mrs. Shawn greeted him as if he were a returning war hero. He put his things in the hall closet, kissed her and their sons, and shook hands all around. The din in the living room continued unabated when he went in: people kept talking, as if they knew that he didn't like his entrance to be noticed. He made the rounds, greeting each person quietly.

One of two facing sofas near the windows, and at right angles to a fireplace that seemed never to have been used, had all along been left unoccupied. Mr. Shawn sat down in the corner seat of that one, with Mrs. Shawn next to him and holding his hand, as if they were newlyweds. Then she got up and busied herself passing around hors d'œuvres—liver pâté, melon balls with toothpicks, and cheese and crackers.

Before the entrance of Mr. Shawn, there had been many little conversations, but now the talk became general and frenzied, with people interrupting one another and vying for his attention. He sat alert, responsive to every change in the current of the conversation, and trying to bring it down to earth when it became increasingly fanciful. But the more rational he was, the more irrational the people around him seemed to become, and there was a part of him that appeared to enjoy this—as if, unable to be outrageous himself, he relished outrageousness in others. (Allen once told me that what his father liked to watch on television were comedians like Richard Pryor and Mel Brooks, or people dancing uninhibitedly, and that Edith Oliver used to tease him that he had a penchant for lowlife.)

At one point, Edith asked him if he had seen the recent flurry of mentions of Thurber's book "The Years with Ross," which was then being praised in the papers as the best book on *The New Yorker*.

I'd thought that the last subject anyone would bring up was *The New Yorker*, since I'd imagined that the party would offer Mr. Shawn one chance to switch off and relax. But it was as if having him as a captive audience gave people an opportunity they couldn't pass up. Although at the office he was always accessible in theory, no one could talk to him for very long, because there was very often someone with him, the telephone was always ringing, and deadlines were looming.

"The book is trash," Edith said. She had a smoker's hoarse voice, and her remarks came out sounding like little barks. "It's all untrue. He might as well be writing about his mother."

"Have a melon ball, Edith," Mrs. Shawn said.

"You're always interrupting serious conversation, Cecille," Edith said.

Mrs. Shawn merely laughed, and told Allen to take the pâté around and give some to Edith.

"Thurber is a horse's ass," Edith continued.

I must have looked shocked, but Mr. Shawn seemed to discount her talk as part of her exuberance and of her loyalty to the magazine. "She doesn't mean it, Ved," he said. (That proved to be his standard phrase at his parties on occasions when there was someone new in the room, who seemed put off by the strident conversation.)

I had become so used to reading ironic interviews in *The New Yorker* in which people, without knowing it, revealed themselves through their speech that I found this social conversation sometimes excruciating. I listened to people talking as if I were reading what they said—or else were going to write it. But Mr. Shawn seemed to ignore the froth of the talk and to listen to the deeper meaning. I became aware of a new dimension in his listening.

"I mean every word I say about Thurber," Edith now retorted.

"I ran into Thurber at the Algonquin, and he was saying an awful lot of bitter things about Bill and *The New Yorker's* fiction department," Joan said, stoking Edith's fire.

"That's because Bill has turned down a lot of his pieces," Edith said.

"His work has really been falling off," Naomi put in. She reviewed books for *The New Yorker*.

"Naomi has Thurber down," Bruce said. The Blivens' solution to the problem of two writers' being married to each other was for Bruce always to reinforce what Naomi said.

"He's become very vituperative since he became totally blind," Philip said.

"Blind people have a lot of anger," Edith said, and then, as if remembering that I was in the room, added, "Ved, of course, is an exception." People laughed uneasily.

Wallace took me aside. "Old-timers at *The New Yorker* really, um, hate Thurber's book," he said. "He glorifies Ross so much that he scarcely even mentions Dad. Dad doesn't care about that, but, although he would never say it, I'm sure he doesn't think the book gives the right picture of Ross. I mean, let's face it, Dad thinks that Thurber makes Ross seem crude but that's probably why Thurber was drawn to him."

We rejoined the general conversation. "Thurber, together with Perelman, has to be one of the greatest humorists of our century," Mr. Shawn was saying, as if he were making an effort to bring Edith—and now Joan, Naomi, and Bruce, too—around to some appreciation of Thurber. He went on to give examples of Thurber's funny writing, and then everyone in the room—even Wallace and his friends, who had been fairly quiet, as if they were spectators at a stage show—began remembering different funny Thurber pieces.

"Of course Thurber is a great genius," Edith said, for the first time sounding calm. Her transformation under Mr. Shawn's gentle prompting was remarkable.

Mrs. Shawn called us in to dinner, asking me to go in with her. I gave her my arm.

"We ordinarily have a buffet, but today, in honor of Wallace's birthday, we're sitting around the table," she said.

The doorway of the dining room was hung with streamers that one had to part to go into the room, and the table was covered with a paper tablecloth, party hats, noisemakers, and party favors. I smiled to myself, thinking how strange it was to have my middle-aged colleagues sitting at what was really a children's table. Otherwise, however, my head was full of the conversation about Thurber—a conversation that for a long time made me wary of putting a word on paper about *The New Yorker* or anything to do with it.

❦

MRS. SHAWN IS naturally sociable. Petite and vivacious, she has about her a quality of adorable girlishness that borders on flirtatiousness. She has a beautiful smile, and she smiles easily. If she hadn't been married to Mr. Shawn, she might have been seen at parties everywhere. Mr. Shawn had no interest in parties, though, and seemed to be most comfortable at home, with the same old friends present. Occasional large parties were given there, but in general, except for the children's friends, there was hardly ever a new face. I was one of just two or three people who somehow got taken into the family over the years—in my case, first because of Wallace, and later, perhaps, because I was single and was away from my family. In any event, I was invited to more and more intimate gatherings—Christmas, Thanksgiving, and, after I became close friends with Mrs. Shawn, even her birthday. At Thanksgiving, I was sometimes the only person at the table who was not a family member. Since Mr. Shawn worked through the holidays, Thanksgiving dinner was in the evening, but in most other ways it was traditional, with Mr. Shawn doing the carving, their longtime nanny-*cum*-housekeeper, Bessie, doing the serving, and Mrs. Shawn using wedding and anniversary gifts, such as lace napkins or a gravy boat, at the table, which was decorated with pumpkins, acorns, and leaves. After I started going there for Thanksgiving, my previous Thanksgivings, with other families, seemed like amateur productions. Shawn Thanksgivings were also memorable for certain eccentric features. One year, for instance, there was a scare that the way cranberries were sprayed might make them carcinogenic, and we had no cranberry sauce.

The typical Shawn party had something of the atmosphere of a get-together of mostly waifs and weak reeds, including me. Except for our writing, we had very little going on in our lives. Many of us were single, and some of us—especially the women—seemed to be conscious of getting old, but everyone valiantly put up a great front. The parties were a challenge for anyone to get through. Elspeth Fraser, Jonathan Schell's girlfriend, who later became his wife, and who was as deeply devoted to the Shawns and *The New Yorker* as any writer, said she often came away with a headache. The group that assembled at Eleven-Fifty, as the Shawn apartment was called, seemed to be calculated to test the endurance of any ordinary person. For one thing, it was impossible to have a conversation with either Joan or Edith. Both were nonstop talkers, and were always telling each other to "shut up, stop yakking." They had met when they were being wheeled around in prams by their Fräuleins—Edith never tired of recalling that hers was evil and Joan's was benign—and they had been classmates in a New York private school from kindergarten right on through. They used to say that there hadn't been a day in their adult lives when they hadn't seen or telephoned each other. Edith, who both handled the assigning of book reviews and wrote the magazine's Off Broadway column—she called herself "the only honest critic"—had been adopted by the Shawns, like many of us lonely drifters, and claimed to be Mrs. Shawn's oldest friend. I found her disconcerting, though, because she often made anti-intellectual remarks. Critics with an intellectual bent, such as Robert Brustein or Eric Bentley, were lambasted by her as "dishonest," on the ground that they reacted to plays with their theories rather than with their hearts. Also, perhaps because she had come to *The New Yorker* from the radio program "The $64,000 Question," she had a tendency to be perky, and called everybody "darling" or "honey"—a habit that was oddly at variance with her acid tongue. Joan was equally frenetic and tough-sounding, and one would never have guessed from her fast, scatter-shot talk that her life's work was the patient, meticulous editing of crime manuscripts. It was as if she had worked on them so long that she had perfected the art of disguise. Olivia was the only one of the threesome whom I could talk with in a natural way. She was quiet and reflective.

In contrast to Edith and Joan, Naomi talked so slowly that I sometimes wanted to push her along to get to the point. As soon as the buffet dinner was announced, she would pick up her plate, make a beeline for Mr. Shawn, and sit down next to him.

Throughout the meal, her voice could be heard over the other conversation, more or less continuously addressing deliberate statements to Mr. Shawn. I once asked Wallace how she managed to edge out Edith and Joan at Mr. Shawn's side, and he said that when Naomi was young she was very beautiful and his father had been quite taken with her, and, though time had moved on, she had continued to enjoy her place.

Naomi's husband, Bruce, was a member of a well-connected journalistic family; his father had been the editor of *The New Republic* for nearly twenty-five years. Bruce himself was a sort of unofficial brother to Jack Kahn, whom I saw quite a lot at the office, but who, for reasons I didn't know, was never at the Shawns'. Bruce and Jack, like Edith and Joan, had been together from kindergarten through high school, and they had also been in the same class at Harvard. I never heard Bruce say an unkind word about anybody, even when Joan and Edith were dispatching reputations right and left. Together, Edith, Joan, Olivia, Naomi, Jack, and Bruce gave me an unsettling view of what it must have been like to grow up in privileged New York.

The other guests generally included Philip and Edith Hamburger. People at *The New Yorker* said that Philip was to our office what Eleanor Roosevelt had been to the White House—not prepossessing in looks but extremely nice, with a highly developed social conscience. He was one of the friendliest people on the staff, and was often seen in the office halls, greeting whatever people were around and engaging them in conversation. His wife was a sensuous woman, who had come from a well-connected family in Cleveland. (Later, she also wrote for *The New Yorker*, under her maiden name, Iglauer. There was mild amusement when her first articles proved to be about Eskimos, because her name sounded a lot like "igloo.")

The group included so many overbearing personalities with strong, conflicting opinions that the parties sometimes had the atmosphere of brawls. At every one of them, especially after

President Johnson got deeply mired in Vietnam, the war, in one or another of its hundred different permutations, came up. Was draft dodging defensible? Should those who carried out the Christmas bombing be prosecuted in a Nuremberg-like trial? Some people were for the war almost to the point of thinking that anyone who wasn't was unpatriotic, and others maintained that the country had gone mad with violence and a misplaced fear of Communism. Mr. Shawn, who in time became profoundly opposed to the war, listened to the arguments with fascination, interested in gaining insight into people's personalities as much as in hearing their opinions. While people talked over one another, interrupted one another, and generally blew off steam, Mr. Shawn patiently waited for an opportunity to get a word in, no doubt in the hope of moderating the extreme opinions. He was so careful of not hurting anyone's feelings that he often listened to utterly fatuous arguments for hours on end. Occasionally, Janet Flanner, perhaps the most intellectually impressive woman I had ever met, came to New York, and she would attend a party with her friend Natalia Murray. She affectionately scolded Mr. Shawn for pussyfooting around people's sensibilities, but she was as much in awe of his manner as the rest of us, and once said, "It's as if, Mehta, he were beyond our human conception."

I often wondered how this noisy, contentious group had ever become established in the Shawn apartment, and the mystery was finally cleared up for me by Bruce. "Immediately after our graduation, in 1937, Jack and I and another Harvard friend got ourselves an apartment on East Fourth Street, between the Bowery and Lafayette," he told me. "We all had parents in New York, but we wanted to live away from them. The neighborhood was so run-down that we could make as much noise as we liked. We would hold regular jazz sessions. I played the clarinet and Jack the drums. Bill Shawn, whom we knew because Jack was already writing for *The New Yorker*, used to come down and play the piano. It was a small, honky-tonk instrument that really sounded like a banjo, but as soon as Bill started playing he was in a world of his own. Daphne sometimes arrived, with her harp. After it was brought downtown and carried up the steps, it was so shaken up that it seemed to play itself. We had a lot of musical instruments lying around the apartment. If you came and wanted to try an instrument, you could—except for the piano, which was always Bill's domain. We would have big musical parties four or five times a year. Jack did the inviting, and I ordered in a case of Scotch. That made my reputation with the local liquor store, because the people there thought I was paying for it. Actually, *The New Yorker* paid for it. In those informal days, such things were simply taken care of. Everyone from the magazine was invited, along with everyone from our families. The party would get going around eight or nine o'clock and would go on late into the night. One night, Ross came, unexpectedly. He picked up the trombone and tried it. It made a terrible noise—it sounded like a cow—and he put it right down again. The parties ended sometime during the war. Jack was one of the first of us to be drafted."

❦

AT THE SHAWN parties I attended, Mr. Shawn could sometimes be coaxed into playing the piano after dinner. More often than not, Edith Oliver or Mrs. Shawn would propose the idea, and everyone else would second it. Much as he might protest, once he sat down at the piano all his constraints seemed to fall away. His playing was as outgoing and social as his manner was private and quiet. Yet it was like him in that it was at once intimate, frank, and truthful, and his piano seemed to be speaking to each person. Even so, the people, knowing that he never liked to draw attention to himself, would go on talking, as if they were at a bar or a night club. Mrs. Shawn would bring out the coffee, and there would be a lot of to-ing and fro-ing as people got up to help themselves to sugar or cream.

In slow pieces, Mr. Shawn's playing had a wonderful, lilting quality, which had to do with the way he used his left hand, in what Allen once described as a stride style: he would play a kind of rolling, broken chord in the bass—as it were, walk from a note to a chord and then break up the chord. Over this stride bass, with his right hand, he would play lively variations of the tune mixed with rich, unbroken chords. When he was playing fast pieces, he had a strong, rolling rhythm. It was inventive, and it was infectiously upbeat, or hopeful, in contrast to his bearing, which gave the impression that he carried the weight of the world on his shoulders—the sorrows of his writers and his friends, the difficulty of bringing out a weekly magazine.

Allen recalls that for some years while he was growing up the family had an indifferent, if not a bad, piano—an upright, which had a banjo stop in it and also something called an orchestra pedal. Eventually, it was replaced by a black Steinway grand, and Allen would sit under it, soaking up his father's playing. He found that a wonderful way to be with his father. Once, when he and a school friend were sitting together under the piano, they noticed that Mr. Shawn's pedal had made an actual hole in the carpet.

Mr. Shawn played completely by ear—he had taught himself to play when he was ten, and had never learned to sight-read, because his ear had proved faster than his eye—and he always played in the key of C. On the few occasions when I talked to him about his playing, he spoke of it very disparagingly. He said, for instance, that he didn't have a very good grasp of harmony. Yet I remember that he was able to play songs with complicated harmonies, like "Downtown," and pieces by Bacharach. Allen, who, on his way to becoming a professional composer, was an accomplished pianist and sight reader, used to say that he couldn't do what his father could do. Partly, no doubt, he was being a modest son, and partly he was saying that as a composer he was being trained in a different kind of harmonic language, with the result that he could pick out a Mozart piece on the piano but would have difficulty improvising harmonies for jazz or popular music. He even had trouble remembering the names of songs that his father played over and over again.

Mr. Shawn's playing was youthful and danceable. Most of the pieces were show tunes from the twenties and thirties, like "Bidin' My Time," "Embraceable You," "Anything Goes," and "Don't Fence Me In"—mostly love songs by Kern, Rogers, Cole Porter, and, especially, Gershwin. Perhaps the song he played most was "They Can't Take That Away from Me." If Janet Flanner and Natalia Murray were there, they would sing along. Many of the other listeners would join in, yet one didn't have to know the words of any of the songs to be swept up in the romance of them. There wasn't a touch of nostalgia about his playing.

Mr. Shawn seemed never to tire of the songs or the words, as if a strong connection existed between them and his feelings generally about female beauty and about love. He responded to any attractive woman on the street or in the office like an excited teen-ager, and he punctiliously observed rituals of love like sending flowers on special occasions. He was moved equally by expressions of such feelings in books, in the ballet, and in *New Yorker* stories, and was completely free of cynicism. His playing of romantic music seemed like a form of affirmation. It had an almost magical, healing quality. When he was not at the piano, one felt that here was a man so urban, so much at home in the glass and concrete of New York City, that he might never have sat on grass, but when he was playing he seemed to be communing with nature. His playing seemed to have a spiritual aspect, a sort of unifying sense of things, as if a being of superior consciousness were speaking to each of us. All the feelings he never voiced but which were palpable when one was with him seemed to find expression in his music. He would cut loose (a phrase he often used) from Mr. Shawn and become Bill—one of us.

VI

JACKKNIFE BEN

A LLEN SAYS THAT NOT ONCE DID HIS FATHER INITIATE TALK about his own family, let alone tell stories about his parents and siblings. He only answered direct questions about them, and then in the briefest possible way, so Allen surmised that his father might not have known much about them himself, since he had been the youngest child and there had been a long span between him and the oldest child, Harold. Or he might have had very complicated feelings about his family. For instance, there was the matter of its name. His brother Nelson had changed his surname from Chon, which he thought sounded Chinese, to Shawn, possibly because he was a songwriter and he knew that Chinese composers had no prospects. None of the other siblings followed his example except the youngest. Allen imagines, however, that this was not an act of rebellion against the family but, rather, an emphatic act of separation. Wallace, however, as if to compound the mystery, recalls distinctly that his father's father told him that the family name had originally been Silberwasser.

It may be that the reason Mr. Shawn didn't talk about his family was that he was a person who naturally avoided the limelight. He enjoyed the fact that all his professional work was done behind the scenes and remained anonymous. Indeed, if there hadn't been a law requiring the name of the editor to be published once a year in the magazine, his name would never have appeared in *The New Yorker*, and that would have pleased him.

Anyway, by temperament he never dwelt on the past, or talked about Chicago, where he was born and reared. Nostalgia was totally alien to him. I never heard him talk about the old days at *The New Yorker,* or about any writers who had died, even when he had edited them for many years, and, indeed, he didn't say much about Harold Ross. Over the years, I heard it said at Eleven-Fifty that Mr. Shawn's father had grown up in Toronto, or perhaps in upstate New York. This inconsistency struck me as odd, since conversation in the Shawn household was always clear and accurate. There were also other areas of mystery about his father: now and again, it was casually said that he had run away from home as a boy and had made his own way in the world, but why he had run away was never discussed. It was also said that he had some acting talent. Once, Allen told me that his grandfather used to sell knives, and that there was a picture somewhere in the apartment that showed him doing just that. Then I heard that the woman he married was named Anna, and often known as Annie, and that her family had lived in England at a certain point. From what I could gather, she was born in Manchester, but her family name, Bransky, strongly suggested that her family had originally come from Eastern Europe. At some point, the Branskys had settled in Detroit. I remember Mr. Shawn's saying to a group in his living room that he had a picture of Anna's parents and that they were extraordinary-looking, but in what way I never found out. Apparently, Anna's brother Sam Bransky had acting talent, like Mr. Shawn's father, and played tough-guy parts in silent films, but, again, I never knew which films or whether he was a walk-on or a major character.

I used to hear from Wallace and Allen that their grandparents on their father's side were Poles from the Russian Empire. Allen felt that somewhere along the way the family had distorted its true origins. He certainly thought that his mother was vague about her background. I asked him why she might have had reason to be, and he said that his mother's mother had perhaps had an extremely painful life, and that his mother had been misled about it or else had decided not to talk about it. "If my mother's mother was Russian, as I believe she was, she may have left her home under very traumatic circumstances," Allen said. "After all, the period in which her family seems to have emigrated was during the pogroms. Initially, I believe, they went to Sweden, but that's not what my mother says. She says that her mother was born in Sweden and that the family had been there for generations." Mrs. Shawn's maiden name, Lyon, bears no trace of her family's Eastern European origins, if those existed.

There were other points of confusion. I heard sometimes that Mr. Shawn's father was the owner of a jewelry shop and at other times that he was also a jewelry designer. It was said that the jewelry shop had caught fire, and that afterward Harold, who had been reluctantly working for his father, became a life-insurance salesman, but it was also said that there had been a fire at the stockyards which had not reached the shop. And so on.

Mr. Shawn's father was apparently no better than Mr. Shawn himself at clearing up confusion. Wallace says that as a boy he once tried to draw his grandfather out, because he wanted to write a little family history. But his grandfather, instead of answering any of his questions, merely made jokes about his project.

The mystery, the secrecy, the confusion—whatever it was—only succeeded in stimulating my curiosity.

❧

ONCE, IN 1972, when Mr. Shawn was editing the biographical portrait of my father, he looked up and said, "Your father reminds me very much of mine."

"In what way?" I asked. Since my father was a doctor and a public-health official in British India, a quintessential clubman, and an inveterate tennis, bridge, and poker player, it was hard for me to imagine how Mr. Shawn's father could have been like him. Still, my pulse quickened in anticipation of having some of my questions about the Chon family answered.

"In so many ways," he said, putting down his pencil. "Like your father, my father started out with nothing and made a wonderful life. Like your father, he came from a large family and had a large family of his own. He was also very worldly, and could get on with practically everybody."

He didn't go on. He picked up his pencil, and we returned to working on the proofs.

Some years later, when Ivan Morris, a noted scholar of Japanese, who was a close friend of mine, died, and I was asked to speak at his memorial service, I remembered that his family had had some connection with Chicago, and inquired of Mr. Shawn if he'd ever come across them. He said that Morris's grandfather Nels Morris was a very important figure in the meat-packing industry, and when I pressed him for more information he directed me to an obscure book, by an observer of the American food industry named Bertram Fowler, that was entitled "Men, Meat and Miracles" and had been published in 1952. In it, along with a story about Ivan's grandfather, was an account of a knife vender in the Chicago stockyards who was known to everyone as Jackknife Ben. His surname was Chon, and, having heard that

Mr. Shawn's family name had originally been Chon, I asked him if Jackknife Ben was any relation. "He was my father," he said simply. The revelation was astounding: the father in the book and the son I knew seemed so different.

Fowler leads off his book with the story of Jackknife Ben—actually, makes him stand for Chicago and, by extension, for American enterprise and industry taking shape there in the nineteenth century. Indeed, according to Fowler, the jackknife might have been the first of many gadgets that proliferated as they became the hallmark of American mass consumer society.

Ben, a small, wiry, tireless man, who was born in Canada in 1863, had, as Fowler puts it, the industriousness of an ant and the irrepressible cheerfulness of a cricket. When he was only thirteen, he left home to make his own living, in the manner of many boys of the period. He belonged to an age of ferment, when men were driven by wild, exuberant dreams of starting with nothing and getting rich. By the time Ben was sixteen, he was the proud owner of a horse and carriage, and used it to peddle tinware from farm to farm in Canada. Then the tinware business began to flag, and he looked southward, to the United States. Having emigrated, he peddled jackknives in various cow towns, often making his pitch on a Saturday night on the main street, or on any other occasion that brought people together in a holiday mood. He was a natural pitchman, and was easy to get along with. He spent the next ten years ceaselessly travelling and hawking his wares. Then he met Anna, and wanted to marry her and settle down by his own fireside. In 1889, he came to Chicago and happened to visit the stockyards. He saw there the whole West converging from the far-flung ranches and ranges of Texas, Montana, Wyoming, and Colorado. "I took one look at the yards and knew that my travels were over," he later recalled. "Why should I chase from county fair to county fair all over the country when every day was county fair at the yards?"

Ben thereupon upended a barrel in front of the old railroad depot on Exchange Avenue and spread out his jackknives. Every night, he stored the barrel and the jackknives in the hallway of the office of the *Drover's Journal*, and every morning, while it was still dark, he retrieved them and set up his stand amid the seething noise and tumult of the stockyards, dimly lit by bobbing lanterns. He never missed a day, no matter how fierce the wind or how bad the snowstorm. Within a year, he had found a little niche inside the depot and opened a booth equipped with one electric light and a small radiator, and also married Anna.

A drover bringing cattle, hogs, or sheep to the stockyards for sale apparently couldn't go by Ben's booth without buying a knife. In those days of simple living, the jackknife was one tool that all men carried. "A man without a jackknife in that age was no man at all," Fowler writes. No matter how many jackknives a man owned, he could always do with one more, and there were always new and better jackknives coming along. Ben imported the best knives from Germany and stamped them "Jackknife Ben," two words that became both his name and his trademark.

The meat-packing industry was different from all other industries. It had an aspect of show, like a fair or an auction. Since it had to contend with the imponderables of the elements, like drought, flood, and disease, it could not have rigid production schedules. Other industries, such as mining, were also changing the face of America, with jerry-built camps and saloons and bagnios, but the meat-packing industry, for all its brutal methods, seems to have had, according to Fowler, a certain wholesomeness about it. People involved in it—drovers, slaughterers, meat packers, and their agents—were rugged individualists. Many of them were moral men, whose attitude toward life had been forged in the solitude of the prairies and the plains, where they lived amid buffalo grass and tall cornstalks. They sealed their bargains with a spoken word. A packer's agent, for instance, would look at an animal and call, "Weigh 'im out," making no note of the sale. He carried all the sales in his head until the end of the day, and then made his report to his boss. It was boasted in the stockyards that no packer had ever gone back on his word and that no drover had ever failed to get his agreed price.

Jackknife Ben, for his part, having built up a formidable reputation, opened a shop called Benjamin W. Chon, and branched out from selling knives into selling diamond necklaces and rings. A drover often picked out a necklace or a ring for his wife and took it on approval. If she liked it, Ben got a check for it at his shop; if she didn't, the drover returned it the next time he came to Chicago.

Jackknife Ben prospered as the city and its meat-packing industry grew and developed under men like Gus Swift, P. D. Armour, Tom Wilson, and Nels Morris, and their names became associated with the great meat-packing houses. He—and they—were in the tradition of pioneers like Long John Wentworth, who came to Chicago barefoot and eventually became its mayor. There was something gargantuan and mighty in the spirit of these pioneers, which made them take huge risks and garner huge returns.

After reading about Jackknife Ben, I often wondered about possible connections between father and son. Could it be that Mr. Shawn's deep aversion to blood and gore (he could scarcely bear to hear about a surgical operation), his bundling up against the cold, his staying close to his home and office, his hatred of any kind of commercialism, and his quietness were all, in one way or another, negative reactions to his father's life? I couldn't think of anyone less likely to carry a pocketknife than he; instead, he always had on him a silver mechanical pencil. And I wondered if his almost total reliance on verbal agreements, his taking huge risks with writers and artists—their lives and their work—and his editing an article or looking at a drawing as if it were a piece of filigreed jewelry, his interest in people, his contentment with minimal comforts, and his total lack of self-importance were positive consequences of his father's early peripatetic life and later stockyard ethics. Such comparisons between the two men might be farfetched, but were they any more so than those between the lives of fathers and sons generally? Then again, such facts were no more relevant to explaining him than were the facts of a poet's life to explaining his poetry.

❧

"MEN, MEAT AND MIRACLES" had only whetted my appetite for Chon lore, and some time after Mr. Shawn died I tried to draw out Wallace and Mrs. Shawn—or Cecille, as I had been calling her for many years by then—about the family background. They were both evasive in their response. I sought to impress upon them that since Mr. Shawn was a substantial figure in the history of letters there was no way he could be kept out of the public eye. Wallace then said that he didn't have much information but would meet me for lunch one day and pass on what he did have.

A vast number of people now know Wallace Shawn as a comic actor in a variety of films. A smaller number, who have seen him in "My Dinner with André" or "Vanya on 42nd Street," know him as a remarkable serious actor, too. A very small number know him as a writer of plays, most of them containing explicit sexual—and, more recently, political—material. He has a cult following, and is as famous as his father was anonymous. On the other hand, Allen, who is married to the flamboyant West Indian-born writer Jamaica Kincaid, has always been somewhat retiring, and seems much more like Mr. Shawn than Wallace does. As Wallace and I walked down the street to an Italian restaurant in my neighborhood, people recognized him.

At lunch, as always, Wallace's manner was punctilious and his expression a little roguish. There is a general rounded quality about his face and his hands which makes him come across almost as cuddly, and he is short and sturdy, yet he seems taller than he is. Even so, whenever I am with him I am reminded again and again of Mr. Shawn. Wallace has a touch of his father's magnetism.

"How old were you when Ben died?" I asked him.

"I was nine—he died in 1952."

"Do you remember him?"

"Of course. Back then, Father was not yet the editor, and we used to go to Chicago. I remember Ben as lean, a little rakish, and dynamic. In his pictures, he looks sportive; one could almost imagine him in a boxing match or running a race. The basic impression I have is that, having started with a junk wagon, he had become respectable and prosperous, and his children grew up in a house with a billiard room. I think they had a maid and, at least for some time, a car with a driver. Apparently, Ben was a little conservative about what his children should do in the world. For instance, Harold had received a very good offer to become a comedian, a violinist, and an entertainer in a vaudeville show, but Ben ordered him to turn down the offer and come and work in his store. Harold exercised his talents for comedy and music by doing shows at his temple. Mike, the youngest brother except for my father, had a similarly lucrative offer—in his case, to play the saxophone in a band—and Ben made him turn that down, too. So Mike, instead of being a professional jazz musician, went into advertising and wrote jingles. He wrote with a friend a very well-known jingle for Wrigley's chewing gum, called 'Double Your Pleasure, Double Your Fun,' and a version of it is still on television. It's generally shown with a motif of twins—twins rowing a boat, and the like. In those days, people did what their fathers told them. Ben was pretty harsh when he was young, particularly with Harold, but he became increasingly mellow as he got older, so by the time Father's turn came he was very permissive. Of all the children, Father was the only one who was allowed to really pursue an artistic vocation, although all the brothers had apparently wanted to do that."

"It's something of a puzzle to me that Mr. Shawn should have turned out to be so open to life, given his conservative background," I said.

"It's a miracle," Wallace said. "I remember poring over his yearbooks of the Harvard School for Boys, a private school in Chicago, where he went from at least the seventh grade on. Clearly, it was a very conservative school. The teachers looked very severe. They had steel-rimmed glasses. The discipline must have been very rigid. Father was one of the regular guys. He was a manager of a couple of sports teams, like the baseball team, and he himself, I think, also played some sports, and not badly. When I was at Dalton, he played in a father-and-son baseball game. Everyone remarked on how agile he was, even though in his literary life he didn't indulge in any sporting activity, of course. He was in the tradition of a scholar who does absolutely nothing in the way of physical activity. It's a very Jewish thing, in fact, that the rabbi—the scholar—is waited on hand and foot."

"Yet I don't remember any Jewish element of any kind at Eleven-Fifty," I said. "Your family observed Christmas and Easter. I remember your mother trimming the Christmas trees, and sewing little Easter bunnies to put in little baskets with grass and jelly beans. I don't remember so much as a mention of Hanukkah or Passover."

"There never was any—probably because Ben grew up in a period when Jews were absolutely bent on assimilating into America," Wallace said. "Their past in Europe was of suffering, which they were determined to forget. It seemed that the general feeling among the Jews of that period was that it was better to be anonymous, not to stand out. If you asked someone whose family had come from Russia about his background, all he would say would be 'It was cold there.' The idea was to be quiet about everything. It had to do with fear—fear that if you talked about things you would stand out and might be killed."

"How did your father and grandfather get along?" I asked. "You must have seen them together."

"I don't remember ever seeing just the two of them together," he said. "I generally saw them in large, noisy family groups. Chon-family occasions such as birthdays and anniversaries tended to be simply enormous. A few were held in hotels in Chicago, with fifty or a hundred relatives, and with many huge red roses, silver implements, and brothers and cousins doing skits for those assembled. Father was by far the quietest among them. He was singular in that way, because all our relatives were very lively, noisy, and theatrical. It was just understood that he was not expected to join in any skits. But they all treated him as beloved. They all admired and esteemed him as a special creature. They thought of him as a genius and also as very sweet and lovable."

"Do you remember Ben's wife, Anna?"

"Yes. Perhaps because I was small, she always struck me as big and peasant-like. She was somewhat heavyset, with gray hair. Her schooling probably hadn't gone beyond the third grade. She died when I was seven, a year and a half before Ben. I know that the date of her death, April 12th, made a great impression on Mother, because it was the sixth anniversary of President Roosevelt's death."

"Did you know your maternal grandmother?"

"Very well," he said. "She died in 1956, when I was thirteen. I remember she usually dressed in black, perhaps because she never stopped mourning for her husband, who died when Mother was three or four years old. Rose—that was her name—was a very striking woman. She had what people think of as a Jewish face— dark hair, a prominent nose. She wore her hair braided on top of her head, and I never knew how long it was until once when she came to visit us, and then I saw it extended to its full length. The braid reached almost to the floor. I couldn't believe it."

We talked on for some time, but he wouldn't answer most of my questions, saying, with a mischievous laugh, that he was under specific instructions from his mother not to talk about certain things. He suggested that I tackle her myself, but warned me, "Don't probe too much into her background. She might get upset."

I said I would tread carefully.

❦

CECILLE HAS AN almost unchanging youthful and sunny disposition, and she has maintained it, even after the loss of Mr. Shawn. She tends to put a positive face on everything; that seems to be her way of surviving the trials of life. As a rule, she is extremely accessible, but she was nevertheless most reluctant to talk to me about anything to do with her husband or with their families' backgrounds. "I can imagine Bill up there counselling me to keep silent," she said.

I said that by remaining silent she would encourage many of the misconceptions that had grown up about him to be accepted as truth.

She didn't seem to mind that, remarking sadly, "His memory has been completely erased."

I told her that in the course of the twenty years or so that Mr. Shawn had edited the autobiographical pieces of my Continents of Exile series for *The New Yorker* he and I had often discussed my writing one day about my years at the magazine. He had acknowledged that he was part of my story, and that there was no way I could avoid writing about him. He had agreed to help me—and, indeed, as she knew, in the last months of his life I had occasionally lunched with him and asked him questions.

"You should write only about your direct experience of him," Cecille said.

I said that that was what I was doing, but that there were many points about the family that I was confused about and needed to clarify.

She suddenly dropped her guard, and began to talk. "Bill's father—my father-in-law, Benjamin—was the oldest of seven children," she said. "He had one brother and five sisters—Dora, Bessie, Sadie, Sam, Birdie, and Rae. Aunt Sadie was the only one who did not marry. The rest of them were all married, with children. Harold, Benjamin's oldest son, who was born in 1891, was sixteen years older than Bill, and died at the age of seventy-five. Melba was two years younger than Harold. She married a barrister in Canada, and lived to be ninety-two. The third child was a boy who died very young. The fourth was Nelson, who was born in 1898 and died of angina at the age of forty-seven. Mike, the fifth child, was six years older than Bill. He was born in 1901, and, like Bill, died at the age of eighty-five. Mike and Bill, being the two youngest, were very close. They were both very sensitive, and Bill was much influenced by Mike. All the children had extraordinary personalities, and it was rather an eccentric family. None of the brothers quite fitted into the conventional world, but it was really Bill who expressed that side of the family the most."

I asked her if the members of the family had resembled one another in looks.

"In some ways," she said. "Both Ben and Annie were what is called short. Ben had blue eyes. Annie was a little plump, and had brown eyes, beautiful skin, brown hair, and, like Bill, rosy cheeks. There was a most interesting set of colors in their family. Melba had fiery-red hair and blue eyes. She was more like her father than like her mother. Nelson and Bill had blue eyes and dark-brown hair. Harold had red hair and brown eyes, and so did Mike."

I asked her where in Chicago Mr. Shawn had grown up.

"When Bill was born—he was born at home—the family lived on Vincent Avenue. After that, they moved to Ellis Avenue. The Chons had the whole first floor. You know, of course, about Ellis Avenue, where Bobby Franks, of the famous kidnapping case, lived. The Chons' house was a couple of doors away and around the corner from the Frankses'. Jack Franks, Bobby's brother, was a very close friend of Bill's. They were at the Harvard School for Boys together, and, as a matter of fact, we went to Little Rock for Jack's wedding."

I asked what the Chon family's life in Chicago had been like.

"Nowadays, everyone has a refrigerator; in those days, everyone had a piano in the house. All the children took piano lessons or played some musical instrument. Harold played the violin superbly. He would march around while he played, holding the violin on his head, resting it against different parts of his body, striking different physical attitudes. He was always interested in music and performing. During the First World War, he directed the Navy orchestra at the Great Lakes Naval Station, in Chicago. Throughout his life, he was a member of veterans' groups. He visited veterans' hospitals, and wrote musical shows for amateur entertainment. The other children were also very musical. Bill and Nelson played the piano, Mike played the sax, and Melba sang. Nelson was also a writer of popular songs. His songs were played a great deal in the big-band days by people like Glenn Miller, and later were sung by singers like Rosemary Clooney. One of his songs, 'Jim,' is still sometimes played on the radio."

"What was Mr. Shawn's upbringing like?"

"Because Bill was the youngest, everybody protected him. In his early years, he didn't see much of his father, who kept long hours at the shop, so he became very close to his mother. Even his phobias of heights, crowds, and close quarters came from her. Several of the other children also seemed to have inherited her phobias. Both Mike and Bill had a phobia of flying, and that was one reason they didn't see anything of each other for the last ten years of Mike's life."

Cecille's mention of phobias reminded me of an awkward situation that my colleague Henry Cooper and I had once got into with respect to Mr. Shawn. Henry and I had suggested him to Yale for an honorary degree, in 1980. He had never sought and never received any honors to speak of, and there was a groundswell of support for the idea from our colleagues, with one significant exception—E. B. White. He wrote to me:

> As far as I'm concerned, Bill should be honored by every college in the land, for his great deeds and great character. Whether I want to put a bee in Yale's ear is another question—one that I have doubts about. Surely Yale is aware of the editor of the New Yorker and his contribution to American letters and the American scene. My tendency in such a situation is to let Nature takes its course, if only because to act in any other way might prove embarrassing to Bill, if he got wind of it.
>
> In any event, I thank you for the suggestion, and, as the politicians say, I will vote my conscience.

When Mr. Shawn was offered the honorary degree, Henry and I wished that we had taken a cue from White. As with all such ceremonies, the honoree's presence was mandatory, but there was no way Mr. Shawn could tolerate being in a crowd, even for a ceremonial occasion. We had not given any thought to his phobia of crowds, because in the office he functioned like anyone else. And so the offer had put him in the terribly embarrassing position of having to decline a degree from a great university without ever being able to state the real reason. I had never mentioned my role in the whole wretched business to him, nor could I mention it now to Cecille.

She went on, "Because Bill was the baby of the family, and because he'd had scarlet fever when he was about sixteen, his mother was overprotective of him. Once, while he was at the Harvard School for Boys, she went to his teacher—or it may have been the principal—and said that Billy was working too hard. The instinct for everyone to protect him continued all his life. He was smothered with attention. Certainly everyone around the office had tender feelings for him. I remember that even my mother and my sister took his side against me if the two of us disagreed."

"How did you and Mr. Shawn meet?"

"I met Bill soon after *The New Yorker* was started, in February, 1925. He fell in love with *The New Yorker* and with me at the same time. We met through the evil designs of Bill's first cousin Marshall Berman. Bill was then in high school, and Marshall and I were both students at the University of Chicago. We had been peeking at each other in the Harper Library there, flirting while we were supposedly studying. It turned out that Marshall and I had no romantic feelings for each other, but we became fast friends. He and Bill were almost inseparable, and he tried to get me to go out with Bill, saying that his cousin needed cheering up. Marshall must have thought that I was nice and silly, and would complement Bill's serious, brooding temperament. I didn't agree for a long time, but finally Marshall hit me over the head and made me go on a blind date with Bill. We went—with Marshall and his date and with my cousin Sylvia and her date, who was a very close friend of Marshall's—to the Chicago Beach Hotel, on the South Side. It was right on Lake Michigan and looked out over the water. That was the style of dates. One would go for the evening to a hotel just to dance. There would be an orchestra, and maybe people would have a sandwich, along with ginger ale or something. Since it was cold, we couldn't have gone out onto the porch to dance, as one did in the summer, when all the doors were open. It was very romantic. Bill lied to me about his age. Although he was seventeen, he told me he was eighteen. Since I was a little older, he was afraid I wouldn't take him seriously. I believed him, since he'd had to drop out of school for part of a term when he had scarlet fever. The evening we met, I simply thought he was a nice young man, but he went home and wrote in his diary that he'd met his future wife. We both went out with other people—he liked girls and had girlfriends—but we quickly became attached to each other."

"How did Mr. Shawn end up at the University of Michigan?"

"Mike had gone there. But, unlike Mike, who enjoyed the university, played the saxophone, wrote the music for the class musical comedy, and graduated, Bill didn't take to the life there. He lived in a fraternity, and that life did not appeal to someone of his temperament. Early in his junior year, when he'd been at the university for a little over two years, his English professor recommended that he leave and go somewhere and write. He dropped out of the university and went to Las Vegas, New Mexico. He wrote some fiction and sent it out to various publications. It was not accepted. Bill was always very quick to decide that he didn't have this or that ability, so he concluded that he couldn't make a living writing fiction, and instead went to work for the Las Vegas *Daily Optic* doing regular reporting. He had to cover stabbings and make frequent visits to the police station. His activities were not yet limited by his phobias. One might say that in those days he was in a pre-phobic phase—he was apprehensive but not immobilized. Also, he must have been able to master his shyness or he couldn't have done his job. Even in his later life, he got tense only when he was heading into a crowded room, and he was always able to conquer his shyness when it came to work or the office."

"When did you and Mr. Shawn get married?"

"Bill returned to Chicago within six months and got a job with International Illustrated News, a Hearst Pictures syndicate. The job consisted of writing captions and headlines for the pictures and ordering them sent out to various papers by wire. In August, shortly after he returned to Chicago, he had announced to me that we would get married in a few days, when he'd turn twenty-one. I had no doubts about marrying him; I already knew that he was the love of my life, and by then we had been going together for three and a half years."

"Were you still in college then?"

"No. I had left the University of Chicago in the middle of my second year, because I had to go to work and earn money to help my mother. Dorothy, my older sister, had done the same thing.

There were just the two of us. We'd been brought up by our wid-owed mother, who was working to support us."

I said to Cecille that I would love to know something about her family, but that she should tell me only what she thought I should know.

Without a moment's hesitation, she said, "My father was an analytic and synthetic chemist. He saw a picture of my mother at the home of her uncle, in Leipzig, Germany, where my father was studying, and he immediately fell in love with her. He went to St. Louis, where she was going to school, to court her. They got married around 1902. I was born in Los Angeles, where my father was working as a chemist for a food-processing company. Apparently, some sort of chemical got into his system during his food-analyzing experiments, and he became ill and died in 1912, at the age of twenty-eight. I have no memory of him. After my father's death, we moved from Los Angeles to Chicago, where my mother's two older brothers and older sister lived. I started at the University of Chicago when I was sixteen—it was not unusual to skip half grades at school then. When I left, I got a job as an assis-tant to the features editor at the Chicago *Daily News*."

"How did your family get along with Mr. Shawn's?"

"Within a year and a half of my first meeting Bill, our fami-lies became very friendly. Whenever Bill was in Chicago, he was always at my house. My mother was much younger than Annie. Annie belonged to a ladies' group that got together for lunches and teas, and did things like rolling bandages for hospitals. My mother, on the other hand, was a working woman. The two mothers became very close, however."

"Did you and Mr. Shawn have a big family wedding?"

"No. On his birthday—August 31, 1928—Bill went to the city clerk to get a marriage license. He'd chosen that date because he would be turning twenty-one and he would not have to ask the permission of his parents. But the clerk didn't believe he was twenty-one, so he had to go home, get his mother, and come back. We were married the next day—the first of September. It was a wedding with just the immediate family, and there was a family dinner. It was not a religious ceremony. Neither one of us was religious. My father had been an atheist, and Bill's father wasn't religious. Bill got the Labor Day weekend off for our honeymoon, and we went to the Edgewater Beach Hotel, on the North Side of Chicago, on the lakefront. In the middle of our second or third night at the hotel, he got a call from his boss to come back, because of something to do with the airship of Ferdinand Graf von Zeppelin. He had to get up and rush to work."

"Did you move in with the Chons?"

"No. We had a little apartment, which we furnished, on the Near North Side, a bohemian part of town. But we often went for dinner to Bill's family. I called Ben 'Dad'—everyone called him that—and I called Annie 'Mother.' The atmosphere in the Chon house was sporting and theatrical. They played poker in the evenings, and every Saturday evening Ben and Annie went to the Palace Theatre to see a vaudeville show. The Palace had the best vaudeville in Chicago. Ben himself liked to act, and had acted in amateur productions of Shakespeare. I remember he would go around the house saying things like 'Alas, poor Yorick!' A year after our marriage, he and Annie celebrated their fortieth wedding anniversary, at his club, which was called Saddle and Sirloin, and was patronized by prosperous farmers and people who worked in the stockyards."

"I've often heard that Mr. Shawn used to play the piano in Paris," I said. "How did that come about?"

"Ben had taken Harold to Europe when he was sixteen, along with a friend who had a son of the same age. The trip was remembered in the family because Ben had actually kissed the Blarney Stone. One evening, when we were all having dinner, Bill and I mentioned to Ben as a piece of news that our cousin Sylvia was engaged and was going to Europe for her honeymoon. Immediately, Dad said, 'You should also go to Europe,' and he offered us the trip, with an impressive sum of money. As it happened, Sylvia broke her engagement, but Bill and I went anyway. In March of 1929, we sailed on the *Nieuw Amsterdam*, of the Holland-America Line. My former boss, Herbert Davidson, had given me a letter of introduction to Paul Scott Mowrer, who was the head of the Paris office of the Chicago *Daily News.* In Paris, Bill was lucky enough to get a chance to play the piano at a café called La Cloche. He played in the early evening, while people had their apéritifs."

"How long did you stay in Europe?"

"I had only a two-month leave of absence from work, but we wanted to stay on. Mowrer was very sympathetic and cabled the editor-in-chief in Chicago on my behalf. A cable came back saying that my leave could be extended indefinitely. We spent three months in Paris and then a couple of months travelling through England and Italy, and we also went to Budapest. We stayed in *pensions,* as part of a student plan through the Holland-America Line. As it happened, this was our only time abroad. We returned to the States the last weekend in August, for my sister's wedding. Shortly after that, the stock market crashed. Bill's father had retired the year before, at the age of sixty-five, and Harold had taken over the jewelry shop in the stockyards. But Harold had never liked jewelry work, and he ended up selling insurance for a living."

"The Depression must have been a very difficult period," I observed.

"Dad had lost some money in the crash, and it was extremely hard for anyone to get a job. Bill started freelancing. He wrote advertising copy—that's what Mike was doing. But it was not satisfying, in terms of either work or pay. He published some short stories in the Chicago *Daily News,* but he wouldn't permit his real name to be used. In the spring of 1932, he was completely out of work. We had some very Spartan times. All along, he had been concentrating on songwriting. Since he couldn't read music, he composed on the piano and had someone to do the writing for him. He was drawn to New York. He hoped to get established there as a songwriter."

"Is that how you came to move to New York?"

"I myself couldn't, because I was working. My feature editor was fired, so I had to take over his job—I cost the company much less than he had. At that time, people were being fired left and right. Bill was so depressed that I thought it would be good for his morale if he went to New York. We gave up our little apartment in Chicago, which we'd got when we came back from Paris, and we put our furniture in storage. I moved in with Bill's parents, and in March he went to New York. He received some commissions there. He was in New York alone for six months. Since I had a job, I sent him money. I was also able to visit him. I brought some of my work with me. Then Bill got a job writing publicity for J. C. Penney."

"When did you yourself move to New York?"

"In October, 1932. I gave up my job and came here. Soon after that, Bill lost his job again. I couldn't get any work, either. Eventually, I had lunch with a reporter from the *World-Telegram,* and he suggested that I try to get freelance assignments from *The New Yorker.* I went to the magazine and met Don Wharton, the managing editor. He was glad to give me some assignments. I came home and turned them over to Bill, so that he would have some work to do. He was immediately able to do them. They required interviews and reporting, so he must have managed to overcome his shyness. At first, he turned in notes for Talk of the Town, and someone at the office—most likely E. B. White, who in those days wrote the whole Talk section—rewrote them. Later, they were rewritten by Russell Maloney. For a long time, I was on the *New Yorker* books as having been given the assignments, but it was actually Bill who did them. So I actually got him his job, but I never told anyone that, because I didn't want people to think he couldn't have got it himself. In the beginning, the contributions were paid for only when the pieces appeared. There was no regular system of payment. He got two dollars for every typeset inch of a Talk story that resulted from his notes."

"When was he taken on by *The New Yorker*?"

"In 1933. He was hired as a Talk reporter. He started going to the magazine, and was given an office, which he shared with Eugene Kinkead. Bill and I would often have dinner with Gene. I would pick Bill up from work —in later years, I never went to the office, because he wanted to keep his private life separate. We would go to a restaurant named the Artists & Writers, also known as Bleeck's. It was where a lot of the *Herald Tribune* people gathered. We often sat with Wolcott Gibbs and his wife, and Ring Lardner and his wife. Anyway, in 1935 Mr. Ross asked Bill to become an associate editor. I think Bill moved into another office, but he didn't start editing pieces right away. There was a news meeting each Monday, and Bill was given the job of idea man. He also contributed art ideas and wrote captions." In all the years that Mr. Shawn was at *The New Yorker*, he published only one piece in the magazine readily indentifiable as his. It was a one-page casual, entitled "The Catastrophe," about the destruction of New York by a meteor while the rest of the world went about its business as usual. In keeping with his self-effacing nature, he signed it only with his initials. "In 1939, Bill became the managing editor of the fact department—journalism only—succeeding St. Clair McKelway." The managing editor for fiction was Gustave Lobrano, and the one for art was James Geraghty. "Bill worked very hard, because that was his nature. As managing editor, he began to build up a group of writers. From the very beginning, his relationships with them were very close. He cared about them, and they were devoted to him. After the war, he expanded the group and instituted the system of staff writers with individual offices and drawing accounts, remembering from his early years at the magazine how hard it was not knowing when, or if, he would be paid."

I asked her what parts of the city they had lived in over the years.

"When we first started living here, we had a room in the Beaux-Arts Hotel, in Tudor City, but once Bill had an office at the magazine we moved to a one-room apartment on Gramercy Park. We then moved to Murray Hill, to an apartment on Thirty-sixth Street, then, after Bill became managing editor, to the Tuscany on Thirty-ninth Street. After than we moved to a newly build apartment hotel called Fifty Park Avenue. We were living there when Wallace was born, in 1943. The apartment was very small, and Wallace's nursery was a converted dining room." She said that in 1949 they started going to Bronxville every year for the summer, renting different houses. They chose Bronxville because some of the *New Yorker* writers lived there and because Mr. Shawn could easily be driven to the office and back every day. He would probably have been just as happy to stay in the city for the summer, but it was wonderful for the children and for her to get out to what the Shawns considered "the country." (Bronxville is actually a suburb of New York City.)

She went on, "We had waited to have children, and I was fortunate in getting pregnant as soon as we decided to try. I had no mind of my own; I always did whatever he wanted me to do. I always enjoyed being pregnant—it was comfortable, exhilarating, and I had easy births. We had five children in six years, but only three survived. My last pregnancy was in 1948, and that turned out to be the twins, Allen and Mary. They were not expected until late October, but they were born in August. Although they weighed four pounds each and were quite sizable, they were put in Davidson beds—with incubators and respirators—and they had to stay in the hospital for six weeks. Mary was less responsive than Allen, or responsive in a different way. She either suffered a brain injury at birth or received too much oxygen."

In all the years I had known the Shawns, I had never met Mary, and I remarked on that to Cecille. She said that Mary was very happy at her school, and that they didn't like to disturb her—the family mostly visited her there. In my experience of the Shawns, the subject of Mary was like an iceberg. The family valiantly kept psychologically afloat, but seemed to feel as if they could be sunk by coming near it. In fact, the mere mention of Mary would bring tears both to Cecille's eyes and to Mr. Shawn's. The boys hardly ever spoke about her. Yet certainly the effect on Allen of his twin sister's missing out on nearly everything that he had must have been profound. I remember once talking to Mr. Shawn about her, and he said that emotionally and intellectually she was like a young child but that she was extremely attractive and lovable and enjoyed things like playing the piano in church.

In my conversation with Cecille, I quickly changed the subject, observing, "After the twins came along, you must have had to move again."

"Yes. We moved to a West End Avenue apartment. It was in an old building in the West Eighties. There was one bedroom for Bill and me, and one for the twins, and Wallace was again in the dining room. Maybe that explains why he likes to eat." She laughed. "We lived there until 1951, when we heard about an apartment at 1150 Fifth Avenue, which we ended up taking. Because it was on the second floor, much was later made of Bill's phobia of living high up. People said he was afraid of living higher than the second floor, but all our earlier apartments had been on higher floors."

"Did Mr. Shawn always work very long hours?"

"Yes. He might have been described as a workaholic—a word he wouldn't have allowed in the magazine. In December, 1971, when he was sixty-four, he had a heart attack. His symptoms, such as pain in the throat, were atypical. He recovered completely, and from then on never had an electrocardiogram that wasn't normal. After the heart attack, though, I never let him do anything that might frighten him and set off palpitations. The only reason he was able to go to the office was that it had become routine. He was very lucky that he found his work totally absorbing and enjoyable. Some people thought he was a benevolent dictator. He was always very firm about editorial matters. It was his nature to be kind, but when something didn't come up to his standards or agree with his opinions he was inflexible—though, of course, he compromised if he was persuaded of the merit of something."

I asked whether Mr. Shawn had kept in touch with his family back in Chicago.

"Yes. Although most of Bill's adult life was spent in New York, he retained a surprisingly deep connection with his family back home. Whenever he could get away, we would have family reunions in Chicago, and Bill and his brothers and sister would get together there and make music, often improvising. After he became the editor, he couldn't get away for reunions. Even when his father died, in December, 1952, he wasn't able to go to the funeral in Chicago, because I was in the hospital with bronchitis. Our last long trip was to Cambridge, in 1970, when Allen graduated from Harvard. But, in 1988, Bill got the idea of our celebrating our sixtieth wedding anniversary in Bronxville, so that he could see all the relatives. When they were gathered, he looked very happy. He was glowing and completely relaxed."

VII

FLIGHT OF CROOK-TALONED BIRDS

E VEN BEFORE I FINISHED WRITING ABOUT THE PHILOS-
ophers, I'd been thinking of tackling the historians and
their theories of history. The greatest ferment taking
place in this subject was also in England, and that very
fact excited me, because I was always looking for an
excuse to go back there. Indeed, except for Mr. Shawn
and *The New Yorker*, everything in America seemed pale to me
compared with whatever was happening in England. Moreover, as
a student of history, I had a head start on the subject and could
see its dramatic possibilities. Some historians, like Arnold
Toynbee, had theories of history so explicit that they were tanta-
mount to a philosophy of history, and invited furious attacks from

other historians, who found any abstract thinking antipathetic. Still others, like A. J. P. Taylor, denied having any theories at all, though theories were implicit in their work. In any event, it seemed to me that philosophy and the philosophy of history, explicit or implicit, were joined like Siamese twins. I worried that writing about two subjects so similar might make the second seem a repeat performance, and somewhat formulaic. Yet, during the year while I was waiting around for the philosophy piece to run, a newspaper item about the historians would come my way every now and then, and would give me a resurgence of interest in the idea. Then, in December, 1961, when I'd hardly got over the sleepless nights I suffered while I was putting the philosophy piece to press, I ran into Mr. Shawn on the nineteenth floor, and he asked me what I wanted to work on next. Having no other strong idea and, as always, fearing that I'd go into debt to the magazine—it seemed that one couldn't lie fallow for a day— I said I would like to go to England and try doing the historians.

"I've always thought that would make a marvellous piece," he said, "and I can't think of anyone else who could do it."

I remembered in a rush the fates of the salt piece and the Technical Assistance piece—fates that were made all the more painful by Mr. Shawn's lack of enthusiasm for a new piece I had meanwhile written, on a United Nations interpreter, George Sherry, since the subject and the writing had turned out to be colorless. "The historians piece might take months or years, and in the end might not work out," I said. "I think I should have a backup piece that I could be doing at the same time. Could I write something about the BBC? I love listening to the radio in England."

Mr. Shawn was resistant to the idea, because, for one thing, institutional Profiles tended to be lifeless.

When I mentioned the BBC's Third Programme, which broadcast the most highbrow and avant-garde material to be found on radio anywhere, he responded by saying, "Radio here is almost dead, and writing about the kinds of things they're doing over there might be very salutary. But your main focus should be the historians."

He sounded so enthusiastic about the historians piece that I ran down the stairs to my office imbued with a new energy. Ordinarily, when I finished something, even just a Comment piece, I would feel that it wasn't any good, become overwhelmed by depression and fatigue, and ask myself, "Who needs more stuff to read? Why produce anything?" Even with the prod of monthly notes from the accounting department listing my credits from and debits to the magazine, I kept doubting whether I should go on writing. But just a few minutes with Mr. Shawn would galvanize me, making me believe that all I did was worthwhile.

In my office, I now started mentally going over the names of historians whose books I should read and whom I should try to interview, and wondering whether they would know about my philosophy piece and, if so, whether it would cause them to be interested in talking to me or would just make them apprehensive.

I sent off letters to historians of different schools—besides Toynbee and Taylor, they included E. H. Carr, Herbert Butterfield, H. R. Trevor-Roper, and C. V. Wedgwood—whose theories ran the gamut from Marxism to Christianity, as their methods did from the analytic to the narrative. But as I began reading their works I doubted whether I would be able to find a thread on which to hang the various schools and theories, as I had succeeded in doing with the philosophers. The same chestnuts had been in the philosophical fire ever since Plato, but these historians didn't even address the same issues. Again, ever since Plato, conversation—and, by analogy, interview—had been a perfectly acceptable means of exploring philosophical ideas, but with historians the situation was far different. Another snag was that, in order to convey the quality of the historians' thinking, a lot of exposition about their books would be necessary. How could I save the piece from being leaden?

I talked over my anxieties with Mr. Shawn. As usual, he was reassuring about the project. "You'll find a way, I know," he said.

The matter of expenses for the English trip was very much on my mind, since Mr. Shawn had not given me any allowance for the philosophy piece, and now I would again have to lay out my own money to get me across to England, get myself a place to stay, and arrange and pay for help. But I didn't say anything about money, imagining that he believed in the virtue of a writer's risking his own capital and living on a shoestring. I concluded that I would have to manage as best I could. Week after week, though, I kept putting off going to England, and continued tinkering with the Sherry piece, feeling that I had to bring it up to Mr. Shawn's standards before putting my hand to the history tiller. He finally said he liked it, but didn't say when he might be able to use it. I concluded that he thought it a second-class effort, and had taken it mainly to keep me going; he seemed to understand instinctively the fragility and insecurity of writers, and how easy it was for them to get discouraged. Finally, some of the financial pressure of the English trip was relieved because I was able to find prospective tenants for my apartment at the Picasso—the New Yorker artist Abe Birnbaum and his wife. Birnbaum had been living in the country and doing his drawing there, and wanted the experience of working in the city.

I had accumulated ten cartons of books for my historians piece, amounting to three or four times the total weight allowed by the airlines. I had bought most of the books so that I could underline passages and hold onto the books for checking and re-checking in the event I was able to write the piece. The only airline that would allow me to take them without charging me an arm and a leg for excess baggage was Air India—and that was only because I had a friend there—so it was on that airline that I booked my seat.

Around the middle of March, I stopped by Mr. Shawn's office to say goodbye. As always, he was busy, but when I told his secretary the reason I was there she interrupted him, and he immediately came out.

"Have a good trip," he said, and paused. "'Trip' sounds quick," he added. "You're really setting out on a journey. Good luck."

❦

THE HILLISES WERE back in London, Arthur having lost his chance to stay on in New York after the death of Hammarskjöld, who had planned to restructure the U.N. Secretariat and put Arthur in charge of the organization's finances. As in the case of the philosophers piece, I preferred to stay in London and make forays into Oxford and Cambridge—and, indeed, onto the Continent, where a couple of my European subjects lived—and, thanks to Mary, I found a small service flat in a lodging house on Draycott Place, in Chelsea, just off King's Road. It was run by a brisk, fierce woman. The house had only one telephone, used by half a dozen tenants and also by her family, and it seemed never to be free. Moreover, she never deigned to take messages, saying that she wasn't paid to be a personal assistant to her tenants. I was therefore forced to rely on letters, and even arranging to see a friend could require several notes back and forth. The worst thing about the house, though, was that it had no central heating—something I had become so accustomed to in New York that it had almost altered my nervous system. Moreover, it happened that England had been—and still was—experiencing its coldest winter in half a century, and I was able to work only when I was wrapped head to toe in blankets. My spirits sank further when I realized that I had arrived in England at the beginning of the universities' six-week Easter break, and therefore many of the historians I wanted to talk to were in such places as San Juan, Padua, and New Delhi.

Surprisingly, Isaiah Berlin was not travelling, and after an exchange of several telegrams—somehow, that had always seemed the best way to get hold of him—we arranged to meet at the Ritz for a drink. After our correspondence over the philosophy piece, I felt that Berlin, whose influence extended to the philosophy of history, was the first trial I had to undergo. Shy and tongue-tied, I sat across from him and probed him to discover the grounds for his attack on historicism, meanwhile trying to draw a portrait of him in my head. I came home and set down some notes on him while our meeting was still fresh in my memory:

By origin, he is a Lithuanian Jew, and, like other Lithuanians I've known, he's very worldly. He has a genial presence, which epitomizes All Souls at its best, and a voice like the gentle popping of champagne corks. Cecil Beaton gets it just right when he describes Isaiah in one of his books as "a bear which has just gorged itself on honey." Indeed, the most striking thing about him is his permanent euphoria, which bubbles up in endless talk and malicious gossip about the historians he doesn't like. He sums them up in thumbnail sketches, precisely describing their weaknesses, faults, and contradictions. He will write off a historian with a chuckle and the words "No good, no good at all, nonono, ohnono, no good at all." In contrast, he seems to take great pleasure in his friends, and to be genuinely delighted at seeing them happy.

He is drawing a lot of fire from people in the New Left, who would have preferred a professor of political theory at Oxford to be someone seething with radical ideas rather than someone sitting on the fence, like him. What he does is bring the paradoxes underlying life into the open by either expounding the ideas of earlier thinkers or raising philosophical objections to ideas he doesn't like. He hates solitude, would rather lecture than write, would a hundred times rather chat than do either.

And so on.

The next day, I ran into a friend, Alasdair Clayre, who was also a friend of Isaiah's and had a message for me from him—that he didn't want any part of our meeting to appear in *The New Yorker*. "I don't know why he wants to be shielded from publicity," Alasdair said. "After all, he has worked pretty hard at being famous."

"I don't know why, either," I said. "But he has a right to his privacy. And there goes the small beginning I've made on my historians piece."

❧

TAYLOR, WHO WAS the object of a controversy touched off by his adversary Trevor-Roper, had remained at home in London, but he brushed off my request for an interview with a blunt letter, sounding his old theme: "I have no theories of History and know nothing about them. Therefore I do not think there is any point in your coming to see me." I spent much of the next month reading Taylor and Trevor-Roper, and trying to work out how I could write an article on them without talking to Taylor, since I had managed to talk to Trevor-Roper in Oxford with better results than I had expected. But there seemed to be no way for me to get Taylor's views at first hand. Disregarding the *New Yorker* principle of never pressuring anyone for an interview, I wrote to him again, asking him if he would reconsider. I mentioned that I had interviewed Trevor-Roper, thinking that that news would make Taylor eager to give me his side of the controversy. My letter, however, succeeded only in irritating an exposed nerve. "I am not a Professor, unlike the distinguished people whom you have interviewed," he wrote back. Trevor-Roper had been appointed the Regius Professor of Modern History at Oxford, a position that many people felt should have rightfully gone to Taylor. "I write history. I do not talk about it," he added.

The day I got Taylor's letter, I was lunching with my friend John Douglas Pringle, the deputy editor of the *Observer*, and I told him that for lack of Taylor's coöperation I was losing heart in continuing with my piece. Unlike some of my other English friends, who wrote cultural pieces for different newspapers, tossing off their requisite few hundred words every week, and couldn't understand why I needed to interview anyone, Pringle immediately grasped my need to talk to Taylor, and, being a friend of his, offered to plead my cause with him.

In the meantime, being cut off from the *New Yorker* offices and Mr. Shawn was taking its toll on me. Having been sent away from home before I was five, I'd always prided myself on being independent, but as far as my writing was concerned I had developed a crippling dependence on him. After reading a new version of the Sherry piece, which I'd left with him, he had decided to run it, and he sent me the page proofs in England. I had trouble revising them without having him at my elbow. It seemed to me ludicrous that I, a grown man, couldn't work on my own, and I struggled on. Somehow, I was able to make the necessary revisions in time for the piece to be published.

❧

ALL ALONG, I had been desultorily working on my piece about the Third Programme. I now decided to concentrate my efforts on it, in case it should turn out to be the only thing I'd have to show for my months in England. At the same time, I finally left the cold, mean house on Draycott Place and moved into a block of flats at 20 Hallam Street, just behind Broadcasting House, where the BBC had its headquarters. Mercifully, both the block and Broadcasting House were centrally heated, and I had a telephone extension in my flat. The building's switchboard was operated by a canny porter, who not only took messages for all the occupants of the twenty flats but soon knew the identity of every caller and the caller's importance to the occupant. In addition to handling the switchboard, he sorted the mail, served tea in the rooms, manned a small bar at the front desk, and cleaned shoes left outside the door at night. (Later, when I mentioned my happy move to Mr. Shawn, he asked me why I had stayed so long in a place where I was clearly miserable. Because it was cheap, I told him. He didn't say, as he had said a year earlier about the Picasso, that *The New Yorker* would have taken care of expenses—I think for at least two good reasons. One was that my income for my first year at *The New Yorker* was fourteen thousand seven hundred and forty-seven dollars and ninety-three cents, which was a princely sum, even for established writers, and if I couldn't bear to use some of the money earned from pieces I'd sold in one year to support myself while I was writing a piece in the next year, because I was constantly fearful of never being able to finish the new piece, that fear, in his view, was merely a psychological problem. The other reason was that Greenstein, who looked after the business side of things on the editorial floors, though he acknowledged my need for assistance, was conscious that *The New Yorker* was paying for it, and felt that additional expenses for me could not be justified.)

At the very moment when I thought things couldn't get any worse with the historians piece, they started looking up. Taylor agreed to see me. All the historians returned from their travels and invited me to join them for lunches and dinners and long conversations. Moreover, while they were away I had gone from being merely a visitor in England to having a settled life with my old friends there, and I was now spending a lot of time with writers and journalists. It was odd to find myself regarded by them as a colleague when inside I still felt like a student. At one point, I met Donald McLachlan, the editor of the *Sunday Telegraph*, at Broadcasting House, and he invited me to one of a series of lunches he regularly held at his flat for his paper's critics. The critics sat around trying out their ideas and talking about politics and art. The gathering was quite different from anything at *The New Yorker.*

Just when I was beginning to feel myself a part of the journalistic and literary communities in London, I finished my research and had to pull up stakes and head back to New York. One cheering aspect of the return was that instead of a student visa, which had allowed me to stay in America since 1949, I now had, thanks to a *New Yorker* petition, a new, H-1 visa, such as was granted to opera singers, ballet dancers, and the like. Back in New York, I was shocked to discover that during the three months or so while I had been fumbling around in England, gathering material for pieces that might or might not work out, the skeleton of a building of no fewer than seventeen stories had been put up almost across from the front window of my apartment.

❦

THE SUMMER WAS dismal and oppressive, not because it was hot—indeed, it was said to be one of the pleasantest in memory—but because from dawn to dusk I was lost in the historians piece, forgetting about time, food, sexual needs, friends, and obligations. And then, when I was asleep, Toynbee, Taylor, Carr, and Butterfield marched through my dreams, rather like Hamlet's father's ghost, and whispered in my ear to get on with the job. But the job had many uncongenial aspects. I had to strain constantly to visualize the historians I was writing about, and then describe them and re-create them as people. I had to adopt the persona of a reporter who was learning for the first time about their ideas and methods. Finally, I had to struggle to come up with a form to accommodate the material, which was by nature vast and intractable. Now and again, I would send up a rough section to Mr. Shawn. With any other editor, I would have been afraid to expose my tentative, fragmentary drafts, for fear of being judged wanting as a writer; after all, the city was full of stories of young writers who had been taken up by this or that editor and then dropped. But Mr. Shawn was able to visualize, long before I could, what my finished piece might be like, and he even saw as merits what I had imagined were obstacles.

On August 10, 1962, seven months to the day from my start on the project, I finished it. Instead of an article, I had written a little book, forty thousand words long. I sent it up to Mr. Shawn. He read it over the weekend, and came down much excited. I must have learned something from the philosophy piece, because he said there was a lot less to be done to the piece about the historians. He wanted to get it into print very soon. But as we started working on it we found that, although individual sections worked well enough, the way they were arranged could be made more effective. It was as if we kept putting up a structure one day and pulling it down on the next in order to start over, each time trying to improve the architecture. I often thought that Mr. Shawn would want me to cut this or that. Critics were always complaining that *New Yorker* articles were too long. But he, like a writer, didn't want to lose a single nuance. On the contrary, he would come down to my office with a new reading and new thoughts about where I could elaborate on an idea or make a point to advantage, as if he felt that in order for a piece to have lasting value it had to be absolutely complete.

At the same time, Ted Weeks was reading the piece, along with the philosophy piece, as the manuscript of my new book to be published by Atlantic-Little, Brown. Even though the book would reach only a few thousand readers, in contrast to the few hundred thousand of *The New Yorker*, he wanted to cut out a lot of the details in order to make it easy to read. One thing he wanted to leave out was the correspondence between Berlin and Carr—what he called the "boxing match" between them— because he found it boring, and he also couldn't see any reason for my including Lewis Namier, whom he found tough going. I pointed out to him that Namier, single-handed, had changed the way English historians approached history. He granted that that might be so, but said that the general public knew nothing about him. And anyway, he added, who would remember him some years down the road? Moreover, he wanted to change the arrangement of the book—put the historians before the philosophers, because he thought that the historians came across as "warmer" and that history was "more accessible" to American readers. He even wanted to replace my title, "Fly and the Fly-Bottle," with "Historians and Philosophers," which, because it was explanatory, would be more salable. The suggestions were drastic, having to do more with commercial considerations than with literary ones.

I consulted Mr. Shawn. He said I shouldn't make any compromises. With his support, I fought Weeks like a tiger for the integrity of my manuscript and managed to prevail on every point.

The historian chapters were published in *The New Yorker* in December as a two-part piece, with the title "The Flight of Crook-Taloned Birds"—from an epigraph to Aeschylus' "Prometheus Vinctus": "I took pains to determine the flight of crook-taloned birds, marking which were of the right by nature, and which of the left, and what were their ways of living each after his kind, and the enmities and affections that were between them, and how they consorted together." In later years, that title would pop into my head for all kinds of controversies between writers and intellectuals, genuine or phony, as if one could do little more than observe and record.

As happened with the philosophers, I received a spate of letters from the historians, amplifying or correcting certain facts, and even offering new interpretations of some. No matter how foolproof one's system of approach seems, gremlins always manage to creep into any published work, as if to prove that perfection is ever elusive. On the whole, however, the historians were much more generous than the philosophers. Toynbee wrote that the article "taught me quite a lot about myself as well as about the others," and went on to say, "[T]here is one thing that I should like to correct. At the top of page 95 you quote me as saying, 'I am a determinist.' I think I must have said 'I am not a determinist.' I probably mumbled and this misled you. I often make this point in order to distinguish my approach from Spengler's." The mistake proved to be less grave than it might have been, since the difference between Toynbee and Spengler on determinism was made abundantly clear elsewhere in the article. But the discrepancy kept me awake at night. Was it caused by my memory, or was it a mistake of the printers? I would, of course, correct the mistake in the book. But how awful to think that hundreds of thousands of copies had gone out without the crucial "not."

❧

SOON AFTER THE publication of the historians pieces in *The New Yorker*, I went to a grand Christmas party, given by the brother-in-law of Queen Juliana of the Netherlands—Prince Aschwin de Lippe—and his wife, Simone, in the Dakota: the apartment house that is New York City's closest equivalent of a castle. Aschwin, who worked in the Asian section of the Metropolitan Museum of Art, was a friend.

The party was very crowded. The moment I entered, Simone conducted me to a line of people waiting to meet Greta Garbo. Standing three or four people away from her, I was mesmerized by her voice, husky and alluring, which I knew from the film "Anna Karenina." My pulse quickened.

A man sidled up to me. "I am George Weidenfeld, of Weidenfeld & Nicolson," he said, speaking with what I took to be a Central European accent.

I had never heard of him or his firm, and I was irritated by the intrusion. "Glad to meet you," I said, in a brusque American fashion, and added, in a sort of stage whisper, "I'm waiting to meet Miss Garbo."

"Garbo can do nothing for you," he said in a loud voice. "I can change your life. Come over into the corner with me so we can have a word *entre nous*."

I was sure that Greta Garbo had heard him, and I was mortified. I hastily left the line, and followed him through a crush of people to a corner.

"I've read every word of your accounts of the philosophers and the historians in *The New Yorker*," he said. "I'll pay you three times what any other English publisher would pay to publish the book in England."

Simultaneously taken aback and tempted, I told him that my book was with my publishers, Faber & Faber, and that I had no intention of leaving them. The truth was that, although I had overruled Weeks's critical suggestions, I secretly feared that I might have destroyed any chances the book had had. In fact, I had so little confidence in it that I wanted the Faber imprimatur.

"Faber is a sleepy firm. My house is extremely active. Three times as much. I'll guarantee you an advance of a thousand pounds."

There was no doubt that Weidenfeld was making a very bold offer.

"Mr. Weidenfeld—"

"George."

"George, then. I can't say I'm not interested in your offer, but I never hold people to what they say at parties."

"I'm a teetotaller," he said. "And I'll expect you for lunch at the Algonquin at one o'clock tomorrow."

He walked away and left me standing there, feeling exposed and not knowing where to turn.

A sympathetic waiter came over.

"Smoked salmon, sir?"

"Miss Garbo."

He was about to move on, as if he thought I was asking for another kind of hors d'oeuvre.

"The lady who was standing over there," I said.

"Oh, the lady in bluejeans? Are you looking for her? She's gone. Only stayed a few minutes."

❦

THE NEXT DAY, I went to Weidenfeld's lunch. He had taken the most conspicuous table in the Algonquin, right in the middle of the Rose Room. I waited for him there for almost an hour, with the waiters circling around me as if to remind me that I was keeping the table from other patrons. I felt increasingly self-conscious and agitated, wondering whether I'd got the day right, and thinking about Mr. Shawn, who was never late by a minute, and who prefaced all his telephone calls with "Is this a convenient time?"

Just as I was about to leave, Weidenfeld arrived, saying he had been tied up on the telephone to London to find out about his mother, who was in a hospital.

As we talked, I discovered that he had only a vague impression of the text of my book, but then I had knocked around Publishers' Row long enough to know that publishers tended to be businessmen, and formed judgments about books by smelling rather than reading them, and that there was no point in measuring them against the standards of Mr. Shawn's reading and rereading.

As it turned out, Weidenfeld's offer was almost seven times Faber's and three times that of the runner-up, Macmillan.

When I told the whole bizarre story to Mr. Shawn, who was involved in every detail of the book, much as he had been in every detail of the *New Yorker* pieces, he said that since Weidenfeld was so enthusiastic I should let him publish the book, provided I got contractual guarantees that I could control how it was designed and presented. This stipulation Weidenfeld readily agreed to, and so it was that in England I became a Weidenfeld author.

❦

SOON I WAS embroiled in conflict with both Atlantic and Weidenfeld over the book jackets. As a matter of course, I sent up to Mr. Shawn roughs of the jacket artwork for his reactions, since he took as much interest in advising me on my book jackets as he did in choosing covers for *The New Yorker*. The American jacket had arrows pointing to a circle, making the drawing look rather like a traffic sign. The English jacket featured an actual drawing of a fly. I wished that both publishers could have used one of three Steinberg drawings that had accompanied the articles in the magazine. One of those drawings showed volleys of words being fired out of cannons and letting off a lot of smoke, for instance. I wished we could have used one of the Steinbergs as a frontispiece, perhaps, if not on the book jacket, but both publishers felt that it would add to the price of the book, and so discourage sales. On the strength of Mr. Shawn's comments, I engaged in battles to get jacket designs in keeping with the spirit of the book. The battles eventually resulted in tasteful, if quiet, jackets, but publishers regard presentation as their preserve, and what they saw as my meddling seemed to have the effect of making them feel redundant. My interference was resented even more when it had to do with the jacket copy. Yet the jacket copy that each of the publishers provided not only was completely at variance with the character of the book but was so badly written that when I showed an example to a colleague, Renata Adler, she exclaimed, "It seems to have been written by a lower form of humanity!" The publishers and I went back and forth on several versions, and finally both just threw up their hands and told me to provide them with something. But I was no more capable of writing my own jacket copy than I was of reviewing my own book. When I mentioned the problem to Mr. Shawn, he immediately offered to write it himself, but said, "I'm not at all sure I can come up with something that will be appropriate." The next day, he brought down a handwritten page with hardly anything crossed out. It captured the spirit of the book so well that scarcely any of the most complimentary reviews the book received measured up to it.

Mr. Shawn wrote the jacket copy for practically all my subsequent books. He was a natural writer, but his writing consisted largely of coming up with thousands of "dummy sentences" every week on other people's proofs, of providing jacket copy for countless books, and of turning out anonymous obituaries for hundreds of editors, writers, and contributors. He wrote quickly and fluently. His prose bore the unmistakable mark of his character—simple, direct, and generous. It was so secure and so well wrought that the words seemed perfectly seated on the page.

As I was about to return the publishers' final proofs of "Fly-Bottle," I brought up with Mr. Shawn the question of the visual elements in my writing, and asked him if anything needed to be said about it in the book. He pondered the matter for a couple of days, and even went as far as to draft a note for inclusion in the book, but then had second thoughts. He said that since my first book had been about blindness, and my point of view had already been explained in the English edition of my second book, he felt there was no need to mention it further. Besides, my book was about philosophers and historians, and to raise the question of whether or not its author could see was distracting, and possibly irrelevant. After that, when I was writing about blindness I wrote like a blind person; otherwise, I wrote like anyone else.

Mr. Shawn was so intimately connected with every word of "Fly-Bottle" that I asked him if I might dedicate the book to him. He thought for a moment, then said that he was honored but that it might not look right. I said that many books were dedicated to him, and that anyway I didn't care what people thought, since I was only expressing what I really felt. He said that in that case it would be all right. I then came up with a quotation from the Bible to express my feelings: "For one day in thy courts is better than a thousand." He said that that might look as if I were comparing him to God. I argued that quotations from the Bible were often used, and no one took them literally. He asked for a day or two to think about it, and in the end he said that he still felt a little embarrassed by it. I then hit upon the idea of printing the quotation in Sanskrit, so that only he and I—and, of course, people who could read Sanskrit—would know what I was saying. The idea appealed to the private side of him, but after I showed him the dedication page with the Sanskrit he thought that it seemed a little coy, and agreed to let me use the quotation in English.

I often wondered how he could find the energy to get involved in the minutiae of the publication of his writers' books, as he so often did, in addition to editing a weekly magazine. Nor was that all: once a book was published, he kept abreast of the letters and reviews it received, as if he were caught up in its fate as vitally as its author was. Once or twice, I asked him how he managed all this, and he said that it was just part of his job. It seemed that anything having to do with *The New Yorker*, however remote, he saw as his own concern.

❦

IN THE SUMMER of 1962, a year before "Fly-Bottle" was published, I met Robert Silvers, who was then an editor at *Harper's* magazine. He said that his friend Walter Kaufmann, a brilliant philosophy professor at Princeton who focussed on such tough subjects as Nietzsche and Hegel, had spoken very admiringly to him about my philosophy piece, and that he, Silvers, would like to publish me in *Harper's*. I told him that I had written a story, "Call Girl," in which a lonely immigrant fantasizes about a call girl and has an innocent encounter with one, but that *The New Yorker* had turned it down, on the ground that it was sketchy. He said he'd like to see it, so the next day I dug up the story, put it in an envelope, addressed it to Silvers at *Harper's*, and took it to Mr. Monsees, in *The New Yorker's* messenger room. "What are you doing sending something to *Harper's?*" he asked. "I thought you were pure *New Yorker*." His remark made me wonder if I shouldn't suppress the story, since I agreed with the judgment of the *New Yorker* editors that it didn't come off. But the temptation to have something—anything—in print was irresistible, and I left the story with Mr. Monsees. Some time later, Silvers returned the story to me with a pleasant note, saying that the *Harper's* editors had liked it very much but weren't buying any new fiction until they had run everything they had on hand. Could I resubmit it in six months? It seemed like a strange policy, not calculated to encourage writers, and I put the story and *Harper's* out of my mind.

Months passed, and then Silvers, though he was on leave from *Harper's*, again asked me to resubmit the story, because, as he put it, "I don't want my good work on behalf of your story to go down the drain." I again succumbed to the old temptation. "Call Girl" was eventually bought, at the end of 1962, and it was published in *Harper's* the following July. In later years, I always regretted its publication. I felt that the story showed me in a poor light, and that its publication must have pained Mr. Shawn, who wanted only the best work of his writers to be published. Besides, it kept me from tackling the subject again, when I had the maturity to deal with it properly. I wondered if I had traded my long-term interests for a short-term gain.

In the meantime, I had been seeing a good bit of Bob Silvers, mainly at the apartment of Cal and Elizabeth Lowell, who had moved from Boston to New York. Among those often to be found at the Lowells' table then were W. H. Auden, Stanley Kunitz, Edmund Wilson, and the Trillings. The table sometimes resembled an informal stock exchange for literary reputations, with barbs flying at a dizzying pace. Silvers, although he was very different from Mr. Shawn, was in his own way a very impressive editor. He seemed to have his antennae in the academic and journalistic establishments of both America and England, and always to know the state of people's reputations. I found it exciting to mix with people outside *The New Yorker* and bring them together with new friends I was making at the magazine.

One evening, back in December of 1962, around the beginning of what turned out to be an almost four-month-long newspaper strike in the city, I had Bob Silvers, the Lowells, and Dwight Macdonald to dinner at the Picasso. At one point during the meal, when I was bemoaning the absence of newspapers, Elizabeth said that the newspapers weren't any good anyway, and it was a relief to be free of them. I said I was grateful for *The New Yorker*, which at least kept me abreast of the things I was interested in. With that, Bob, Cal, and Elizabeth all turned on *The New Yorker*. They said that the magazine suffered by not publishing hard-hitting articles. Dwight, who was proud of his credentials as a New York intellectual, expressed agreement. (Dwight was one of many *New Yorker* writers who treated the magazine as a Rock of Gibraltar, which could be battered but would always be there.) I said that Mr. Shawn felt there was so much destruction and violence in society that he wanted his magazine to be a force for good, and that anyway he didn't want to devote precious space in *The New Yorker* to attacking people unless they were doing something pernicious or dangerous.

My guests then shifted their attack to other magazines. *Harper's* and *The Atlantic* were middle-brow—literature for people who avoided anything really taxing or troubling. The writing in *The Saturday Review* was "pap," and *Commentary* was Zionist. The *Times Book Review* was disgraceful: its editors treated books like merchandise rather than like literature.

I suggested to Bob that maybe he should try to become the editor of the *Book Review*.

"I'd rather start something new," he said.

Dwight said that this was the best time to start a new magazine, because, with the newspaper strike on, people were hungry for something to read. So it was that the *New York Review of Books* was conceived.

In subsequent days, there was a lot of excitement about the new publication—about who should be approached for financial backing, which people were the right sort to be associated with it, and when the first issue should come out. I was not privy to many of these discussions. The project soon became the property of people with more knowledge of printing and publishing, and more financial resources and literary clout, than I had.

❧

AT THE TIME of the newspaper strike, Gavin Young, a corre-spondent for the London *Observer,* was haunting the New York scene. He was a rather solitary figure, yet liked to go to glam-orous parties, and he was always looking for new subjects to write about. He spotted one in the inception of the *New York Review of Books,* and on February 3, 1963, the *Observer* carried this story:

Growing discontent with the standards of book criticism in leading American papers has led members of the literary "establishment" to take mat-ters into their own hands, reports our New York frontiersman, Gavin Young.

On February 16 the *New York Review of Books* will appear for the first time. Its 48 pages will be edited by Bob Silvers (an editor of *Harper's Magazine* now on leave of absence) and Mrs. Jason Epstein, whose hus-band is vice president of Random House and one of the liveliest and most enterprising publishing people in New York. The first issue will print 100,000 copies and will sell at 25 cents.

Fifty books will be discussed in each number by top contributors like W. H. Auden, Dwight Macdonald, Gore Vidal, Robert Penn Warren, Norman Mailer, Mary McCarthy, James Baldwin, Muriel Spark, Ved Mehta, Virgil Thomson, and Arthur Schlesinger. Special cartoons are being drawn by Jules Pfeiffer.

The editors point out that the paper will not simply fill the gap created by the two-month-old newspaper strike in New York. No, they intend it to be a kind of literary Design Centre, with models of what every good literary review should be, thus paving a way to better criti-cism in the United States.

For some weeks, Bob had been inviting me, as a founding member, to write something for the first issue. At the time, I had what seemed to be a kidney infection, and was having trouble doing even my *New Yorker* work. I called him and said I would pass up the chance of being in the first issue, but he wouldn't take no for an answer. By then, though, all the good new books seemed to have been chosen by other reviewers. The only one left that he thought could rate a review in his magazine was "Lawrence Durrell and Henry Miller: A Private Correspondence," edited by George Wickes. Durrell and Miller were by no means my favorite writers, and, speaking in the *New Yorker* tradition, I told Bob that I would rather write about writers I had some enthusiasm for. He said that he liked polemics. While I conceded that polemics had a noble literary tradition, from Jonathan Swift, through George Orwell, to Dwight Macdonald, I said that temperamentally I was unsuited to that kind of writing. Yet I allowed myself to be persuaded to review the book, even as I knew that I wouldn't succeed. I wrote something quickly and sent it in. It was no surprise to me when he didn't publish it.

I soon received a kind letter, dated February 12th, from Elizabeth Hardwick, who served as a sort of literary guardian of the magazine. It read, in part:

I'm sorry about your book review. We are having it re-typed today and will send it to you. Naturally, most of it is very good, as one would expect, and it would have only needed another going over, but we are this moment putting the dummy together, having changed printers last week, and so there isn't time for anything. Can't tell you how grateful all of us were for your willingness to help. Please, if we go on and we assume we will, do something for the next issue. We need you.

The book review is very good, quite amazing in fact. Our worry is how, on such short notice and so little money, to make it look as good as it is. In any case, we have no intention of giving up after this first try and hope we are at the birth of an important magazine.

Much love and many thanks. Do call us soon.

However, I never have written anything for *The New York Review of Books*, a publication I much admire—perhaps because after that episode I retreated more snugly than ever into the safe shell of *The New Yorker.*

❧

ONE OF THE first things I noticed when I started writing for *The New Yorker* was that the New York journalistic community was split among many competing magazines, which seemed to be forever engaged in gunning for their competitors, whether imagined or real, as if the country weren't large enough to accommodate them all. I sometimes thought that New York's publishers and editors took their cue from the city's profit-hungry real-estate contractors, who in the very process of putting up a building began to imagine tearing it down and putting up a bigger one. For both groups, it seemed, everything was fair game for immediate profit, and nothing else was sacred. I, for one, was not at all prepared for the continuing poisonous attacks gratuitously aimed at *The New Yorker*, some of them the result of careful planning. In fact, the editors of some publications seemed to seek out *New Yorker* writers who were willing to attack other *New Yorker* writers. I recall meeting the English sometime-*New Yorker* theatre critic Kenneth Tynan in London in 1965 and learning that he had been asked by the London *Observer* to review Truman Capote's "In Cold Blood," which had appeared in *The New Yorker*. "I'm going to cut Truman off at the knees," he told me, "and everyone will know about it from London to Los Angeles." He seemed to think that the more scathing he made his attack the greater the glory that would accrue to him. I myself was once coöpted into doing down another *New Yorker* writer, just after I had started writing for *The New Yorker*. Rochelle Gerson, the book editor of the *Saturday Review*, asked me to review a book about India by Emily Hahn, and insinuated that an assault that would get people talking would be welcome. I was young and fell into Miss Gerson's trap. But I quickly came to realize that such assaults served the same function for the intellectual press that sensational stories of crime and mayhem served for the tabloids—simply to increase circulation—and thereafter I refused to take part in such internecine warfare.

It has to be said, however, that there were some circumstances peculiar to *The New Yorker* which made it a particularly inviting target for other magazines. When I began writing for it, *Time* had still never forgiven *The New Yorker* for Wolcott Gibbs's 1936 Profile of its founder and editor, Henry Luce, "Time . . . Fortune . . . Life . . . Luce," which parodied, among other things, *Time*'s backward writing style, marked by the use of awkward, forced syntax and portmanteau words. ("Backward ran sentences until reeled the mind," Gibbs famously quipped.) Similarly, *Reader's Digest* had not forgotten John Bainbridge's 1945 Profile of its founder, DeWitt Wallace, which was entitled "Little Magazine" and ironically compared the *Digest* to the Holy Bible. (*The New Yorker* was a holdout among publications in its later years in never allowing its articles to be condensed and reprinted in the *Digest*.) Many magazine editors fancied their publications to be intellectual competitors of *The New Yorker*. One notable example was Francis Brown, the editor of the *Times Book Review*. As if to make it quite clear that his publication was intellectually superior to *The New Yorker*, Brown often buried reviews of *New Yorker* books in the back pages, or insured their being panned by assigning them to reviewers who were known to be totally opposed to the authors' fundamental point of view. Characteristically, the reviewer he chose for Hannah Arendt's book "Eichmann in Jerusalem," which criticized the conduct of the Eichmann trial, was one of its witnesses, Judge Michael

Musmanno, and Musmanno's attack was scathing. The review resulted in such an outpouring of condemnation by the intellectual community that Brown was forced to devote a great deal of space in the *Book Review* to responses to it. There was no hint of apology, however: he merely published a "statement from Miss Arendt" and a "reply from Judge Musmanno," along with nearly two pages of letters attacking and defending the review—a recourse calculated to create a sensation at the expense of *The New Yorker*. It was said that he might have a personal vendetta against the magazine, and, indeed, Greenstein once showed me a long list of manuscripts by Brown that had been submitted to *The New Yorker* in his early years and had been rejected. Some magazine editors who were not sympathizers with Luce, Wallace, or Brown were no doubt simply irritated by the extraordinary success of *The New Yorker*. It ran more advertisements than any other consumer magazine—at its peak, in 1966, over sixty-two hundred pages. On top of that, the use of weekly newsbreaks, poking fun at journalistic lapses in newspapers and magazines, gave an impression of superciliousness which must have irked the publications ribbed.

Nevertheless, no newspaper or magazine, critical as it might be of *The New Yorker,* could dismiss it completely. The one general method of dealing with its persistent success was to pay it a backhanded compliment by dredging up just a few well-known pieces for commendation—John Hersey's "Hiroshima," Rachel Carson's "Silent Spring," James Baldwin's "The Fire Next Time," and short stories by John Cheever, J. D. Salinger, and John Updike—as much as to say that the rest of it was of little consequence. The fact was, of course, that *The New Yorker* had unwaveringly published some of these writers for years while they were little known or were out of fashion, and had been condemned for doing so by the very publications that later went in for the backhanded compliments.

From a somewhat different perspective, some of my truly literary friends patronized *The New Yorker* by dismissing it as merely a glossy publication, because they confused the advertisements with the editorial content, failing to grasp that the latter was as sensitive and liberal as the former were crass and snobbish, and that this irony was at the heart of the magazine. The business office and the editorial department were on separate floors, and there was no contact between them. Certainly no one in the editorial department had any use for the glossy advertisements. They were tolerated as a fact of life, and many of the magazine's devoted readers often concentrated on the editorial content to the point of not even seeing them.

Unlike other magazine editors, who gave as good as they got and viewed the cut-and-thrust as free publicity, Mr. Shawn was pained by everything adverse he read or heard about *The New Yorker,* and he was such a pacifist by temperament and conviction that he always resisted joining the battle, whatever the cost—this despite the fact that he thought of the magazine as a fragile institution. Like Ross, he believed that putting out an issue was as precarious as opening a play. Some people would have liked *The New Yorker* to look to its security by becoming an economic empire, in the manner of Luce's *Time,* say, which seemed to be continually launching new and bigger magazines. (Now Time, Inc., having joined forces with Warner Bros., is one of the world's biggest entertainment companies.) But Ross and Mr. Shawn were interested only in putting out one good magazine, and that magazine's assets, both at the start and sixty years later, were largely its people, who went down in the elevator at the end of the day. Ross and Mr. Shawn had gathered under one roof writers and artists so individualistic, and often fractious, that it was hard to understand how they could have been made to hold on and pull together. But then Mr. Shawn's charity and tolerance for people had no limits. I sometimes heard writers pleading with him not to publish this or that other writer, because he or she had attacked the magazine, but Mr. Shawn was no more influenced by what one writer said to him about another than by what any of the writers said in print about each other. He felt confidence in his ability to sift through a writer's pieces and distinguish those of lasting value from attention-getting ephemera, and he acted accordingly. One effect of this attitude of Mr. Shawn's was that *New Yorker* writers seemed to be constantly shooting off their mouths to the press with impunity, as if each of them were the magazine's official spokesman.

❦

IN APRIL, 1965, in the dying days of the New York *Herald Tribune*, Tom Wolfe, a writer with a Ph.D. in American Studies from Yale, published a two-part article about *The New Yorker* in the newspaper's Sunday-magazine section. The first part was entitled "Tiny Mummies! The True Story of the Ruler of 43d Street's Land of the Walking Dead!" and it portrayed *The New Yorker* as a morgue—a mere relic of Ross's magazine—and Mr. Shawn as the mortician, reverently preserving it. The second part, entitled "Lost in the Whichy Thicket," made fun of *New Yorker* writing as convoluted, and choked with qualifying subordinate clauses. The articles were simply a pernicious attack. Wolfe had never visited the *New Yorker* offices, never interviewed any of us, and never met Mr. Shawn. His only glimpse of the staff of the magazine had been at one of the anniversary parties that the business office gave every year in a hotel, with food, drink, and music, and which Mr. Shawn never attended. It was Wolfe's stroke of luck that a new member of the staff, a young woman who wasn't aware of a policy at the time of not inviting dates and spouses to the party, brought him along, and he was able to slip in.

In the articles Wolfe had editors at *The New Yorker* rewriting pieces at will, without the approval of their authors. And, altogether gratuitously, he had Mr. Shawn as a schoolboy being the intended kidnap victim of Nathan Leopold, Jr., and Richard Loeb, the two notorious wealthy University of Chicago students who in 1924 had kidnapped and murdered fourteen-year-old Bobby Franks merely for thrills. According to Wolfe, the trauma that Mr. Shawn was supposed to have suffered was documented in court records, and explained his shy and retiring nature. Both Wolfe articles—described in the *New York Review of Books,* among other publications, as "new journalism" or "parajournalism"— were such murderous inventions and such a brutal caricature of Mr. Shawn that all of us at *The New Yorker* felt that the random violence of the city streets had suddenly entered our lives.

When Mr. Shawn saw the first article, he wrote a private letter to the publisher of the *Herald Tribune,* John Hay Whitney, protesting against it as "gutter journalism" and trying to stop the publication of the second article. As if to humiliate Mr. Shawn further, Whitney released the letter to the press, thereby confirming many of us in our opinion that he was much more to be blamed for the *Herald Tribune* affair than either Wolfe or Wolfe's editor, Clay Felker: there was always gutter journalism around, but respectable publishers saw to it that it didn't get into their pages.

Scores of us also wrote letters and sent telegrams to the *Herald Tribune* refuting everything in the articles, but the newspaper published only five of the letters—comments from E. B. White, Richard H. Rovere, Muriel Spark, J. D. Salinger, and me—and these to little effect, since they were printed alongside letters that praised Wolfe's articles. One of the latter, from the writer William Styron, for example, read, in part, "I was quite amused to read in *Newsweek* that William Shawn feels that Tom Wolfe's brilliant study of himself and *The New Yorker* 'puts the *Herald Tribune* right down in the gutter.' I have become fairly resilient over the years in regard to criticism, but since the only real whiff of the gutter was in a review of one of my books in the pages of *The New Yorker*, I found Shawn's cry of Foul woefully lacking in pathos." (Styron was referring to a 1960 review of his book "Set This House on Fire," which Donald Malcolm described as "pages of indifferent prose.") Wolfe, instead of dealing with our rebuttals, let alone retracting anything he had written, or apologizing for it, dismissed us with one characteristic gibe: "They scream like weenies over a wood fire."

Practically every respected publication weighed in with an article of its own on Wolfe, the basic point being that he had, of course, gone too far but had put his finger on something real. Mr. Shawn's advisers, like Greenstein, told him to ignore the attack and maintain a dignified silence in the pages of the magazine, as he had always done when it underwent previous attacks, however false or misguided. But practically all of us writers on the staff pressed him to respond, if for no other reason than for the record. I wrote to him, "To follow up on our telephone conversation regarding Wolfe. No doubt it has been urged on you—and the case may even have its strongest advocate in you—that silence in the pages of *The New Yorker* is the best course, that it alone is the dignified way out of this filthy mess, etc. Yet if the House of Commons had been attacked, who would have been in a better position to defend it than a Member of Parliament, and would the fact, say, that Churchill or any other politician was an interested party have automatically disqualified him? You know my feeling that history should not be allowed to be made by default."

Mr. Shawn met with any of us who wanted to talk to him. Some of us prepared notes that might be used in formulating the magazine's response. Renata Adler, on her own initiative, flew to Chicago and combed through court records in Cook County, where Leopold and Loeb were tried, and her research conclusively showed that the records contained no reference to Mr. Shawn. She went on to compile, together with Gerald Jonas, then a young *New Yorker* reporter, what amounted to a legal brief cataloguing the spurious facts and factual errors in Wolfe's articles. But the conclusion that all the researches and deliberations led to was that a smear could not be refuted with facts. In the end, nothing about the attack was published in the magazine.

I continued my crusade outside the magazine, even after Kenneth Tynan assured me that Wolfe was no threat to anyone, because he wrote "like toothpaste," and after Ted Weeks sent me a letter he had received from Walter Lippmann, whose column was then appearing in the *Herald Tribune*. "I have read the piece in the *Herald Tribune* about *The New Yorker*," Lippmann wrote. "The author of it is an incompetent ass. And, though while I realize that his intentions were to murder, the effect, so far as *The New Yorker* is concerned, is nothing at all. He tried to throw a bomb. All he could manage was a rotten egg." With Lippmann's permission, I got the letter into print in the *Village Voice*. It was a small step, but I felt that at least it was something. At the same time, I entered into correspondence in the columns of the London *Observer* with Irving Kristol, who had published there a scurrilous piece entitled "The New Yorker Bitten by a Wolfe." Kristol's piece was littered with factual errors, and I wrote a letter to the *Observer* listing some of them, but only a truncated version of my letter was printed, and that brought a reply to the *Observer* from Kristol, which contained more factual errors. This exchange only served to prove the futility of trying to correct the public record. In a private letter to me Jasper Griffin summed up the exchange: "We have followed with amusement your attempts to get some change out of the *Observer* and Irving Kristol. You should know these journalists—rogues—the last disciples of Napoleon, who 'never explain and never apologize.' I must say it is amazing, the way in which writers in the *Observer* and elsewhere assume that they can say anything, and then if some spoilsport like Mehta points out that what they've said isn't actually *true*, then the writer need say nothing whatever in reply. O blessed state of irre-sponsibility!"

It's now a matter of history that Wolfe's articles helped to launch the magazine *New York*, which in 1968, two years after the New York *Herald Tribune* folded, rose from the paper's ashes and was soon presenting itself as "the new *New Yorker*." After all but appropriating the *New Yorker's* name, it grew fat on cigarette ads that Mr. Shawn had banned after the Surgeon General's report, in 1964, established that there was a connection between cigarettes and lung cancer. In due course, Wolfe and *New York* won respectability, and became one of many successful new magazines being published in big cities from Boston to San Francisco.

However, *New York* failed to dislodge *The New Yorker* from its preëminent place. Mr. Shawn's magazine continued to prosper. There was a little weekly intramural handout—a sheaf of Xeroxed papers distributed by the business department as an aid to the salesmen of advertising space—that reproduced favorable mentions of *The New Yorker* in the press. From this we gathered that a whole breed of *New Yorker* watchers, posted all across the newspaper and magazine world, reported on every little twist and turn of the magazine. (When, in 1969, Mr. Shawn finally included a table of contents in the issue—something he had resisted for years, because he wanted to maintain a feeling of informality and to feature good writing and art rather than specific contributors—newsweeklies, among other publications, carried big stories on the change.) Contrary to the fears of Wolfe, Felker, and their friends, it turned out that their magazine and Mr. Shawn's had their distinctive audiences, and one did not have to destroy the other in order to survive.

VIII

PINNING THE
BUTTERFLY

J UST AT THE TIME THE HISTORIANS PIECES WERE
appearing, Gigi a dancer in the Metropolitan Opera
ballet, whom I had been going out with for some months,
abruptly ceased to be a part of my life. Looking back,
I took this as a sign that my life would be turbulent and
would veer from the lives of my Oxford friends, who
seemed to be settling into the groove of their lives. Now and
again, though, a letter from one of them would lead me to realize
that, despite the outward stability of job, marriage, and children,
their lives were not as enviable as I had imagined them to be. For
instance, in April, 1963, Jasper Griffin wrote from Oxford:

During the very cold weather, in February, I went for a walk on the
frozen Cherwell, and as I stood on the ice at a point where I have often
punted in Summer, I had a sudden and rather intense realization that

the whole future of my life had taken shape in the last couple of months: with Geoff's death, getting the job at Balliol, and Miriam becoming pregnant. I stood still on the ice for a few minutes, and thought to myself that in later years I must remember that I had recognized at the time that this was the turning-point after which everything would be predictable.

Geoff, Jasper's younger brother and only sibling, had died of a rapidly progressing cancer while we were up at Oxford.

Now everything in my apartment reminded me of Gigi and my new loneliness, so, a bit like Melville's Bartleby the Scrivener, I practically moved into the office, haunting its corridors and going to the Picasso only to sleep. Before long, I decided to escape from the Picasso entirely, as a way of escaping from my memories of Gigi: a change of apartments, I hoped, would calm my spirits.

As it happened, in February, 1963, I had met a couple named Sidney and Maria Rolfe at a party. Sidney, a real-estate developer, and Maria, the daughter of a Greek shipping family, who had grown up in London, were rich and had come to be known as patrons of the arts. They expressed great enthusiasm for my historians pieces, and we became friends almost at once, and started seeing each other frequently. They owned two apartments in the Dakota, they told me, having recently moved from a five-room apartment there into a much larger one, and, without any preliminaries, they offered to sell me their old apartment at cost, which was nineteen thousand five hundred dollars—an amount that chanced to be most of my savings.

I thought of the Dakota, at 1 West Seventy-Second Street, as a little piece of England in the middle of New York; it reminded me of the Albany in Piccadilly, where I had visited the writers Harold Nicolson and Graham Greene. Built late in the nineteenth century, it was the first large luxury apartment building in Manhattan. Massive and imposing, it had got its name because it was so far uptown from the then familiar part of the city that people said going there was like going to the Dakotas. It had a gate large enough to admit horse-drawn carriages, and a courtyard like a cloister in an Oxford college. Despite all this, I had contradictory feelings about the Rolfes' offer. On the one hand, I had a secret fantasy of following the example of my Oxford friends, many of whom were getting married, buying houses in London, and living the lives of aesthetes or gentlemen. Although after Gigi I had assumed that I would never get married, I still wanted to live like them—to come across as worldly, however alone I felt. On the other hand, I was afraid of getting trapped by financial obligations, for I'd heard that serious writers unable to meet their obligations were often forced to turn commercial. I felt that a writer should be unencumbered—should be able to pick up and go anywhere at a moment's notice. Indeed, by now I had become so deeply influenced by the Balliol and *New Yorker* tradition of plain living and high thinking that even indulging in a glass of wine at lunch made me fear that I was headed for a fall.

I voiced some of my feelings to the Rolfes, but they pressed me just to see the apartment, and when I did I immediately took to it. It was on the eighth floor, the same floor as that of Prince Aschwin and Simone de Lippe, at whose party some months earlier I had nearly met Greta Garbo, and it was so baronial that I could almost imagine Prince Philip playing polo in one room and stabling his ponies in another. I began having visions of grandeur. But then I learned that the monthly maintenance charge was three hundred and seventy-two dollars, and I sobered up. That was more than twice my Picasso rent and came to half my drawing account, so I told the Rolfes there was no way I could afford it.

The apartment had two bedrooms, and Sidney and Maria now offered to keep one of them, which was very large, even for a Dakota bedroom, and had its own bathroom and its own access door from the public hall; they could use it either as an office or as a guest room. Sidney made some fast calculations and said that this arrangement would bring down my maintenance charge to two hundred and fifty dollars, because he and Maria would assume a hundred and twenty-two dollars of the maintenance, and that it would also reduce to fifteen thousand dollars the purchasing price of what would now be a four-room apartment. The offer was so generous that there was no way I could resist it.

I consulted Greenstein. "You want to blow all your savings on buying a coöp apartment, which is nothing more than buying a lease?" he asked. "When you own a coöp apartment, all that you really own is shares in the corporation that owns the building."

"Maybe *The New Yorker* would help me take out a mortgage," I said, glossing over his objection.

"*The New Yorker* is not in the business of mortgages," he said. I then recalled that I had once asked him to sign my application for a credit card, certifying that I was on the staff of *The New Yorker*, and he'd refused, saying that *New Yorker* writers were really like agents for an insurance company—independent operators, who had only an association with the magazine. "But why do you think a writer needs more than a room and a kitchen to live in?" he now went on. "A painter needs a studio and light, but all a writer needs is a pencil and a desk, which you have at the office anyway. Kafka probably just lived in a lonely little room somewhere."

"But, Milton, I've fallen in love with the apartment," I said.

"In my experience, love is always what gets writers into trouble," he said, with a laugh. But, as if there were no legal argument he could advance against love, he then put me in touch with Alexander Lindey, whom I had previously met when the libel problem with "Indian Summer" arose. I retained him to consummate the purchase of the apartment, and no sooner had I done so than I was bedevilled by a series of Dakota problems.

It turned out that the Dakota building board was planning to wall off the access door to the bedroom that the Rolfes had decided to retain, and, if it did so, the apartment could not be divided. Sidney was confident that in time he could get his way with the board, but we were both advised that meanwhile I should only rent the apartment from the Rolfes with an option to buy the four rooms at the agreed price within two years. The arrangement was satisfactory both to them and to me, since the Rolfes were keen to sell the apartment, and I wanted some protection against a rise in its price. We executed the necessary contractual documents, and in March I moved in.

Lindey had advised me to "camp out" until the uncertainty about the access door was resolved—to be cautious about spending much on furnishings and decorations. But there was no way for me to live in the Dakota simply. The entire apartment needed a coat of paint, and I had to pay for that. I felt that for my books I must have built-in bookcases with a special kind of molding to match that of the apartment, and obtaining them required the services of a cabinetmaker. More important, none of my Picasso furniture was appropriate: the Dakota seemed to call for antique furniture. If I had been born into the aristocracy, perhaps I would have had the self-confidence to live there without a paint job, with my books in cartons, and with only my shoddy Picasso furniture, but in my living quarters, as in my personal appearance, I wanted to present a pleasing front to the world, so that I wouldn't be excused or pitied. And no sooner had I moved in, with nothing but my books and records and a couple of pictures, than I was caught in a web of rug merchants and antique dealers, drapers and upholsterers, and the money was draining out of my savings account as if I were a rich traveller recklessly throwing gold coins in the Fontana di Trevi.

On top of everything else, getting to the office and back was inconvenient. In the beginning, I would take the subway. Then, one day, I ran for the train, thinking I had heard it pull in, and all but fell headlong onto the track; in fact, I caught myself with one foot suspended over the gaping track, and saved myself from being electrocuted only by falling backward. After that, I never trusted myself to take the subway alone, and the route to and from the Dakota with the least number of crossings of two-way streets and with good restaurants for dinner on the way home required taking a bus up Fifth Avenue, changing at West Fifty-seventh Street to a West Side bus, and walking home from Broadway. If I didn't stop along the way, it usually took me forty-five minutes from door to door, and I dreaded waiting for the buses during the bitter-cold months.

Now that I was on the West Side, going to Les Escargots for dinner was out of the question, but in due course I discovered another French restaurant, wonderful in its own way, called the Fleur de Lis, on Sixty-ninth Street, just east of Broadway. Walking home from there along Sixty-ninth Street and up Columbus, which in those days meant picking one's way through garbage cans and garbage bags, I would find myself mindlessly repeating the title of a popular book I had heard about but never read— "The Loneliness of the Long-Distance Runner"—and thinking about the women in my new restaurant: there was Gilberte, the hat-check girl, who always greeted me as if she'd been waiting for me; Anna Marie, a tragic-sounding woman, who liked to wait on me, and who I fancied was involved with a married man and would never get married herself; and elderly Marie, who as she passed by my table always scolded me for looking too thin.

One day, I had an inspiration, and I made up a parcel of my books and *New Yorker* articles and sent them to Gilberte at the restaurant. The next time I saw her, she thanked me awkwardly and said she was not much of a reader but her husband was. "He has your books on the bedside table," she said. After that, it was some time before I could bring myself to walk into the Fleur de Lis again.

There were, however, certain perks to living in the Dakota. Merely by doing so, I became part of a little artistic community of writers, actors (Zachary Scott, Jason Robards, Judy Holliday), and a sprinkling of patrons and heiresses. I didn't quite fit in, but

I enjoyed going to the parties of, for instance, Susan Stein, a Music Corporation of America heiress, who threw some of the most decorous parties in the city. She had furnished one room with a standard-size pocket-billiard table, which was lit by a low-hanging Tiffany lamp. Just outside the billiard room, in part of a long hall, she had made a bar by panelling the walls with the interior panels of one of a pair of the old Dakota hand-driven elevators, which she had bought when the building changed over to automatic elevators, and adding a couple of mirrors. Her apartment was so big that she was able to fit the whole cage of the other elevator into one end of the living room. The cage, which was the size of a small room itself, was an antique curiosity. She turned its interior into a powder room and its roof into a dining area, complete with railings and special ladders. The ceilings in the apartment were so high that there was almost more headroom on top of the cage than there had been in my Picasso apartment. It always gave me a special thrill to be ensconced up there, with a huge party flowing below, and the waiters bringing up wine and food: I felt as if we were all characters in a play of some kind and the elevator cage were a stage set.

A year or so after I moved into the Dakota, my youngest sister, Usha—she was twenty-seven then—called me from Ohio, where she was living, to tell me that she was getting married. I was thrilled. When she was eighteen and was studying at Delhi University, she had waked up with a couple of little white spots on her face—one on her cheek and one on her neck. The diagnosis had been leucoderma, a permanent loss of pigmentation, but people had started treating her as if she had leprosy. The most beautiful of my four sisters, she had suddenly come to be regarded as a pariah because of the loss of a little pigment, and this blow had almost brought on a nervous breakdown. My father and I had brought her out to the Western world, where, in contrast to the situation in India, a physical defect was not a bar to leading a full life. Subsequently, she had got an M.A. in political science at

Cornell and then a job as a sort of housemother at the Western College for Women, in Oxford, Ohio. She now told me that she was marrying a naval officer from Watervliet, Michigan, named Arthur Helweg, whom she had known for some time. Flying out to India for an elaborate three-day Indian wedding was out of the question, not only for her but also for her future in-laws, so she asked me if I could arrange a New York wedding for her.

Our family was then in such straitened circumstances that no one except my father could come over from India, and it fell to me to give her as grand a wedding as I could. We arranged for a small ceremony in the Fifth Avenue Presbyterian Church, and I made up a list of some four hundred guests, most of whom had never met Usha, to be invited to a reception in my apartment. I borrowed the Rolfes' extra room and got it cleared out for dancing, and engaged a dance band to entertain some of the younger guests. I asked my Indian-diplomat friends to lend me their servants to serve at the reception, so that the wedding would have an Indian aura—something that Usha very much wanted. All my *New Yorker* colleagues and Usha's Cornell friends rallied around, and nearly everyone I invited came to the reception. My father and I were able to marry Usha off with all the traditional trappings, from the bridegroom's bachelor dinner at a club, which was organized by one of my friends, to a big send-off with the pelting of rice (at the gate of the Dakota). I remember thinking that New York was the only city where a comparative stranger could have organized such an event. Years later, when Usha, Arthur, and I looked back on the wedding, we always blessed the Rolfes for getting me into the Dakota. It was as if the apartment had fallen into my lap only so that I could get my little sister married.

A few months before the wedding, I got a letter from Maria's lawyer saying that the board had finally decided to seal the access door but that Sidney wasn't giving up. I was just settling in with some of my newly acquired possessions—an eighteenth-century dining table and some Georgian silver. Given my precarious life as a writer, I have no simple explanation of why I went in for such trappings; either I was always trying to put up a dazzling front in order to guard against any unwarranted pity or I was just born extravagant.

The lawyer said that the battle had now moved to the city's Building Department, where the Dakota's certificate of occupancy was pending, because the building had become a coöperative only recently, and the city's approval of its layout was required. The Building Department eventually denied Sidney's application to keep the access door open, on the ground that doing so would create a single-room occupancy. Soon after the wedding, therefore, jackhammering and bricklaying began, and the door was quickly sealed. The only access that Sidney, Maria, and their guests now had to Sidney's reserved room was through my front door, so I had to give the Rolfes a key to it. At the oddest hours, I would hear the key turning in the lock. The moment I heard it, I would drop whatever I was doing, run to my bedroom, and silently close the door behind me, before the front door opened. It was invariably Sidney. In my mind, he came to seem like one of the many Dakota ghosts who were rumored to haunt the building.

In April, 1965, a month before my lease and my option to buy were to run out, I received word that the monthly maintenance on the whole apartment had jumped from three hundred and seventy-two dollars to six hundred dollars. That put an end to any lingering hope I had had of continuing to live at the Dakota.

Since then, the apartment, which I could have had for nineteen thousand five hundred dollars in 1965, has changed hands several times and, thanks to inflation, has sold for a million and more. Not long ago, I calculated that if I had bought it and stayed in bed all day, drinking champagne and eating caviar, I would have probably fared better economically than I fared as a result of what I did do, which was to move out and go on trying to earn my living.

Because I had found travelling between my office and the Dakota burdensome, I was determined to find an apartment that would require only a single bus ride and a minimal walk each way, so I restricted my search to Fifth Avenue. Because good apartments there were snapped up before they could ever be advertised, a friend kindly walked along the avenue inquiring of the doormen whether any apartments in their buildings were available for rent at about two hundred and fifty dollars. What turned up was an apartment on the thirteenth floor of 1010 Fifth Avenue, at Eighty-second Street, which was light, cozy, and adequate for my needs. Its rent was two hundred and thirty-five dollars a month, and was "stablilized"—a legal term that meant that the rent could go up by only a small percentage whenever the lease had to be renewed. However, the whole apartment, which had just two rooms, could have almost fitted into my Dakota bedroom. My Dakota furniture took up most of the available space. After moving in, I realized that in the Dakota I had had room to expand—perhaps get married and raise a family—but in the new apartment I had settled for the diminished life of a single man and had also become the custodian of antique furniture I should never have bought. I lived there for fourteen years, riding the bus between a cramped office and a cramped apartment, but taking comfort in the thought that I was leading the austere, dedicated life of a monkish writer—a life that Mr. Shawn must surely approve of.

❧

THROUGHOUT 1963 AND 1964, not only was I under pressure to find good material and to write about it in a way that would come up to Mr. Shawn's standards but I was also tormented by the feeling that the financial screws were constantly tightening. I was in England in the summer of 1964, working on a couple of pieces, and Bill Maxwell, my fiction editor, sent me a small check for a reprint fee from a publisher, along with a note saying, in part, "I don't know whether the enclosed will lighten your financial worries, but I hope so. The well always fills up during these trips to England. I don't think you should at the same time think about money. Especially since there are no debtors' prisons." Maxwell's thoughtfulness was a small comfort. Being the son of a man who never stopped quoting "Neither a borrower nor a lender be," I was always trying to pack as much research and writing as I could into the shortest possible time. But all I had to show for all of 1963 and 1964 were two long pieces—the one about the Third Programme, and a new piece about Blackwell's, the celebrated Oxford bookshop—when one generally needed four long pieces a year to keep from piling up a *New Yorker* debt. Debt, I thought, made Mr. Shawn as anxious as it made me, since I imagined that he always worried about his writers' financial well-being.

After the historians piece, I had got involved in a long project on theologians, and had been working on it off and on for more than two years. Writing about God presented special difficulties, both because of the nature of the subject and because of the sensibilities of the various believers. (I myself had lived through the Partition of India, a sort of religious war between Muslims, on the one hand, and Hindus and Sikhs, on the other, and had long been fascinated by the power of religion over people's minds.) Nor were those the only difficulties: the theologians I was concerned with were wrestling with such explosive questions as whether Christ's miracles were merely a reflection of the period in which he lived, whether it made any sense for Christians in the twentieth century to believe in a personal God, and whether Christianity could be demythologized to fit a scientific age. The piece had involved not only backbreaking reading but also trips to England, Switzerland, and Germany. In August, 1965, I finally handed it in. By that time, I had lost all perspective on it, so I immediately started fretting that it was deficient in a hundred respects and that Mr. Shawn would reject it. Anyway, I couldn't imagine that he would be able to read it quickly. I often had trouble reading even the *New Yorker* pieces of colleagues who were good friends of mine; in fact, many people in the office took a long time to read one another's published pieces, if they got around to them at all.

Mr. Shawn, however, now read my new piece within forty-eight hours, and he accepted it with enthusiasm. His intellectual energy never failed to impress me. I was hungry for his detailed reaction—what he thought of this or that section. As always, he was pressed for time, but when I tried to draw him out he got interested in talking about theology and was in my office for more than half an hour. Other editors or publishers, I thought, would have sent my piece to scholars or colleagues for an opinion. But he had such confidence in his own judgment about any piece of writing that he then and there committed himself to publishing this one in its entirety, which would take up the better part of three issues.

Astonishingly, when the piece was finally about to make its début, in the middle of November, articles on the subject suddenly seemed to spring up everywhere, mostly under the rubric "God is dead." I was appalled at the sensationalism of the articles, and felt that my labors had been scooped, even as I realized that all the public interest made my piece more topical. People around the office marvelled that Mr. Shawn should have approved the idea two years before. He seemed to be always a step ahead of the crowd, they said. Mr. Shawn and I had given my piece the flat but accurate title "The New Theologian," and we firmly turned away a suggestion by Weidenfeld, who was considering publishing it as a book in England, that I should entitle it "The New Man of God," because having "God" in the title would triple or quadruple its sales. Then, after the first part, "Ecce Homo," had gone to press, such unprecedented and unnerving things happened that I wondered if all of us might have brought down the wrath of God upon our heads.

A little after five on a Tuesday, as we were preparing the second part, "The Ekklesia," to go to press (Mr. Shawn was closing it early), we suddenly discovered that all references to "church" in this part had been capitalized, when in fact capitalization was intramurally reserved for the Catholic Church. I ran to Thelma Sargent, the O.K.er, and told her of the problem. She said that she herself had been puzzled by the capitalization, and she immediately riffled through her notes, in which, amazingly, she had jotted down the page and line of every proper noun in the piece, and thereupon made the necessary corrections.

Just as I got back to my office, my assistant said that the office light was growing dim. I picked up the telephone to call the messenger room for a new bulb, but she exclaimed, "Horrors! All the lights in New Jersey are going out!" She sat facing the window, and could see across the Hudson River. Simultaneously, I heard a commotion in the halls. People were calling to one another that the lights were going out everywhere. My first thought, and probably that of everyone else in the office, was that a nuclear war had started, and that Doomsday, which was never far away from our nightmares, was at hand.

Without thinking, I ran upstairs to Mr. Shawn, passing anxious members of the staff along the way.

"Have the missiles started flying?" I cried.

He was very calm. "Maybe it's just a sunspot," he said.

I had no idea how a sunspot could put out the lights, but I felt reassured.

Mr. Shawn and I walked down the corridor to the office of the editor Hobart (Hobey) Weekes, who had a battery-powered radio. People were huddled around it. The broadcasters seemed to be as confused as we were, but they reported that the lights were going out in Albany, in Boston—all over the Northeastern United States—and in two provinces of Canada.

"It somehow seems fitting that we should be working on a piece about God when all this is happening," Mr. Shawn said wryly.

As we waited for the lights to come back on—the blackout, we eventually learned, was caused by a glitch that had turned off the whole electric-grid system—the office, for once, had an atmosphere of community, almost of euphoria. People who would ordinarily pass one another in the hall, sometimes with just a dour look, were talking and kidding around. The blackout stretched on for hours. I thought I'd never been so hungry.

Finally, around eleven o'clock, John Murphy, from the makeup department, led a party of us down the building's old fire stairs, fighting the darkness with the unsteady flame of his cigarette lighter. It was bitterly cold on the stairs, and the stairs themselves were so rickety that we weren't sure we'd ever reach the ground. Once we did so, Hobey and I made our way along Forty-third Street to the Century club. There Mario, the manager, cooked us steaks on a kerosene stove, and we ate standing up at the bar, by candlelight. Then we took a bus up Madison Avenue. The city had an eerie atmosphere. The streets were empty, none of the streetlights or the traffic lights were working, and the bus careered up the avenue with the help of nothing but its headlights. Fortunately, by then Madison and Fifth Avenue were both one-way—Madison going north and Fifth south.

In the morning, when life had returned to normal, I came into the office and encountered Mr. Shawn getting into the elevator to go and get some breakfast. Because of his fear of heights, he had stayed in the office. He had had no dinner, and had sat up all night, in touch with Mrs. Shawn by telephone. He does everything for everyone, but no one ever seems to know what to do for him, I reflected. It was as if we were all children, and couldn't imagine that a parent might have any needs. I remembered having once stood near Mr. Shawn in a group when he got a fit of sneezing. He must have sneezed a dozen times, and not one of us, including me, said anything, as if saying something as simple as "God bless you" were beyond us. How could Hobey and I have eaten our dinner without making any effort to get some food up to him? There were no shortages of alibis for us, not the least being that he had very special food requirements, but at least we could have tried.

Mr. Shawn now said to me, "Makeup did get the theologians piece to the printers last night," and added, "If you think of anything to say about the blackout, could you send it up in the next two or three hours? We'll be preparing a Talk Department on it." That week, he wrote the whole Talk of the Town section himself, from bits and pieces of reporting that we sent in to him.

❧

EVER SINCE I first set foot in the *New Yorker* offices, I had toyed with the idea of going to India and writing about it. It was unquestionably a natural subject for me: I knew several Indian languages, and I had a network of relatives spread across the country. Over the years, I often talked with Mr. Shawn about how I might best do it, and my plans for the project grew. What I wanted was to travel around India and write a series of articles describing it—articles written as if I could see—which could become a comprehensive, timeless book on India, on the order of the great works done by Victorian English travellers. But all along I had reservations. I felt that I needed much greater technical competence to respond to the challenge. I also had to be emotionally ready to treat India as a place that was part of me, and not as a place that I was trying to escape from, which was how I had treated it in "Walking the Indian Streets." Many awful things had happened to me there, beginning with going blind and being sent away to an orphanage, and it was hard for me to rise above them. Besides, I seemed to be always waiting around for pieces already written to be edited and published, so I could be paid for them, and then to oversee their appearance in book form, with the result that in the long run I didn't have the money to stake on such a big project so far away. But now, thanks to *The New Yorker's* generous payment for the theologians pieces and to advances from Harper & Row and Weidenfeld & Nicolson, which were publishing the book in America and England, I had money in the bank. Also, I told myself that now, having published three books and having two more in the process of being printed (one was a comic novel), I should feel professionally more confident about tackling India, and that there was no excuse for putting it off.

I talked to Mr. Shawn. He was very encouraging about the idea, but told me that *The New Yorker* would not be able to help me with any expenses for such a vast undertaking, since it was something *The New Yorker*, in the normal course of things, would not be interested in doing. There were a lot of stories closer to home. Still, if I wrote good pieces he would, of course, try to get them in.

It was a hallmark of his character to be very enthusiastic about an idea when it was a distant prospect, but then, as it got closer to being realized, to put up cautionary flags. Perhaps his greatest caution and resistance came at the moment he started thinking about publishing a piece, when all considerations except that of the magazine seemed to fall away.

Despite these cautions, I set out for India near the end of November, 1965, as soon as the last part of the theologians piece had gone to press, and almost from the moment I arrived in New Delhi I felt desperate. Although only my parents and my young brother, Ashok, were living at home, relatives and neighbors were constantly turning up, and it seemed that there was no quiet corner of the house in which I could be alone and think. To be sure, there was my father's desk, with his lightweight, portable typewriter stored under it and a bookcase above it, but it was in the rather small drawing room, and seemed to be more for decoration than for work. And now that I was actually in the country I had no idea where I should go, whom I should see, or how I should get started. Everyone I met kept saying that there was nothing in India worth writing about—that since Nehru's death, early in 1964, no Indian leaders of any consequence had emerged, and that internal problems, like the Sikhs' demands for a country of their own in the Punjab, could be of little interest to the outside world. Even the foreign correspondents who had rushed to India to cover the recent Indo-Pakistan War had left, people pointed out. I didn't care so much about politics. I wanted to travel the length and breadth of the country. But my family treated me as if I were a child; they seemed to see me as naïve and out of touch with every aspect of Indian reality. When I wanted to go and see someone right there in New Delhi—an Oxford friend or a writer I had met during my earlier visit—a servant was sent on a bicycle to a taxi stand to get me a taxi. Then the whole family would troop after me to say goodbye and wish me luck, as if I were setting off on a momentous trip, and when I returned to the house everyone would come out to receive me and ask how I had got on and if I had got some good material. Or else my father would insist on driving me to my appointments, and then he and anyone else who was in the car with us would be invited in and, in accordance with Indian custom, offered tea. That had the effect of diffusing and dulling my impressions. I wanted to get out of my father's house, get out of New Delhi, go to the hinterland. But how? Knock around from hotel to hotel? Camp out in villages? I suddenly discovered that in India my blindness was an enormous impediment, and also that even journalists who could see went around with attendants.

I wrote to Indira Gandhi, the Minister of Information and Broadcasting, whom I knew slightly, telling her that I wanted to write something about India for *The New Yorker* and would need some official help. She invited me to a social lunch, as if that answered my needs. The most maddening difficulty was that many places I wanted to visit required not only government permission but also government transportation and accommodations. I spent a full three weeks appealing to one bureaucrat after another, only to be continually put off. The officials sometimes spoke as if they would prefer to gather the information for me, and not risk letting me out on the Indian streets. I got the feeling that I was up against the same old misjudgment about the blind—the assumption that the blind were helpless—that had denied me education in India and forced me to go abroad for it.

Then I ran into Cyril Dunn, a correspondent for the London *Observer*, in the lobby of a hotel. A rather gloomy man, who had the reputation of being a misanthrope, he didn't invite confidences, but I found myself telling him of my frustration.

"In the Indian government, there is only one man who can get anything done, and that's because he's actually a West Indian," Cyril said. "His name is I. J. Bahadur Singh, and he is the press-relations officer for the External Affairs Ministry."

I rang up Bahadur Singh from the hotel, and immediately got through to him. He asked me to come and see him in the secretariat that very afternoon. No sooner had I sat down in his office than he said, "Where would you like to go?"

"Nagaland, NEFA, and Ladakh," I said, thinking I would test him by mentioning places that were off limits to foreign correspondents. (NEFA was an acronym for Northeast Frontier Agency.) While I had an advantage in that I was an Indian citizen, I was writing for a foreign publication—a fact that he could obviously use as an excuse to deny me permission. But he said, "That's easily done. Where else?"

I told him I wanted to go to important cities in every state, and reeled off the names of many politicians and leaders I wanted to talk to. Visits to villages, I said, I would arrange on my own.

"How much time have you allowed for travelling?" he asked.

"Two or three months," I said.

"Two or three years would be more to the point," he said, with a laugh. "But let's work out your itinerary, and I'll send off telegrams today. You can catch a plane tomorrow."

Within an hour, I had received my typed itinerary, along with the names of government contacts and, most important of all, arrangements for accommodations. In most places, hotels were nonexistent, and the only accommodations were government rest houses built in the British times for government officers on tours of inspection.

From the start, my father had been against my travelling, saying that India was full of all kinds of physical dangers. He had pleaded with me to request a government officer to accompany me. But I wanted my impressions to be wholly my own, and anyway my pride would not allow me to ask for a personal attendant, so just a couple of days after my visit to Bahadur Singh I set out on my travels.

❧

IN THE DAYS that followed, I got up each morning at five or five-thirty in a different city or village and kept going until I all but dropped from exhaustion. I made my way from place to place by one-engine plane, rowboat, train, or jeep, or on foot or on the back of an elephant, the last two methods usually being the only available means of transport in the interior. I was fortunate in that as I travelled I was often able to speak to people I met along the way in their own languages and on their own terms, and then evaluate what they said and did on the basis of my Western education. Yet, no matter how frenetic a schedule I kept, I always took a few minutes at night to dictate my impressions into a tape recorder I carried for the purpose, because if I waited until the next day my impressions became so fuzzy and confused that they were as good as lost. All along, I had the feeling that I was gathering a lot of disparate material, which could provide me with no particular theme. I was overwhelmed.

In the meantime, important news stories seemed to be breaking every day: Prime Minister Shastri died, and after a political struggle Mrs. Gandhi was elected Prime Minister. I had the impulse to interrupt my travels and cover what seemed like momentous events. After all, I was a journalist, on the staff of a weekly. I cabled Mr. Shawn for advice on what I should do. He cabled back, "AS FOR REQUESTED LINE OF ADVICE ON YOUR INDIAN PIECE OR PIECES COMMA EYE WOULD STILL RECOMMEND THAT YOUR POINT OF DEPARTURE BE CHANGES AND EVENTS THAT HAVE TAKEN PLACE IN YEARS SINCE YOUR LAST VISIT PERIOD THAT IN ITSELF WILL SET LIMITS ON SUBJECT AND MAKE IT LESS OVERWHELMING PERIOD. . . . EYE STILL THINK THE JOURNAL FORM MAY WORK BEST BUT FORM CAN BE DETERMINED BY MATERIAL YOU FIND PERIOD . . . EYE THINK HOWEVER WOULD DEFINITELY BE MISTAKE TO LET YOURSELF BE DIVERTED FROM LONGER HYPHEN VIEW KIND OF PIECES BY NEWS PERIOD THEREFORE EYE WOULD BE AGAINST PIECE ON SHASTRI AND IMMEDIATE POLITICAL SITUATION PERIOD KEEP TO THE LONGER VIEW EYE THINK AND SET DOWN YOUR IMPRESSIONS PERIOD YOUR IMPRESSIONS ARE WHAT WOULD BE OF GREATEST VALUE PERIOD AND YOU WILL NEVER RUN OUT OF THINGS TO WRITE ABOUT IN INDIA PERIOD OR ELSEWHERE FOR THAT MATTER PERIOD."

Once, in the course of gathering those impressions, I spent six weeks in the remote Himalayas. There was no convenient way of communicating with my home, in New Delhi, and in my hurry to get started on my travels I had neglected to leave with my father the name of Bahadur Singh, who could have got in touch with me anywhere through government channels. When I had been gone only a few days, my father had what he called a premonition that I had met with an accident and died. He was already anxious about Ashok, because his own long absences abroad on medical assignments for Mrs. Clyde had caused the boy's education to be neglected, and now Ashok had become a hippie, recklessly driving around the city on a motorbike. At twenty-one, he showed no signs of settling down. As for my father, he was seventy-two, and his constant worrying, capped by the premonition, brought on a heart attack. He was hospitalized for three weeks.

When I got back to New Delhi after the Himalayan trip, I felt so guilty that I promised him I would never again do any travelling anywhere without making sure that we could keep in touch. He rallied quickly, helped by the good news that Ashok, in spite of everything, had been accepted as an officer in the Indian Navy.

☙

DURING THE FIRST few weeks after my return to New York after six months' travels in India, I began to realize that the scope of the Indian series would be much greater than anything Mr. Shawn and I had projected. Even though publishers commonly believed that the subject of India was of no interest to the general public, and so there was no market for it, not once did he ask me to curtail the project. Like editors from an earlier period, he thought that his job was to educate readers by exposing them to thought-provoking material, irrespective of how many of them would actually read it. He once said in an interview with Anna Beeke in the Dutch publication *Hollands Diep*:

We sometimes publish something which I am convinced only a few people would be interested in. Perhaps a hundred, perhaps six. Every now and again, even people on our editorial staff are not interested in what we print. Sometimes it's very specialized or unusual, but if I think that it's important and really worth someone's time I think we have to offer it to people. We must make it accessible to them. It is an obligation to make it public, even if they don't want to read it.

For example, when I read something that means a lot to me, I don't want to withhold from the reader the chance of reading it himself. Whether it's a poem, an article, or a short story—and sometimes I really think it concerns only a minimum number of readers—it doesn't matter. It's got to be outstanding. Actually I think that it's the other way around: a privilege, a gift to the reader.

When I find that I am changed, cheered up or enriched by something of ours, an article, a story, I think we must give the reader the same opportunity. For this reason, we are sometimes rather eccentric. We publish a lot of pieces that are unusual, sometimes difficult, not easy to read because they are complicated, even obscure. We don't want to be difficult or obscure, but some things are complex. . . . These things are difficult by nature but when pieces are written about them that are really good and have real significance and value, they get into the magazine and then people read them, or don't read them; that's how we work. And that's the only way we can work.

Still, I was worried that I might go for years writing in a vacuum, as it were, and that in the end Mr. Shawn would find either that the articles were not good enough or that he simply couldn't find the space for them. I therefore arranged with him to submit my pieces as I wrote them, so that he could evaluate them one by one. That was not difficult, since in my head each piece was to be self-contained and built around a particular theme, such as music, Hinduism, Islam, or economic development. So it was that, once I had a backlog of India pieces, he was able to stagger the series, publishing two or three pieces a year, with the result that by the time my book was ready he had published nearly a quarter of a million words on India. (Many of my subsequent pieces—a biography of Gandhi, portraits of my father and mother, and my autobiographical narratives—started out as ideas for short pieces, but, as I went through the process of learning, thinking, and writing, I turned them into books.) "Portrait of India," as I called the book, was rejected by both my American and my English publishers, because they found the book too big and too detailed to sell. It was ultimately published successfully by other houses to warm critical acclaim but cool sales. What I found most satisfying about its publication was that it led to my receiving letters from fellow-workers in the vineyard—like this one, from the writer Ruth Jhabvala. (She had gone from England to live in India at about the same time that I had come to America as a boy, and we used to joke that I was the only non-Indian Indian she knew and that she was the only Indian non-Indian I knew.) She wrote about the book:

> I knew that your travels were extensive in scale but had no idea how extensive—in both scale and conception. Then you went back and spent the next few years travelling the same ground again, and my God what effort and strength you've brought to those second, more terrible travels in this terrifying place. I hope it's doing very well but I wonder about that. It's not only that there are not enough people to care about India but even of those few how many are in any way informed enough to realise what sort of a book you've written?

Even around the office, very few people cared enough about the India pieces to read them, either in the magazine or as a book. Mr. Shawn alone seemed to care. He edited every last word of every one of the pieces, reading and rereading them with unflagging zeal.

❧

IN LOOKING BACK on what I came to think of as my relationship with India—travelling there, living with my family, and spending upward of four years writing about my experiences—I long felt that it was inextricably bound up with a romance I became caught up in with a young woman I met there, whom I'll call Lola. She was a Eurasian, born of a German mother and an Indian father, and seemed to me to embody my own split Eastern-Western identity. In some ways, we were both reflections of the India I wanted to write about, which was itself a palimpsest of Hindu and foreign influences. Anyway, whenever I thought of that India in retrospect, I thought of Lola—enticing, mysterious, confused, and, essentially, unreachable. But I'm getting ahead of my story.

I met her soon after I arrived in New Delhi. She turned up, on impulse, at the door of my father's house, because she had heard through a friend of both of us that I was looking for secretarial help. She was so beautiful that she created something of a stir in the house as soon as she walked in. Fair-skinned, with green eyes and long auburn hair, she looked completely European except that she had the generous mouth and the full figure characteristic of Indian women.

I went into the drawing room, where she was waiting for me. She was dressed in a silk sari and sandals, and greeted me, Indian fashion, by folding her hands.

"I understand that you need help," she said, without further preliminaries.

"But I don't know a thing about you," I said. "I don't even know if you can type."

"I wouldn't be here if I couldn't type, would I?" she retorted, rather haughtily.

"I need to feel comfortable with the person I'm working with," I said. I was stalling.

"Do I make you uncomfortable?" she asked, with a little laugh.

"Who's interviewing whom?" I asked, defensively, in return.

"What do you need done?" she asked.

"Don't you want to know how much I pay?" I asked.

"Not really," she said.

She is both selfless and self-possessed, I thought.

"Would you like me to start now or would you prefer that I come back some other time?" she asked.

The idea of her starting before I knew what she could do and before we had settled anything seemed totally unprofessional, and yet the thought that she might just get up and go was disturbing; in fact, I felt as if on some level I were already personally involved with her. I had ordinarily kept my personal life separate from my working life, thinking that if the one invaded the other

I would be distracted and so would be unable to work. In every way, she is the wrong person, I reflected. But what I said to her was "Where did you go to college?" That was one of a set of standard questions I asked when I was interviewing an amanuensis or a reader.

"I didn't go to college," she said matter-of-factly.

My interest in having her work for me immediately flagged. I felt sad, but could think of nothing to do except politely take leave of her.

Just then, though, a servant came in with tea.

"Ah, *chai!*" Lola exclaimed. She spoke English like someone from England, without the singsong accent of an Indian, so hearing *chai* in her voice was something I found charming. In a small way, it made me feel as if I were back in the British raj.

"Do you speak Hindi?" I asked.

"Of course, and Punjabi, too," she said, in perfect Hindi. "Dad was a Punjabi. Can I pour you some tea?"

I nodded.

Over tea, she told me that her father was dead, that she had three older brothers and one older sister, all of whom had settled down, and that her mother, from a small flat on the western side of our colony, carried on what seemed a bit like the life of a merry widow, working as a secretary during the day and gallivanting in the evening. Lola also told me that she herself had lived for some time in Hong Kong, and simply by her way of referring to it she made it sound like the most romantic place on earth.

"What were you doing there?" I asked.

"Secretarial work. But that was a small part of what I did. When I wasn't watching the lights on the harbor, I was sitting in the Peninsula Hotel and watching the pukka British mem-sahibs drink tea. They didn't miss a day, year in and year out, and the tea had to be brought to them just so on the trolley, with a jug of hot water and a pitcher of hot milk, and served with crumpets and scones such as you can never get in India."

"Have you lived in other places?"

"Yes. Australia, England, and Germany."

Her voice, her manner, and her talk gave the impression that she was in her teens, yet what she said made her sound as if she had been in Hong Kong for a long time and had drifted around in many countries. I asked her how old she was.

"Now who's interviewing whom?" she said saucily, but added, "Twenty-five. And you?"

"Thirty-one. But I feel like an eighteen-year-old inside my head."

"So do I," she said, and we both laughed.

"Do you have a full-time job?" I asked her.

"You've lived too long in the West," she said. "You've forgotten that in India girls of good family don't work. But I do. I'm different."

I involuntarily sniffed, and noted that she didn't emanate the powerful scent of coconut hair oil that all my women relatives did, for instance, but had an aura of some scent I couldn't identify.

"Of course you're different," I said, half ironically.

"So are you," she said.

She went on to tell me, with refreshing humor, that girls of good family could work in supposedly glamorous jobs, like some offered at the New Delhi station of All India Radio, and could even keep late hours reading newscasts, putting on skits, or just hanging around the station.

"Do you work there?" I asked.

"I go there as little as I can," she said. "It's a depressing place, very amateurish and bureaucratic, with a lot of very pretty girls thinking they're at the BBC."

I felt we were talking as if we had known each other for a long time. I could talk to her as naturally as I would talk to a close English or American friend, yet we were talking in Hindi or Punjabi. I had never imagined that there could be such a person. Since Gigi and I broke up a few years earlier, I had been somewhat shell-shocked. But Lola seemed to be slowly awakening something in me which I was afraid to acknowledge but which seemed tantalizing.

I asked her why she hadn't gone to college.

"I wish you hadn't asked me that," she said, "because I have to be truthful, and the reason is very embarrassing." She sounded sad, rather than coy.

"I don't need to know," I told her.

She seemed relieved, but then said, "I don't want you to think it was because I couldn't go to college. I had the highest marks in my school, and I got into Miranda House, which here is thought to be the tops."

I wanted to say that I liked the fact that she cared what I thought, but I couldn't say it. I was still confused about whether she would be working for me or we would be friends.

We finished tea, and she stood up to go.

"Would you like to do a little work for me today?" I asked suddenly.

"I had decided that you didn't need me."

"No, I do," I said, and, as much as anything to keep in contact with her, I gave her hundreds of scraps of cheap Indian paper I had been carrying around with the names and addresses of people whom I'd met during my travels through India and whom I might have to get in touch with if I ended up writing about them. The papers, of all shapes and sizes, and written on in a variety of legible and illegible hands, were scrunched up from being carried in my pockets.

"Could you type these onto index cards?" I asked, and then explained, "It's not busy work. Once I leave India, my readers will be hard put to it to make out the names."

She immediately sat down to work at my father's desk.

I left her to her task, and when I came back, after several hours, she was gone, leaving me neat piles of cards on which she had typed out all the names. On her own initiative, she had made a second set of cards, cross-referencing people according to their towns or villages, as if instinctively sensing that when I came to write about them, months or years later, I would look them up according to where I'd met them. She had left no address, not to mention a bill, and I realized that I didn't even know her surname.

After some trouble, I got hold of her through the radio station, and thereafter whenever I returned from one of my trips I gave her my rough notes that I had made along the way, and she organized and typed them.

One day, she said to me, out of the blue, "How is it that you knock about all over this country on your own? People here always go around with a retinue."

"Can you imagine me with a retinue?" I asked. "I gather my best impressions when I am a sort of fly on the wall."

"It must be very hard, though."

There was something in her tone of voice—more concern than sympathy—that made me realize I'd never before done anything so physically difficult. The absence of even the most basic Western amenities, like lavatories, paved roads, and sidewalks, and of any semblance of order or organization, like the consecutive numbering of streets, lanes, houses, or huts (people often used their lucky numbers for their addresses), created frustration at every turn.

"It's manageable," I said, putting the best face on things.

"The places you go sound so alluring," she said, a little dreamily.

"Would you like to come along?" I asked, without thinking—almost as if I were asking her whether she would like some more tea.

"Yes," she said simply.

No sooner had the words come out of my mouth than I began imagining all kinds of obstacles. For an unmarried man and an unmarried woman to travel together was unheard of in India in the mid-sixties. In many places, it was hard enough to get accommodations for one person, so how could I get rooms for two? And how would Lola's mother feel about it? How would my family react? Then I thought I saw a way out. I had heard her mention that she had a boyfriend—something that was unusual in those days among girls from good families, for whom marriages were arranged, but was condoned in her case, because she was only half Indian.

"Your boyfriend would never let you travel with me," I said, and then caught myself, because I seemed to be insinuating that our relationship would go beyond work.

"I always do what I please," she said.

I had been feeling for some time that in four and a half months in India I had been missing a lot. Everything about the country, with its colorful landscape and people, was visual. I had to strain constantly to imagine it, and the problem of describing it so that it would stand up in print seemed insurmountable. It was one thing to describe, for instance, scholars, their habits, their studies, and their houses, as I had done in the past—I could glean such information with the judicious use of my four senses—but quite another to describe a whole country. My friend Dom could write pages about the view of a mountain outside his window. I wanted to measure up to him, but how was I going to do it? The thought that I might have a companion along, with whom I could compare notes—through whose eyes I could, as it were, see—was thrilling. Moreover, I sensed that I would see through her eyes what I would have seen if I could have seen through my own, because I had not met anyone else, with the possible exception of my father, whose way of thinking and feeling seemed so close to mine.

"It will be fun to travel together," I said. My forthcoming trip, which was scheduled to be my last one, would also be the least rigorous. It was to be mainly to big cities, where there were taxis and hotels, but this meant that it would also be the most expensive. How could I justify paying for two, especially since the reams of notes I had collected seemed so chaotic and intractable that I feared I might not be able to shape even one *New Yorker* piece out of them? But I told myself that Lola might make the difference between going back to New York with the promise of a piece and going back with nothing.

We started talking about what part of the Indian picture still needed to be filled out, and planning where we would go and whom we would try to see.

"I thought you said it was going to be all fun," Lola said abruptly.

"Did I say that?" I asked. "I'm sure we'll have fun, but it has to be a working trip."

When I told my father about Lola, not only was he relieved that I would have someone with me when I was travelling but he immediately started talking about her as a life companion for me.

❦

AT THE AIRPORT in New Delhi, Lola's boyfriend came to see her off. My heart sank, though I told myself that his doing so was completely appropriate. After all, she was coming along only as my secretary-*cum*-assistant.

Lola and her boyfriend exchanged a long kiss—something so out of the ordinary in India, where all public kissing was banned, even in films, that my parents, who had come with me to the airport, looked away. But they understood that, as a Eurasian, she was free to observe European customs, and they greeted her warmly.

The flight was called, and my parents left, but then the weather suddenly turned bad, and the flight was repeatedly delayed. When we were finally up in the air, we bounced around as if we were being carried along on a kite. The way the plane rattled and shook suggested that it was poorly maintained.

"We're going to die," Lola moaned.

In all the time I'd known her, I had never so much as shaken her hand—we always greeted each other from a distance, Indian fashion—but now, disregarding convention, she grabbed my hand, and clutched it so tightly that I myself began to be frightened.

"No one is going to die," I said weakly.

"I didn't tell you," she said, "but I'm very afraid of flying. It's almost the only thing I'm superstitious about."

We were to fly to Nagpur, in central India, and then drive to Bhilai, a new steel town, with a steel plant that had been built with the help of the Soviet Union. In fact, there was a whole colony of Russian advisers and engineers there, and I had thought that the building of a steel plant with foreign collaboration would make an interesting story about Indian industrial development. But, because of the weather, we were stranded for the night in Bhopal, the desolate capital of Madhya Pradesh. There seemed to be no accommodations available. When I was on my own, I had often spent nights at the airport, dozing off on a chair or a bench, regardless of the hubbub around me, but now I had to worry about Lola, and I wondered aloud what we should do.

"We can just camp out here at the airport," Lola said. "It's very romantic."

She's a girl after my own heart, I thought.

At that moment, we were directed to an official who was able to locate a room for us in a tourist bungalow.

"We accept," I said, thinking that Lola could take the room and I could perhaps have a charpoy set up on the veranda. But when we got to the bungalow the night watchman clearly assumed that since we were travelling together we were husband and wife, and he put our luggage in the room. I expected Lola to say something, but she started unpacking both my things and hers, as if she thought that that was part of the arrangement. I recalled that I had never mentioned to her that I had planned to take two separate rooms.

That night, I cautiously reached out for her, and she responded without hesitation. My happiness knew no bounds.

❦

LATER, WE ASKED each other what we had imagined it would be like to travel together. She said that she had never given it a thought, that she simply loved travelling and was excited by the idea of helping me, that typing my notes about my going hither and yon had made her feel she knew me and liked me, and that anyway she took life as it came. For my part, I had never allowed myself to think that anything would happen between us. I had merely wanted to be worthy of her trust. Yet, once she yielded, I felt that it was meant to be, and I was suffused with confidence. A moment before, I had assumed that I was much less desirable than her boyfriend, because he could see, but now I felt cockily sure that I was superior to him, because of my intelligence. I went from thinking I was nothing to thinking I was everything.

Temperamentally, I was not much given to flights of fancy. From a very early age, I had always had to deal with harsh reality, and hadn't allowed myself to want things I couldn't have. Lola's life seemed to have been the opposite of mine, and to have made her a free spirit. I was a little frightened by her, even as I started evaluating her as a prospective wife. To imagine myself as a blind person getting married was scarcely more possible for me than to imagine myself as a centaur. Still, most of my daydreams had long been about an ideal wife, and Lola seemed to have come out of them. She was just the right height—about three inches shorter than I was. Her father belonged to the same caste that we did, and came from our Punjabi community. She and I even had the same birthday. She would fit into my family perfectly, and, at the same time, she would adapt easily to my life in the West.

Without my asking her, Lola had brought along a shorthand book and a pencil, and in Bhilai the next day, as we walked around the town and the steel plant, she unobtrusively took notes, as if doing so were second nature to her. I continued to make my own mental notes, since I had no idea what she was picking out and writing down—whether what she found interesting corresponded to what I found interesting. I just took pleasure in having her at my side. Her hand reached down just to mine, so we could walk together with our hands barely touching. I noticed a perceptible change in people's attitudes toward me when I was with her, as if I were someone to be envied rather than pitied or patronized.

That evening, when I was about to tape-record my impressions of the day, as was my custom, Lola started reading me her notes. The writing was rough and telegraphic, but her perceptions were so rich and full that I was staggered. Until then, I'd had no idea of what I was missing by not seeing things. She had an amazing eye. She picked up just the right details, and in a few words she could describe a person's face or gesture in a way that made the person jump off the page. One note read, "Interviewed Zathenko through an interpreter, a Russian girl called Lena. Lena was wearing a plaid skirt and scarlet cotton knit top. Her hair had been dyed with henna and some bits were redder than others. Very pleasant girl who said she was a Persian scholar. Zathenko wore a dark green bush shirt, a very neat man, with clear-cut features, white white hair, perhaps a hard face but for twinkling blue eyes." I felt that as long as she was with me I need never again strain to get visual information. I felt lightheaded. Thereafter, I relied on her to do all the note-taking, and when it came time to type the notes we would exchange impressions, elaborating on this scene or that, and prompting each other. I started feeling that I would finally have a piece, maybe a series, and possibly a book that Mr. Shawn would be proud of. The work was no longer drudgery.

As Lola and I spent more time together, my only reservation about her—that she had not gone to college—melted away. I found her to be not only naturally intelligent but also, perhaps because she was self-educated, more intellectual than many university women I had known in America and in England.

Lola and I travelled together near the end of my stay in India. We were together only for five weeks out of my six months there—from late April to early June of 1966—but those weeks gave me a totally new perspective on how I might write about the country. We went first to the east, then to the south, then up to the north, and on to the west, and the names of the places we visited—Calcutta, Madras, Mahabalipuram, Trivandrum, Quilon, Kottayam, Brnakulam, Bangalore, Mysore, Hyderabad, Nagarjunasagar, Bombay, Panjim, Margac, Mermugao, Vasco, Kengaryal—became a romantic incantation in my head.

In later years, people often asked me how I managed to write so visually about India, but there was no easy way to explain the frustration of months of solitary exertion and then the gift of Lola, and what I had learned by concentrating on her notes—how, for instance, capturing a character on the page was a little like pinning a butterfly—so that long after she became a memory she had continued to influence my writing.

❧

UNBEKNOWNST TO ME, in India, as soon as my theology articles were published in *The New Yorker*, and the theologians I wrote about had read them and had learned that they were being collected in a book, they started writing one after another to Cass Canfield, the president of Harper & Row, which had become my publisher (sadly, Ted Weeks and I had parted ways), to protest against how they were portrayed and to demand extensive revision of the text.

From the outset, I had taken extra precautions with the theologian series. I knew I was writing not only about public men, who, like the historians and the philosophers, were regularly on television and radio and in the newspapers, but also about people who, by virtue of their religious study and their faith, held high ecclesiastical offices, like the Archbishopric of Canterbury and the Bishoprics of Southwark and Woolwich, or were chaplains at ancient seats of learning, like Cambridge. They had often spoken to me in a collegial atmosphere, over sherry or lunch, treating me as a fellow-pilgrim in search of truth, and had made statements like "No intelligent man today can believe in miracles" and "The idea of resurrection is clearly nonsense in our scientific age" and "We have to try Christian beliefs on our pulses and, if they don't suit, discard them"— things they would obviously never have said from the pulpit. I was fully aware that when they read their words in cold print they might have second thoughts, or even try to retract some of the things they had said to me, and that I would have no way of proving the authenticity of my record. Braille did not lend itself to taking notes, and I did not carry a tape recorder, because I thought that doing so would be intrusive and would detract from the spontaneity of my interviews. Instead, I relied on my memory, underlining in my mind the remarks I wanted to remember and set down. The checker and I had checked and rechecked the facts in the series, and Greenstein was satisfied that it was legally in the clear. Still, in most instances, because of the sensitivity of the subject, I went to the length of submitting proofs of my interviews to those I had interviewed and modifying my text in line with their comments—a departure from the general policy of the magazine, which was to avoid passing editorial control to the subjects, because most people liked to read only flattering copy about themselves. Nevertheless, after the *New Yorker* publication the theologians contended that they were seeing the full text for the first time, and that anyway magazine articles were fugitive but a book was a permanent record. They said they would not allow the book to be published as it was, and the principal method they chose for forcing revisions was to deny me permission to quote passages from their books unless I incorporated all the new changes they were making in the record of the interviews. This seemed preposterous, since the legal doctrine of fair usage allowed anyone to quote printed passages as long as they were brief and were part of an argument, and my quotations met both those conditions.

During several months in India, I knew nothing about these protests, in part because the storm was slow in gathering—some of the theologians objected only after they heard that others were objecting—and in part because Cass Canfield and Mr. Shawn didn't want to disturb me in India until they had a consolidated report of all the objections. When I saw that report, late in April, just as I was setting off on my travels with Lola, I was as stunned as I was baffled. The book had long been in page proofs, and I took the view, which was shared by Mr. Shawn and Greenstein, that I was under no obligation to accommodate the theologians' second thoughts. But Canfield took the view that Harper & Row might be exposed to legal action in Britain, where libel laws were more stringent. Moreover, it turned out that Harper & Row was the American publisher of almost all the theologians, and that their books were so commercially successful that Canfield didn't want to offend them.

For my part, while I sympathized with Canfield's dilemma, I didn't want to compromise the integrity of my account. To Mr. Shawn, who had agreed that in my absence he would handle everything about the book, from various stages of proofs to the jacket copy, I sent this cable: "IF THERE IS ANY DANGER THAT REVISIONS WILL EMASCULATE THE BOOK THEN I AM PREPARED TO FORGO ITS PUBLICATION AND RETURN HARPERS ADVANCE AND INDEMNIFY THEM FOR PRINTING COSTS ET CETERA STOP MY BEST IS

IN THE ARTICLE THE NEW THEOLOGIAN AND AS ALWAYS I WAS INTER-
ESTED ONLY THAT YOU SHOULD LIKE IT AND THAT IT SHOULD BE
PRINTED IN THE MAGAZINE STOP REST WAS AND IS ICING ON THE CAKE
STOP I AM PAINED AND EMBARRASSED ABOUT THE TROUBLE I HAVE
CAUSED YOU AND CANFIELD STOP"

Mr. Shawn cabled back that he thought I should return from
India, because, although he didn't believe that the problem could
be serious, it would help for me to be on the spot. His cable put
me in a great quandary, which had to do with Lola. I wanted to
stay in India six months longer and gather more material for the
book by travelling with her, and also come to know her better
and possibly get married. During our travels, we would talk
vaguely about getting married, but I never actually proposed to
her in so many words. Still, I had fallen completely in love with
her, and couldn't imagine being without her.

Appeals to officials in the American Embassy to let Lola
go with me to America, even if just as a tourist, fell on deaf
ears, however. Her application to go abroad, even if only as far
as England, was blocked, for at the time England was going
through one of its waves of anti-Asian sentiment. Having once
allowed all Commonwealth citizens to come and settle in
England, its government was now keeping out even legitimate
Asian visitors, for fear that once they came they would never
leave and so would swell the numbers of its "colored" popula-
tion. Consequently, I was confronted with a stark choice: either
to return to America and try to rescue my fourth book or to
stay back with Lola for however many months it would take for
her to get an American visa to accompany me. On top of that,
her passport had expired, and in India getting a new one was no
easy matter. As it turned out, bureaucratic and legal delays
wreaked havoc with our hopes for perhaps making a life in
America.

ON MY WAY back to New York, I stopped over in Germany and in England to talk to some of the protesting theologians and was relieved to find that I could take care of most of their objections without much difficulty. Canfield, however, continued to worry that they might make trouble after the book was published, and he and his law firm, Greenbaum, Wolff & Ernst, would not allow me to quote more than five hundred words from a book by any theologian without the author's legal release. They were so insistent on this point that in the case of one theologian—A. H. Williams, Fellow and Dean of Trinity College, Cambridge—they made me paraphrase an excerpt from his book "Objections to Christian Belief" because the word count was five hundred and one. All this required a certain amount of rewriting, and the rewriting itself involved more time and more correspondence. In addition to landing Harper & Row with a legal bill of three thousand dollars, the revisions delayed the publication of the book by six months, with the result that the book never did as well as it might have done.

In the midst of all this, I was having a hard struggle to get the projected India series off the ground. For one thing, I was surfeited with six months of notes I'd made and with endless books, leaflets, and newspaper cuttings I'd gathered up during my travels, so every time I thought I was getting a handle on the material it slipped away. For another thing, I didn't have the slightest idea what form the writing should take. I started out recording my impressions in a sort of journal form, but the writing became episodic, devoid of any sense of architecture. Mr. Shawn and I spent some time talking about it over lunch and came up with the idea of using the journal form but combining it with narrative, and organizing each piece around an implicit theme. That would give me the greatest freedom to write about India's history, geography, religion, and people.

I finally learned that Lola was coming to New York, after all. More than four months had passed since we parted, and I knew from her letters that—impulsive, as always—she had become involved, in the interval, with someone else and now felt torn between him and me. I wanted to sweep the whole business under the carpet, but I wasn't prepared for the profound change in the way she acted around me when I went to receive her at the airport.

"I hope you're up to a party," I said casually, pretending that nothing had changed.

"Whatever you say," she said. I took her compliance as a willingness to adapt herself to anything that came along.

I brought her up to the apartment, she changed quickly, and I hurried her along to the party, plunging her into a crowd of strangers. It was the continuation of my pretense that we were picking up where we'd left off. Neither one of us was much given to talking or analyzing. She took life as it came; I was so mesmerized by being with her again that I was afraid of making a misstep. That night, we resumed our affair, as if there had been no interruption.

The next day, she got ready to come to the office. I suddenly realized that she was thinking we would be working together, as we had done in India. But her talent for quick, spontaneous impressions and her secretarial skills, though they were valuable in the field, were of little use in the office, where my work now involved literary and historical skills—sifting through innumerable facts, consulting hefty tomes in the library, and editing and revising dozens of drafts. I recalled that in all the time we were in India she had never had the patience to read an entire newspaper story to me. By temperament, she was restless, not suited for intense intellectual work. But she knew no one in New York and had nothing to do during the day, so I took her along to the office. I escorted her upstairs and introduced her to Mr. Shawn, and it was evident that he found her magical. He immediately grasped that there was no room for her in my office, for I was then working with both an amanuensis and a typist in my little cubicle, and he arranged for me to borrow the empty office of a colleague. There I put her to work organizing some letter files. It was soon clear that she missed being part of the book, even though she was the first to acknowledge that she was not equipped for the kind of work that preparing it required.

Lola finished up the filing job within a few days, but she didn't then sit around in the apartment. Since she didn't have working papers, the only place she could get a job was in an international organization. She went across town to the U.N., took a test, and did so well that she got a good secretarial job right away.

Our life settled down on what I felt was an even keel. We both had our work, my friends took to her, and she seemed content, so I didn't give as much thought to her feelings as I should have.

In later years, I lacerated myself for not taking a break from my writing to concentrate on her—spend more time with her, show her around, and, above all, get her started on college courses. She had helped me, and I should now have helped her take advantage of the opportunities that the new country offered her. But through long years of hard work I had had the illusion that if my writing was going well the details of my life didn't matter, and Lola became, in a sense, merely a detail. After a few months in New York, she left me for the other man.

Three years later, when the series was finally finished and was being turned into a book, I got in touch with her again. She was married to the other man, had a daughter, and was living in a middle-class suburb of London.

"Can I dedicate my book to you?" I asked on the telephone.

"Why, sweetheart?" she asked, as if no time had passed.

"I always wrote it with you in mind, wondering what you would think when you read it. In a funny way, it's about you."

"But I travelled with you only for a month," she said, adding that she thought her husband would be seriously upset if he were to see her name in my book. "He's very jealous, you know," she explained. "He doesn't let me have any book of yours in the house."

Despite her protestations, I felt that I had some claim on the memory of the life that we had had together, brief and turbulent though it was, and so I did eventually dedicate the book to her, by using just her initials. That way, I reasoned, only she and I would really be certain whom the book was meant for. With some trepidation, I sent her a copy of the book, with a note of explanation, and was relieved at this response: "The book discovered an unexpected streak of egotism—I found myself rather pleased at having my initials in such grand print. Thank you. I'm deeply touched."

In later years, whenever I picked up the book I thought of her, but I was never able to explain to myself satisfactorily what there was about India and about her that invariably stirred me. What was there about them that held me in their grip? I was scarred by my love for her even as I had been by the experience of having passed my childhood in India. But my passion for both her and India was undiminished. She was therefore a station on a longer journey—a journey of which the travels in India, with and without her, had been only a small part.

IX

UNDER A TOLERANT ROOF

MY EXPERIENCE IS THAT AN INSTITUTION IS ONLY AS good as its head. Many of us arrived at the magazine intolerant, but under Mr. Shawn's influence we didn't stay that way for very long. Indeed, Ebba Jonsson, the magazine's longtime, nonpareil librarian, used to say, "I can't imagine a place where nicer people could be gathered under one roof." Nevertheless, I doubt if any us were able to live up to Mr. Shawn's generosity of spirit. It seemed that the often most impossible but always most talented characters were drawn into his ken and, before any of us knew it, were testing his charity, in the original sense of the word. They were not necessarily our most illustrious colleagues, but his patience in coping with them not only added to the nurturing atmosphere of the place but also revealed some of the deepest instincts of his being. We often wondered among ourselves where and how he had developed those instincts. One mentor was surely Harold Ross. Thomas Kunkel, in his thorough, thoughtful, and lively book "Genius in Disguise: Harold Ross of *The New Yorker,*" writes:

> Talent, [Ross] understood, was the key. He never stopped searching for it or, once he had found it, nurturing it. . . . Ross had a respect for creative people that bordered on veneration; everyone else, himself included, was meant to be in their service. Needless to say, this was an attitude that writers and artists didn't come across every day. . . .
>
> Add to this Ross's intrinsic understanding that writers and artists are different from other people and must be treated—tolerated, he would more likely harrumph—as such. He believed that the same unique vantage point that made creative people insightful could also render them vulnerable, impractical, and maddeningly unreliable.

Ross himself has often been portrayed in books by memoirists who knew him as so vulnerable and impractical that he was incapable of even tying his shoes, as if *The New Yorker* had been started and published not because of him but in spite of him. Joe Mitchell used to say, "Often Ross is depicted as, you know, kind of a rube. But that was a pose, I do believe, like those characters in Mark Twain who don't know anything and then get in the poker game and walk off with all the money." Kunkel is too young to have ever met Ross, but, perhaps as a result, the Ross that emerges from his book is a fuller and more complete person—an impractical rube and a visionary but also a civilized, savvy, and determined sponsor of the writers and artists he understood and admired.

Both Ross and Mr. Shawn took in their stride the peccadilloes, the misadventures, and the nervous breakdowns of the writers and artists under *The New Yorker's* roof. They even saw to it that the debts of the writers and artists did not become altogether overwhelming. As a rule, a writer or an artist who came to be in a financial scrape was likely to turn to either Ross or Mr. Shawn. But, since *The New Yorker* was a business, however unconventional, and therefore the editorial department was accountable, in the last analysis, to the publisher and the share-holders, neither man was always in a position to help writers and artists financially every time he would have liked to. Indeed, I remember reading that Edmund Wilson didn't file an income-tax return or pay any taxes from 1946 to 1955—because, he said, he didn't realize the seriousness of the omission. When, in 1955, in his sixtieth year, he was hit with a big bill for back taxes, plus ten years of compounded interest as penalty, he was so outraged that he wrote a whole book about the iniquity of the American income-tax system in squandering most of the taxpayers' money on defense and the Cold War. To raise the money to pay his back taxes, Wilson sold his papers to the Beinecke Library, at Yale. Still, that didn't bring in enough, and he tried to get Mr. Shawn to publish part of his book. But Mr. Shawn passed on it, because it read like a ratio-nalization of a silly mistake. Wilson wasn't happy, but there was little that Mr. Shawn could do about it. (The book, entitled "The Cold War and the Income Tax" and published by Farrar, Straus & Giroux, eventually came out in 1964.)

Still, there were numerous occasions when Ross or Mr. Shawn did help out, but, in general, matters like who fell behind with taxes and alimony payments, how they were taken care of, and who was forgiven how much were never discussed around the office. The last thing that Ross or Mr. Shawn wanted to do was to encourage contributors to take a cue from wayward colleagues. Yet if people could not sell enough pieces to *The New Yorker* to make ends meet they were not forced to leave. Many of them stayed around, supplementing whatever they could get from *The New Yorker* with advances from publishers, with sales of articles to other magazines, with the income of a spouse, or, in rare instances, with the cushion of family money. Those who lived almost exclusively on their writing for *The New Yorker* were grateful for the drawing account. Even so, some of them could never get used to the system, and would have preferred to get a regular salary, which went up with seniority, as was the standard arrangement at a newspaper or at any other conventional organization. Joe Mitchell, one of the most deeply revered *New Yorker* writers, told me once that he was so terrified of the drawing account that he would never have left his job at the *World-Telegram*—as he did, in 1938—in order to come to *The New Yorker* if Ross had not made an exception in his case and offered him a steady salary. In fact, money was never far from the minds of any of the writers and artists, no matter how well the magazine paid them. Geoffrey Hellman, one colleague of mine who was well heeled even before he came to the magazine, in 1929, and who wrote for it until he died, in 1977, at the age of seventy, was always complaining about not being paid enough for his pieces. One day in 1936, he confronted Raoul Fleischmann, the founding publisher, on that subject. Fleischmann made a rude remark in reply, and Geoffrey immediately jumped ship to Henry Luce's new magazine, *Life,* for a considerable increase in remuneration. But *Life* was no place for a subtle, urbane writer like Geoffrey, and within two years he was back at *The New Yorker.* He found his office exactly as he had left it, with his mail piled up, as if Ross had always expected him to return.

Then, there was the example of a younger colleague, Hendrik (Rick) Hertzberg. He was a Talk reporter, and in 1976 he told me that one of the reasons he was leaving was that if he stayed around the magazine he would never be able to earn enough to let him get married and have a family. At the time, I thought he was exaggerating, but in subsequent years I came to appreciate his view. I sold more pieces than many other *New Yorker* writers did, but always felt economically pressed. Even though I realized that such insecurity is a writer's lot, it took its toll. Like Rick, I sometimes thought that I would never be able to support a family, indeed, that I would never have enough money to pay rent and readers, and that I had brought off my latest piece by some stroke of luck, which would never be repeated. During most of my years at *The New Yorker,* my drawing account was eight hundred dollars a month, which was not enough to meet my basic expenses, so I was continually sending up a stream of notes to Mr. Shawn asking for advances. I don't remember his ever failing to respond to them, but I would usually have to submit part of a manuscript to get him to O.K. some kind of advance. Except once, when I referred to my financial problems in an interview I gave to the *Times* on the occasion of my receiving a MacArthur prize fellowship, in 1982, he never lost his patience with me. This was astonishing, considering that I was one of hundreds of writers in his care, and not only was I just doing my own writing, for the most part, rather than helping him to get out the magazine from week to week—the way people who, for instance, regularly wrote Comment and Talk stories and critical columns did—but I was also writing pieces of such enormous length on such out-of-the-way subjects that he was always hard-pressed to justify publishing them in the magazine. When a manuscript was in its initial stages, he never wanted to choke the flow by mentioning (to me or to any other writer) any constraints, such as length or complexity. For instance, he would O.K. a short piece about a part of my life and then be confronted with a whole book. But as publication neared he would study the piece repeatedly to see if it could be reduced in length with no sacrifice of its integrity. In any case, he had a problem with processing a final payment until such time as he knew how long a piece would be. That was true of most of the seventeen books of mine that first appeared as articles in *The New Yorker* under his editorship. As it turned out, over the years I made a better living at *The New Yorker* than most writers and journalists I knew made elsewhere, and I always lived comfortably. This makes me wonder how much reality there ever was in my fear of not having enough money.

The office, despite harboring a great many vulnerable creative people, was in some respects a happy place. No piece of writing or work of art was published for any reason other than that Mr. Shawn thought it to be good, and in such matters he was impervious to flattery or personal appeal. The place was remarkably free of office politics; indeed, there was no one there who was not touched in one way or another by the gentle and civilizing person of the editor. But in other respects the place encompassed a lot of inner turmoil. After all, how could turmoil be avoided among a collection of self-centred writers and artists who were there only because they had sold something to Ross or Mr. Shawn and had then been tapped to become members of the staff on Forty-third Street?

The place was such a cauldron of neurosis and frustration that even when people agitated for change they didn't like it when it came. I remember that in 1964, when the magazine changed printers—moving from our old faithful Condé Nast printing plant, in Greenwich, Connecticut, to a new, up-to-date R. R. Donnelley printing plant, in Chicago—everyone fretted because the yellow paper we had always written our manuscripts on was replaced by heavy white paper, and our soft pencils were replaced by hard pencils, because, for some reason, such paper and such pencils were better suited to the electronic age. E. B. White ironically noted, in a Comment piece on the change, "We have just discovered, to our great satisfaction, that this new heavy white paper gives everything we write, irrespective of merit, an appearance of natural grandeur, which in the past we arrived at only by straining." The doubters, however, were somewhat reassured that literary standards, at least, would be maintained when they saw that the first Donnelley issue, dated May 9, 1964, contained the first of two parts of a novel by Vladimir Nabokov. The whole story had to do with chess and a chess player, but some of the writers thought that Nabokov was in fact using those subjects as metaphors for writing and writers, and that perhaps it was actually about our emotionally wrought situation at *The New Yorker*. I know that it seems ludicrous for anyone to have believed that Nabokov had *The New Yorker* in mind when he was writing his novel, especially since the book was actually published first in Russian in 1930. Yet when I once wrote a Comment piece attacking Prime Minister Indira Gandhi's policies one staff writer came into my office and said he was sure that I was attacking him for one of the short book notes he had written for the magazine. (He later spent some time in a psychiatric hospital.)

Even for ancillary positions, the magazine drew people who sometimes seemed to become more frustrated the longer they stayed. Yet, paradoxically, most of them wouldn't have dreamed of leaving. Many of them would have preferred to write or draw, and some of them were by no means devoid of talent, but instead they got stuck in jobs like typing manuscripts or collating proofs. Their lack of success did not prevent some of them from having exalted views of their own talent in comparison with that of some writers or artists whose works were chosen for publication. They loathed working on the writing of certain run-of-the-mill authors, disparaging the pieces as "dirty laundry," and maintaining that such pieces would never have seen the light of day if it were not for their own washing and ironing. In fact, even some of the better writers around the office didn't think that certain pieces of journeyman writing deserved to be published. I once asked Mr. Shawn delicately why he included one such piece in the magazine at all. He avoided giving me a direct answer but implied that it was published for its information value: that the magazine needed to be balanced with ordinary journalistic fare, and that it would be a pitfall to fill *The New Yorker* entirely with difficult writing—to make it a sort of literary spree.

Every year, it seemed, Mr. Shawn was inviting new writers onto the magazine. Although a few times he brought writers from other magazines, or recruited people from *The New Yorker's* newsbreak department or messenger room, or took on spouses or grown children of staff members, many of the new arrivals were recent college graduates, for he preferred to bring people onto the magazine while they were still in their twenties, so that they could develop into writers familiar with its values. I remember that there arrived in 1961, the year I came onto the magazine, Jane Boutwell, Gerald Jonas, and Susan Lardner; in 1962, Renata Adler; in 1963, Jane Kramer, Tony Hiss, Jeremy Bernstein, and Calvin Trillin; in 1965, John McPhee and Fred Shapiro; in 1966, Susan Sheehan, Michael J. Arlen, William Whitworth, and George Trow; in 1968, Jonathan Schell and Ellen Willis; in 1969, Rick Hertzberg and Kennedy Fraser; and, in later years, Victor Chen, Ian Frazier, Suzannah Lessard, Jamaica Kincaid, Bill McKibben, Bill Barich, and Jim Lardner. Other writers, among them Tom Meehan, Paul Brodeur, Henry Cooper, and Donald Malcolm (he died at the early age of forty-three, in 1975), were more or less of my vintage, had come along a few years before me. The situation was a little like having a new class entering college each year. New blood was all very well, but, in contrast to what happens in college, the old blood stayed around, with the result that it became harder and harder for anyone to get pieces into the magazine. The new arrivals were enthusiastic, eager, and full of talk and questions, making us feel at once young, in the sense that we had to reëxamine what we had started taking for granted, and old, in the sense that we had already lived through similar beginnings. All the newcomers—and the sixties newcomers in particular—had their own interests, passions, and insecurities, of course, and those added to the general angst of the place. At first, we who had already arrived couldn't understand why Mr. Shawn had chosen them—so many of them seemed callow and unsophisticated—but after their pieces began appearing we thought that, despite certain differences, we and they had a lot in common. Like us, they didn't quite fit into the world outside, and therefore observed it and wrote about it with a certain detachment and irony. It was as if we were all members of an extended family in one of Salinger's stories—troubled and eccentric, following our own strange paths.

❧

ON THE EIGHTEENTH floor, whenever we took a break we gravitated to the only open space, near the watercooler, which was just outside my door. That space, a widening of the hall, served as the landing for the staircase between the eighteenth and the nineteenth floors. Shelves next to the watercooler haphazardly held current newspapers and magazines, along with a copy of Webster's unabridged dictionary. Above the shelves was an electric wall clock, and nearby were a dingy wood-backed sofa and some chairs. Against another wall were a couple of glass-fronted bookcases holding a miscellany of books and called, for some reason, the Writers' Library. Around the corner, near the fire stairs, was our bulletin board. People would stop at the watercooler to read the newspapers or flip through the magazines, they would pass through the hall on their way to and from the nineteenth floor, or they would just hang around waiting to talk. During the day, most of us would have more than one drink of water in a flimsy paper cup from the watercooler. The area was the closest thing to a collective space we had. In fact, it was our little version of an Athenian agora, and at any time of the day one could hear vigorous debates about the merits of this or that *New Yorker* piece (or a piece from another magazine or a newspaper). Some of the watercooler criticism could be discounted as jealousy, because, for every piece that got into *The New Yorker*, a dozen pieces were either held over—sometimes indefinitely—or rejected. Young Talk reporters were especially eaten up with jealousy, because Mr. Shawn, despite his best intentions, could never find enough time to explain to them why he had published other Talk stories instead of theirs. Moreover, Mr. Shawn, in contrast to most writers, who liked only the kind of writing they themselves did, had eclectic tastes, and in practically every issue there would be a piece that raised the hackles of one group or another.

The grumbling on the eighteenth floor was generally kept in check—such was the esteem in which even the grumblers held Mr. Shawn—but once it did get out of hand, when, in August, 1966, a Comment proof went up on the eighteenth-floor bulletin board. An ironic rumination on modern man, who was said to have lost his spiritual way in his preference for information over knowledge, the Comment was written by an imaginary theologian named Alotrios and had been sparked by a casual remark of John Lennon's in the press that the Beatles were more popular than Jesus. Comment pieces, of course, were published anonymously, but everyone knew the identity of the writers—in this case, Niccolo Tucci—because, despite Mr. Shawn's wishes, a tradition had grown up of posting Talk proofs, along with the names of the authors, on the bulletin board just before the issues containing those pieces went to press. (The names were easily obtained from the makeup or checking department.) Some writers gathered around the watercooler and expressed outrage at Tucci. They felt that his writing style was convoluted, his point of view reactionary, and the persona of Alotrios a heavy-handed device. As they saw it, a Luddite had been allowed to use the *New Yorker's* Comment slot as a soapbox. It was perfectly understandable that Tucci, as a European Catholic, might hold such views, they declared, but he should not have been allowed to attribute them to *The New Yorker* in the Comment voice. The protesting writers wanted the Comment to be pulled. But they didn't know how to go about it. We later learned that Mr. Shawn, whose antennae seemed to pick up everything, instantly detected the discontent. But he said nothing and did nothing.

In September, a second Alotrios Comment by Tucci went up. If anything, the protest was shriller than the first. Again, it registered with Mr. Shawn, and again he decided not to take any notice of it. And then, in October, a third Alotrios Comment by

Tucci was posted. This time, Alotrios delivered a diatribe on the mechanization of culture, prompted by the American government's decision to build a supersonic jet. Part of the Comment read:

"A bicycle will not improve your thinking," my father said to me when I was thirteen. "Your ignorance of Latin syntax will be the same out in the country, at the beach, or in the city as it is here," he told me, "so you'd better stay here and change your inner world, and then introduce the outside world to a new man." This was ridiculously true in the case of a thirteen-year-old boy who wanted a bicycle, but it is tragically true in the case of the grown men who want the supersonic jet, because grown men are infinitely more virulent in their ignorance of what it takes to live in a civilized world than thirteen-year-old boys are, and when grown men use grown material means to travel faster than sound in metal monsters, they can turn into barbarians who leave Attila, on his horse or in his chariot, far behind.

These words touched off what was almost a full-scale rebellion, and Mr. Shawn came down to the watercooler. This is the only time I can remember a general confrontation with him. He patiently heard everybody out but would not be drawn into an argument or a defense of his decision. Yet his mere act of listening, without contradicting anybody, had a most extraordinary effect on those assembled. As they listened to their objections with, as it were, his ears, most of them seemed to realize that their reaction was more emotional than reasoned, and the tide of opinion turned, going out to sea as swiftly as it had come in. There were a couple of holdouts, however, and to them Mr. Shawn simply said that he didn't think a magazine could be edited by a committee, any more than a symphony could be conducted by more than one conductor. Then he walked back upstairs and went ahead and printed the third Comment, which also turned out to be the last.

Years later, I heard several of the writers who had initially been the most outspoken against Alotrios refer to the three Comment pieces as some of the best diagnoses of what was wrong with modern society and culture.

❧

NOT ALL WRITERS subscribed to the general view that Mr. Shawn had created ideal conditions for writing and drawing. Under the pressureless pressures of being left alone to do whatever they liked, and meet no demands of any kind, people fell apart: they had nervous breakdowns, or developed writer's block, which sometimes lasted for years. (Joe Mitchell didn't publish anything new from 1964 on. Indeed, toward the end of his life the corpus of his writing was so small that it was bound up in one volume, entitled "Up at the Old Hotel," and was published in 1992. He died in 1996.) But there wasn't any particular anathema attached to such vicissitudes. Some people who might have blossomed as writers in the fast-paced environment of a newsroom became intellectually and emotionally paralyzed at *The New Yorker*. One writer told me that Mr. Shawn's benevolence made him feel that he was being smothered with pillows of kindness. He left. Others complained about the individual cubicles, which they felt sealed them off from their colleagues. "It's sheer torture to come in in the morning and sit in front of the typewriter all day in a room little bigger than a telephone booth," I was told by one of them. "In fact," he went on, "the only human contact I have is with the telephone operators, Marie or Anne, when I pick up the phone to call somebody." Sometimes, late in the evening, when I was getting ready to go home, I would smell pungent, smoky fumes in the hall and hear rock music coming out of the office of one of the young writers, Tony Hiss. In time, Tony found the most unexpected person to hang out with—the elderly *New Yorker* editor and writer Rogers E. M. Whitaker. A large, gruff man, he wrote from time to time about football, supper clubs, and jazz, and with him Tony shared an enthusiasm for trains. (Whitaker, who collected railway timetables and could tell you when any particular train left or arrived anywhere in the world at any time during the twentieth century, rode trains as a hobby. At one point, late in his life, it was calculated that he had ridden a total of 2,748,636.81 miles across six continents in six decades.)

Plenty of my colleagues, young and old, were restive, and were often angry at Mr. Shawn and at the world because their promise remained unfulfilled, or because they had made one or two big splashes and had then been forgotten everywhere except at *The New Yorker*—because their lives hadn't turned out the way they wished. Some older writers had grown up with Ross's magazine and wanted *The New Yorker* to be trenchant and funny, which was how they remembered it. They complained about Mr. Shawn's publishing long pieces on out-of-the-way subjects and on serious or abstruse social and political issues. The only long pieces they liked were the ones they had written themselves, and they were always declaring that this or that writer was deadwood, forgetting that they themselves were considered deadwood by someone else. I recall Geoffrey Hellman repeatedly railing against Mr. Shawn and his choice of pieces about the poor and the underclass. In contrast, admirers of Mr. Shawn who had not grown up with Ross said that Ross's magazine published pieces about blacks only if they were entertainers or sports figures, and embraced simplistic, apolitical causes, and then only if one came along, such as moving an information kiosk in Pennsylvania Station or banning the broadcasting of music in Grand Central Terminal. They said that in Ross's *New Yorker* such subjects as Zionism, homosexuality, and cancer had been taboo, and that promiscuity could be written about only with extreme tact. This was, of course, a caricature, which overlooked, among other things, the fact that Ross's *New Yorker* belonged to a different age, and that, anyway, as it grew and developed it distinguished itself by publishing letters from *New Yorker* writers in all corners of the world and also some of the nation's most memorable war reporting. In any event, I don't remember Mr. Shawn's *New Yorker* publishing anything about Zionism, homosexuality, or cancer.

No doubt the opinions expressed on both Ross and Mr. Shawn bordered on caricature. As far as I could tell, Mr. Shawn's magazine was evolving from week to week, in response to the interests and obsessions of its writers and artists and to the pressures and concerns of the day, while trying to maintain its original character, which was conceived and elaborated by Ross. I could pick up an early issue of *The New Yorker* and recognize it as the same magazine as the one I was writing for. The fact that writers from the twenties and writers from the eighties could work under the same roof and could write for the same *New Yorker* was testimony to the magazine's continuity and to Mr. Shawn's ability to assimilate in his magazine styles from many generations of writers.

That assimilation, of course, was never easy. In 1968, Mr. Shawn hired Pauline Kael to join Penelope Gilliatt in writing film criticism for *The New Yorker*. At that time, Pauline was forty-nine years old and was already established as a film critic in California. In 1980, after taking a break from the magazine for a brief stint in Hollywood as a film producer, she became *The New Yorker's* sole film critic, and held that position until her retirement, in February, 1991. Her writing had such energy, precision, and biting wit and evinced such encyclopedic knowledge not only of American and British but also of French and Italian films that she quickly acquired a loyal following among the magazine's readers. Her taste in movies, however, couldn't have been more different from Mr. Shawn's. She thought movies were a popular medium, and liked those with blood and horror, while Mr. Shawn couldn't bear to see violence in any form. Although he would never have dreamed of interfering with her judgment as a critic, she constantly challenged his editorial judgment. Like the theatre critic Kenneth Tynan, perhaps the only weekly critic who could hold a candle to her, she had a penchant for scatology and kept complaining about the prudishness of *The New Yorker.* She was fairly amenable to having her copy improved but fierce when she spotted editorial changes that might curtail her frank, conversational writing style, as when Mr. Shawn would suggest that she change "ass" to "derrière," or "crap" to "ordure," because those terms were more in keeping with the tone of the magazine. In the course of her years at *The New Yorker,* she underwent remarkable changes, developing some scandalous, intolerant opinions, such as despising art and gentleness. Mr. Shawn had ceaseless battles with her, because many of her views were antipathetic to him. But one of Mr. Shawn's most essential qualities was that once he had committed himself to a writer he never withdrew his support; it was as if only death could part the two. Often, when I was in his outer office waiting to see him, I could hear them arguing about his editorial suggestions— Pauline's voice loud and strident, Mr. Shawn's calm and persuasive. (He planned to open the magazine up to four-letter words, as she wanted, but very gradually, and only when it was appropriate and necessary, not as a form of exhibitionism.) Even after their battles, her copy just skirted the edge of what he found acceptable. Few writers could have been more preoccupied with perfection than she was, and she was always revising and amplifying her copy until it was time to go to press. Indeed, she used her film criticism as an occasion to write brilliant essays of social commentary, and these frequently ran longer than the space allotted to Cinema, so that in order to accommodate them Mr. Shawn had to add extra pages at the last minute, at great expense. (Raoul Fleischmann and his son and heir, Peter, had allowed Ross and Mr. Shawn to determine their own budgets and to add extra pages to issues at will, irrespective of the cost.) There had always been things that Mr. Shawn could not or would not allow to be published in *The New Yorker,* and it seemed that Pauline went out of her way to violate every principle that Mr. Shawn held sacred. The more constructive he tried to be, the more destructive she seemed to become, and in the end their relationship became toxic.

For the twelve years from 1967 to 1979, Penelope Gilliatt had alternated with Pauline Kael as film critic for *The New Yorker.* I had first met Penelope around 1961, in London. She was then in her late twenties and was being courted by leading papers to become their regular film critic; as I recall it, she was offered the job by the *New Statesman*, the *Spectator*, and the London *Observer* all at the same time. This was quite remarkable, because she had none of the usual British credentials, like an Oxford or a Cambridge degree, for getting a foothold in what were then considered to be the most intellectual papers in Britain. (Born in London, in 1932, she had attended America's Bennington College when she was sixteen but had dropped out within the first year to begin her writing career, at British *Vogue*.) At our first meeting, I don't think we spent more time together than the few minutes it took to drink a glass of hock in a pub, but she came on so forcefully in an upper-crust English voice that I could scarcely get a word in. In 1961, she accepted the job at the London *Observer,* and she remained one of its fixtures until she joined *The New Yorker* and moved to New York.

I remember that once when Penelope came for a dinner at my apartment someone made an innocent remark such as that he had been to a festive party somewhere, and suddenly she was off on a monologue about all the famous houses in which she had dined and all the famous people whom she had met. Although there wasn't a hint in her manner of the ordinary name-dropper—she talked as if she herself were one of the famous people—her descriptions were so elaborate and baroque and so unmistakably touched with the magic of a fiction writer, which she was, that none of us could tell what was true and what was imagined.

Over the years, her conversational flights of fancy became wilder and wilder, and one wasn't always sure that she knew when she was being fanciful. At the office, she would suddenly embrace receptionists and colleagues one day and look right through them the next day. Similarly, her film reviews and the factual pieces she did for *The New Yorker*, such as Profiles of Woody Allen, Jean-Luc Godard, and Luis Buñuel, had a touch of the surreal about them.

English friends of both of us told me that *The New Yorker's* editing system, with its endless questions about meaning and fact, was unhinging Penelope—that English reviewers were used to being free with their opinions, and even with their facts, and were not used to being constantly challenged and asked to substantiate them. Many of us who were her friends thought that there was also a painful personal explanation of her problems. She talked to us openly about her sadness at the breakup of her second marriage, to the English playwright John Osborne. (Her first husband had been an English neurologist, Dr. Roger Gilliatt.) In New York, she was bringing up her only child—a daughter named Nolan—as a single parent, and differences had arisen between her and Osborne, the child's father, over custody and so on. Meanwhile, things had not worked out with the American actor and director Mike Nichols, whom Penelope had very much hoped to marry. She had once been a highly visible and social person in both London and New York, and ever since I had known her she had been a heavy drinker, but now, as time went on, she was drinking more and more, and people started avoiding her. I remember going to her apartment for an early supper and not being allowed to leave until very late at night. It was as if she craved friends and feared being alone, and there seemed to be no way of diminishing her drinking. Her friends, who were mostly in the arts, had their own emotional problems and evidently found it too difficult to take on Penelope's. Her loneliness became achingly apparent when Osborne took their daughter away from her, claiming that her drinking made her an unfit mother.

At another magazine, Penelope would have been put in the care of a doctor and not been allowed to continue her column until her condition improved, but Mr. Shawn, once he had put his trust in a writer, backed that writer to the end, and as long as she was doing her work tolerably well and was managing to function he clearly didn't want to interfere. He had seen plenty of drinking among writers, especially in *The New Yorker's* old days, and he seemed to think that it was an occupational hazard. An editor other than Mr. Shawn might have taken her off Cinema, but he believed in her critical talent and kept patiently waiting for her health to improve.

Then, in 1979, the magazine published a Profile of Graham Greene, by Penelope. Greene publicly denounced it as largely fabricated, and the writer Michael Mewshaw demonstrated that some of the material in her Profile had been lifted from an article of his about Greene which had been published in *The Nation* two years earlier. Greene's denunciation could be disregarded, since it was not unusual for the subject of a Profile to be furious about the way he or she was depicted. But Mewshaw's charge was of another order: plagiarism was an attempt to steal someone else's kudos and profits, and, as Greenstein often remarked, that was one charge a writer should never have pinned on him or her. Penelope's "plagiarism" was probably unconscious: she was said to have a near-photographic memory, and she was such a gifted writer that she certainly had no need to stoop to purloin anyone else's material. But whether it was a form of kleptomania or a matter of deliberate theft seemed to be beside the point. Mewshaw demanded a financial settlement and a printed apology in *The New Yorker*. Mr. Shawn agreed to the former but managed to persuade him to forgo the latter, on the ground that she was in poor health. Mr. Shawn then put her on an indefinite leave of absence for medical reasons and restricted her writing to fiction. She published twenty short stories during the remaining years of his editorship. Two factual pieces by her appeared in *The New Yorker* only after Mr. Shawn was gone from the magazine. She died in London, in 1993, at the age of sixty-one.

❧

MY NEXT-DOOR neighbor at the office for many years was a writer named Kevin Wallace—a tall, pale ghost-like figure. He never said so much as good morning to me—or, as far as I knew, to anyone else—and, no matter how early I came in or how late I left, he was there, typing away. His door was always shut, but I could hear him through the wall that separated his cubicle from mine, typing without a pause, rather in the manner of a star typing pupil doing his exercises. Even the changing of the paper in the typewriter seemed somehow to be incorporated into the rhythmic *rat-tat-tat*. Kevin Wallace's first piece in *The New Yorker* had appeared in 1958, and his sixth, and last, piece appeared in 1963. (His pieces tended to be on offbeat subjects, like psychical research.) After that, year after year went by to the sound of his typing but without a word from his typewriter appearing in the magazine. People often wondered why Mr. Shawn didn't ask him to leave, for his own good, since perhaps he might do a different kind of writing in a different place or find a different occupation altogether—and, in either situation, might excel. As it was, he seemed to be casting a shadow on the office. He was rumored to have three children, but when he saw them or how he paid his bills none of us knew.

One day in the winter of 1974, I came to my office and immediately felt that something was missing. I soon realized that I wasn't hearing the sound of the typewriter banging away next door. Days and weeks went by, and his typewriter remained silent. I now missed that sound, for over the years I had got used to it as a sort of white noise in the background, constantly and subliminally reminding me of my own purpose.

I made some inquiries, and learned that Kevin Wallace had gone to the San Francisco *Chronicle,* which was where he had got his start as a reporter. For several years, his office was left empty, as if Mr. Shawn expected him to come back. But he never did. In fact, he died in 1979, at the age of sixty.

I later learned that Kevin Wallace had long suffered from crippling depression—and, indeed, many of my colleagues were manic-depressives. Christopher Rand, who, beginning in 1947, wrote for the magazine from practically every continent but seemed to live nowhere, and who for many years found refuge from deep depression in Buddhism, jumped out of a window in a hotel in Mexico City, in 1968, when he was fifty-six years old. Richard Harris, a longtime acerbic reporter of American politics, left *The New Yorker* in a fit of anger in 1978 over the lack of a dental plan for the writers and artists, and he jumped out of the window of his apartment, on the twelfth floor, in 1987, when he was sixty-one years old; the cause, friends said, was the misapprehension, probably induced by a hallucinogenic drug, that he could fly. Rand had a family to mourn him and Harris a girlfriend and ex-wives to do so. But other writers who met similar fates seemed to have no one.

I remember speaking to Dwight Macdonald at the office one day in the summer of 1966. He had just got a call from the desk clerk of a hotel in Times Square. The clerk told him that a guest who had not been identified had died, that his body was lying unclaimed in the morgue, and that the only name he had had on him was Dwight's. The clerk said that the police wanted Dwight to come to the hotel to see if he could identify the guest by the belongings left in his room. Dwight didn't want to go alone, so William Knapp, a *New Yorker* editor, and I accompanied him. As it turned out, the guest in question was the well-known poet Delmore Schwartz. He had suffered a heart attack and died, at the age of fifty-two. For years, he had been drinking excessively and relying heavily on drugs. Dwight couldn't figure out why Schwartz had been thinking of him just then. Was this a sign that the poet, in such an extremity, had no one else to turn to—that he felt completely alone in the city?

❧

OF ALL THE people I knew at *The New Yorker* who were eccentric, none was more captivatingly so than St. Clair McKelway. He had come to *The New Yorker* in 1933, at the age of twenty-eight, and was around right up to his death, at the age of seventy-four, in 1980. The son of a prominent Southern family, which numbered notable journalists among its members (a great-uncle of his, also named St. Clair McKelway, had been the editor of the Brooklyn *Eagle,* and from 1946 to 1963 his brother, Benjamin Mosby McKelway, was the editor of the Washington *Star*), he was an impressive figure in the office and on New York streets, for he had the air of a patrician about him.

In Ross's day, when the office was small, McKelway did some of everything—hiring people, coming up with ideas for articles, encouraging newcomers, and editing their copy—and for three years, from 1936 to 1939, he functioned as Ross's managing editor, or "jesus" (a corruption of "genius"): a sort of messiah that Ross was always searching for, to bring order to the chaotic office. As a jesus, McKelway is remembered for splitting *The New Yorker's* editorial workings into two distinct divisions: one, called fiction, which encompassed not only short stories but humor, poetry, and memoirs; and the other, first called journalism but later fact when the term journalism proved too narrow to accommodate the wide range of creative nonfiction material that the magazine soon started publishing. Prior to this reorganization, editors had shuttled back and forth between different kinds of pieces, but afterward they concentrated on pieces within their own fields of expertise. Indeed, those divisions, together with the art department, became fixtures of the magazine.

McKelway is also remembered as a great spotter of talent. He brought in many of the writers—Joe Liebling, Joel Mitchell, John Bainbridge, and Philip Hamburger, to name a few—who during the war years developed a form of reporting that distinguished *The New Yorker* and set it on its course of profound writing done in a seamless narrative style. Nor was that all: it was McKelway who first recognized Mr. Shawn's gifts, when young William Shawn was a Talk reporter, still a little wet behind the ears. Around 1937, McKelway made him one of his two assistants—the other was the esteemed and much beloved editor Sanderson Vanderbilt—and so prepared the way for Mr. Shawn to succeed him as Ross's next, and last, jesus. Moreover, McKelway had a hand in some of the longest-remembered Profiles to appear in Ross's *New Yorker*. He wrote a dissection, in no fewer than six parts, of the gossip columnist Walter Winchell; collaborated with Liebling on a sendup of the Harlem evangelist known as Father Divine; and was a valuable researcher for Wolcott Gibbs's classic examination of Henry Luce and *Time*. On top of that, McKelway wrote and published in *The New Yorker* not only amusing pieces—about impostors and outlaws, among others—but also remarkable short stories, some of them set in the Orient, where he had spent five years before coming to the magazine. But what he will perhaps be most remembered for are his wild narratives about himself, which, as far as I know, have no parallel in the history of letters.

One narrative tells how during the Second World War, when he was serving as a lieutenant colonel in the United States Army Air Forces in Guam, he took it into his head that the illustrious Admiral Chester W. Nimitz was a traitor, and how he then set about exposing him by sending a radiogram to the Pentagon. The idea of the admiral's treachery was a vast misinterpretation of events by McKelway, and General Curtis E. Lemay eventually had to apologize to the admiral in person on behalf of the Army Air Forces. McKelway ended up, as usual, in what Ross used to call "the bughouse." Another narrative tells how during a vacation in his ancestral Scotland in the summer of 1959 he imagined that he had stumbled upon a Russian plot to kidnap President Eisenhower, Queen Elizabeth, and the Duke of Edinburgh. Fancying himself an instrument of a counterplot run by British and American secret agents, he started chasing after any cars whose license plates happened to bear the initials of some of his *New Yorker* colleagues. What prompted these pieces were experiences he had had during periodic nervous breakdowns, but his talent was such that when he recovered he was able to write about his bizarre experiences with humor and grace, rather in the manner of a sane doctor observing the antics of an insane patient. "I have pretty much come to the conclusion that I have a great many heads," he asserted in one piece. "I've counted and identified twelve separate and distinct heads, or identities, that I know I possess." Mr. Shawn, who wrote many anonymous obituaries of staff members which appeared in *The New Yorker*, characterized him at his death in this way:

McKelway saw events, people, facts—what is ordinarily regarded as reality—through his own particular prism. He must have known that the reality other people accepted was coarse, cruel, and painful, so he avoided it and devised an alternative reality—one that was bearable to him and was a source of endless pleasure to his colleagues and his readers. He was no moralist. The behavior of nearly all people, including rascals and criminals, and plainly including him, came through to him as inherently funny. From time to time, he entered what was technically a manic phase but what he experienced as anything from "feeling good" to boundless euphoria.

McKelway became so used to his breakdowns that as soon as he felt one coming on he would check himself into a psychiatric hospital. Sometimes he was gone for months at a stretch. Whenever he reappeared, he seemed rested and cheerful and full of plans for catching up with all the things he had missed out on. But the process wasn't as easy as it sounds. I remember that once a fellow-patient of his at the hospital was Robert Lowell, who was probably the only established American poet never to have appeared in *The New Yorker,* and whom the magazine would have very much liked to publish. At the hospital, Lowell, himself suffering from a nervous breakdown, wrote four lines of what were mainly gibberish and showed them to McKelway, and McKelway accepted them on the spot, as if he were the editor. In due course, he presented them as a done deal to the real editor, whereupon Mr. Shawn was faced with the unenviable task of rejecting Lowell, and doing so in such a way that the poet would not feel snubbed.

McKelway once told me that if he had had his choice he would have lived right in the office when he was not in the hospital, because the office was where his "real life" went on every day. The jacket copy of his book "The Edinburgh Caper," expanding on his Scotland article, noted that his "birthplace is rumored to have been a corridor near the watercooler in *The New Yorker* offices." In all the years I knew McKelway, he never had an apartment of his own but lived in rundown residential hotels within walking distance of the office. I remember that once he was determined to upgrade his accommodations, but the place he chose was the Iroquois Hotel, just opposite the Forty-fourth Street entrance of our building. He rented by the month an inexpensive room that had a steam pipe running right through the middle of it, which left floor space for little more than a single bed and a couple of chairs. Although he was glad that it was already carpeted and that it would not require any new furniture, he was dismayed to learn that he was responsible for his own bed linens. At just about that time, he happened to meet a friend of mine named Marguerite Lamkin, a divorcée with a charming Southern accent, and he immediately asked her if she would go on a shopping expedition with him. (By then, he had been married and divorced four times. Although he had such a way with women that he was said to be friends with all his ex-wives, he seemed to think that they knew him too well for him to ask them to go shopping for bed linens with him.) Marguerite was a great fan of his writings and readily agreed, and they spent an afternoon getting the bed linens and a few sundries for his room. By the end of the expedition, McKelway had fallen in love with her, and he proposed marriage. An extremely civilized woman, she turned him down without making him feel bad, and afterward they remained good friends.

Most of the time I knew McKelway, he was single, and, like a number of us on the magazine who either were not married or had trouble staying married, he was at loose ends at mealtimes. One could cadge breakfast on the run, and one could find people to lunch with, but in the evenings married people disappeared into their own nests. They might invite friends like McKelway once in a while for a family meal, but most of the time he was left to fend for himself. He couldn't cook and found little pleasure in sitting down to a lonely dinner.

On the same side of Forty-third Street as *The New Yorker* offices was the Century, a men's club for writers, artists, and amateurs of the arts which served in the evenings as a watering hole for many bachelors and widowers. (It was so close to the office that when I was put up for the club I almost missed becoming a member because, on being asked by a worthy at my interview why I wanted to join, I failed to give an earnest answer, and said flippantly, "It'd make a great canteen.") Every evening during the week, members gathered at six o'clock for drinks at the Round Table, on the second floor, and at seven-thirty they went up for dinner at the Long Table, on the third floor. The evening atmosphere was very much that of a Balzac boarding house. The group might contract or expand, but essentially it stayed the same, for its core came month after month, year after year, and, in doing so, became increasingly set in odd habits and quirky ways. Ned Perkins, a retired Yankee lawyer, who was one of the oldest members of the club, was convinced that Arthur, the waiter who got the drinks from the bar for everyone, was half deaf. At the Round Table, Ned would ring the bell furiously and shout out his order for a drink, even though Arthur knew exactly what he had every evening and had already assembled the makings on his tray—a shot glass of freshly squeezed lemon juice, a little baking soda, and water, along with a shot of Jack Daniels. Lewis Galantière, a rather quarrelsome French-American man of letters, seemed never to leave the club until he had complained to the manager about something—stale bread, hard macaroons, unripe cheese. Jo Mielziner, the Broadway set designer, who was ordinarily a mild-mannered man, was always getting into a hot dispute with Galantière about who was going to pay for the taxi ride home to the Dakota, where they both had apartments. (The rest of the members simply split the fare when they shared a taxi.) There was Dr. Stewart (no one called him by his first name, Harold), a gentleman from the South, who was always so cold that he if he could have he would have worn his overcoat to the Round Table. Charles Saltzman, a partner in Goldman, Sachs, who had been a general in the Second World War, was sure to lose his cool if someone came up and greeted him as General, for he insisted that such titles were appropriate only for professional soldiers, and he was not one. Hobey Weekes, an elegant bachelor and born club-man, was known to drink his way through the day—beginning at the Princeton Club, going on to the Coffeehouse, and ending up at the Century—without his storytelling faculties' being in the least impaired. A few times, he invited McKelway as a guest, and McKelway took to the life of the Round Table and the Long Table and immediately became eager to join the club. Those who knew of his turbulent nature were a little wary of putting him up for membership, since there was no telling what capers he might get up to while covering the short distance from the Iroquois or *The New Yorker* to the Century. Still, with his eccentric talent, easy charm, and courtly demeanor, he was a born Centurion. He was duly proposed and quickly elected. For some months, he was happier than I had ever known him. But, as he later said, "every apple has a worm in it, and the club is no exception."

McKelway was a member for four years, from 1961 to 1965. He would arrive at the club at eleven in the morning and drink well into the evening, oblivious of the sure fact that at the end of the month there would be a reckoning in the form of a hefty bill. He was now carried by this member, now rescued by that. Every so often, he got a bit of money from *The New Yorker* or from a publisher and made a payment, but he could never catch up with his debts, and they kept on ballooning. He was warned that practically the only way a member could be expelled was by not paying his bills, and he was put on notice several times. He always pointed out that he would not have got into trouble if the club had required him to pay cash for whatever he ate or drank. The club tried to accommodate him, but in the end taking cash from only one member proved a nuisance for the bookkeeper. Anyway, the combination of his debts and the sight of him drunkenly stumbling down the grand staircase finally proved enough to get him ousted from the club.

Like many single people, McKelway used to get especially depressed during the holidays. He wished he were a minor Rip van Winkle, and could sleep through Christmas and wake up in the New Year. One winter, he hit upon what he thought was a marvellous way of getting through Christmas Day. He equipped himself with an impressive-looking briefcase, stuffed it with newspapers, donned a three-piece suit, as was his wont, and boarded a train for Albany. He got a table in the dining car and ordered an elaborate meal. Just as he had expected, the waiters were extremely deferential: they took him to be an important politician, whose business was so urgent that, Christmas or no, he had to travel to the state capital. In Albany, he got off the train and killed some time in the men's room. Then he boarded a train back to New York, feeling sure that he would get the same deferential treatment from a new set of waiters. He marched into the dining car. To his horror, the same staff was on duty and recognized him. His Christmas Day was spoiled, because he was sure that its members had guessed his ruse. He had always been mesmerized by impostors, since he himself was at the mercy of a number of identities at any given moment.

Another time, when McKelway was in his manic phase but was on the verge of tipping into a depression and a psychiatric hospital, he took a fancy to a young Englishwoman, Kennedy Fraser, who was a writer at the magazine. She was only a third his age, but he was smitten by her and proposed to her. She laughed the proposal off, thinking it a sweet compliment and nothing more. Thereafter, he started scribbling meaningless words on the walls of the eighteenth floor. (It was a habit he shared with at least one other *New Yorker* writer, James Thurber, who went in for doodling on his office walls as he became totally blind.) Kennedy's rejection only made McKelway more obsessed with her, and one night he persuaded the police that she had been murdered. He must have told them a plausible story, because he arrived at her doorstep in the middle of the night with a posse of half a dozen policemen. When she opened the door, she was stunned by the crazy lengths that McKelway had gone to.

The next morning, when Mr. Shawn was apprised of this mad intrusion, he advised Kennedy not to discuss the matter with anyone and to stay away from the eighteenth floor for a time. Soon McKelway was back in the hospital, and Kennedy, shaken up, was back among us.

Mac's fourth, and last, wife, to whom "The Edinburgh Caper" was dedicated, was Maeve Brennan, a diminutive, red-haired Irishwoman, whom he married in 1954, when she was about thirty-seven. The marriage lasted only a few years. At the time I knew her, she had an office on the twentieth floor. She wrote short book reviews and also a series of Comment pieces, which were published as "communications from our friend the long-winded lady." The central irony of these Comment pieces was that they were vignettes—minutely observed impressions of how the city felt, looked, and sounded at a given moment. What she was best known for, however, were beautifully written *New Yorker* short stories, generally set in her native Ireland; they were collected in two volumes, "In and Out of Never-Never Land" (1969) and "Christmas Eve" (1974). Temperamentally a gypsy, she was drawn to run-down neighborhoods and to transients, and she camped out in a series of small hotels near the office. She was paid well for her work, but she was incapable of holding on to money. When she had it, it seemed to slip through her fingers, as if there were no tomorrow. Mr. Shawn often rescued her from going hungry and having nowhere to lay her head by seeing to it that, if she wanted to, she could go to a place in the city where she would have food and shelter.

Sometime in the early nineteen-eighties, Maeve began to haunt the nineteenth floor like a waif. Imagining that she was destitute, she moved into the office, did cooking in her cubicle on the floor above, and slept on a daybed in the nineteenth-floor ladies' room. The women on the nineteenth floor accommodated her behavior, even though it could sometimes turn violent, as if that were the fate of writers. Whenever we brought up the subject of her erratic behavior with Mr. Shawn, he would say, "She's a beautiful writer," and quickly walk away. He seemed to be at a loss to know how to handle her.

One morning, after Maeve had been living in the office for several months, we heard that she had thrown a chair through the top part of Greenstein's office door, which was opaque glass. "It's a cry for treatment," one colleague said to me, and Mr. Shawn and Greenstein finally entered her in a hospital. She was in and out of hospitals for the next decade, and died in 1993, at the age of seventy-six. In her last years, she was often seen on East Forty-fourth Street, a block or so away from the office, sitting on the sidewalk amid shopping bags and discarded papers.

Maeve seemed unaware of what was happening to her. In contrast, McKelway was an expert at knowing when a breakdown was coming. One morning in the nineteen-seventies, however, when he was hailing a taxi in Boston, he failed to catch the telltale signs. He stepped into the cab, leaned back in his seat in a princely fashion, and said, "Twenty-five West Forty-third Street, please."

The driver turned around and gave him a sharp glance. "That's in New York, Mac," he said.

"I know," McKelway said irritably, as if his intelligence were being questioned. As usual, he was wearing a finely tailored three-piece suit, and the driver decided to take him at his word. "O.K., if that's what you want, Mac," he said, and put down his flag. "You know I'll have to come back without a ride, so you'll have to pay double what's on the meter."

"Of course," McKelway said dreamily. He thrust his hands in his pockets and sat back for the ride to the office.

Four or five hours later, the taxi pulled up in front of 25 West Forty-third Street, with several hundred dollars run up on the meter.

McKelway got out, thanked the driver grandly, as if he were speaking to his private chauffeur, and started to walk into the building.

The driver threw a fit. He leaped out of the taxi and chased McKelway up to the eighteenth floor, bellowing that if he didn't get his fare there would be murder to pay. The receptionist was terrified and called Mr. Shawn, and he came running down from his office, with Greenstein close behind. The two of them calmed the driver by assuring him that he would be paid, and then they ushered an oblivious McKelway out of the reception area. It was late afternoon, and the banks were closed, but somehow they scrounged up the cash, and the driver was paid.

McKelway later told me that if the driver had not called him Mac, his nickname, an alarm would have gone off in his head, and he would have realized what he was doing.

X

EARLY
TREMORS AND
SHOCKS

I N RETROSPECT, I REALIZE THAT THE FIRST OF A SERIES
of tremors that would eventually alter *The New Yorker* as
we knew it came when, in the nineteen-seventies, Peter
Fleischmann and Greenstein compelled Mr. Shawn to
adopt a policy of mandatory retirement for editors sixty-
five or older. Fleischmann, the only issue of Raoul
Fleischmann's three marriages, had succeeded his father as publisher in 1969, at the age of forty-seven, when his father died.
And Greenstein, who as a college student, in 1931, had started
working in the law offices of Hawley Truax, the liaison man
between Ross and Raoul Fleischmann, had officially joined *The
New Yorker* staff, in 1945, as a reader for libel, and had become an

officer of the company in 1962. After Truax retired, in 1966, Greenstein served as the liaison man between the business office and the editorial department. The retirement policy that Fleischmann and Greenstein initiated, at the end of 1975, immediately forced out some of the most deeply respected *New Yorker* editors. It aroused the indignation of many people around the office not only because it ignored the fact that people age in different ways but also because the editors who were to be retired, having all been at the magazine for decades, were much the most experienced and were unquestionably just as alert as any of the younger editors. (Such policies became illegal in 1987, when Congress eliminated mandatory retirement in most public and private businesses.) In the years leading up to the retirements, there had been a vigorous struggle with the business office over the policy, during which some of us got together and protested to Greenstein that editors had previously stayed around until they dropped dead. He retorted, "This isn't an old people's home, it's a magazine. Younger plants can't flourish if they are always in the shadow of old oak trees." We argued that *The New Yorker* had always tried to be a home away from home, and that to get rid of people merely because of their age was contrary to the spirit of the place. But he was immovable, and it was evident that without him there was no hope of getting the business office to rescind the policy. Besides, the policy was not wholly unreasonable. As Greenstein reminded us in later years, young editors, like Charles (Chip) McGrath and Dan Menaker (they were inseparable, and had become known around the office as the Rosencrantz and Guildenstern of *The New Yorker*), would never have come into their own if they hadn't had a chance to take on the responsibilities of older editors.

In 1975, Mr. Shawn was sixty-eight—three years over the new retirement age—but he was exempted, no doubt because the business office had grasped the fact that there was no way the magazine could get along without him. He continued to fight hard against the policy right up until the day the retiring editors left—in fact, Mrs. Shawn later told me that the effort had almost killed him—yet in the end it was he who, as the editor, had to enforce it. Mr. Shawn tried to soften the blow to the retiring editors by offering each of them an eighteenth-floor office, where any who wanted to could write for *The New Yorker*, and a couple of them took up the offer. But at least one editor, William Maxwell, seemed too proud to accept any such diminished role. As he left, he observed sadly that he might just as well stay in his pajamas in the morning and write at home.

And so it was that in short order the magazine lost the services of—in addition to Maxwell—Robert Henderson, Robert MacMillan, Hobart Weekes, and Rogers E. M. Whitaker, leaving Mr. Shawn isolated at the top. Those editors were well aware of how hard Mr. Shawn had fought against the policy. Even so, one of them, Hobey—to whom Mr. Shawn had given a post-1975 office and the make-work job of revising *The New Yorker's* style guidelines—said to me that Mr. Shawn could certainly have reversed the policy if he himself had threatened to leave, yet Hobey knew as well as I did that Mr. Shawn would never have made such a threat unless he was prepared to carry it out, and that if he had done so there would, of course, have been an upheaval from which the magazine might never have recovered. In fact, the policy seemed to be essentially a thinly veiled notice that he shouldn't lose any time in grooming a successor.

I remember asking Mr. Shawn once if the business office could ever force him to leave. He said without a moment's hesitation, "No. I'll be here as long as the writers and artists want me."

❧

A TREMOR MORE severe than that first one came the following year, in the form of a letter that *The New Yorker* received from the Newspaper Guild of New York. Dated October 6, 1976, it was addressed to Mr. Shawn and to George Green, the president of the company, and it named twenty-two salaried editorial employees who had asked the Newspaper Guild to help them organize a labor union at the magazine.

I recall that Mr. Shawn was stunned. He had always handled employees individually, settling the question of their salaries and of their advancement—always, of course, with their agreement. He could scarcely believe that people who worked with him day in and day out had clandestinely gone to an outside entity instead of approaching him directly to explain their grievances. Green sent the company's formal acknowledgment of the letter to the Newspaper Guild, leaving it to Mr. Shawn to deal with the potentially explosive situation in the office. Employers were under legal constraint not to interfere with the union process once it had begun, but Mr. Shawn took the view, possibly with dubious basis in law, that he was technically not an employer, because he did not hold a corporate position in the company. He immediately called a meeting of the salaried editorial employees. Since there had never been editorial meetings of any kind at his *New Yorker,* this was an extraordinary departure. He spoke for nearly two hours. One editor who was present told me later that Mr. Shawn didn't seem to realize that unhappiness about salaries was not confined to just a few junior members of the staff but had become almost universal by that time. "But I don't think many people held him personally responsible," the editor added. "The house lawyer, Greenstein, was generally perceived to be the villain." (Greenstein was the intramural jury to whom Mr. Shawn had to justify his financial decisions, so he was an easy target for the staff.)

Mr. Shawn followed up the meeting with a personal letter to the staff on October 12th, saying that he was not opposed to unions in principle but felt that the introduction of a union in the office would be harmful to the well-being of both "the staff" and "the magazine"—which in his mind were indistinguishable—

and observing along the way, "If the magazine publicly stands for high principles and is privately unfair to the people who work here, it is a sham." He acknowledged that some staff salaries had not been increased recently, as a result of oversight and overcautiousness, but said that the magazine's business had picked up in the first six months of the year, and certain salary increases had already been decided upon. He went on to say that he felt it would be wrong to hold off on those just because they might be misinterpreted as an attempt to derail the union process. He stressed the fact that throughout the magazine's existence it had hired people who not only were qualified for a specific job but also showed promise of being able to move into more satisfying and better-paying jobs, and he pointed out that over the years dozens of people had moved from jobs such as messenger or typist to more demanding and responsible positions, with some ending up as writers or editors. Far from thinking of people on the staff in terms of job categories, he—and, by extension, the magazine—had thought of them as individuals, and had given them, on the basis of their temperaments, a good deal of latitude in their work habits. He therefore feared, he wrote, that the installation of a union might inhibit free movement among jobs, and might even polarize the office. He was sure that whatever had gone wrong could best be corrected from within, and he invited staff members to come and talk to him. "I believe we have at *The New Yorker* a friendly, gentle, free, informal, democratic atmosphere," he concluded. "It took several decades to achieve this atmosphere, and I think it would be tragic if we lost it."

To the cold eye of an outsider, Mr. Shawn's letter might have seemed self-serving, in that it could be read as trying to head off a threat to his own freedom of action, and to gloss over the possibility that he had been out of touch with his staff's economic concerns. Many of us, however, thought that he was the most self-sacrificing person we knew, and that he was fighting to rectify a grave mistake, which had already opened up divisive, hierarchical distinctions—for instance, between, on the one hand, the writers and artists, who were generally paid only for what work of theirs was published in the magazine, and, on the other hand, the salaried staff, who helped to improve and perfect the material.

Mr. Shawn's letter provoked many meetings of the salaried staff, in the office and in the apartments of the members of the organizing committee. As a rule, we writers and artists were excluded, simply because we weren't salaried. Still, we were jolted out of our cocoon-like existence upon discovering that the office, which had once been blissfully free of politics and factionalism, was suddenly awash with them. I remember walking along the halls and encountering so many people in huddles, hotly discussing the pros and cons of joining the Guild, that I wondered how anyone had time to do any work.

In those days, I was involved in some delicate negotiations with publishers, and so was in and out of Greenstein's office. I was surprised to discover that what was usually a purely businesslike place had suddenly come to resemble a little war room. Greenstein consistently had with him a young assistant, Joseph Cooper, who ordinarily helped him read *New Yorker* proofs for libel but had now become caught up in the effort to frustrate the movement for a union. The two did a lot of boning up on the finer points of labor law—specifically, the National Labor Relations Act—in preparation for possible challenges in National Labor Relations Board hearings, which were conducted if, for example, there were disagreements between employers and employees (as there invariably were) about just who in a company were eligible to vote on the union question. Many of the jobs at the magazine were so undefinable that there was certainly plenty of room for such challenges, and Greenstein and Cooper were therefore working up arguments against the Guild on the ground that it had precipitated the closing down of newspapers and thus brought about the loss of the very jobs it was meant to protect. Greenstein conceded in those arguments that during more prosperous periods many people at the magazine had done jobs such as typing for two- or three-year stints while they were waiting to find themselves as writers or artists, or were deciding whether to attend graduate school or law school or whether to get married and move out of the city, and that the idea of a *New Yorker* union had taken root in recessionary times, when people had started worrying about security and holding on to whatever jobs they had.

The organizing committee sent its formal response to Mr. Shawn's letter on October 27th, two weeks after receiving it. Although the response was respectful, even reverent, it disclosed that in the interim the committee members had gone ahead and petitioned the National Labor Relations Board to hold an election in the office in order to ascertain whether the majority of the employees were in favor of a union. The committee members contended in their letter that *The New Yorker*, though it was a profitable company, had not been paying its employees adequately, and they attached to the letter a table comparing its salaries with those at *Time* and *Newsweek*, from which it appeared that *The New Yorker's* salaries were woefully low. While some employees immediately seized on the table as an indication of *The New Yorker's* neglect of its employees, Greenstein rejected the comparison, saying that it made no sense to compare salaries at mass-circulation newsmagazines with the salaries at *The New Yorker*, a magazine that had a comparatively small circulation and whose raison d'être was to publish good writing and good art. In the letter, the committee members tried to justify themselves for not having gone to Mr. Shawn in the first place by saying that most of their concerns were financial, and therefore decisions about them would, of necessity, be made by the company. They said that they had ruled out the notion of an in-house union, because they could not afford the cost of lawyers, whom they would need if they were to negotiate with the "management" as equals rather than as supplicants, and that was why they had turned to the Guild, which could provide them not only with legal advice but also with expertise. Then, too, they wrote, they felt that joining the Guild would put in place an enduring labor organization. "Some of those who have expressed support for Guild affiliation have worked for and trusted the magazine for more than thirty years," they concluded, with a nod to *The New Yorker's* paternalism. "We feel it is now time for the magazine to trust its employees."

On October 28th, the day after the organizing committee sent the letter, Robert Bingham, who had been a fact editor at *The New Yorker* since 1964 and had assumed the additional duties of executive editor in 1972, sent around a letter to the staff. As the executive editor, he directly monitored the work of the salaried staff, and he said to several of us that he felt he had little excuse for not having picked up the whiff of discontent; in fact, he added, he felt so guilty that he had resumed smoking after giving it up some years before. This was something he never tired of repeating in the days that followed. Because his letter to the staff was clearly based on Greenstein and Cooper's legal research, it made chilling reading. He pointed out that anyone who was asked to join a union had the right to inquire about, among other things, information pertaining to its "projected dues, possible assessments and fines, the character and history of the union's membership, and the record of its strike activities." (The Guild was notorious for being financially strapped.) He pointed out, further, that in the inevitable process of give-and-take between a company and its unionized workers some of the old benefits voluntarily granted might have to be withdrawn to make way for new benefits. Moreover, if a strike against the magazine should be called, the company would have the right to suspend payments and benefits, and the employees, before voting a union in, would do well to find out what strike benefits the Guild would be able to pay. In any event, once there was a union, the company would have to negotiate salaries on the basis of job categories rather than of individual merit and might also, in its sole discretion, reduce the number of employees, with those most recently hired being the first to be let go. (The people at *The New Yorker* most passionate about the union were recent recruits.)

Bingham's letter had its intended effect: it gave people pause. It succeeded in widening the split between, on the one hand, some of the messengers, receptionists, and secretaries, whose involvement in putting out the magazine was secondary, and, on the other hand, query editors, page editors, proofreaders, and checkers, whose involvement was primary. But we were having a belated version of the sixties rebellion in the country, and there were a lot of cross-currents. One or two receptionists were as strongly against the union as one or two of the checkers were for it. The attitudes of the staff had as much to do with their larger political leanings as with specific grievances.

There was so much turmoil that Mr. Shawn was prompted on November 11th to write a second letter to the staff, and this one ran to more than seven single-spaced pages. It was remarkable, not least because it was the first time that he had ever broken his silence about the history of the mysterious workings of *The New Yorker* and his part in it.

He said that, beginning in 1939, when he became the managing editor, he and Hawley Truax met every autumn with Ross to review both the salaries of all staff members and the payment rates for writers and artists. Though Truax was on the payroll of the business office, he worked out of the editorial department, the reason being that he was an old friend of Ross's. At those meetings, Mr. Shawn made recommendations, and, after discussion, Ross accepted them. Truax then formally took them to Fleischmann, and Fleischmann invariably accepted them, in his turn. After Mr. Shawn became the editor, in January, 1952, he stepped into Ross's role in the meetings, and Leo Hofeller, who then had the title of executive editor (though he never edited anything but, rather, was a jesus, in charge of all the departments), stepped into Mr. Shawn's old role. (As for Truax, he continued in his old capacity until he was succeeded by Greenstein, his assistant and protégé, in 1966. Similarly, when Hofeller retired, in 1972, he was succeeded by Bingham.) The old procedure from Ross's day was followed throughout, with all of Mr. Shawn's recommendations being accepted, in turn, by the publisher. "At any time in those fifty-two years," Mr. Shawn wrote, "the publisher (from 1925 to 1969, Raoul Fleischmann, the business founder of *The New Yorker*; and from 1969 to the present, his son, Peter Fleischmann) had the right to exercise his authority and either say no to a given recommendation or simply take the whole matter of editorial expenditures into his own hands. But the point is, he did not. He said yes to everything we asked for, and he took what we asked for on faith." Ross and then Mr. Shawn, for their part, in making their recommendations took on faith what the liaison man told them about the financial state of the company, and were sometimes persuaded to exercise financial restraint, but whenever they insisted on certain increases they got their way. Mr. Shawn noted that the arrangement was unprecedented in the publishing world, but that it worked at *The New Yorker*, because it was based on mutual trust between the successive editors and publishers.

Mr. Shawn then turned specifically to the organizing committee's October 27th letter to him. He reiterated that, contrary to what it asserted, all financial decisions about editorial matters had been his the whole time, and he explained how it was that he had acquired such authority: the publisher had technically appointed him editor, but he had actually taken the job because Ross and the staff had wanted him. He wrote:

The authority has been granted me, or entrusted to me, by the editorial staff, the writers, and the artists of this magazine, in accordance with what can be called a silent, unwritten compact among us—a compact that I think of as being renewed every day we work together. As I see it, I cannot impose myself on the other editors here, or the writers, or the artists, and I cannot be imposed on them by the publisher. Even though Harold Ross was the founder of the magazine, I suspect that exactly the same thing was true for him. He could not have functioned as the editor of *The New Yorker* unless he knew that he had the confidence of the editorial staff, the writers, and the artists. And it will be true for whoever succeeds me, unless the workings of *The New Yorker*—and thus the magazine itself—are drastically altered. For the financial decisions are simply a monetary reflection of the final editorial decisions.

Pointing out that "the extraordinary working arrangement we have had between the business office and the editorial department would not have been possible if the four 'business' people involved had not been extraordinary men, with a rare, even eccentric approach to their business life," Mr. Shawn went on to argue that *The New Yorker* was no ordinary "profit-making corporation." Of course, the company had to see to it that dividends didn't fall below a safe level, but the Fleischmanns had derived "a businessman's satisfaction in seeing the enterprise they headed flourish." From having engaged hundreds of people at the magazine, he could confidently assert that many of them would have worked for much less than *The New Yorker* paid them, but he'd always believed that the company should pay its employees the maximum it could, and acknowledged again that salaries had indeed not been recently increased. "As for the future, I intend to do everything I can—and I have already done much—to make sure that the editorial and financial policies of the past will continue under whoever succeeds me as editor," he wrote. "There is a reasonable chance that that can be accomplished. The Guild, however, can do nothing at all to guarantee that either our editorial policies or our financial policies will be continued. On the contrary. In my judgment, the arrival of the Guild in our office will be the beginning of the end of the very policies that have made *The New Yorker* what it is."

His letter continued:

The Organizing Committee, in its October 27th letter, writes, "*The New Yorker* is a place where high editorial standards and artistic expression have always counted more than the demands of the market. Most of us came to work here for that reason." But who established those standards? The standards did not establish themselves. They were established by people (and I am only one among many) who resisted the various pressures exerted by the outside world—to be popular, to be commercially successful (with the financial rewards that would accompany that), to be fashionable—and who played their part in fending off the big corporations that wanted to buy *The New Yorker* and might have been prepared to make tempting offers to our publishers. And our publishers were subject to another sort of temptation: the temptation, after the magazine became successful, to exploit our prestige, our literary and journalistic preëminence, either by selling the magazine or by using it as a base on which to build a number of other, related businesses, like book publishing and book clubs, as other publications have done, or by using our good name and, whatever the risks, gradually popularizing the content of the magazine, increasing our circulation, raising our advertising rates accordingly, and thereby putting themselves in a position, at least, to make enormous profits. They did none of these things. Again, going counter to almost every normal business impulse, they went along with us—the editorial staff—not only in letting us run the editorial department but in letting us knowingly, consciously maintain our "high editorial standards" in defiance of the "demands of the market." We were getting out the best magazine we knew how, with no concessions to fashion or popular taste, and that kind of magazine, clearly, would appeal to a relatively small public and was, on the face of it, "non-commercial." Publishers who do that are something more than just "management" or "a profit-making corporation." Our "high editorial standards" did not come about by chance and were not immutable; they were established—and, in the business office, tolerated—by actual men and women, and were hard-won, and were vigilantly guarded. The New Yorker as a company is singular, just as *The New Yorker* as a magazine is singular. One cannot find another like it.

Mr. Shawn then came back to the organizing committee's idea of "management," noting that for more than half a century the magazine had got along without the word in its vocabulary. He feared that the Guild would bring management into being on one side and bring labor into being on the other, and turn the magazine from an unconventional, idealistic enterprise into a conventional, conflict-driven "business." He wrote:

If you examine most other publications, you will find that their editorial departments strive for independence and either fail in the effort altogether or achieve only a degree of independence—that the publishing offices either play a direct part in the day-to-day editorial workings of the publications or exert diverse kinds of pressure to influence not only how the editorial departments are run but even their editorial policies and decisions. With most publications, no matter what the pretense, it is the business people who, in the final analysis, determine what the publications are. *The New Yorker* has stood at the other extreme. We have not had a degree of editorial independence; we have had total editorial independence. And, most peculiarly, that independence has included financial independence.

Mr. Shawn asked if the organizing committee had given informed thought to the consequences of inviting, as it were, the business office onto the editorial floors, and so bringing an end to the financial and intellectual independence of the editorial department, for soon management would feel the need to interfere with the editorial policies, editorial substance, and editorial character of *The New Yorker*, and possibly begin playing the ruthless game of an adversary. He said, in closing, "*The New Yorker* has been a miracle, but it is a miracle that can be extinguished.

Nothing like it ever happened before, and nothing like it will ever happen again."

Mr. Shawn's letter was an extraordinary document. In addition to serving as an explanation of how the union would destroy the magazine's fragile mechanism that separated the editorial department from the business office, and as a means of setting forth his ideals and principles, it was a powerful political gambit. He appealed to the nobler impulses of one and all without making any distinctions between, for instance, messengers and page editors.

The committee's reply came eleven days later, on November 22nd, and it was clear that Mr. Shawn's high-minded approach had succeeded better than the legalistic blandishments of Greenstein and Bingham, for the committee members said that they were suspending the National Labor Relations Board election and instead were proposing that an in-house committee regularly meet with Mr. Shawn and sit in on periodic salary-review sessions, and were setting the additional condition that the minutes of any and all meetings be made available to salaried employees.

To many of us writers and artists, the committee's proposals, though far preferable to the Guild-driven union, still seemed onerous: the committee was trying to formalize an informal, ad-hoc system that had worked well for more than half a century. But Mr. Shawn quickly acceded to the proposals, setting the condition, in his turn, that the in-house committee act only in an advisory capacity and deal only with low-level salaries. This was agreed to.

The whole union movement changed the atmosphere of the office. The new in-house committee, with its campaigns, its elections, and its circulated minutes, brought a certain mundane fractiousness into our midst, and turned out to impose a great strain on Mr. Shawn's time and energy. Although the almost dour individualism of the office was tempered by a new community spirit, especially when it came to making people in routine jobs

feel that they were part of the magazine, still, because of increases in their salaries and an attrition in publishing jobs in the city,
there was even less turnover in the salaried staff than before, and
as people made almost lifetime careers of routine jobs some began
to stake out their turf and consider themselves important.

☙

IN 1977, ON the heels of the 1975 mandatory-retirement
policy and the 1976 union disturbance, there came another
shock. This time, it was from Washington—from the United
States Treasury Department. Since 1944, each *New Yorker* writer
or artist who had a yearly contract—a short letter setting out a
rate of payment in return for agreeing to give the magazine a first
look at his or her work—had been covered by the magazine's pension plan, and since 1963 each had also been included in its
extremely modest profit-sharing plan, which paid a percentage of
the magazine's yearly profit based on each person's earnings. The
money could be drawn out only when a writer or an artist left
The New Yorker or reached retirement age. (Whether a person
was offered an agreement and, sometimes, an office was always
decided on an individual basis, and had to do with Mr. Shawn's
sense of the needs of a given writer or artist and his sense of the
balance of people and interests he wanted represented on the
magazine.) For signing the annual contract, we received a few
hundred or as much as a thousand dollars; that was the extent of
our retainer, and we came to think of the small benefits we would
also receive from the two plans, along with the company's
medical insurance, as part of our emoluments. The system was
perfectly suited to us. It allowed us to work in an atmosphere
of complete freedom—the atmosphere, of course, that enabled
people to do their best work—and, as a result, the best work of
anyone who was talented turned out to have value. The magical
thing was that, along with these freedoms, we still had our con-

tinuing association with *The New Yorker*. It was a tie that was not only emotional but also nourishing, because underlying it was a sense of economic security.

The government had not questioned that eccentric arrangement until 1977, when new regulations required that pension plans be submitted for its approval. Officials in the Treasury Department immediately disqualified *The New Yorker's* plans, on the ground that the magazine was giving independent contractors tax benefits that were intended by the government to be granted only to employees. Since independent contractors were self-employed, they were entitled to take tax deductions for business expenses, whereas salaried employees, since they were not allowed to take such deductions, were entitled to tax deferment for money put aside for their pensions. *The New Yorker's* writers and artists were being paid as independent contractors but were being treated as salaried employees with respect to the pension and profit-sharing plans. The government's denial of the plans, while legally indisputable, seemed to loosen the ties that all of us writers and artists had with *The New Yorker*.

The magazine, in its traditional paternalistic way, immediately started paying us outright the money we would have received if we had continued to be included in the plans. To many of us writers and artists, however, this was insufficient recompense: not only was that money taxed but we were under such constant financial pressure to begin with that all of it just dribbled away on daily expenses.

In 1981, thanks in part to New York's Senator Daniel Patrick Moynihan, who, having written for the magazine, in some measure grasped the peculiarities of our system, Congress passed special legislation which was applicable only to *The New Yorker,* and President Carter signed it just before leaving office. It allowed sixty-four *New Yorker* writers and artists—the number who were on the books as of December 31, 1977—to remain in the plans, the justification being that it would be unfair to take away a benefit from those who had enjoyed it unchallenged for so many years. This special arrangement was to cease once none of the sixty-four were any longer with the magazine.

Those of us who were thus grandfathered in had much to be grateful for, but the law was galling to the new contributors with contracts who were constantly joining the staff; thus the legislation had a negative effect in that it undermined a fraternal feeling that all of us were equal, regardless of when we came to *The New Yorker* or how frequently we contributed to the magazine. It struck for the first time a dissonant note among us.

XI

THE

SUCCESSION

PROBLEM

MUCH OF WHAT FOLLOWS WAS LONG A MATTER OF CLOSELY
guarded confidences. The way I came to know any of the
story at the time is that a couple of the participants,
faced with a dire emergency, started talking to the staff.
Later, however, the very reasons for keeping things under
cover were made irrelevant by events that took place outside *The New Yorker.* But I'm getting ahead of myself.

Almost from the time I came to the magazine, the problem
of who could succeed Mr. Shawn had been on people's minds, and
the mandatory retirement of editors in 1975 had put additional
pressure on him to come up with a successor. Indeed, Cecille
Shawn believed that the difficulties he faced over the retirement

policy had brought on a heart attack, which he suffered in 1971, when he was sixty-four. Although the attack was minor and he bounced back, as vigorous as ever, it had made the need to find a successor all the more urgent. Greenstein liked to say that our fate should not be trusted to a one-horse buggy, however great the horse.

Soon after the retirement policy went into effect, Greenstein, acting on behalf of Fleischmann, all but forced Mr. Shawn to appoint Bingham the emergency editor, in case something suddenly happened to Mr. Shawn himself. Once that was accomplished, Greenstein, still looking to the interests of the magazine, started pressing Mr. Shawn to select a deputy editor from the staff who could be trained in the intricacies of his job. According to Greenstein's and Fleischmann's lights, they were right: since Mr. Shawn did practically everything himself, no one could conceivably step in and take over without years of training. But Mr. Shawn felt that a wrong person selected in a hurry would get in the way of the right person, who was bound to come along sooner or later, and that if, for some reason, that person didn't, then the magazine was better off stumbling along as best it could, the question of training being beside the point. He had always taken huge risks with every issue of the magazine, and he felt that if the magazine was to remain a creative force he would have to take equally huge risks in finding the right successor. Merely having a successor in place, as if *The New Yorker* could run just like any other business, went against everything he believed in. It was a battle of wills between those who were thinking of *The New Yorker* in conventional ways and someone who was so imaginative that to him *The New Yorker* was a world unto itself.

❧

LIKE MOST OF my colleagues, I usually stayed in my office from morning to evening, carrying on my own unequal struggle with words. Now and again, though, I would take a break in the afternoon and go and chat with a colleague. One of the colleagues I most enjoyed chatting with was Jonathan Schell, who had become a close friend through the Shawns.

Ever since Jonathan was a small boy, he had been going to Eleven-Fifty. Jonathan and Wallace had grown up together. One of Jonathan's earliest memories of the Shawns was receiving notes from Wallace in *New Yorker* envelopes. He once told me that every time he saw a *New Yorker* logo he got a thrill. Both boys had gone to Dalton, on to Putney, and then to Harvard, and at Putney and Harvard they had been roommates.

After graduating from Harvard, in 1965, Jonathan had gone to study in Japan for a year, and on his way back he had got himself over to Vietnam and had written a horrifying story about the American destruction of a pastoral South Vietnamese village called Ben Suc. It described how American troops, in order to flush out the Vietcong, had evicted and relocated thirty-five hundred Vietnamese peasants at gunpoint, and it portrayed the peasants' anguish and suffering in vivid terms. It was a classic *New Yorker* piece, in that by telling a story of a few people in a small place he had told a larger story—in this case, of the wanton destruction of a poor country and the futility of America's military effort.

Jonathan submitted the piece to Mr. Shawn, and Mr. Shawn edited it, and published it, in 1967, in *The New Yorker*, under the title "The Village of Ben Suc." It created a sensation. People had come to think of the Vietcong as the enemy, and the papers had been printing their body counts as if they were mere statistics. "The Village of Ben Suc" suddenly brought these Vietnamese to life on the page as real people, with their own concerns and aspirations. It was a catalyst in changing Americans' consciousness of Vietnam: they began perceiving the military effort not as a war to check the export of a world Communist revolution but as a brutal attempt to quash the national struggles of a people. As for Jonathan, on the strength of "The Village of Ben Suc" he became a staff writer, and was soon turning out a steady stream of Comment pieces.

One afternoon in the spring of 1977—some months after the Newspaper Guild strife—I dropped in on Jonathan, and he told me that from then on he would be Mr. Shawn's deputy editor; in fact, he would be moving from the eighteenth to the nineteenth floor and into Bingham's office, near Mr. Shawn's, in preparation for becoming the editor.

I had an irrational twinge of jealousy. I'd always thought of Jonathan, who was now thirty-three, as a younger brother, and suddenly the father had chosen him as son and heir.

Jonathan said that the arrangement had been under discussion for years, in part because Mr. Shawn, who hated to hurt anybody's feelings, had been searching for the right way to tell Bingham that he would have to vacate his office, thereby disappointing his hopes that, as the executive editor and also the emergency editor, he would one day succeed Mr. Shawn.

In 1977, Bingham was fifty-two. He was an excellent fact editor, and before coming to *The New Yorker,* in 1964, he had been managing editor of *The Reporter*. Because he had a conventional outlook, he had quickly become popular with the worldly writers, if less so with those who were more eccentric. But, as Jonathan put it, in the five years that Bingham had been executive editor he had failed to demonstrate to Mr. Shawn that he had the talent to be the editor of the magazine. Jonathan added that, of course, if he himself should be chosen to become the editor he would have to be acceptable to the writers and artists. I replied that I, for one, supposed that, given Mr. Shawn's support of him, that would not prove difficult.

As I started taking in the ramifications of Jonathan's momentous news, however, I was bowled over.

The question of succession was, naturally, of paramount importance to the Fleischmann family, since the magazine was its main asset. Yet for all of us writers and artists the question was equally important. Since we had no tenure, no salary, and no guarantee of publication, or even of being on the premises from year to year, our relationship with *The New Yorker* was our relationship with the editor. Indeed, I couldn't imagine anyone besides Mr. Shawn wanting the kind of pieces I wrote. Almost every idea I had ever proposed to him was originally intended to be a possible piece for a single issue but turned out to be complex, involved, and extremely long, presenting him with the problem of how to fit it into the magazine. He used to say that almost every piece of mine that he published seemed to test how far back the walls of *The New Yorker* could be pushed. In 1974, when I was working on my Profile of Mahatma Gandhi, he had sat around in my office wondering aloud what the justification for publishing it would be. *The New Yorker* had scarcely ever published a Profile of a dead person, and, although Mr. Shawn was not answerable to anybody, he always liked to have it clear in his mind why he was planning to publish any given piece. Finally, he had said, "Gandhi is a world figure, and that is a justification in itself." As he was leaving, I had proposed a Profile of my mother, who was as far from being a world figure as anybody could be. He had laughed—he could never resist irony—and, recalling the Profile of my father which he had published a couple of years earlier, he had O.K.'d the idea on the spot. After he published the Profile of my mother, he O.K.'d my writing a few pages about my experiences in an orphanage in Bombay, where I had spent three years, between the ages of five and eight. In the writing, the few pages grew into a whole book. He liked it so much that he wanted it to have its début in *The New Yorker,* but there was no existing heading under which it could be accommodated. I finally suggested Personal History, and he inaugurated that as a new department and published my piece. For years thereafter, Personal History was used only for my autobiographical pieces, since he thought of a personal history as an exception—not something *The New Yorker* should publish as a matter of course.

I often wondered who, when Mr. Shawn was no longer at the magazine, would encourage me in my mad projects. I would conduct a mental worldwide search for a possible successor and come up with no one. But here was Mr. Shawn proposing, of all people, Jonathan, who had been right under my nose all along, but whom I had not once considered. In fact, I couldn't take seriously the idea that Mr. Shawn was actually tapping somebody who was ten years younger than I was. I reassured myself that there was no possibility of Mr. Shawn's leaving any time soon. People could succeed others to carry on ordinary jobs, but how did one succeed a genius? There was no point in even thinking about it. I was like most other people in the office in ultimately not facing up to the problem.

I congratulated Jonathan somewhat disingenuously and beat a hasty retreat. My thoughts as I returned to my office were of how I could get some kind of job with regular pay, as Jonathan seemed to have done. I wanted to take on more and more ambitious, challenging projects, which would require years of servitude. Even though I published more than many other staff writers, *The New Yorker's* generous payments were not enough to begin to cover my expenses, and I had been supplementing them with fellowships and grants. For several years now, I'd been casting about for some extracurricular work to do at *The New Yorker*—something that would be unconnected with writing and would bring in a regular income. But the jobs at the magazine were so specialized that I was stymied. Seventeen years of earning my keep by writing as if I could see had worn me down. I wanted to have less anxiety and some steady income, which might allow me to move out of my small apartment, and perhaps have a real home and a family. (I eventually got married—and had a family—but the marriage didn't come about until I was forty-nine years old.)

When I next met Mr. Shawn, after hearing Jonathan's tidings, our talk was about the future of the magazine, and eventually I broached the subject of a salaried job. I told him that I was tired of living like a troglodyte and wanted to expand my horizons. I didn't get anywhere. He said he was so confident of my talent that I would be able to afford everything I wanted by just going on writing as I had been doing. His confidence was flattering, but it did nothing to alleviate my anxieties.

I then asked him how it was that he had stopped thinking of Jonathan as a writer and started thinking of him as his deputy editor.

He said that, while he admired Jonathan enormously as a writer, he hadn't initially thought of him as an editor, and certainly not as the editor of *The New Yorker*. But over the years, working with him on Comment pieces week after week, he had become impressed by the subtlety and the intellectual breadth of his mind. He said that the more he worked on Comment pieces with Jonathan, the more he came to believe that Jonathan just might have the qualities to lead *The New Yorker* after he had gone.

It was in 1968 that Jonathan had started contributing Comment pieces to the magazine, and he had gone on to write hundreds of them. Those pieces, though they were written about current events, had such an ironic and literary turn to them that they resonated in the mind long after they were read. Indeed, he had invented a whole new way of writing about politics and expressing opinions, and as a journalist he had few equals. No more than a handful of people in the office were capable of working in the disciplined yet elusive Comment form. Although there were some *New Yorker* aesthetes who regarded the magazine's journalism, however brilliant, as inferior to its fiction and poetry, Mr. Shawn thought of it as being the magazine's raison d'être.

Jonathan's having gone on to become the primary Comment writer meant that he had spent more time than anyone else with Mr. Shawn, for Mr. Shawn lavished a great deal of attention on each Comment piece. Since Comment was the closest thing to an editorial in the magazine, it had to correspond to his judgment and opinion. If Mr. Shawn hadn't long since decided to devote himself to other people's writing, he would surely have written Comment himself. For some years, therefore, Mr. Shawn had been seen going into Jonathan's office most afternoons and spending an hour or more there. No one else, it seemed, had had that kind of access to him since he became the editor. Some people couldn't imagine how he could spend so much time in the company of a man less than half his age. To anyone who knew both the men as I did, though, there was little mystery about why they needed to meet, especially after Mr. Shawn had tapped Jonathan to be deputy editor. Mr. Shawn, the most discreet and secretive of men, was trying to pass on to his apprentice what he knew about the place, and about the idiosyncrasies of various staff members, in the hope that our peculiar traditions and relationships would survive him in Jonathan's hands. If Jonathan did sooner or later become the editor, he would have to set aside his own creative work for the most part in order to minister to that of others. The job of editor of *The New Yorker* was nothing if not selfless.

❦

WITHIN A WEEK of his appointment, Jonathan burst into my office just before he left for home on a Friday to tell me the news that the first piece Mr. Shawn had given him to edit was a story of mine, on becoming a naturalized American. He was excited, and he showed it. One of his most lovable qualities was his warm reaction to everything. In that, he was truly akin to Mr. Shawn.

I hadn't thought of my citizenship piece as a strong one, but it was important to me, because it dealt with my complicated emotions as I finally decided, some twenty-eight years after I first arrived in America, for a high-school education, to renounce my Indian citizenship and become an American.

On the following Monday, Jonathan walked into my office much as Mr. Shawn might have, even to the point of knocking in Mr. Shawn's characteristic way—*tap-tap-tap-tap*—and told me that he had turned in the edited manuscript to the makeup department, and that Mr. Shawn had asked for "working proofs" of it—an arrangement whereby a piece was still treated like a manuscript and the proofs were distributed only to Mr. Shawn and the editor and the writer involved, rather than to all the people who would ordinarily be dealing with it. The piece had been sitting around for a couple of years, and I was delighted to learn that things were now moving, but when I saw the proof, the next day, I was filled with dismay. Jonathan had made substantial cuts, causing some of the deeper resonances in the piece to sound hollow. He had also flattened out my distinctive voice, so that it sounded somewhat the way it might have sounded if he had been recounting the experience. In fact, it bore the marks of another writer rather than those of an editor—or so I thought, in my anxiety, which was heightened by the dread that one day he might have a say concerning my destiny much as Mr. Shawn did.

As an adult, I should have battled out Jonathan's editing with him. Instead, I ran to Mr. Shawn. He immediately decided to edit it himself, and eventually did so while explaining everything to Jonathan, who sat next to him. He restored all the material Jonathan had cut, and accepted scarcely any of his other editorial changes.

❦

JONATHAN HAD MANY admirers—especially among the younger staff writers, some of whom identified with him—yet, as Mr. Shawn went around to different offices and told people about his decision to make Jonathan the deputy editor, opposition mobilized against it so quickly that Jonathan didn't even get a chance to move into Bingham's office. As a rule, except in the fiction department, editors didn't write, and writers didn't edit. *The New Yorker* tended to compartmentalize people according to what they were good at, and Jonathan was typed as a very deft writer on politics. Unlike many editors, he hadn't worked his way up; indeed, he had never been tested on editing a single manuscript before mine, let alone on difficult or messy ones, which Mr. Shawn had used in trying out fact editors who wanted to work at *The New Yorker*. That the editors who opposed Jonathan's becoming deputy editor could not have written a Comment piece, for instance, meant nothing to them. They had competence in technical matters, and used that as their yardstick for taking the measure of Jonathan. Also, they were all much older than he was, and were doubtless consumed with jealousy, for even stronger reasons than I had been.

Some of the staff writers, too, who were dazzled by the technical competence of these editors and imagined that Mr. Shawn's successor would have to be a technical wizard like him, were indignant at the choice of a person who had been appointed deputy editor before he had put as much as a pencil mark on someone else's copy. They thought of editing *The New Yorker* as an art form in itself and as one of Mr. Shawn's greatest gifts, for, rather like a Talmudic scholar, he responded to any piece of writing on the basis of close reading and mastery of the text. It was an education to see how he read a manuscript: he would clap his eyes on a page, absorb every last detail, and go on to the next page with the rapidity of someone flipping through a picture book. Since Jonathan didn't have any such gift, he could at best succeed to only a part of Mr. Shawn's job, but then that would have been the case no matter who succeeded Mr. Shawn. Those writers—or, rather, I should say all of us, in varying degrees—never grasped the point that Mr. Shawn's technical abilities, however stunning, were not essential to an editor of *The New Yorker*. Deep down, what informed and animated his editing were his judgment and wisdom, his thinking and vision. Every issue that came out under his stewardship was marked with these qualities. Although his work was so subtle as to be all but invisible, the results of his labor were there for the world to see, week after week, but were somehow not recognized by many of the staff members.

Some of them enthusiastically put forward William Whitworth as their candidate, in place of Jonathan. Mr. Shawn himself thought that Whitworth was one of the finest editors of fact pieces that he had known. Moreover, in 1977 Whitworth was forty years old, had been an editor at *The New Yorker* for seven years, had at one time been a fellow staff writer, and was widely liked. But in 1981 he left *The New Yorker* to edit *The Atlantic Monthly,* whose new owner, Mortimer B. Zuckerman, had been courting him for some months. At the time, Whitworth didn't give any clear reason for leaving. Years later, however, he wrote to me that he'd believed that Shawn had still not given up on Jonathan, so he himself might come to be cast in the role of a "usurper." He added, "Mr. Shawn presented the prospect of my succeeding him as a terrible, depressing burden I might have to bear, while Mort Zuckerman depicted the *Atlantic* job as a joyous opportunity." Also, the talk around the office was that, for family reasons, Whitworth might have needed the money Zuckerman was offering. Although Mr. Shawn strongly and repeatedly urged Whitworth to stay, at no point did he offer him monetary inducement, possibly because for him working at *The New Yorker* was a sacred trust, and if anyone had to be bargained into staying on there, then, by definition, he didn't belong there.

Apart from technical objections, some crotchety older colleagues, including salaried staff members, objected strongly to Jonathan's thinking. They didn't like his Comment pieces, hammering away week after week against Vietnam and President Nixon and Watergate, and so on. They said that the pieces were too strident, even unpatriotic. Some of Jonathan's critics not only favored the Vietnam War but also looked back nostalgically to simpler days, when *The New Yorker* had seemed to ignore politics. They thought that if Jonathan became the editor he would turn *The New Yorker* into a sophisticated version of *The New Republic*, running, in addition to idealistic political Comment pieces, even more "bleeding-heart" pieces about the poor, the blacks, and the disenfranchised than Mr. Shawn ran. Pointing out that some advertising pages had been lost around the time of *The New Yorker's* turning "political," they said that as an editor Jonathan would chase away a lot of the magazine's advertisers. Moreover, not knowing Jonathan very well as a person, they thought of him as naïve and ingenuous, noting that he had been an enthusiastic supporter of George McGovern, the Democratic candidate for President against Nixon, in 1972. (For a time, Jonathan had taken leave from writing Comment in order to write campaign speeches for McGovern.)

These colleagues regularly disagreed with Mr. Shawn on the choice of what was said and published in *The New Yorker*. In fact, some of their criticisms of Jonathan were really directed at Mr. Shawn. Over the years, however, many of them had developed confidence in Mr. Shawn's ability to balance things. For instance, he published both Jonathan's anti-war Comment pieces and Robert Shaplen's pro-war reports, sometimes in the same issue. If there seemed to be too much political content in one issue, Mr. Shawn could be counted on to balance the next issue with extra fiction and humor. Jonathan never got a chance to earn such confidence, because there was such an uproar over his selection that within ten days Mr. Shawn officially withdrew him as a candidate.

The way that Mr. Shawn had chosen his putative spiritual son as his possible successor was abrupt, and admirers of Jonathan later wondered whether he wouldn't have been better served if Mr. Shawn had laid the groundwork by trying him out as an ordinary editor, the way he'd done with Whitworth, for instance. Mr. Shawn himself had become the editor in a curiously

roundabout way. Ross had told the staff as early as 1946 that
he wanted Mr. Shawn to succeed him, but when he died, some
five years later, on December 6, 1951, he had not publicly
declared his preference. In theory, there were three possible can-
didates for his job: Jim Geraghty, the art editor; Gus Lobrano, a
long-time fiction editor; and Mr. Shawn. In practice, though,
Mr. Shawn was the only candidate. He had been the managing
editor since 1939, and during much of the Second World War
he and Ross had edited the entire magazine. After the war
ended, Mr. Shawn, for the first time since coming to the magazine, left it in order to write—something he had always wanted
to do—and his long-standing editorial colleague Sandy
Vanderbilt had taken over his job. But the duties proved too
onerous for Vanderbilt. In any event, not long afterward
Vanderbilt scalded himself with boiling-hot water in his bath-
tub at home, and it seemed that he would be unable to work for
quite some time. Ross asked Mr. Shawn to come back, with the
result that his considerable talent as a writer was permanently
sacrificed to working on other people's copy. Whenever Ross was
on holiday, Mr. Shawn was the acting editor. Indeed, during the
months of Ross's illness that led up to his death Mr. Shawn had
all but assumed his duties. Yet Raoul Fleischmann had had such
a rough time with Ross, whose independence and unchallenged
authority over everything to do with *The New Yorker* had all but
made him feel like a subordinate, that he was reluctant to put
another powerful editor in his place. It was said that his old
friend Hawley Truax, who on many previous occasions of dispute
between Fleischmann and Ross had saved the day, now intervened again. He explained to Fleischmann what Mr. Shawn could
not explain—why Mr. Shawn was not just the best but the only
person for the job. Still, Mr. Shawn did not become the
editor officially until January 21, 1952, six weeks after Ross's
death, when he "accepted" the job from Fleischmann. As the late
Brendan Gill pointed out in his book "Here at The New Yorker,"

William Shawn. New York. ca. 1952

Mr. Shawn was not "appointed or elected or designated"; rather, something was "offered to him and upon due consideration" he "consented to accept it." Of course, Mr. Shawn would never have accepted the job if he hadn't felt that he enjoyed the confidence of the writers and artists.

Now, a quarter of a century after all this, Jonathan found himself in a very awkward bind. He had been taken out of consideration for the job of deputy editor, but many people continued to regard him as the heir apparent, since it was common knowledge that Mr. Shawn was working ceaselessly behind the scenes to get people to accept Jonathan as his possible successor. Jonathan, for his part, seemed, perhaps unconsciously, to be conducting himself a little differently with his colleagues, whom, after all, he might still be in charge of one day. Always one of the more spontaneous people around the office, he suddenly seemed self-conscious. I remember going to a lunch with him, Penelope Gilliatt, Edith Oliver, and Kennedy Fraser, at the Teheran, across West Forty-fourth Street. He seated us at the table very carefully, much as Mr. Shawn might have done, with Edith on his right and Penelope on his left, and he tried to listen to us with Mr. Shawn's intensity. But his manner didn't ring true. He seemed like a kid brother trying to act like a father.

Not surprisingly, many of Jonathan's colleagues were constantly pondering his every utterance and action to see if he could ever measure up to the standards that Mr. Shawn had set. He had always seemed to walk, talk, and behave like Mr. Shawn, although physically he bore little resemblance to him. (He was tall and had a good head of hair.) After all, Mr. Shawn had been his mentor from childhood. But some of Jonathan's Shawn mannerisms that had heretofore gone unnoticed now seemed like affectations and came in for a certain amount of derision. People who were resentful of his new status began attacking him as a caricature of Mr. Shawn. Some old-timers who recalled what a complete contrast Mr. Shawn had been to the brash, jocular Ross started saying that they didn't want Mr. Shawn's successor to be a pale shadow of him—they wanted someone who was his own man. In one form or another, the wrangling over succession continued right through 1977 and 1978.

Few staff members stopped to dwell on Jonathan's personal and intellectual qualities: that he had a sweet, kind nature and a quick intelligence, and was nearly always in a good humor, and that, contrary to the perception of those old-timers, he was very much his own man. His designation, however, had brought into play a combination of political forces that seemed to threaten the very continuation of Mr. Shawn himself as the editor.

❦

TECHNICALLY, PETER FLEISCHMANN, as the publisher, had the prerogative of appointing the new editor. However, he had understandably left the choice to Mr. Shawn, since no one else could know what the job entailed. People acquainted with Fleischmann said that he would never override Mr. Shawn's choice, but that Jonathan later told me, Mr. Shawn believed otherwise, because he felt that Gardner Botsford—a long-time fact editor who was Raoul Fleischmann's stepson and Peter Fleischmann's half brother—had enormous influence on Peter. Botsford was a trim, extremely energetic man, with a brisk manner and a ramrod—an almost military—bearing. He wasn't much for nuances and seemed to be free of the doubts and hesitations that bedevilled the rest of us. Although he had a complacent air, one felt that he could be galvanized into action at any moment. He walked around the office as if he owned the place. In fact, he was intellectually superior to Peter Fleischmann, and Mr. Shawn believed that Peter stood in awe of his half brother. Therefore, Mr. Shawn felt that if he himself chose a successor, and if Botsford was convinced that the successor was not in the best interests of the magazine, Botsford would do his best to interfere.

A powerful figure on the scene, Botsford was reported to have said at one point that Jonathan might be up to working on the copy desk but that was about it, and that Mr. Shawn was actually incapable of retiring and therefore of choosing a real successor. Believing that Mr. Shawn couldn't imagine the magazine going on without him, Botsford apparently felt that there had to be an interim editor to conduct a search for an inspired successor, and rumor had it that he thought he himself was the logical choice for that interim job. Although he had always been a great admirer of Mr. Shawn—and often spoke of him the way he also spoke of Ross, as a genius—in his later years at the magazine he was out of touch with Mr. Shawn to such an extent that he scarcely knew what Mr. Shawn did day in and day out, how he held the magazine together, and how easily it could have run aground without him at the helm. Not surprisingly, Botsford thought—so he once told me—that any one of a number of people in the office could have been a caretaker editor, for doing that job would have been just a matter of "driving a well-oiled machine along its groove."

Though in 1977 Botsford was fifty-nine, he seemed much younger, and he was energetic and self-assured. (A widower, in 1975 he married Janet Malcolm, a writer who was as psychologically astute as she was intellectually sharp.) He was also an able editor, but because his job was that of a fact editor he could edit only pieces that Mr. Shawn initiated, bought, and assigned to him, whereas fiction editors often developed stories on their own with writers and then presented them to Mr. Shawn for approval. Since Botsford knew the workings of the editorial floors at first hand and was mindful of his family's business interests, he was seen as having a foot in both camps, and, indeed, he had a baronial manner, quite at variance with the manner of any of the other fact editors. Despite that manner, however, he came across as someone who was not interested in taking on any onerous duties—would never aspire to become the permanent editor himself—and yet he was no ordinary subordinate. One felt that he would enjoy having a backstage role as a kingmaker.

In the months following Mr. Shawn's announcement of his choice of Jonathan as deputy editor, very few people knew what diplomatic moves and elaborate schemes Mr. Shawn was devising or how many consultations with Greenstein and others he was having in the hope of turning things around for Jonathan. He did everything quietly, because he thought that any talk in the press of dissension at *The New Yorker* would be very damaging to the magazine. The strain on him during this period was so great, however, that now and again he was overcome by exhaustion and had to lie down on the sofa in his office for a short time in order to recover his spirits.

Peter Fleischmann, taking his cue from Botsford—who, people said, believed that there would be a wholesale exodus if Jonathan became the editor—concluded that the editorial floor was in turmoil, although in fact most members of the staff were ignorant of these moves and countermoves over Jonathan, so the turmoil existed only in the heads of a few editors. Still, Fleischmann apparently came to believe that the only way the situation could be resolved was for Mr. Shawn to resign. Sometime in 1978, a message to this effect was sent up to Mr. Shawn through Greenstein. Mr. Shawn dragged his feet for several months, and then, in December, obliged, sending in a letter of resignation. Afterward, there was open talk in the office—spread by Jonathan and Lillian Ross, who were privy to many of the goings on, and who, upon being faced with an extreme situation, had decided to reveal what Mr. Shawn had told them in utter confidence—that he had been fired. (They were Mr. Shawn's only confidants—Jonathan because of his involvement in the succession, and Lillian because of her intimate relationship with Mr. Shawn, which went back to the time before he became the editor. Mr. Shawn, desk-bound as he was, and hemmed in by his phobias, had long relied on Lillian as his special eyes and ears, to keep him abreast of things going on in the city and in the culture at large. She seemed to have an unfailing sense of people and of trends in the making.) No one believed Jonathan and Lillian, and they told the skeptics, "Go and ask Botsford." That had the effect of both smoking out and frustrating a coup—as it was soon spoken of— which had been in the making by Botsford, Bingham, and Roger Angell to take over from Mr. Shawn. The plan appeared to be that Botsford would become the caretaker editor; that Bingham, a handsome man with an impressive head of rich brown hair and many years of experience in putting *The Reporter* to press, would manfully shoulder the day-to-day responsibilities of getting out the magazine; and that Angell, who was the head fiction editor and was also an accomplished writer, would have complete control over fiction and would be in the background, supporting them in putting out the magazine. At one time, people had thought that Angell, who in 1978 was fifty-eight years old— younger than Botsford but older than Bingham—had aspired to be Mr. Shawn's successor himself. He was the son of Katharine White and the stepson of E. B. White, and so had grown up with *The New Yorker* even more closely than Jonathan had. But he had no experience editing fact pieces. Moreover, he had long since become interested in doing his own writing, and it was generally thought that temperamentally he was cold and irascible, and lacked the nurturing qualities that were a *sine qua non* for the job of *The New Yorker's* editor. He seemed to lack Botsford's self-confidence, too. In fact, he seemed to be stuck with a boyish face. (Even a mustache he sported was short and timid.) The motives of the three men, like their take-over plan, were only a matter of speculation, but one or another of us had heard one or another of them criticize Mr. Shawn's magazine as self-indulgent and full of long fact pieces that went unread, humor that was too gentle to have any bite, and short stories that didn't go anywhere. These were standard criticisms pressed home daily by people who seldom read the magazine. Anyway, the idea behind the coup seemed to be that instead of having one man, Mr. Shawn, make all the decisions, the kingdom would be divided among the three of them. Apparently, the plans had gone so far by December that Botsford had typed out a note for the office bulletin board reporting Mr. Shawn's decision to resign, and was only awaiting Fleischmann's assent to tack it up.

However, when it came right down to it, what Fleischmann would actually do when he had to choose between Botsford and Mr. Shawn could be only a matter of conjecture. Some felt sure that Botsford would win out, because Mr. Shawn was seventy-one, because he had designated no alternative deputy editor, because there was a total vacuum of authority under him, and because, philosophically, he was a pacifist. Moreover, Fleischmann had long been in poor health, and he had to look to his own succession, whereas Botsford was in rude health and had a youthful disposition. Others felt equally sure that Fleischmann would never lift a hand against Mr. Shawn, not only because he had always deferred to him in editorial matters but also because he sensed that his interference would have an extremely destructive effect on the magazine. Something like a consensus soon developed, which was that if Mr. Shawn had not had to back-pedal on Jonathan he would have carried the day, but that since Fleischmann was confronted with a nebulous situation Botsford would prevail.

Mr. Shawn, soon after submitting his resignation letter, wrote a letter telling Fleischmann why he should not have been forced to resign. As far as I know, the only account of this letter—which was apparently twenty-five pages long—and of some of the pressures that had prompted Fleischmann to ask for the resignation letter in the first place is in a book entitled "The Last Days of the New Yorker," written by Gigi Mahon and published by McGraw-Hill in 1988. The book attracted little attention, perhaps because the author was unknown. (In any case, her account of the events in the editorial department is muddled.) Mahon was the girlfriend of George Green, who was the president of The New Yorker Magazine, Inc., from 1975 to 1984, and she seems to have had an inside track on what was happening in the business office. In fact, she may have seen a copy of Mr. Shawn's entire letter to Fleischmann. She writes:

A distraught Shawn took a drastic step: In December 1978, he submitted his formal resignation to Peter Fleischmann. At the same time, he made a proposal to Gardner Botsford that he be allowed to stay on for two more years, until the end of 1980, to aid in the search for a successor. Botsford replied that the proposal was unacceptable; it would be better if Shawn left immediately. Fleischmann, in turn, was inclined to accept the resignation which he had precipitated.

But Shawn, for all his vaunted timidity, was not one to be quietly ushered out. He wrote Fleischmann a long, anguished letter in which he refuted each of the charges against him. It was not true, he wrote, that his staff was demoralized: "No writer has left." As for editorial criticisms, those went back twenty-five years, to the time when people started complaining that *The New Yorker* wasn't funny anymore. He noted that ten or fifteen years earlier, there were many unfavorable reviews of *New Yorker* books that had gone on to criticize *The New Yorker* itself. But in defense of his magazine, he quoted sources he clearly considered worthy and astute. J. D. Salinger, "who is a genius and who admires almost nothing about our contemporary culture," had spoken of his pleasure at reading *The New Yorker,* and his hopes that it would not change. . . . Saul Bellow had recently sold a story to *The New Yorker,* even though he would receive far less money than another magazine had offered him. . . .

Shawn outlined for Fleischmann the qualities that made a great editor. He must have art sense, editorial instincts, the feeling for a good story, but most important, the ability to establish a good relationship with writers on the staff, and the skills to help writers cope with their inevitable insecurities. Botsford didn't have a rapport, Shawn declared.

Shawn recited his résumé. With Ross's encouragement, he had broadened the magazine's journalistic scope, given it new dimensions, both intellectual and spiritual. He had served as editor for twenty-seven years; he had built a staff. "Gardner doesn't have that," Shawn protested.

"But when it's time to make the most important decision, you turn to him, not me."

Were Botsford to become editor, declared Shawn, it would be "a disaster." Botsford would bring in more writers, try to make the magazine more popular. Botsford would delegate to the editors. The editors, Shawn wrote, were "incompetent." [Mahon fails to mention that his term "incompetent" applied only to their being editor of the magazine, and not to the work which they were already performing and for which he considered them extremely talented. He told this repeatedly to Jonathan.]

"I am seventy-one," Shawn told his chairman, "but I am neither old nor tired." He listed the great contributions throughout history of men of advanced years. Verdi, he pointed out, wrote "Falstaff," one of his greatest operas, when he was seventy-nine. Picasso and Titian painted masterpieces in their eighties. Casals and Stokowski conducted when they were ninety. Balanchine directed the New York City Ballet at seventy-four.

Yet he, Shawn, was being dismissed. "I am not being gently eased out," he stated. "I am being brutally thrown out."

I had heard that the question of Mr. Shawn's resignation would be decided at a meeting scheduled to take place at Fleischmann's apartment on the Sunday before the Shawns' 1978 Christmas party, and that the meeting would consist of just four people: Fleischmann, Botsford, Greenstein, and Mr. Shawn. By the time the party began, I was on tenterhooks, because I was afraid that Botsford might have already taken over, and that heads (including mine) would roll as the New Year was ushered in. Botsford—unlike many of us, who had no private means we could fall back on—was well off, and it was rumored that he didn't care for some of the plebeian writers (of whom I considered myself one) that Mr. Shawn gathered around him, nor did he care for certain pieces about the poor that Mr. Shawn often ran (some of them, of course, by me). And I was aware that Botsford's solution to a problem in a manuscript was often to cut: he was known among the people in the makeup department, who saw his proofs regularly, as the Slasher. I myself had had only one direct editing experience with him, and it had been unsettling. In 1963, Mr. Shawn had assigned to him my Third Programme piece, perhaps because he wanted me to have the experience of working with someone else at the magazine. By then, I was so used to Mr. Shawn's proofs, where the reasons for his suggested changes had become self-evident to me, that I was shocked when I received my Third Programme proofs from Botsford. Many of his changes struck me as arbitrary. I rushed up to Botsford's office, as I might have to Mr. Shawn's, and then, suddenly remembering whom I was dealing with, took a step back. Quaking, I approached him. He had his feet on his desk, and was reading a newspaper. I told him as politely as I could that I objected to some of his changes, such as the substitution of Americanisms in English speech for Anglicisms. He said, "I'm editing for an American magazine." Instead of treating editing as a collaborative experience, I thought, he has become the authority figure and has made me the suppliant. I hated to run to Mr. Shawn, but I did appeal to him nevertheless, only to discover that he preferred to have me work things out with Botsford myself, because he felt that once he had assigned a piece to an editor he could only suggest changes, and not second-guess changes that the editor had made. I rationalized that I would reconsider Botsford's changes when the piece appeared in a book. But before the piece went to press Botsford made a move that I couldn't overlook: he disregarded my various suggestions for a title and put on a title of his own, which I didn't like. Since I knew that titles were the editor-in-chief's prerogative, I went again to Mr. Shawn. He didn't like Botsford's title, either, and said he would find a way of talking to him about it. He eventually arranged to have the piece called "The Third," an enigmatic title that both he and I liked.

At the Christmas party, after giving some thought to Botsford's personality, I was left wondering whether, instead of dismissing people, he might simply reject pieces and allow attrition to do the nasty work for him. That evening, however, Mr. Shawn seemed calm and collected, as always. If the meeting had indeed taken place, the coup had failed or, if for some reason it had been postponed, he was assuming that Botsford—or, rather, the Botsford-Bingham-Angell triumvirate—would not be able, when it came down to it, to go through with what was analogous to patricide.

After Christmas, a note did appear on the office bulletin board, not over Botsford's signature but over Mr. Shawn's. Just two sentences long, it said that he had been asked to continue as the editor, and added, "I have agreed to do that in an atmosphere of friendship and understanding." There was great relief among those of us who knew how close Mr. Shawn's departure had been. Most of my colleagues, however, still having no idea what it was all about, barely glanced at the note. The announcement soon found its way into the newspapers, but without any of the background information, so readers were left to wonder why such an announcement had been necessary. Before the year was out, I heard that the meeting had been anything but conclusive, and that Greenstein—much like his mentor, Truax, in earlier crises—had saved the day by siding with Mr. Shawn. Yet for some time afterward, despite repeated requests, Mr. Shawn was not able to get his resignation letter back from Fleischmann. One could only assume that Fleischmann, once he had acquired the ace, didn't want to surrender it.

❦

ALMOST BEFORE THE year 1979 got under way, the press fastened onto two *New Yorker* pieces and provoked public controversy, suggesting that Mr. Shawn's authority in the office had weakened. Indeed, the controversy was especially damaging to

Mr. Shawn in the office, because his authority had been so recently challenged for the first time. One controversy concerned a Profile, by John McPhee, of an anonymous chef—of an anonymous restaurant—identified only as Otto, which was published in February. Otto cast aspersions on the celebrated New York restaurant Lutèce by saying that the turbot served there was frozen. McPhee had been so keen to prevent anyone from discovering the identity of Otto that he had requested that the piece not be checked in the regular way. Actually, since the quality of the turbot could have been ascertained from someone at Lutèce, that point could have easily been checked without endangering Otto's anonymity. But, in deference to McPhee, one of the magazine's most talented fact writers, it was not. When the piece came out, Lutèce set up a hue and cry, and provided proof that its turbot was always fresh, so McPhee had to publish an apology. No sooner had the dust settled from the turbot mistake than the second controversy erupted—this one over the charge of plagiarism in Penelope Gilliatt's Profile of Graham Greene. The press, having sniffed out trouble with succession, turbot, and plagiarism, kept up its baying.

Mr. Shawn, seeking to put the controversies in perspective, broke his traditional silence. In an interview in the New York *Times,* he sadly dismissed the idea that there was anything new about such controversies, or that *The New Yorker* never made any mistakes, saying that, in addition to overlooking typographical errors now and again, it had once published a whole story plagiarized from another author, and that dead people had inadvertently been recalled to life and persons still living killed off in error. "Falling short of perfection is a process that just never stops," he observed wryly.

❦

IN 1984, MR. SHAWN was engulfed in yet another press storm, this time over Alastair Reid, who had been a staff writer

on the magazine since 1959 and was also well known as a trans-
lator and a poet. In June of 1984, the *Wall Street Journal* ran a
front-page article written by a young woman named Joanne
Lipman, who had heard Reid speak some time earlier in a seminar at Yale, where she had been an undergraduate. In her article
she reported him as saying that in writing his *New Yorker* pieces
he sometimes took liberties with facts. Her most notable example was a "Letter from Barcelona" written in 1961. In it Reid had
described watching a speech by Generalissimo Francisco Franco
on television in a bar and listening to villagers discuss it, whereas
in fact he had actually watched the speech at a friend's house—
the bar had been shut down—and the villagers whose reactions
he had cited were composites. In the seminar, he had justified
such techniques by saying that a reporter had to be faithful to the
spirit, rather than the letter, of the truth.

The *Wall Street Journal* had its own reasons for playing up the
story and sullying the good name of another publication. Its reputation had recently been besmirched when one of its reporters,
R. Foster Winans, was caught regularly tipping off a stockbroker
named Peter Brant on the stocks that he was about to recommend
in his influential column "Heard on the Street." On the strength
of the column, the stocks would go up, and Brant would pocket
the profits. Winans had been prosecuted and sentenced to an
eighteen-month jail term, and the case had received an enormous
amount of attention in the press.

In any event, Joanne Lipman's article touched off a spate of
attacks on *The New Yorker* from newspapers across the country,
which called into question the long, distinguished record of the
magazine's factual accuracy. The press was soon equating Reid's
techniques with *The New Yorker's* techniques and then comparing
them with those of the so-called "new journalism," which played
fast and loose with facts in order to achieve fictional effects in
reporting. Nothing was more galling to Mr. Shawn than having
The New Yorker associated in any way with the new journalism,

whose techniques were, of course, anathema to him. He reluctantly gave an interview to Maureen Dowd, of the *Times*. "We don't have a single fact presented as a fact that isn't one," he said. The interview, instead of calming the waters, as he had hoped, churned them. Dowd's article, which read like the account of a scandal, was put on the front page, and the *Times* was prompted to publish a holier-than-thou editorial, beginning, "The end of the world seems near now that our colleagues at The New Yorker, that fountainhead of unhurried fact, turn out to tolerate, even to justify fictions masquerading as facts." Mr. Shawn pointed out to anybody who would listen that if Reid had made the bar and the villagers identifiable he would have risked bringing reprisals upon them. After all, Reid was writing about conditions in Franco's Spain, notorious for its brutal dictatorship, and when newspapers and magazines wrote about such regimes they regularly used disguises and composites. In fact, Mr. Shawn held to the view that Reid had done nothing wrong—that his only mistake had been to discuss the refinements of reporting techniques in a forum such as an undergraduate seminar, where he risked being misunderstood. But Mr. Shawn's explanation got lost in the general clamor, and, as was so often the case when *The New Yorker* was under siege, there seemed to be no way to get any attempt at explanation into the papers. Since the magazine would not stoop to defend itself in its own pages, the impression was left that *New Yorker* writers and editors were cavalier about facts.

As it happened, just before the time of the Reid uproar Maureen Dowd had written a feature article about me for the *Times Magazine.* It was full of inaccuracies; for instance, it asserted that I had a "comfortable salary" at *The New Yorker*, and this statement was particularly damaging, because I had received a number of grants and fellowships based in part on the fact that I had no salary. Dowd asserted, further, that I had renounced my Indian citizenship and become a naturalized American as a form of protest against Prime Minister Indira Gandhi's declaration of a state of emergency, in June 1975, when she suspended all civil liberties in India; in reality, my citizenship process had been started before the emergency was dreamed of. Since I regularly reported out of India for *The New Yorker,* Dowd's factual error would—and did—make trouble for me during my subsequent visits there. Moreover, in the article she used the very techniques that the *Times* and the *Journal* had attacked Reid for using: without telling the reader, she transplanted to my apartment conversations that had been held in my office. Reid at least had the excuse of trying to protect his sources; her only excuse could be that she did it for effect.

After reading Dowd's article, I sent a letter to Edward Klein, the editor of the *Times Magazine,* citing a total of thirty-one factual errors. When I got no response, I telephoned him, only to be told by him, "Everything in the article is on tape, so there can be no factual mistakes." When I persisted, he made a veiled threat, saying that such articles were done as favors, and that if I didn't desist I could expect no further favors from the paper. I then wrote a letter to A. M. (Abe) Rosenthal, the executive editor of the *Times,* who was a friend of mine. I thought that he would be deeply embarrassed and would want to set the record straight. In my letter I alluded to the parallel with the Reid affair, which was very much on all our minds, but when I finally spoke to him on the telephone he pounced on that allusion, as if it were the reason for my letter. I objected, and said that in my mind Reid had been a tangent—that I was interested only in correcting some of the most damaging of Dowd's errors. He refused point-blank to do anything about them. I realized that, in a small way, I had got caught up in the crossfire between *The New Yorker* and the rest of the press. I told him that I would then be forced to write an article about the whole experience for a journal like the *Columbia Journalism Review.* He thereupon relented somewhat and agreed to publish corrections of a couple of the most egregious errors. However, the corrections would appear not in the

Times Magazine, where they would have stood out, but in the body of the Sunday paper, where they could be easily buried. Still, some corrections somewhere were better than no corrections anywhere. And thus, in accordance with our agreement, I got the *Times* to recant on the salary and the citizenship points.

The cumulative effect of the press storms over McPhee, Gilliatt, and Reid between 1979 and 1984 was to create a public impression that *The New Yorker* was slipping because Mr. Shawn was aging. At the time of the Reid affair, he was just a few months short of seventy-seven. Those of us who read the magazine week after week and worked with him day after day saw no sign of any diminution of his mental energy and acuity. We could only wring our hands at the portents that his distinguished career would have an inglorious end.

❧

IN FEBRUARY, 1982, two years before the Reid affair, Jonathan published a highly acclaimed series of articles on the threat of nuclear destruction, called "The Fate of the Earth," and when it appeared in book form, a couple of months later, under the same title, it became a best seller. The publication of the book established Jonathan as an important political thinker in the world at large.

That June, Bingham died of a brain tumor, at the early age of fifty-seven, and so put an end to Botsford's hope of installing Bingham as a stand-in editor. The coincidence of the book's publication and Bingham's death prompted Mr. Shawn to attempt quietly to put Jonathan across as the deputy editor, but he still could not overcome Botsford's opposition. Since four years had been taken up with the struggle, Mr. Shawn's advanced age drastically reduced the time left to him to find and train a new successor.

Mr. Shawn must have continued to be haunted by a sense of failure, because one day in 1984 he dropped by my office after lunch and wanted to know what, if anything, I had said to any-one about my editing experience with Jonathan.

I was taken aback and stalled for time. I had only breathed a word or two of that experience to Eleanor Gould, and that was when she was doing her final work on my citizenship piece. I was sure she hadn't mentioned it to anyone. Still, I sometimes thought that if I had been a more generous person I would have assumed that Jonathan, if he'd been given a chance, would have developed as an editor, much as all of us had developed in our var-ious ways under the nurturing guidance of Mr. Shawn. I worried that by objecting to Jonathan's editing I might have put the fate of one of my fugitive pieces ahead of the future of *The New Yorker*. I felt that even alluding to the subject to Eleanor had been a form of betrayal. The allusion had all along bedevilled my feelings about Jonathan as Mr. Shawn's successor, making me feel less effective as Mr. Shawn's ally than I might otherwise have been.

I now asked Mr. Shawn, in my turn, why he wanted to know, after all this time, whether I had said anything about my experience.

"Just for the sake of history," he replied.

The editing incident was many years old but very fresh in my mind, and I told him that I had mentioned it only to Eleanor. "Do you think I played any part in his failing to get the job?" I asked.

"No," he said reassuringly, and he got up to leave.

"Then what difference does it make?"

"I wanted to be sure that I had the history straight."

"Are you thinking of doing anything with it?"

"Oh, no," he said, sounding alarmed. He added, "It's just for my own information," and he was gone.

I later learned from Jonathan that the reason for Mr. Shawn's visit was that, even at this late stage, he was privately trying to work out what had gone wrong, in 1977 and 1982, for he was wondering if he should try Jonathan out for a third time as his successor, in case things had changed in the politics of the office and of Fleischmann's family. He finally decided against it once and for all.

The Jonathan struggle had to do with Mr. Shawn's wish to leave in the best possible hands an institution that he had helped to create through nearly fifty years of unremitting work. Yet he did not so much as utter a word in self-defense when, in his later years, the press continually poured scorn on him for neglecting the question of succession. He never approached any of us—let alone the press—with his side of the story. Some of the facts about the matter of succession dribbled out only because people involved had mentioned this or that part of confidential conversations with him on the subject. He himself never mentioned anything about any of them. It may be that in the private files of colleagues there are buried papers, such as confidential letters he wrote, but, if so, the papers have not, to my knowledge, surfaced so far, and, for all anyone knows, some of them, by design or by accident, may have been destroyed. All his editorial work on manuscript and proofs was, of necessity, silent and invisible. Still, there was something ironic about his self-imposed silence concerning general office matters, in that, being a man of prodigious curiosity, he wanted to know every last fact about every last thing, yet when it came to talking himself he said nothing unless there was a good reason to say it. He knew no other way of functioning effectively, and he seemed to think that as long as he could feel sure he was doing the right thing it didn't matter what other people thought. He never felt the need for public approval of his actions. He seemed to take it for granted that no one would be able to understand all the ramifications of what was happening and why, so there could be no way to clear up the misconceptions and confusions that were always swirling around in the press. Approval by the staff was another matter. That was the silent, unwritten compact that was the foundation and continuation of his editorship, as he had said during the union agitation.

And even then he had relied on his actions to speak for him. Later on, he couldn't say to the staff why he had passed over the senior editors in his search for a successor. Perhaps the basic reason for his silence on this particular point, about which he was often questioned, was more human than political: he didn't want to hurt anyone's feelings. Indeed, as he saw it, his personal relations with people counted much more than his professional reputation. (For most of the history of the magazine, it had no public-relations department. When one was established, in the late sixties, it was so inept that Mr. Shawn ended up drafting most of the advertising copy himself, and the result was so subtle and low-key that, like him, it was almost invisible.)

❧

IN NOVEMBER, 1984, only a few months after what turned out to have been Mr. Shawn's exploration of resurrecting Jonathan as a candidate for editor yet once more, Mr. Shawn announced the appointment of Chip McGrath, who had taken over from Angell as head fiction editor, and John Bennet, a fact editor, as co-managing editors, and thus designated them as his possible joint successors. Both McGrath, a tall, thin man with a self-effacing manner, and Bennet, a portly and extremely serious fellow who could almost pass for a businessman, were much loved by their writers, and both were under forty. Yet the appointments were seen to have been more forced upon Mr. Shawn by circumstances than to have emerged as his recommendations by choice. Indeed, as the appointments were interpreted around the office, he might almost have been saying, "My successor must come from inside, and, of all the editors on the magazine, no one editor here can do my job." Certainly his solution was eccentric. Even though it had always been taken for granted that once Mr. Shawn ceased to be the editor the job he had done alone would have to be done by half a dozen hands, it had also always been understood that one person would have to be at the helm, since, as he himself had previously observed, two people could no more lead a magazine than two conductors could conduct a symphony.

I remember asking Mr. Shawn how he expected McGrath and Bennet to work together as the editor.

Mr. Shawn hedged, and then offered a theoretical justification: McGrath and Bennet would collaborate on policy matters and look after the magazine's general interests but would handle different kinds of writers; and McGrath, who had an interest in art, would also choose the art with the art editor.

"So they wouldn't be equal," I said. "McGrath would end up being the editor."

Mr. Shawn replied that things were still being worked out.

All the same, the writers who did mostly journalistic pieces couldn't understand how a fiction editor could ever run the magazine, while the writers who were of a more literary bent couldn't imagine how a fact editor could play any part at all in handling fiction, poetry, and criticism—not to mention art—so it was evident that neither of them was seen to be cut out to be the editor on his own, as Mr. Shawn's resort to a diarchy had seemed to suggest. But, given Mr. Shawn's nurturing temperament, he was often able to bring out qualities in people that they themselves didn't know were there. There was always a chance, therefore, that McGrath or Bennet, or the two working together, could surprise us.

It soon became clear, however, that the arrangement was floundering even before it could get going. For instance, I was matched up with McGrath, but he had no independent authority, and whatever I discussed with him he said he would have to take up with Mr. Shawn. Then Mr. Shawn had questions of his own, which McGrath had to take up with me. Soon Mr. Shawn and I were dispensing with the intermediary and talking together directly, as we had always done. And all the other writers, after badgering their assigned editors, were also soon running to Mr. Shawn.

346

Yet, unwieldy though the arrangement was, Mr. Shawn persisted with it. In the following months, he regularly had two or three lunches a week with McGrath and Bennet, during which he tried to impart to them the intricacies of *The New Yorker*. For a time, he also had them sit in on all his private conversations with writers, artists, and editors, as if he thought they could learn by osmosis. But that turned out to be an excruciatingly painful experience for everyone concerned. People didn't like to have their conversations with Mr. Shawn overheard by anybody, and Mr. Shawn didn't feel comfortable speaking freely in the presence of two reluctant eavesdroppers perched on his sofa. Consequently, the arrangement of Bennet and McGrath collapsed on its own.

Indeed, Mr. Shawn sometimes talked as if he were waiting for a talented young person to get off the elevator, join the staff, and quickly prove himself to have all the qualities needed to become the editor. He hoped that he would have enough years left to him to train such a person. It was taken for granted that no established person from the outside, however illustrious, could do the job unless he had had a period of training under Mr. Shawn. As it used to be said in the office, Ross had gone through no fewer than seventeen managing editors—or jesuses—before he found Mr. Shawn.

Mr. Shawn generally read undergraduate publications of leading universities and in that way often spotted talented writers, who later became stalwarts of the magazine. Around this time, he happened to read some pieces by William McKibben, who was an undergraduate at Harvard. As soon as Bill McKibben graduated, he became our colleague, and was soon writing some of the most brilliant and perceptive stories ever written for the Talk department. Mr. Shawn tried him out as an editor; indeed, I think Bill cut his teeth on some autobiographical pieces I wrote about Arkansas. Many of us writers were much excited at the thought that Mr. Shawn might have finally found a successor, and that this was someone in his early twenties who was both a marvellous writer and a promising editor. But, in our euphoria, we forgot about the competing egos of the older editors, who either wished they could have the job or were being tried out for it. Consequently, the experiment with Bill, as with Jonathan, came to nothing. Bill went back to writing. For a time, Mr. Shawn tried to groom Bennet alone, but, while Bennet was brilliant with pencil in hand, he turned out to lack a head for administrative details. Mr. Shawn then approached McGrath and asked him if he would consider being his sole heir apparent. McGrath thereupon made it clear that he didn't like the ambiguity of his position. He felt he didn't know where he stood with Mr. Shawn, and doubted whether Mr. Shawn really thought he was worthy of the editor's mantle. He certainly didn't want to be the choice of last resort, but he agreed to undertake the job, as he later told me, for the sake of the magazine as much as anything. They soon developed a relationship of trust and mutual regard.

❦

ALTHOUGH NONE OF us on the editorial floors were aware of it, there had long been great disarray in the business office. In fact, ever since George Green became the president of the company, in 1975, certain missteps had been taken which made the company increasingly vulnerable. As a matter of principle, the company had never owned anything except the magazine, but after Green took it over it went on an investment spree. Ignoring Mr. Shawn's objections, Green persuaded the board in 1978 to take a minority interest in the Teleram Communications Corporation, which made portable computer terminals, and then to take majority interests in the magazine *Horticulture,* in 1981, and in the magazine *Cook's,* in 1983. Along the way, under Green's initiative, *The New Yorker* also founded Boulder Enterprises, a printing company that made computer business

348

forms. These subsidiary investments all proved unsuccessful. The only saving grace was that the expenditures on them had been negligible.

Green, always restive and expansionist, cajoled Fleischmann in 1978 into appointing a couple of outside directors to the board—William C. Eiseman, a senior vice-president of Morgan Guaranty (the magazine's bank), and Philip Messinger, a private investor. Messinger, who by 1984 ended up owning a thirteen per cent share of *New Yorker* stock—second only to the holdings of the Fleischmann family, which owned thirty-two per cent—eventually played a decisive role in putting an end to the family control of the magazine. Like Green, Messinger thought that *The New Yorker's* business practices were too conservative: the magazine had no debt and hoarded cash, even to the point of husbanding money from subscriptions. In the late nineteen-seventies, Fleischmann fell under the influence of Green, and treated him almost like a son. But in the early eighties differences emerged between them, for one had been brought up in the *New Yorker* mold, while the other was a young Turk looking to conquer new worlds. (Green was only thirty-seven in 1975, when Fleischmann chose him to take over as president.) In 1984 the two openly clashed. The immediate cause was Fleischmann's decision to have his son Stephen, a dropout from Yale College, elected to the board of directors. (He had another son, James, who was retarded and, coincidentally, attended the same school as Mary Shawn.) Green offered his resignation, and Fleischmann made no move to keep him on. Messinger had looked to Green to expand the business and to raise the value of the company's stock, and upon hearing that Green was gone he started reconsidering his investment in *The New Yorker.* His disenchantment with the company, combined with the fact that Fleischmann was in extremely poor health, caused the company to seem ripe for the picking.

Messinger's actions in the early autumn of 1984 made the sale of the magazine almost a foregone conclusion. Business was bad just then, and the problem of succession, in both the editorial department and the business office, was in limbo. Messinger was a former stockbroker, and, as a director, he felt increasingly frustrated at not being able to find out even how the writers and artists were paid, how the ever-growing inventory of their work was valued, or what kind of contract or salary Mr. Shawn had. He was applying accepted standards of accountability and information for ordinary businesses to *The New Yorker*. But *The New Yorker* was no ordinary business. On top of everything else, Fleischmann ran the magazine all along as if it were a family company, even though over the years there had been many opportunities when the stock was cheap and he could have made the company private. But he didn't, for he was confident that he had enough stock to run the company any way he liked and to keep any prospective raider at bay.

Messinger, in the hope of getting the highest premium on his stock, started exploring ways of selling it in a block, and, behind the backs of his fellow-directors, he joined forces with William J. Reik, an investment counsellor at Paine Webber Mitchell Hutchins, who over many years had been accumulating *New Yorker* stock for himself and for rich clients, on a discretionary basis. Indeed, Paine Webber itself had acquired a block of stock that once belonged to Jane Grant, Ross's first wife, and Reik had been given the job of placing it where it would make a big profit. All told, Messinger's, Reik's, and Paine Webber's blocks added up to seventeen per cent of *The New Yorker's* stock, or of the total 833,000 shares then outstanding. This meant that at a single stroke a prospective buyer could acquire a big stake in the company and so leave *The New Yorker* vulnerable to a potential takeover. Reik and Messinger quietly sold their seventeen per cent as a package to Advance Publications, Inc., the family holding company of Samuel Irving Newhouse, Jr. (As it happened, the conjunction of these forces took place that November, which was when Mr. Shawn finally settled on the co-managing editors—a move that, ironically, seemed to resolve, at least temporarily, the succession problem.) When the sale was completed, in January, 1985, S. I. (pronounced "sigh") Newhouse had bought the stake at a hundred and eighty dollars a share, for a total of twenty-six million dollars, with a proviso that if in the future he acquired any more *New Yorker* stock for a higher price per share he would have to make up the difference to the original holders of the stock. But the price that Newhouse paid for his stake was so much above a hundred and thirty dollars, which was where the *New Yorker* stock had been trading at the time (in my day, it had sold for as little as thirty dollars a share, before a five-for-one split in November of 1981), that it was clear that Newhouse was positioning himself to make a bid for the magazine. We all took fright. We thought that we were on the way to becoming part of the media empire of Newhouse and his younger brother, Donald. According to *Forbes Magazine,* the brothers ruled over the fifth-largest communications conglomerate in the nation after ABC, CBS, Time, Inc., and RCA—and the only one in private hands, with no publicly traded shares.

S. I. Newhouse, Jr., who was born in 1928, had joined the family business as a dropout from Syracuse University. When he and Donald inherited the business, upon their father's death, in 1979, he went on to become the seventeenth-richest man in America, with Donald the eighteenth. The brothers together owned twenty-nine newspapers (including the Newark *Star Ledger*, the Cleveland *Plain Dealer,* and the New Orleans *Times-Picayune),* a Sunday supplement *(Parade)* distributed in three hundred and fourteen newspapers, nine Condé Nast consumer magazines (*Vogue, Mademoiselle, Vanity Fair, House & Garden, Glamour, Gourmet, Self, GQ,* and *Bride's),* a book publisher (Random House) and its half-dozen subsidiaries, an assortment of television and radio stations, and one of the country's largest cable-television systems. They more or less divided the management of the company between them, with S. I. looking after the magazines and books, and Donald the newspapers and television stations.

The founder of the Newhouse family fortune was their father, Samuel I. Newhouse, Sr., whom A. J. Liebling, the writer of some of the nation's best commentary on the press, once described as a "journalist chiffonier," a "rag-picker of second-class newspapers," and a man with "no political ideas, just economic convictions." Newhouse, Sr., had also liked to buy magazines. Indeed, one of his favorite presents to put under the Christmas tree for his wife, Mitzi, was said to be a new magazine. Once, many years ago, around Christmas, he called up Raoul Fleischmann and asked him what it would cost to buy *The New Yorker*. Fleischmann spat out some obscenities and hung up on him. For Mrs. Newhouse *The New Yorker* might have been a bauble, but for her husband it seemed a crown jewel, which he apparently thought would make his magazine empire complete. After Newhouse, Jr., purchased his stake in it, we worried, because we felt that if he put through a similar call to Raoul Fleischmann's son, Peter, the inquiry might not be dismissed. The mere idea of such a call was unsettling.

Newhouse, Jr., was quick with assurances to Fleischmann and to the press that he intended to be merely a passive investor, and that, in any case, he had no interest in making a hostile offer. Many of us on the editorial floors, however, felt that Newhouse could make even a friendly offer and still win control. We felt that his initial investment was a gambit—part of a well-thought-out strategy. He himself later said that he had got interested in buying *The New Yorker* in a very mundane way. An investment banker had called him and told him that a minority interest in *The New Yorker* was up for sale. He snapped it up, and subsequently observed, "There's an expression attributed to Napoleon: 'First charge and then see what happens.'"

Nevertheless, Fleischmann seemed to take Newhouse's assurances at face value. Indeed, Fleischmann was so naïve about the cutthroat world of mergers and acquisitions that he refused to hire an investment banker to advise *The New Yorker's* board on how it should proceed.

On February 12th, Newhouse, only a few weeks after the completion of his seventeen-per-cent purchase, made an offer for a "cash merger" of The New Yorker Magazine, Inc., with Advance Publications, Inc.: he proposed to buy the eighty-three per cent of the stock he did not already own for a hundred and eighty dollars a share, which is to say for a total of a hundred and twenty-four million dollars. Magazines were generally valued on their cash flows, and the offer was twenty times the cash flow of *The New Yorker*, so in purely financial terms it was deemed to be very generous. At the time, *The New Yorker* had about twenty million dollars in cash and marketable securities, and no debt. In 1983, the last full year for which figures were available, it had cleared nine million dollars before taxes and interest on its investment. In fact, *The New Yorker* had borrowed money from a bank only once, in 1930, and since the Second World War there hadn't been a single year when it failed to clear a good profit. Although in 1984 the earnings had dropped off to less than thirty-five million dollars from a peak, in 1982, of fifty-six million three hundred thousand dollars, that was not really significant, since the earnings of magazines were volatile and the advertising revenue generally followed the peaks and troughs of the economic cycle. And *The New Yorker* had managed to clear five million dollars after taxes. Anyway, there was no way to price the knowledge and the experience and the skills of *The New Yorker's* staff. How did one go about pricing a man like William Shawn? As Joseph R. Perrella, a First Boston managing director, who was the investment banker hired to advise *The New Yorker's* board of directors after the cash-merger offer, succinctly put it, "this is an unusual situation, because the assets go up and down on the elevators each night."

Fleischmann alone owned twenty-five per cent of *The New Yorker* stock. (The rest of the Fleischmann family owned seven per cent.) Fleischmann's stake was sufficient to allow him to exercise a veto on the sale. We hoped against hope that he would. We tried to believe that he was his father's son, and would think of *The New Yorker* as a family heirloom. And, in fact, it seemed that he had tried to pass it down to his son Stephen, after Stephen was brought into the company, in 1980, with a view to his being groomed as his father's successor. But Stephen hadn't worked out, and had left. (He had eventually been elected to the board, but more as a mark of affection for his father than for any experience he'd had with the workings of the magazine or with business in general.) Not only had Peter Fleischmann been disappointed in his son but, at sixty-three, his health had worsened still further. In his youth, he had been a great athlete, but during the Second World War, as a forward man to the artillery in the Army, an extremely dangerous post, he had been badly wounded twice, and after the war he had suffered a broken neck in a car accident. Later, he was afflicted with diverticulitis. Moreover, he was a heavy smoker and a heavy drinker; he developed cancer of the larynx, and in 1980 he underwent a laryngectomy. Thereafter, he could speak only by holding a device with a microphone against his throat, an arrangement that gave his speech an eerie monotone. (He used it without any self-consciousness, however, much as other people might use eyeglasses or hearing aids.) In the face of all these circumstances, it was perhaps unrealistic for any of us to expect that he would be able to resist the huge financial windfall that Newhouse was now offering him.

On the advice of First Boston, *The New Yorker* directors held out for two hundred dollars a share—a price that, in March, Newhouse quickly agreed to pay. In other words, he was now offering a hundred and forty-two million dollars for the eighty-three per cent (or 705,500 shares) of the total (850,000 shares now outstanding) which he didn't already own. This amount, when combined with his initial stake of twenty-six million dollars and an additional two million dollars to the sellers of the original seventeen-per-cent stake, brought the total purchase price to a hundred and seventy million dollars. The sale was a fait accompli.

❦

GREENSTEIN ONCE TOLD me that over the years Mr. Shawn, Truax, and he had considered the idea of establishing a trust that would own *The New Yorker,* so that the magazine could continue as an institution independent of the Fleischmann family. Indeed, at one time he had spent days and weeks studying the instruments of various publishing trusts and had given his stack of notes to Truax, and Truax had then discussed them in several meetings with Raoul Fleischmann. "Truax didn't get anywhere with Raoul on the trust matter," Greenstein recalled, "possibly because Raoul may have had it in mind all along that someday, in different times, the magazine might have to be sold. He was always very proud of being the owner of *The New Yorker,* but he didn't think institutionally. For him, it was just another magazine—to be sure, a successful magazine. He simply didn't like the idea of surrendering control. The freakish thing about *The New Yorker* was that neither of its publishers was a reader. Raoul read *The New Yorker* spottily, when he liked the sound of a title or when a friend of his mentioned a piece to him. Though Jewish, he was like an old-school, Viennese aristocrat, but if you removed the polish he was a fairly simple man. He loved the races—he loved to look at horses. He loved the women. At the end of his life, he wound up marrying his nurse, who was some thirty-five years younger than he was. The subject of establishing a trust didn't come up with Peter, because we sensed that there would be even less chance with him than there had been with Raoul."

Writers and artists never had any say in the matter of the trust, primarily because, from the very beginning, they were always discouraged from owning any shares in the company. Mr. Shawn felt that the writers and artists already lived under such financial pressure that it would be a mistake for them—or any other editorial-staff members—to get involved in the business of the company. If it soured, they would be in double jeopardy: they would lose money on their stock, and they would perhaps be able to publish less of their work in the magazine. In 1983, however, in large measure on Green's initiative, the business office offered to include writers, artists, and the salaried editorial staff in a stock-purchase plan that permitted all of us to buy, with a designated portion of our earnings, *New Yorker* stock at a fifteen-per-cent discount. "Shawn was much upset by the plan, because it was very obvious that it was the tail of the dog downstairs," Greenstein told me. "A few people in the business office had doped out a technique for enriching themselves with company stock, and then decided that they had to do something for the whole staff, upstairs and downstairs." Mr. Shawn had little choice but to assent to the plan—in part because no one was excluded from it, and in part because he himself had owned twenty-five hundred shares until 1981, a year in which a share ranged in price from thirty to sixty dollars. He had sold his holding on the advice of Greenstein, who thought that the stock had gone up precipitously with no relationship to the real worth of the company. Otherwise, allowing for the shares' subsequent five-for-one split, Mr. Shawn would have owned twelve thousand five hundred shares, with a value of two and a half million dollars, at the time of Newhouse's cash-merger offer.

XII

"BEING HONOUR BRED"

I T WAS FRIDAY, MARCH 8, 1985, LESS THAN A MONTH after Newhouse's cash-merger offer, and it seemed no different from any other day at the office. But a little after four o'clock in the afternoon there was a commotion around the watercooler, and I stepped out of my office to see what was going on. Mr. Shawn, looking very sombre, was coming down the stairs. Every day, he went up and down those stairs dozens of times. This time, however, there was something grave in the deliberate way he walked. Moreover, he was accompanied by a lawyer—Peter Ryan, of Fried, Frank, Harris, Shriver & Jacobson—whom he and a group of writers had retained after Newhouse's appearance on the scene, in order to see

357

how the magazine's editorial independence could be guaranteed. Mr. Shawn stopped three steps short of the eighteenth-floor landing—just above the watercooler, where he could be easily seen and heard. Although there had been no prior notice that he wanted to say anything to us, people came out of their offices spontaneously and gathered in the hall.

Mr. Shawn, with tears in his eyes, read us a formal statement announcing that earlier that day the board of directors of *The New Yorker* had voted unanimously for the sale of the magazine to Newhouse. As we listened to him, we all felt, successively, angry, dismayed, betrayed, and hopeless.

Halting frequently to master himself, Mr. Shawn read what at first sounded like fighting words: "The editorial staff was not a party to these negotiations. Nor were the views of the editorial staff solicited during these negotiations. We were not asked for our approval, and we did not give our approval. When there are further developments, I will meet with you again."

He started to leave, but by now scores of people had gathered around him on the landing in the hall, and everyone had a question: Could anything be done to stop the sale? Was our *New Yorker* finished? What could we do?

In his answers he recounted the history of the sale, telling us, to begin with, that, at Fleischmann's urging, he had met twice with Newhouse in the previous weeks. "I described to him some of our peculiarities, and he listened attentively," he said. "I explained to him how strange we were, how fragile the magazine was. I thought that he should know what he would be walking into. I told him that *The New Yorker,* as it is, is not a good investment—that it is a speculative business venture, and that there is no way to put a value on it. I told Mr. Newhouse that the kind of money he is offering for the magazine makes no sense—that with that kind of investment he would need a return that *The New Yorker* couldn't possibly provide. Once he paid a big price for it, then it would be natural for him to expect a twelve- to twenty-per-cent return on his investment. But then, of course, the magazine would no longer be free to do what it liked. It would inevitably make the kind of commercial compromises that it has avoided through all of its history. I told him that the reason we could take the kind of editorial risks that we've been taking for the past sixty years is that the magazine had practically no debt and nobody's money was riding on it."

He paused, as if he were wondering whether he should say anything more, and then resumed: "At one point, Mr. Newhouse told me that he was buying *The New Yorker* in the same spirit in which he would buy a Rembrandt. As you may know, he's an art collector. In other words, he was saying that he doesn't want any return on his investment. He would just like to own it for the pleasure it would give him. That could be true. In that case, it could turn out that he would be an owner in the tradition of the Fleischmann family."

It was characteristic of Mr. Shawn to put the best face on things—even on the sale of *The New Yorker*. But then I imagined *The New Yorker* as one of the Condé Nast magazines: magazines that, according to the newspapers, were constantly "redefining themselves," "turning themselves around," getting a new look, a new editor—in short, trimming their sails to the prevailing winds of fashion. What could such commercially driven magazines conceivably have in common with our *New Yorker*? I warned myself that the Newhouses built up their magazine and newspaper empire not by sitting around like aristocratic art collectors but, rather, by taking an active hand in the growth of their business. Moreover, a Rembrandt could hang on the wall for hundreds of years unchanged, whereas every week *The New Yorker* was a blank canvas.

We later read in the newspapers that Fleischmann had dismissed Mr. Shawn's protest against the sale that afternoon as "emotional." Indeed, the Los Angeles *Times* described at some length what Fleischmann and his friends had to say about our impromptu gathering:

> Extremely close friends describe the chairman as "crushed" by what they call the "grossly unfair" reaction of Shawn and his staff. "You've got an extraordinarily spoiled group of writers and editors, and it has been brought to their attention that they work for somebody," one of Fleischmann's friends said. "They lived in a hothouse created by Raoul Fleischmann and perpetuated by his son. They should have recognized that Peter was not very well. . . . Peter had to think of the succession of the magazine."

It was because the Fleischmanns had, as Mr. Shawn put it during the struggle over the union, "a rare, even eccentric approach to their business life" that I don't think any of us ever believed we worked for Peter Fleischmann, although, of course, in the sense that we were paid by a company in which he held the biggest block of shares, we did. We believed we worked for Mr. Shawn: that was the reason we were preoccupied with who would be his successor but never gave a thought to who would be Fleischmann's. We blithely assumed that the business office could not affect our lives—that, at best, it was a handmaiden there to serve us, rather than a master expecting us to serve it. I realize now that in practically denying its existence we were courting disaster. Fleischmann might have felt isolated from the very people whose support he needed, or so I thought when, although hardly any of us on the staff knew him personally, each one of us received a letter from him (all the letters sent to our home addresses) giving his side of the story about the sale. As well as I can remember, this was the first time we had ever received any kind of communication from him. In his letter, dated April 19th, he wrote, in part:

> I did not seek a change in the ownership of *The New Yorker*. When Mr. Newhouse first approached me, I tried to discourage him. I hoped

that he would lose interest and go away. I did not want to give up the special relationship I have enjoyed as a result of my father's stock ownership and my own. I did not want any change.

But as time passed, I came to think that my feeling was unrealistic and that change was inevitable. I was, of course, influenced by the fact that Mr. Newhouse, if he so wished (though there was never a hint of such a desire on his part), could unilaterally accomplish what he sought; but beyond that, there was the inexorability of death and taxes. The day was bound to come when my death and the resulting estate taxes would require an uncontrolled sale and bring some new and unknown owner. If the change were unplanned and forced by circumstance, a smooth transition might be impossible, and permanent damage might be done to our fragile institution, which consists essentially of the interpersonal relationships among dedicated people of good will, ability, and creative genius. I decided that it was in the best interest of *The New Yorker* as an institution to have the change in ownership take place smoothly and agreeably on the basis of commitments that our people and our practices and traditions would be continued.

Fleischmann, throughout his tenure, had acted like his father, but in this instance he was almost repudiating his father's behavior. After all, his father, too, had faced the problem of estate taxes; in fact, his father could have sold out and retired as a rich man. But he didn't, purely for the sake of the magazine. Peter Fleischmann, however, now seemed to be acting like any ordinary businessman, looking to his own interests and to those of his heirs. And yet one has to weigh in the balance how the deterioration in his health, which we on the editorial floors, with the exception of Mr. Shawn—and, of course, Botsford and Greenstein—were scarcely aware of, must have affected his decision to sell.

I myself heard Fleischmann's eerie, mechanical voice only once, when he was talking in the elevator to a friend of his. It was heartrending. Also, his father had had a capable heir ready to step into his place, whereas Peter Fleischmann did not have that luxury.

Because we felt some sympathy for Peter Fleischmann over his illness, we never felt anger toward him. All of us were thinking only about Mr. Shawn, who we thought owned *The New Yorker* in a moral sense. He had shaped its editorial content for much of its life; in fact, its great reputation was based on the material he selected and published, and that material was responsible even for the magazine's carrying a certain class of advertisements. Indeed, one could argue that the value of Fleischmann's stock was mostly due to Mr. Shawn, who had been the sole arbiter of *The New Yorker's* editorial material for thirty-three years. But the ultimate power, we were now forced to acknowledge, had never rested with him but always with Fleischmann, as the major stockholder. (Ideally, it should have rested with the staff, and there were some who said that our failure to exercise it had created a vacuum that allowed Fleischmann to step in. But the lesson driven home by subsequent events was that ultimately the staff was powerless, since the game was now one for money and we couldn't even sit at the table.) But neither before nor after the announcement of the sale did Mr. Shawn say a word against Fleischmann's decision. He remained true to his pacifist principles, and his self-discipline was impressive.

❧

"THE BASIS OF commitments" that Fleischmann had referred to in his letter to the staff, and which seemed to be a salve to his conscience, was formally set forth in a legal instrument called the Agreement and Plan of Merger. Executed on the day of the sale announcement, it acknowledged that the unique quality of *The New Yorker* was the result of the magazine's personnel and operating practices, including "complete editorial independence" and editors' "total control of the magazine's editorial character,

policies, procedures and content." The Agreement then gave
assurances that all those practices and all the personnel would be
preserved, and an article headed "Representations and Warranties"
went on to state, "Advance further intends that the Company
President, Publisher or Chairman will consult with the editor of
The New Yorker on advertising-acceptance policy, on the magazine's own advertising, promotion and public relations, and on
circulation policy." Ross and Mr. Shawn had both set the broad
outlines of the advertising policy, and Mr. Shawn was, if anything, stricter than Ross, since Ross had allowed, for instance,
some advertisements for lingerie, whereas Mr. Shawn banned that
subject and also persuaded the business office to reject all advertisements for feminine-hygiene products, for tourism in
Apartheid South Africa, and, of course, after the Surgeon
General's report of 1964, for cigarettes. The separation of church
and state, as the editorial department and the business office were
sometimes referred to intramurally, applied to prevention of the
business office's interference in editorial material, not the other
way around. Both Ross and Mr. Shawn had also avoided gimmicks used by other magazines for building up circulation, such
as promoting individual issues. Those prerogatives of the editor
had never sat well with the magazine's advertising salesmen, but
the Agreement guaranteed that even those prerogatives would
not be interfered with. And, on top of that, the Agreement went
as far as to give the staff a role in the appointment of the editor,
in a statement reading, "The final decision will be made by
Advance, but Advance will consult with, and seek the advice and
approval of, a group of staff members to be selected and to function in a manner then deemed to be appropriate by the present
senior editorial staff." Newhouse seemed to be bending over
backward to promise that he would act the way the Fleischmanns
had acted—ostensibly surrendering the time-honored prerogative of a magazine publisher to have his own man as the editor.
Another article, headed "Covenants," stated that *The New Yorker*

"will be operated on a stand-alone basis as a separate company," and added that "all present departments, including accounting, circulation, personnel and production, will be maintained independently from those of Advance's other magazines." The final article proclaimed that all the assurances and promises in the Agreement would survive the merger.

But, of course, once the merger had taken place, the only man who could enforce its provisions was Newhouse, for what he was left with was an agreement essentially with himself.

Throughout the Fleischmann-family era, an unwritten constitution governed our lives. Mr. Shawn said to the *Times* on the occasion of the sale, "If Mr. Newhouse turns out to be the man who comes into the situation, I will try, as I do with anyone who comes here to work, to establish a relationship of mutual trust. I would hope that as man to man we could work things out." He seemed to be implying that Newhouse would be working for him rather than vice versa. He continued, "You can make a magnificent document. If the people who draw up the document, or even sign the document, want to get around it, they can. And if they want to live up to it they will. It isn't documents in the long run. It's what the people's real intentions are."

The editorial department's full public statement about the sale was set out in a long Comment piece, written by Mr. Shawn—but, of course, unsigned—and published in the issue of April 22, 1985. It said that when the magazine was launched, in 1925, it had to grope its way and discover its natural character, like any new publication, and that the arrangement for the separation of the editorial department and the business office was never spelled out, because it was impromptu and ad hoc, but, as a result of it, the magazine had enjoyed complete editorial independence, which was rare in the annals of publishing. The Comment said that in sixty years neither Raoul nor Peter Fleischmann "ever made an editorial suggestion, ever commented favorably or unfavorably on anything we published or on any editorial direction the magazine was taking, or ever permitted the advertising or circulation or accounting people to bring any pressure to bear on us." No doubt, it continued, there had been occasions when both publishers had been unhappy or puzzled by what the editorial department was publishing, but they had exercised self-restraint and held their tongues. The Comment then noted that soon the magazine would be merged into the conglomerate, and it cited the assurances spelled out in the Agreement, as if publishing them in *The New Yorker* might sanctify them. It then made this clarion call: "We reassert our editorial independence. We reassert it with these few formal words. We feel certain that the Newhouses will respect it as rigorously as the Fleischmanns did."

The Comment went on:

But what does this editorial independence mean? What is it, actually? It is simply freedom. It frees us to say what we believe to be true, to report what we believe to be true, to write what we want to write, to draw what we want to draw—to publish what we want to publish—with no outside intervention, without fear, without constraints, in defiance of commercial pressures or any other pressures beyond those of our own conscience and our own responsibility. It also frees us to be open to experiment and innovation, to new forms and styles, whether journalistic or literary. The freedom that the editorial office enjoys includes the freedom of every staff writer and every staff artist and every editor (and every non-staff contributor) to follow his or her own impulses, inclinations, aspirations, passionate interests. No writer or artist or editor is ever given an order. When a journalistic writer undertakes a new project, it is always done in full agreement with the editor; the two have to bring to it the same enthusiasm. And no editing is ever imposed on a writer; every editorial suggestion is presented in the form of a question, and is settled by agreement between writer and editor. The artists are similarly free. And our editors edit only what they are willing to edit.

We edit *The New Yorker* as a magazine for readers, not as an advertising medium. We regard our readers as readers, not as consumers or as a "market." Just as advertising is an essential part of our country's life, it is an essential part of *The New Yorker's* life. But it must not be linked to the editorial content of the magazine. They belong in separate realms, and the two realms must remain separate, must remain cordially apart. In this atmosphere of freedom, we have never published anything in order to sell magazines, to cause a sensation, to be controversial, to be popular or fashionable, to be "successful." We have published only what we thought had merit of one kind or another.

The business ownership of *The New Yorker* may change hands, but the idea of *The New Yorker*—the tradition of *The New Yorker*, the spirit of *The New Yorker*—has never been owned by anyone and never will be owned by anyone. It cannot be bought or sold. It exists in the minds of a group of writers, artists, editors, and editorial assistants who have been drawn together by literary, journalistic, aesthetic, and ethical principles they share, and by a shared outlook on the world. Whatever else may happen, it will endure. We need not name or define our principles or standards, for they are implicit in what we publish in our pages each week. Yet this may be the moment to say that if *The New Yorker* could be everything we want it to be it would unfailingly combine thorough, accurate, fresh, inspired reporting with fiction that runs deep and says something that hasn't been said before; it would be funny as frequently as possible; it would contribute something of worth to the national discourse; it would cast light; it would be well-wishing; and it would be humane. In an age when television screens are too often bright with nothing, we value substance. Amid a chaos of images, we value coherence. We believe in the printed word. And we believe in clarity. And in immaculate syntax. And in the beauty of the English language. We believe that the truth can turn up in a cartoon, in one of the magazine's covers, in a poem, in a short story, in an essay, in an editorial comment, in a humor piece, in a critical piece, in a reporting piece. And if any single principle transcends all the others it is to try to tell the truth. *The New Yorker* will continue to change, as it has changed through the years, but our basic principles and standards will remain exactly what they have been. With that knowledge, and with the assurance that we freely asked our prospective publishers to give us and that they freely gave, we are confident that we will preserve *The New Yorker*—not merely a magazine that bears its name but *this* magazine: *The New Yorker* itself.

The people in the makeup department, the moment they saw Mr. Shawn's copy, made Xeroxes and circulated them throughout the office. Many members of the staff who read it were thrilled by his words. I was, too, but I had a sinking feeling that the fact that he had to state our credo—something he had never done before— meant that in some part of his mind he already knew that it was about to be lost.

Over the next few days, other people, too, must have had second thoughts about the Comment, because a profound unease returned to the editorial halls. Newhouse's corporate and expansionistic culture seemed utterly alien. There was no way *The New Yorker* could truly be a "stand-alone" company within the Newhouse empire. Some of my colleagues who had long hated the squalor of our offices went around saying disingenuously that we would soon have spiffy new offices with potted plants and glamorous receptionists and secretaries.

The press counselled us to be grateful that Rupert Murdoch wasn't buying us. We were. But we thought that we might better have been bought by the brilliant investor Warren Buffet, who was known for never interfering with the management of companies that he bought. In the mid-nineteen-sixties, he had acquired some *New Yorker* stock, and by 1973 he had obtained sixteen per cent of the company's shares. He had wanted to acquire the magazine but had been rebuffed by Peter Fleischmann. All of us were only too well aware of what had happened to other publications when they changed hands. Once Rupert Murdoch had bought the venerable London *Times* and appointed his man as the editor, the entire complexion of the paper had changed. Even respected old hands had started writing news stories as features, thinking—correctly, it turned out—that that was what the new editor and the new owner wanted. Newhouse was far from being a Murdoch, but who could blame him for wanting to make a profit from his huge investment in *The New Yorker*?

There were, however, some dissenting voices among us. One of them was Brendan Gill's. "I'm considered Judas Iscariot around here," Gill told the press. "But it strikes no terror in my heart to think we could become part of the Newhouse kingdom. . . . People like the Newhouses are infinitely more sophisticated and much more intellectually and culturally oriented than ninety per cent of the staff of *The New Yorker*. S.I. is an intellectual. He's not the head of a shoe conglomerate." Gill had been writing for *The New Yorker* for forty-seven years. Mr. Shawn often designated him as a spokesman for *The New Yorker* on public occasions. Gill's endorsement of the sale publicly must have been especially painful for Mr. Shawn, though he said nothing.

On the morning of May 7th, a couple of months after the announcement of the sale, the directors met with the shareholders in the Bar Association Building, on West Forty-fourth Street, in order to consummate the merger. Neither Newhouse nor Mr. Shawn was present, but staffers, many of whom had recently become shareholders through the stock-purchase plan, were there in force and used the opportunity provided by a public forum to air their grievances about the sale. They pointed out that Fleischmann was walking away with fifty-three million dollars and that the other directors were also being rewarded handsomely. They complained that in the previous two years four top officers of the company had awarded themselves large amounts of stock, ranging from twelve hundred to nearly four thousand shares each. J. Kennard Bosee, who had been the company's president for less than a year, received two thousand shares when the sale seemed imminent—and, indeed, it was just two weeks later that Newhouse made his cash-merger offer—so, including eighteen hundred and thirty-three shares he had been awarded some months earlier, as compensation, he pocketed nearly eight hundred thousand dollars as a result of the sale. Similarly, three other officers who had voted themselves compensation stood to profit from their stock awards. In contrast, staffers and other contributors who had devoted their working lives to *The New Yorker* were not getting a penny of compensation.

Bosee defended the awards to the top officers, saying that such compensation was a common practice among companies that were being bought out. He then pointed out that Newhouse had generously offered to make payments to valuable members of the editorial staff but that Mr. Shawn had refused to accept any money on their behalf, on the ground that he could not say which employees were more valuable than others, since, as far as he was concerned, they were all valuable. Those of us who were familiar with Mr. Shawn's principles concerning the magazine could have predicted his refusal, since he would not want to participate in any way in the sale. Still, some of the writers and artists expressed resentment, and later contended that he could have accepted the money and put it in the profit-sharing plan. Since the plan was based on each contributor's annual earnings, that would have been a fair and equitable method of distributing Newhouse's largesse. The truth was, however, that Mr. Shawn looked upon money the way he looked upon the advertisements in the magazine—as a fact of life that had to be tolerated but was separate from the heart of the work. (Years later, I found out that for many years of his editorship Mr. Shawn himself had not received a raise in his basic salary: Fleischmann had never offered him one, and Mr. Shawn's temperament did not allow him ever to bring up the subject.)

The shareholders' meeting was soon adjourned; a pro-forma gathering, it was merely the final curtain to a drama that had concluded.

❦

ON THE VERY day that S. I. Newhouse acquired *The New Yorker,* he made his first appointments as owner: he named Steven Florio the magazine's publisher and Jonathan Newhouse, a cousin, its business manager.

Among the people standing around the watercooler and, as usual, looking at newspapers and magazines, there was an audible gasp at the news of the appointment of Florio. He was a total outsider and knew nothing of our traditions or operating practices. It was reported that he had made a great success of *GQ* (*Gentleman's Quarterly*), but that magazine was as different from us as the Folies Bergère from the Bolshoi Ballet. Florio was described in the press as brash and aggressive—he was all of thirty-seven—and as not letting anything get in his way when it came to business. Such personal qualities might be in demand at dozens of magazines, but they were wholly inappropriate to *The New Yorker.*

Before the day was out, I ran into Mr. Shawn. "It seems as if the workings of *The New Yorker* are about to be drastically altered," I said.

"That's not going to happen," he said. "I think I've established a relationship of mutual trust with Mr. Newhouse, and I think he understands how important it is to respect our traditions."

"But Florio is such an odd choice."

"It's understandable that Mr. Newhouse would want somebody in the business office whom he knows and trusts," Mr. Shawn said.

"How are you going to stop Florio from making changes for commercial reasons?" I asked.

Without missing a beat, Mr. Shawn said, "Mr. Newhouse has given me his word."

As a rule, conversations with Mr. Shawn were reassuring, but in this instance I got the feeling that he was making an unusual effort to do what he did so often, which was to put the best face on things. Still, what other choice did he have?

In the following months, Mr. Shawn and all the rest of us sustained one painful shock after another as the business office under Florio made a series of radical changes from our accepted ways. One shocking change was the firing of seventy-five per cent of the business staff, including all the members who had been top officers under Fleischmann. Some winnowing might have been expected as Florio tried to put in his own people, but at what was soon being referred to by many writers and artists as "the old *New Yorker*" all the employees, even in the business office, had been treated as family, and people had hardly ever been fired. By January of 1986, even Fleischmann felt redundant and quit; although he had enjoyed still coming to his office during Florio's first months, what was happening to his colleagues depressed him, and he himself had nothing to do. (His health was deteriorating, and he died in April, 1993.) Another change was the launching of a big promotional campaign, involving direct-mail solicitations and also expensive television advertisements, which were broadcast during prime-time shows like the flashy police series "Miami Vice." As a result of the campaign, circulation rose from four hundred and eighty thousand to five hundred and seventy-five thousand between June, 1985, and January, 1987. (*The New Yorker* had begun with a circulation of about five thousand, but the circulation had more or less grown steadily, if slowly, ever since—from a hundred and fifteen thousand in 1952, for instance, to four hundred and ninety thousand in 1976.) These techniques of Florio's were a sharp departure. As a matter of policy, the old *New Yorker* had turned down all kinds of reader surveys, and, besides, Mr. Shawn had always been of the opinion that raising circulation by artificial means was self-defeating. He thought that television advertising was a waste of money, since its viewers were not natural *New Yorker* readers—or, at best, were merely transient readers, whose loyalties would be fickle. Still

another change initiated by Florio was the publishing of advertisements that were completely out of kilter with *The New Yorker.*
One was a "cover gatefold"—a double-page layout that, swinging
out from the cover like a map, required the cover to be narrower,
and therefore to abridge the art on it. Another was a proliferation
of advertorials—advertising copy laid out like editorial text and,
moreover, inserted between the pages of a story, so that, for the
first time in the magazine's history, a story was interrupted
and continued elsewhere. (One advertorial ran thirty-six pages.)
Then came horizontal advertisements, which broke up the vertical-
column layout of the magazine. There were even provocative
spreads for Calvin Klein's Obsession perfume which featured glossy
nude models. In the old *New Yorker,* Mr. Shawn would have banned
all these innovations, and nothing more would have been heard of
them, for the business office deferred to Mr. Shawn's judgments—
as it had, earlier, to Ross's—about nearly all advertisements. But in
the new *New Yorker* Mr. Shawn's words of displeasure and protest
were ignored. Under the new regime, not only was Mr. Shawn's
power over the business office being whittled away but the wall
between it and the editorial department was being breached.

The savvy business people we met around town gave Florio
high marks, saying that it had been his and S. I. Newhouse's mis-
fortune to inherit the magazine when it was less successful in
attracting advertisers than it had been in the past. One of these
business people, who was a publisher of a mass-circulation magazine, gave me a long account of what he thought had happened:
"New York no longer has those exclusive shops which made *The
New Yorker's* success possible—you know, the great stores that
used to cater to the carriage trade and your readers, and which
used to be independent boutiques. All those specialty merchants
were local and conveyed a sense of intimacy to *New Yorker* readers
and shoppers. Those merchants wanted to reach these readers,
who were very different from consumers across the country that
national advertisers were trying to reach. There was a kind of

symbiotic relationship between *The New Yorker* and upscale shops, but all those shops have now become part of national chains. They are no longer the exclusive preserve of the rich but, rather, are appealing to middle-class consumers across the country. Besides, in the sixties and seventies new city magazines sprang up and went after the same advertisers as *The New Yorker.* Your business office used to guarantee that a large proportion of your readers lived on the East Coast and could get to New York shops, so it was worthwhile for these shops to place ads in the magazine. In *The New Yorker's* heyday, the East Coast was where the financial and political establishment was based. Now it's dispersed all over the country—in Chicago, Dallas, Los Angeles. This is an age now of pop culture and mass media. You have to attract national advertisers, which means you're competing head on with television and with magazines whose circulation is in the millions. In this new environment, *The New Yorker* is an endangered species and requires bold intervention to save it. You people are lucky that you have men like S. I. Newhouse and Florio on your team."

Maybe so. But it was hard to imagine how the magazine could be kept afloat by changing its distinctive advertising character so that it felt and looked like other magazines and by artificially pumping up its circulation with steroids, as it were. Mr. Shawn, for his part, had believed all along that if *The New Yorker* ever fell on hard times it would be better for it to reduce its circulation and its number of pages and to stay true to itself, even if that meant eventually going out of business, rather than to dilute the editorial content and give in to gimmicks and fads. In fact, Ross and Raoul Fleischmann originally did not want the circulation of the magazine to exceed sixty thousand—their estimate of total natural *New Yorker* readers. When, in 1935, it reached a hundred and twenty-five thousand, they took alarm and arranged to have *The New Yorker* telephone number unlisted, so that prospective subscribers wouldn't be able to call the magazine. During the era of the old *New Yorker*, the editorial department sometimes acted as if the lower the circulation became, the better it was for the quality of the magazine. Any such option, of course, was foreclosed once the magazine was acquired for a hundred and seventy million dollars.

The advertising pages were so plentiful in the nineteen-sixties that advertisements were being rejected in the autumn issues leading up to Christmas, because our standard binding could hold no more than two hundred and fifty-two pages; in 1966, in fact, the total number of advertising pages for the year reached an all-time high of sixty-one hundred and forty-three. The salesmen got so used to simply waiting by their telephones for the advertisers that they almost forgot how to call on accounts and solicit them. In the early seventies, there were some lean years, but the number of advertising pages picked up again in the late seventies, then reached a peak of forty-five hundred in 1981—a year that was especially good financially, because of an increase in the magazine's advertising rates. The number of advertising pages then dropped off to thirty-five hundred in 1984, just before Newhouse arrived. Under him, the magazine started losing money, for the first time since its inception, and, despite all of Florio's efforts, the financial slide gathered momentum. The number of advertising pages dropped off by ten per cent in 1985 (from twenty-nine hundred and ninety to twenty-six hundred and forty-four), and, indeed, the magazine's total revenue dropped twelve per cent in 1985 and another twelve per cent in 1986. The business office laid the blame for the decline on the sluggish economy. And yet *The New Yorker* had had some of its best years during recessions—including some of the years of the Great Depression, when other magazines had suffered but *The New Yorker's* advertising pages and revenue had gone up.

Florio and his associates complained about certain entrenched practices of the editorial department. For instance, Florio said that Mr. Shawn had not alerted the business office to the fact that the magazine was publishing a two-part article on Wisconsin in upcoming issues, and so had deprived the business office of a chance to drum up advertisements and sell extra copies in that state. (Just as a matter of course, many magazines and newspapers would not publish a piece about a particular place unless they could sell space to advertisers with an interest there.) Actually, Mr. Shawn had never alerted the business office to any material he was planning to publish, for he maintained that involving any business people in editorial decisions was dangerous. Moreover, he had always resisted the prevailing trend among publishers to win readers with subjects popular at the moment rather than with interesting subjects and good writing.

❧

ON THE AFTERNOON of Tuesday, January 13, 1987, around two o'clock, Mr. Shawn came down to the eighteenth floor, at our invitation. He again stood three steps from the bottom of the staircase, above the watercooler, just as he had done when he made the announcement of the sale, in March, 1985. This time, he had Milton Greenstein at his side. As on the earlier occasion, a hundred or so of us gathered around Mr. Shawn on the landing in the hall. Many of us had been kept awake all night by the shocking news we had heard the day before: that Mr. Shawn had suddenly been fired, and that Robert A. Gottlieb, who was the editor-in-chief and the president of Alfred A. Knopf, a subsidiary of Random House, had been appointed by Newhouse to be the new editor, and to take charge on March 1st, a little less than six weeks away. The fact is that from the very day Newhouse became the owner there had been newspaper stories about his choosing one of two outsiders to replace Mr. Shawn—either Gottlieb or Robert Silvers, the editor of the *New York Review of Books,* both of whom were in their fifties and were friends of Newhouse. It was subsequently reported that Silvers was not interested, and that

Gottlieb had characteristically given out a non-denial denial statement. ("It is very flattering . . . [but] I have a great job. . . . *The New Yorker* has a great editor.") None of us had given credence to the stories, not only because of the warranties, representations, and covenants in the Agreement and Plan of Merger but also because the same newspapers that reported the rumors had earlier quoted Newhouse as saying that Mr. Shawn could go on being the editor as long as he wished. The Washington *Post* of May 7, 1985, for instance, had run this quotation from Newhouse: "Mr. Shawn is a very young 77. I've had several meetings with him. I found him very vital intellectually and physically. I hope he continues to edit the magazine for a long, long time. Obviously Mr. Shawn will continue to be editor as long as he wants to continue to be editor. He is so much *The New Yorker*. To say he is there at my sufferance would be presumptuous. He's going to be there because he's Mr. Shawn. Just as I wouldn't change the name of the magazine, I wouldn't change Mr. Shawn."

Now, nineteen months later, Mr. Shawn had been abruptly dismissed, and we had asked him to come down to acquaint us with the circumstances. This time, in contrast to the occasion when he announced the sale, he had no prepared statement. His words were impromptu.

"As recently as two months ago, I discussed with Mr. Newhouse my choice of Mr. McGrath as my successor, and, as far as I understood, he approved the choice," Mr. Shawn said. "I told him that Mr. McGrath was coming along well and that I was training him." He had made McGrath deputy editor earlier—he had long since abandoned the idea of co-editors—and McGrath had been scheduled to move into a refurbished office next to him that very week in preparation for succeeding him. "I kept Mr. Newhouse abreast of all the steps I was taking to insure an orderly succession," Mr. Shawn went on. "I heard nothing different from Mr. Newhouse in our conversations until yesterday. Then, around four o'clock, he came to see me in my office and handed me a memo, which he said had already been sent out as a press release dated for today."

Although the memo was addressed to us, we had had to read it that morning in another publication, the New York *Times,* to know its content. It read:

To: The New Yorker Staff
From: S. I. Newhouse, Jr.
Date: Jan. 13, 1987

Recently, Mr. Shawn informed me that he will retire on March 1.

During 35 years as editor—capping his 50-year career here—this remarkable man invented and maintained a standard for *The New Yorker* that is unparalleled in world journalism.

Mr. Shawn's personal qualities of professionalism, high intellect and honor <u>are</u> this magazine. Knowing him and working with him have been a source of pride and pleasure for his staff and for generations of writers and artists . . . and for myself in our too-brief association.

Mr. Shawn, in short, has been the finest editor of his time.

*   *   *

It will take a brilliant editor to succeed this brilliant editor. I have asked Robert Gottlieb, editor and publisher of A. A. Knopf, to become the third editor of *The New Yorker* and Mr. Gottlieb has agreed to accept this responsibility.

Some editorial staff members know Bob Gottlieb personally through the extensive interaction between *The New Yorker* and Knopf. But I believe everyone is aware that he is a unique figure in book publishing whose reputation in his field is comparable to Mr. Shawn's in the world of magazines.

Finally, I will say about Mr. Gottlieb that his range of interests runs from humor to the arts to current affairs to fiction— a gamut that is quite concurrent with *The New Yorker*'s.

* * *

Please join me in expressing my profound gratitude to Mr. Shawn and my appreciation of his lifelong dedication to our magazine.

And join me in also wishing Mr. Gottlieb well in his challenging new position.

Outsiders might have seen nothing extraordinary in the firing by a fifty-nine-year-old tycoon of one of his employees who was nearly eighty. They might have thought that the employee's retirement was long overdue. But we were devastated. There had been no diminution of intelligence or energy in Mr. Shawn's work. Besides, he had made it known that he would be passing on his responsibilities to Chip and staying around to make sure that the transition was a smooth one. It seemed that in one stroke Newhouse had destroyed *The New Yorker*, into which Mr. Shawn had poured his heart and soul for fifty-four years of service. I found myself remembering a poem by W. B. Yeats, "To a Friend Whose Work Has Come to Nothing":

> Now all the truth is out,
> Be secret and take defeat
> From any brazen throat,
> For how can you compete,
> Being honour bred, with one
> Who, were it proved he lies,
> Were neither shamed in his own
> Nor in his neighbour's eyes?
> Bred to a harder thing
> Than Triumph, turn away
> And like a laughing string

Whereon mad fingers play
Amid a place of stone,
Be secret and exult,
Because of all things known
That is most difficult.

"Mr. Newhouse told me that I had indicated to him March 1st as the date of my retirement," Mr. Shawn was saying, "but in fact he had chosen the date. I had discussed my retirement with him, and several dates had been mentioned, including March 1st, but I had never meant to suggest that I planned to leave then. It's possible that he may have misunderstood me, however. I was also stunned by the news of Robert Gottlieb's appointment. Although I've never met him, after the newspaper stories that he might be coming over here he called me at least twice to say that he had no intention of ever becoming the editor of *The New Yorker*. I believed him."

Mr. Shawn stopped for questions. People wanted to know how Gottlieb could possibly learn the ropes in such a short time.

"I will try to meet with him and to familiarize him with everything that goes on here as best I can in the time I have," Mr. Shawn said.

Someone asked Mr. Shawn how long he would be staying around. He didn't respond immediately. Gottlieb couldn't have known, but, despite the brutal circumstances of his coming, Mr. Shawn's nature was such that he would have completely overlooked them and would have stayed around to help him as long as his successor needed him. In any event, Mr. Shawn had a vested interest in insuring the future of his magazine.

While Mr. Shawn was pondering his reply, someone else asked him if he could stay around for a year or two, until Gottlieb understood at least how the magazine worked. Mr. Shawn finally said that Mr. Newhouse had told him that he should be out of his office by March 1st, and that one of

Gottlieb's conditions for coming had been that Mr. Shawn should not remain on the premises. That condition seemed heartless. I recalled that when Ted Weeks was retired from *The Atlantic Monthly,* some seven years earlier, he was allowed to keep his office and his secretary. In fact, that was a common practice in publishing and other businesses when people who had given long years of service to a company were leaving the scene. Mr. Shawn, however, was not to be extended such a courtesy.

It was spontaneously agreed by all of us, following a suggestion by Lillian Ross—and our group had grown to include almost the entire editorial staff—to send a letter to Gottlieb asking him to withdraw. Mr. Shawn warned us that nothing we could do would change Gottlieb's—or Newhouse's—mind. Still, a committee of half a dozen writers went upstairs to draft the letter, and some of us started calling contributors who were friends to ask if they wanted to sign it. As word got out, people called in from all over the country, wanting to add their names.

The letter was written in an hour. It read:

Dear Mr. Gottlieb:

At a spontaneous meeting this afternoon on one of the editorial floors of this magazine, there was a powerful and apparently unanimous expression of sadness and outrage over the manner in which a new editor has been imposed upon us—and opposition to the fact of that imposition. The meeting appeared to include every member of the editorial staff and a great many of our writers and artists. Mr. Shawn, who addressed the gathering at the invitation of those present, told us that, contrary to Mr. Newhouse's announcement distributed to the staff, he had not planned to retire on March 1st, and that the appointment of an editor not heretofore affiliated with the magazine had halted the orderly process, already well along, of providing the magazine with a new editor from within its present ranks. After many years of painful uncertainty about the succession, the magazine has at hand—or had at hand—a successor to Mr. Shawn whom the staff overwhelmingly endorsed. Our hopes were high.

This carefully thought-out procedure, which had been understood and supported within the magazine, would have safeguarded the unique editorial independence— inviolate in our sixty-two-year history—that we feel is essential to the magazine's operation and to its future. *The New Yorker* has not achieved its preeminence by following orthodox paths of magazine publishing and editing, and it is our strange and powerfully held conviction that only an editor who has been a long-standing member of the staff will have a reasonable chance of assuring our continuity, cohesion, and independence. (All through the day, spontaneous messages and calls and cables from our contributors have come into this office, in support of the beliefs stated here.)

We wish to assure you—and we should have done so long before this point—that none of these feelings or reservations were directed against you. Many of us know you personally and professionally, and admire your splendid record at Knopf. We also know that you are a reasonable person. With this in mind, and cognizant of your expressed deep admiration and affection for this magazine, we urge that, after consultation with our owner, Mr. Newhouse, you withdraw your acceptance of the post that has been offered to you.

Sincerely and hopefully,

The letter had many of the marks of Mr. Shawn's *New Yorker.* It was understated and polite, and had to do with convictions, feelings, and principles. No rancor was expressed against either Newhouse or Gottlieb, nor was there any threat of non-coöperation or of a walkout. Mr. Shawn obviously had not helped to edit the letter—or else "imposed," "opposition," and "imposition" would not have appeared together in the lead sentence—and at no point did he comment on it. Rather, it was checked, like any other *New Yorker* copy. It was then circulated for signatures and was signed by a hundred and fifty-four people. Then it was hand-delivered to Gottlieb, with a copy to Newhouse.

I think all of us knew that neither Newhouse nor Gottlieb would back down—they held all the cards. With every one of us gone, the magazine could still come out with pieces that had accumulated on the bank over the years. Anyway, the general view outside the office was that there was no shortage of writers and artists, and everyone could be replaced.

After the letter was sent, Renata Adler and I happened to walk together to the Madison Avenue bus. Renata, along with Brendan Gill, Pauline Kael, John Updike, and Lee Lorenz (the art editor), had declined to sign the letter. She thought that the choice of Gottlieb might turn out to be "great for the magazine." Her remark gave me pause. But then I recalled that she had shown remarkably poor judgment in attacking the movie version of Truman Capote's "In Cold Blood," in the New York *Times,* in 1967, and also in attacking Pauline Kael as a movie critic, in the *New York Review of Books,* in 1980. (After March 1st, Gottlieb always spoke of Renata as "our Renata Adler.")

Later, I read in the press a statement by Brendan Gill that if Gottlieb had heeded the request in the letter he would have committed "professional suicide." But, since Gottlieb had never been an editor of a magazine, his main credential for the job could only be that, like so many people who succeeded in New York, he was confident he could tackle anything. He could have stayed on at Knopf, and the public would have encouraged his good opinion of himself. As a rule, an editor of books is not held accountable the way an editor of magazines with devoted readers is, because books are not associated with their publishers the way such magazines are with their editors. A book publisher may have a hundred and one commercial or noncommercial reasons for what he chooses to publish, but a magazine editor—especially one with a devoted readership—does not have that kind of latitude. At Knopf, Gottlieb had published, along with books of literary distinction, commercial ephemera such as biographies and autobiographies of Hollywood stars. In the opinion of most of us at the magazine, he had compromised the integrity and dulled the lustre of the house of Alfred and Blanche Knopf, who in more than fifty years of publishing together had made their imprint probably the most distinguished in American publishing in the twentieth century. If Gottlieb had been reared in the *New Yorker* tradition, he would surely have withdrawn upon receiving our letter, since he would, of course, have realized that he would be coming aboard to face what was a form of mutiny against his employer and our new owner. But he brushed our letter aside, much as Newhouse did. Ours was "a very emotional reaction . . . part of the *New Yorker* culture," Newhouse told the press. "It is an intense magazine. People are strongly involved in it."

As if the Agreement and Plan of Merger and Newhouse's public assurances had never existed, the press attacked our letter to Gottlieb, accusing us of behaving like spoiled children. The public-relations department of Advance Publications was so powerful that we were like David fighting Goliath, except that we were not in a position to win. The upshot was that our version of the story never got out. Despite Florio's antics, *The New Yorker* had been losing money, and Newhouse might have seen the appointment of Gottlieb as a way of stanching the losses, since Gottlieb was an editor with a considerable public reputation, which, of course, Chip McGrath lacked. In any event, it was no secret that Chip was far from being Mr. Shawn's first choice—that he had been forced upon Mr. Shawn by desperate circumstances. Mr. Shawn's preference for Jonathan never wavered, but he also felt that the editor of *The New Yorker* should ideally come from the fact, rather than the fiction, side of the magazine. Moreover, in the previous month Newhouse and Florio had met with Chip over dinner and asked him many questions, to which, as a very recently designated successor, he could as yet have had no answers. After all, his real training had just begun.

But Newhouse and Florio might have surmised that he wouldn't do. They might have sensed Mr. Shawn's ambivalence toward Chip— that is, if they hadn't already decided that Gottlieb was their man.

❧

ON WEDNESDAY, JANUARY 14th, the day after the cataclysmic public announcement, Mr. Shawn lunched with Gottlieb at the Algonquin. Much was made in the press of the fact that Gottlieb, known for his casual dress, had put on a jacket and tie for the occasion. Over lunch, Mr. Shawn urged Gottlieb not to come to the magazine, since he couldn't imagine how Gottlieb would be able to function in the face of such resistance. His urging, however, had no effect. He then started the process of familiarizing Gottlieb with what went on at the magazine—who the various writers and artists were and what they were working on.

After the lunch, Mr. Shawn was surprised on the street in front of the hotel by a photographer. (Paparazzi had been stalking him and Gottlieb even as they were eating.) He instinctively covered his face to shield his eyes from the glare of the flash. The next day, that awkward picture appeared on the front page of *Newsday* alongside the headline "Up in Arms at The New Yorker." At the time, Mr. Shawn was nearly eighty. He had a right to expect a civilized exit. In the thirty-five years of his editorship, he had never let us write about anyone who didn't wish to be written about: he had always respected people's privacy. But at the end of his long career he himself had to bear the indignity of having his privacy invaded on a New York street.

Gottlieb had handed Mr. Shawn a reply to our letter, and it was posted on the office bulletin board. It read:

Of course I understand the feelings you expressed in your letter, and can even sympathize with them. I also appreciate the fact that your resistance to my coming is not personal.

But I do plan to take up this new job as soon as is convenient and practical, and can only add that I'm looking forward to knowing and working with you all.

As we saw it, Gottlieb's note, lacking the elegance of feeling and language which was the mark of even the most fugitive sentence from Mr. Shawn's hand, was a harbinger of the new *New Yorker.*

The result of our letter, and of Mr. Shawn's wrongly assumed role in prompting it, was that Newhouse moved up the date of Gottlieb's taking charge as editor from March 1st to February 15th.

Mr. Shawn later told me that he actually believed that, as soon as Gottlieb came over, all of us who had signed the protest letter would go down in the elevator and never come back. He came to realize that that was a romantic view. Over the years, he had helped writers and artists to pay school fees for their children and make payments on mortgages for their homes, so he was aware of the practical difficulties of obeying the dictates of one's conscience. Still, he was, to put it mildly, a little bit taken aback when almost all of us acted as if we had never signed and sent the letter. Calvin Trillin went one step further than the rest of us: he signed the letter for Gottlieb not to come, but after seeing Gottlieb's note he sent a welcoming letter to him.

Jonathan Schell was one of a handful of staff members to leave the magazine in protest. In a parting statement, put up on the eighteenth-floor bulletin board, he reviewed the events that had culminated in Mr. Shawn's firing, and concluded, "My objection is not to Robert Gottlieb, either as a person or as an editor; it is to this series of actions. As I see it, they tear up the unwritten charter that until now has guided *The New Yorker.* They annul its crucial editorial independence. They breach its humane traditions. They compromise its integrity. They overthrow the magazine that I and so many others have loved and believed in and worked for over the years."

Jonathan came out of the whole affair with his integrity intact. His critics said that he couldn't possibly have stayed around, because he had at one time been slated for Gottlieb's job. That was unfair, since Chip had also been slated for the job—and more recently than Jonathan—and he was staying around.

"Maybe Newhouse intended to keep his word to honor all the fine representations that Peter had got from him in the Agreement and Plan of Merger," Greenstein told me in the middle of all the turmoil. "We don't know what pressures were brought on Newhouse to change his mind—who scared him, maybe emphasizing to him that his editor was seventy-nine years old, the readership was falling off, advertising was off. All that wasn't anyone's fault—it was simply the change in the whole country. Our salesmen were reporting that they would call on an advertising agency to sell space, only to discover that no one there was reading the magazine—reading anything. In fact, people were coming out of colleges who couldn't read. Sure, *The New Yorker* had a wonderful renewal rate—from seventy-five to eighty per cent—but what was happening was that, while our old faithful readers were renewing, others were falling off or dying and no one was taking their place." (Like Greenstein, I thought that Newhouse intended to honor his representations in the Agreement. In my own case, he continued to provide me with an office and an amanuensis after the magazine gave me my walking papers, and thereby honored my unwritten agreement with Mr. Shawn.) In fact, I myself wondered if behind what some of us perceived as the tremors and shocks that brought down the old *New Yorker* there weren't large economic and social forces at work, beyond anyone's control, such as the eclipsing of the print medium by new technology, which ultimately made the continuation of our protected life at the magazine merely a dream. Certainly the consolidation of newspapers, magazines, and television channels in fewer and fewer hands and their exploitation for primarily commercial reasons did not make for a hospitable climate—the kind of climate in which not only the old *New Yorker* but also publications like the London *Observer* had been able to flourish. In fact, one could argue that it was impossible for the old *New Yorker* to survive in the absence of support from other publications aspiring to high standards. One indication of the depths to which those standards had fallen was that even news stories in the few serious newspapers that were still around had begun taking their cue from the tabloids.

❧

ON FRIDAY, FEBRUARY 13TH, Mr. Shawn left *The New Yorker* as inconspicuously as he had arrived, in 1933. On the previous day, he said farewell to us in this letter, delivered individually to our offices and also posted on the bulletin board:

Dear colleagues, dear friends:

My feelings at this perplexed moment are too strong for farewells. I will miss you terribly, but I can be grateful to have had your companionship for part of my journey through the years. Whatever our individual roles at *The New Yorker*, whether on the eighteenth, nineteenth, or twentieth floor, we have built something quite wonderful together. Love has been the controlling emotion, and love is the essential word. We have done our work with honesty and love. *The New Yorker*, as a reader once said, has been the gentlest of magazines. Perhaps it has also been the greatest, but that matters far less. What matters most is that you and I, working together, taking strength from the inspiration that our first editor, Harold Ross, gave us, have tried constantly to find and say what is true. I must speak of love once more. I love all of you, and will love you as long as I live.

William Shawn

Although it would be some time before we realized it, the process of erasing our memory of Mr. Shawn began almost at the moment that Gottlieb took over.

XIII

AFTERMATH

 N JANUARY 15TH, THE DAY AFTER MR. SHAWN'S LUNCH
with Robert Gottlieb, and on the days following, papers
and magazines were full of complaints, most of them old
and well worn, about *The New Yorker:* that its format was
stodgy; that its articles were long-winded, tedious, and
abstruse; that it was bloated and arrogant; that all magazines had to undergo a revamping from time to time and *The
New Yorker* was long overdue for it; that *The New Yorker's* writers
and artists were coddled, cosseted, and spoiled. Indeed, our reaction to Mr. Shawn's leaving was described as "whimpering" and
childish. Liz Smith, in her widely read column, called us "pam-
pered, self-indulgent refugees from the hard world of publishing."
Richard Cohen wrote in the Washington *Post,* "The *New Yorker*
writers, including some who you might have thought were dead,
and others who write as if they were, were piqued that Shawn had
been replaced in what they felt was an abrupt manner—after only
35 years." And Jonathan Alter, in *Newsweek,* compared us to the
"self-important, dewy-eyed disciples" of the Reverend Jim Jones.
He said that in our frenzy to spurn Gottlieb we were sacrificing

the good of the magazine, and thus, like them, were willingly helping ourselves to ladlefuls of lethal Kool-Aid. Despite all the years of such attacks, we hadn't become inured to them, and the invective took its toll, especially since, as always, we chose to maintain a dignified silence rather than slug it out.

Gottlieb had earlier announced to the press that in his first issue of *The New Yorker* he was going to publish a piece entitled "The Catastrophe," by Doris Lessing, which Mr. Shawn had rejected—an announcement that served to make it clear right away that he, Gottlieb, was not beholden to Mr. Shawn's *New Yorker* and was his own man, for Lessing was one of Gottlieb's Knopf authors. As it happened, the issue in question had been scheduled to carry the first of three autobiographical pieces of mine on my years in California, but now, in order to make room for Lessing's article, my series would, at the very least, have to be bumped to later issues. I had barely got used to the disappointment when Gottlieb sent down word to me that the whole series was being killed. He had already let it be known that, after a careful review, he was killing nearly all of the huge inventory of unpublished manuscripts that Mr. Shawn had accumulated over the years in order to have a greater variety of pieces on hand to choose from and also to keep the staff writers going. But there was all the difference in the world between killing some of the manuscripts in the inventory and killing a piece that was in finished page proofs and ready to go, as mine was. No piece I had written since I first started making submissions to *The New Yorker*, some twenty-eight years earlier, had been treated that way. Although I could console myself with the thought that the series would eventually be published, since it was part of the California book that I was in the middle of writing (the book came out two years later, as "The Stolen Light"), still, the rejection by Gottlieb boded ill for my future at the magazine.

A couple of days after receiving the news about my series, I happened to be speaking to Mr. Shawn on the telephone, and told him about it. If anything, he sounded more shocked than I felt—possibly because I was prone to a kind of Hindu fatalism, whereas he was, in his quiet way, used to leaning against the prevailing wind.

"I am going to call Gottlieb," Mr. Shawn said.

I tried to dissuade him. I didn't want to put him in an awkward position on my account, nor did I myself want to antagonize Gottlieb, for he could very well take offense at my appealing to Mr. Shawn and make things even more difficult for me.

Within hours of my conversation with Mr. Shawn, Gottlieb walked into my office. "Mr. Shawn just called me and scolded me for substituting a poor piece for a brilliant one," he said, with a short laugh, and added, "But I am the editor now, and I think Lessing is a very important writer."

His use of the word "important" reinforced my feeling that all of us writers and artists were now living in a different world—a world where the notoriety of the writer would, for the first time, be a factor in what was published, and even take precedence over the quality of the writing.

Now, thinking that Gottlieb was ready to leave, I stood up. Instead, he stayed around and, suddenly becoming extremely affable, talked to me about his second wife, the actress Maria Tucci; her father, the writer Niccolo Tucci, who had been the author of the Alotrios pieces; and her mother, Laura. I had once known all three of them well. When Gottlieb finally left, he said, "I'll look at your series again." The remark was well meant and seemed almost reminiscent of Mr. Shawn. I took heart. I told myself I should try to suspend judgment on Gottlieb and give the man a chance.

Gottlieb called me a little while later and said, "Maybe I can carve out an article from your California material after all."

I should have felt happy. Gottlieb was offering to salvage something from my series. Something was better than nothing, and he was trying to be nice. Instead, I felt uncontrollably sad.

"Carving out" implied cutting and pasting, taking paragraphs from here and there and trying to fit them together, the editor imposing his vision on the piece—not honoring the writer's vision.

How different Gottlieb's editing was from that of Ross and Mr. Shawn! If either Ross or Mr. Shawn admired a piece of writing, he published all of it, long or short, for he saw it as a piece of architecture, and saw publishing only part of it as erecting only part of a house that an architect had designed. Indeed, in publishing whole works they followed the tradition of great nineteenth- and twentieth-century editors.

Soon after Gottlieb's call, a reporter from *Newsday* who was doing a piece on the succession called me and asked if it was true that Gottlieb was killing a series of mine that Mr. Shawn had been about to run. I said that Gottlieb was probably going to reduce it to one part but that I was still waiting for the final word. (In fact, he not only reduced it by two-thirds but also cut out any intellectually demanding material, such as a favorite quotation of mine from the "History of Philosophy" by the German philosopher W. Windelband.) I added that it was Gottlieb's prerogative as editor to run what he liked. The reporter published my remark that the piece was being cut down but not my qualifying comment. No sooner had the story appeared than I got a stern note from Gottlieb saying that I had no business talking to the press about private matters at *The New Yorker*. I felt frightened in spite of myself. Indeed, all of us at the office were soon watching what we said, not only to the press but to one another, and some people were going out of their way to praise Gottlieb, in the hope of currying favor with him. Overnight, the atmosphere of freedom had been transformed into one of fear.

❦

GOTTLIEB'S FIRST ISSUE, which came out after the kerfuffle over my California piece, was anything but reassuring about his editorship. The Lessing article, which was a long piece on the Mujahideen, the "holy warriors" of the Afghan resistance fighting against Russian invaders, violated principles of reporting that we'd grown up with at *The New Yorker*, such as to refuse favors from people one is writing about and not to be partisan. It was clear from the text that her expenses for the article had been paid by an interested organization, Afghan Relief: she wrote that she had been involved with it for some years. Indeed, good chunks of her article were verbatim transcriptions of self-serving statements by her hosts. But, of course, since the author was Lessing, the article was not without interest.

Then, there was the Comment, leading off the issue, which Gottlieb had written himself. From beginning to end, it read like p.r. copy—completely out of key with anything I'd ever read before in the magazine. Here is its text:

In these past weeks, scores of news stories, feature articles, and editorials about *The New Yorker* have appeared in the press, and, more important, a flood of letters has reached us here—letters that have made one thing clear: *The New Yorker* matters to its readers in a special and very personal way. Nothing else could explain why, at this public moment in our history, so many people have written to us with the most thoughtful expressions of anxiety, encouragement, and concern. This close bond between our readers and the magazine is the foundation on which we hope and plan to build our future.

In Mr. Shawn's day, if by some mischance this copy had got set up, it would have been chock-a-block with editorial queries: "Want to use 'flood of letters'? It's a cliché." "Any reason to repeat 'letters'. . . 'letters'? Sounds rhetorical." "Want 'public moment' and 'history'? Sounds odd. Avoid?" "'Bond' and 'foundation' are a mixed metaphor. Any reason for using it? Anyway, why 'foundation,' since magazine in existence for sixty years plus?" And so on. Since most of us were perforce staying around, we tried feverishly to find alibis for Gottlieb: it wasn't fair to subject his copy to such niggling criticisms; it was the man's first issue; he wasn't a writer; he was an intelligent man and would learn in time; in a sense, any copy subjected to close scrutiny could be found wanting in one respect or another. Indeed, we all tried to wish him well, because our future was bound up with his. But, as it turned out, the lapses of Gottlieb's Comment were soon cluttering his magazine. The simple truth was that the tradition of meticulous writing and reporting which had grown up in Ross's and Mr. Shawn's *New Yorker* was alien to him. He had never had any experience of running a magazine, and it was soon woefully clear that he was floundering.

❦

GOTTLIEB CAME FROM Knopf with the reputation of being so effective at firing up his salesmen at sales conferences with enthusiasm for the books he edited that he was as deeply revered by the salesmen as he was by the books' authors. Consequently, according to *Advertising Age*, the advertising industry's trade magazine, his appointment as editor of *The New Yorker* was "welcomed by members of the advertising, marketing and media communities." They believed that, as a super book salesman, he would be more closely attuned to business and advertising at *The New Yorker,* because, as Newhouse had pointed out to *Advertising Age* at the time of Gottlieb's appointment, "there's no question that in book publishing there's a traditional proximity to best-seller lists, to sales of books and the sales department." Yet Gottlieb had to tread a fine line, *Advertising Age* observed, for "there could be trouble if editorial changes under Mr. Gottlieb are simultaneously not enough to satisfy critics clamoring for new approaches, and too much for the weekly's longtime readers."

Gottlieb had to be especially watchful because he had come to *The New Yorker* under very difficult circumstances—against the will of the staff. He coped with this difficulty shrewdly: he made Chip his deputy editor and started working with him hand-in-glove. Even so, in the early days Gottlieb seemed extremely nervous. Whenever I had a conversation with him, I got the impression that he had trouble concentrating, for he jumped from subject to subject like a grasshopper. Greenstein was astonished that Gottlieb never asked questions of people who had been at the magazine a long time; it seemed as if Gottlieb felt that he could run it perfectly without any reference to how things had been done in the past. "Gottlieb just doesn't want to know what came before," Greenstein said. But then Greenstein, who died in 1991, had no experience of the corporate culture in which Gottlieb had been reared, and which must have led him to believe that running one business was much like running another—that whatever had worked at Knopf would work at *The New Yorker.* Anyway, Gottlieb gave the impression that he wanted to write on a tabula rasa. We could only marvel at his chutzpah. He initially brought with him from Knopf only two allies: a longtime associate of his, Martha Kaplan, and a protégé and former *GQ* editor named Adam Gopnik.

❧

DESPITE GOTTLIEB'S TREATMENT of the one California piece that he did publish, I continued to submit additional parts of "The Stolen Light" as I wrote them—much as I would have submitted them to Mr. Shawn. I expected nothing but was cheered up when he accepted three of the six I had submitted. My good cheer dissipated quickly, however, when two of the pieces started going through the hoops of the editorial carving-out process. Yet the third, along with two pieces about Indian politics, which I wrote later, went through much as I had written them, so I was left confused about what to make of him, especially since his proofs on all the pieces showed him to be a brilliant textual editor. Indeed, his suggestions on sentences and words were reminiscent of those of Mr. Shawn himself. Certainly his editorial decisions, whatever one thought of them, were based on close reading of texts. Moreover, in many respects he came across, perhaps by instinct, as a conservator, and seemed to want to preserve the magazine's heritage. Outwardly, his *New Yorker* looked like the old *New Yorker*, for revolutionary departures in format, such as publishing a photographic essay, were few and far between.

Gottlieb, however, either never grasped the form of various departments or chose not to honor them. In fact, he showed himself here to be out of key with the tone of the magazine. Under him, for the first time, *The New Yorker* started running out-and-out opinion pieces without labelling them as Comment or some similar rubric. For instance, there were one-sided pieces against the United Nations and against New York City's Human Resources Administration. One entire Talk of the Town section was given over to a partisan attack on the nomination of Robert H. Bork to the United States Supreme Court. Gottlieb also went in for kitsch and camp. He published a piece by Knopf authors who were friends of his, Jane and Michael Stern, about the annual convention of the Wee Scots, an organization of collectors of Scottie-dog memorabilia. Meanwhile, he himself collected women's plastic pocket books from the nineteen-fifties and was known to make "jaunts," often in the company of Kaplan, to flea markets and vintage-clothing stores far and wide in search of them. "I keep them now on glass shelves around my bedroom, on bookshelves in halls, on the floor, under my bed," he wrote in a book he published about his collection in 1988, the year after he became editor. "Since my wife doesn't totally grasp the charm of this collection, she shares the bed but leads the waking hours of her home life outside our bedroom."

Like the shrewd publisher he was, Gottlieb soon began assiduously mining old issues of the magazine in order to cull material for books, and published the books under the Knopf imprint: "The Complete Book of Covers from The New Yorker," "The New Yorker Book of Doctor Cartoons," "The New Yorker Book of Lawyer Cartoons," "The New Yorker Book of Cat Cartoons," and "The New Yorker Book of Dog Cartoons." There had been *New Yorker* collections in the past, but what made these new ones different was a lack of thought and care, and, in the case of the cover collection, even a lack of attention to how the art looked. It was so reduced—there were twelve covers to a page— that some of the artists whose work was represented told me they were embarrassed at having appeared in it. (The commercial gimmick was so irresistible that five years after Gottlieb had gone from the magazine Roger Angell brought out a collection of *New Yorker* stories with love as its theme. The whole approach of focussing on collections suggested a greeting-card store, which has cards for every occasion.) Soon Gottlieb was also running in the magazine pieces whose appeal was based not so much on good writing as on apparent business considerations. As a result, many of us felt that even in his dealings with his "important" writers he was governed more by commercial values than by literary ones. For instance, in half a dozen successive issues he published weak and discursive excerpts from John Cheever's journals which posthumously portrayed the author as an alcoholic, an adulterer, and a homosexual. *The New Yorker* had begun publishing Cheever's short stories in 1935, when he was living in Greenwich Village, in a room he rented for three dollars a week, and had continued to publish them, whether he was in or out of fashion; in fact, during many of his *New Yorker* years he had had no commercial success but had enjoyed a growing reputation. The publication of his journals, however, revealed his private maunderings to be sensational, in contrast to his marvellous old *New Yorker* stories, which had been profound, and it sullied his reputation. In addition, it confirmed the impression that readers could no longer be certain they would be reading the best work of the writers who appeared in the magazine, whether they were established or were just starting out.

❦

EARLIER, I HAD discussed with Mr. Shawn whether I could do an autobiographical series on Oxford as a follow-up to the California series. Now I asked Gottlieb what he thought of the idea. To my surprise, he was extremely enthusiastic. On the strength of my conversations with him, I moved my family to Oxford and spent a year in England gathering material and doing research. As with all the pieces I'd ever written for *The New Yorker,* I invested a lot of my time and money in them. After further months—these devoted to reading and writing—I started submitting my Oxford pieces to him. He rejected seven of them in a row. Then I submitted three new Oxford pieces, and these he accepted. This was a bittersweet blessing: neither he nor I could explain why the first lot had been rejected and the second lot accepted. Anyway, the latter lot, read in *The New Yorker* in isolation from the former, was bound to give a weird impression both of Oxford and of me. The whole business made Gottlieb seem capricious and unpredictable, and thus compounded my confusion about my place in his magazine.

Meanwhile, the wall between the editorial department and the business office was being demolished, and that did not augur well for *The New Yorker.* Not only was Florio seen going in and out of Gottlieb's office regularly but the writers and editors were flying to retreats organized by the business office, and consequently they were, for the first time, talking and worrying about the number of advertising pages.

❦

GOTTLIEB AND STEVE FLORIO introduced many changes in our day-to-day office life. I still can't make up my mind whether they were necessary improvements or merely corporate gilding. One of Gottlieb's first acts as the editor was to install a coffee machine and make free coffee available to everyone. The machine produced such a strong brew that all the editorial floors seemed to be permeated with the aroma of a café. There was something inviting but also offputting about the smell: it made the office homier but changed its monastic atmosphere. Gottlieb turned up at the office in sneakers, chinos, and shirt-sleeves, and insisted that everyone call him Bob; soon surnames almost disappeared from our social intercourse. He transformed Mr. Shawn's old office, making it his own by introducing touches like an oversized poster of Joan Crawford. He also let it be known that he would be publishing four-letter words in the magazine—an innovation that made possible in it the inclusion of a certain kind of modern fiction. Moreover, he said he had no objection to terms such as "glitz," a Yiddish word that had been appropriated by the fashion industry and spurned at the old *New Yorker*. The press interpreted his informal, campy style as a sign of greater accessibility and contemporaneity than had been provided by Mr. Shawn, but many of us saw it as a form of exhibitionism and an easy way to court popularity with the fashionable crowd.

In addition, there were more substantial changes:

Gottlieb jazzed up Goings On About Town with drawings related to the listings—a move that, though it was visually engaging, amounted to supplying free advertising for stars and shows. He also brought in some new critics to cover regular departments. They drew a mixed reaction, but then it was obvious that there was no one who could replace Pauline Kael, for instance, any more than there had been anyone who could replace Kenneth Tynan in Mr. Shawn's day.

Computers replaced typewriters in the typing pool, and it was renamed the word-processing department. No doubt the time had arrived to change over, but the new name didn't seem altogether felicitous, since it conjured up for some of us the image of a sausage factory.

The printing of the magazine was moved from the R. R. Donnelley plant in Chicago to a new Donnelley plant, in Danville, Kentucky—a move that that gave the magazine three extra days of lead time in distributing issues to newsstands and to subscribers but similarly reduced the lead time for closing the issues. This meant that if something significant happened after Comment, the Talk stories, and the art had gone to press, readers would find no mention of it, for there was no way to bring the copy up to date. (The problem of needing extra lead time at the office seemed to come up every month or so, but the most notable example, which no one who was on the staff in the early days ever forgot, had to do with the attack on Pearl Harbor. When it happened, parts of the magazine had already been printed, and Ross had barely a day in which to shift the tone of the magazine from its usual gaiety to an appropriate seriousness.) Gottlieb's change of printing plants also meant that the issues, instead of being folded in half and wrapped in kraft paper, so that they could be stuffed into readers' mailboxes, would now be sent flat and wrapped in clear plastic. The artists, though, were much pleased by this change, because their art would no longer be creased.

Under Gottlieb's regime, Florio contracted out some of the functions of our accounting department, which was at the heart of our institution, and this change turned the system of the drawing account into what amounted to a salary system. Getting a salary lowered our anxiety level but also had the effect of somewhat corrupting our austere ways. Gottlieb and Florio also adopted a new policy for managing our profit-sharing plan. Now, instead of the company's choosing investments for us and directing the money manager accordingly, each participant was asked to fill out a form every quarter designating how his or her share in the plan was to be invested. Some people protested, saying that they were not savvy about the market, but Gottlieb told them, in my hearing, that the new policy was a way of ending the old *New Yorker's* paternalism, which, he maintained, had reduced us to acting like children. Apparently for the same reason, the woman to whom we had submitted our medical bills for filing insurance claims was let go, and we were asked to deal directly with the insurance company ourselves.

Perhaps the change that was the most disorienting, however, was that, early in 1991, we were moved out of our run-down but homey offices on the north side of Forty-third Street, where the magazine had been quartered since 1935, and into extremely smart offices on the south side, which provided a third more space. The old offices had been a warren of small, dingy rooms with linoleum floors, with doors that often had a top panel of opaque glass, with thin partitions for walls, and with individual air-conditioning units—rooms that were all periodically rebuilt, in helter-skelter fashion, as the need arose, and were all laid out in a maze of narrow, cramped halls. (They reminded me of drafty garrets to which some of my Oxford friends liked to retreat in order to study or to write.) For all their dust, squalor, and discomfort, they helped us feel part of a community, because one could hardly stir out into the hallway without running into colleagues. The new offices, however, were a succession of large rooms with carpeting, solid doors, stoutly partitioned walls, and centralized air-conditioning—all spread along wide, airy halls. They reminded me of the offices of a law firm. For all their comfort and splendor, they made us feel isolated and cut off from one another. (The only feature common to both sets of offices was that many of us had individual windows that we could open and close.) The new space had recently been vacated by a telephone company, and no time or expense was spared in remodelling it. House architects working for our new owners were asked to draw up plans that emphasized special touches, reflecting the new corporate status of the magazine. Thus an open area near the editor's office had an elegant staircase in the middle of it, leading to the floor below. The space was designated the "piazza," and there, in due course, parties would be held and the office would shell out money for champagne, canapés, and farewell presents. The offices also included a lunchroom, which provided not only tables and chairs but a lounge-*cum*-kitchen, complete with vending machines, microwave ovens, a television, and a jukebox. Such changes at every turn made clear how Gottlieb, Kaplan, and their architects envisaged the new, modernized, corporate *New Yorker*. A great deal of time had been spent deciding exactly where the various editorial departments should be situated and which person should occupy each. Some clever gestures were made in homage to our old offices which predictably attracted a lot of press coverage, the principal gesture being to bring over to the new offices a couple of sections of Thurber's office wall, preserving those sketches he made on it before he became totally blind.

In the new building, the floors of the business office, which had formerly been situated under the editorial department, were now situated above it. Moreover, Gottlieb liked to say that Florio had insisted on having an office bigger than his, and that, while that kind of thing was important to Florio, it wasn't to him. In one sense, such distinctions were inconsequential, yet in another they were symbolic of the new corporate culture.

The prospect of the move from the familiar to the alien terrain created a lot of agitation. To calm us all down, Gottlieb had told us from the start that the rationale for the move was that we needed more up-to-date electrical wiring for computers and other modern equipment. He didn't explain, though, why the old building couldn't have been fixed up and rewired. I, for one, wondered if there was a subtext to the decision to move, especially when I read that there had been a debacle over *The New Yorker* archives. In more than half a century in the old building, the magazine had collected a huge quantity of manuscripts, proofs, and correspondence in its basement. Every little piece ever published generated a score or more drafts and proofs, and all of them were saved, originally for legal reasons. Prior to the move, Newhouse had donated all the archives to the New York Public

Library. The Reverend Timothy Healy, then the president of the library, told me that by making such a gift Newhouse would be saving at least a hundred thousand dollars a year on storage costs. During the move of the offices, just across the street, at least forty large boxes of archives destined for the library were accidentally taken off to the dump. No packing lists had been made, but Mimi Bowling, the person at the library in charge of *The New Yorker* archives, told me that all the manuscripts and proofs for the first twenty-five years' worth of issues—from 1925 to 1950—were lost.

One reason for the egregious blunder might have been that the new regime was not as careful with the archives as its predecessor had been. For example, Eleanor Gould told me that at a farewell party for a departing staff member she noticed some open file boxes of correspondence sitting around in an inconspicuous corridor off the new piazza and obviously waiting to be stowed away. Out of curiosity, she looked in one of the boxes under "P" to see if there might be something about her late husband, Freddie Packard, who had been, among other things, the head of the checking department; instead, she happened upon a letter from Mr. Shawn to Pablo Picasso, rejecting three poems he had submitted. Later, when I was consulting the archives in the Public Library in preparation for this manuscript, I wondered if other papers of Mr. Shawn's had been destroyed or mislaid. All his papers were conspicuously absent from the library's collection, nor was a significant quantity of them to be found at Eleven-Fifty.

At some point, all the meticulous records of word counts and of the resulting payments for individual articles and art work to all of us, along with clippings about our *New Yorker* books, copies of those books which the business department had kept in its files, and copies of the weekly in-house handout that had quoted favorable mentions of *The New Yorker* and had been circulated weekly to the sales staff, were chucked out as if memories of the glory of the magazine were irrelevant to Newhouse's *New Yorker.* The move certainly seemed like the last gesture in the erasing of the memory of Mr. Shawn and of his *New Yorker.* Essentially, we were like children of divorced parents: our father had been kicked out and we had to accommodate ourselves to the presence of a stepfather and forget whose place he had taken.

The process of wiping the slate clean of the magazine's institutional memory started, in a sense, when Gottlieb eliminated the system of checking all proposed Talk ideas against previous published Talk stories. Eugene Kinkead's department, which had performed this function, was done away with, on the ground that no one remembered Talk stories published even a few months earlier—never mind decades. The slate-cleaning process picked up breakneck speed in the fall of 1992, when Gottlieb was suddenly replaced by Tina Brown, a thirty-eight-year-old Englishwoman who had been the editor of the British magazine *Tatler* and then of the American magazine *Vanity Fair* and was also the author of two aptly titled books, "Loose Talk" and "Life as a Party." Why Newhouse relieved Gottlieb of his job was never explained in so many words, but the changes that came with Tina Brown were so radical that they constituted an explanation in themselves. Although she kept the magazine's old type for department headings, she abandoned its body type, New Yorker Caslon, which had an airy, classic look, for Adobe Caslon, which had a tighter, more modern look and could fit more text onto a page. Also, whereas the old body type had had to be customized, the new type, which was used by other magazines, too, was available off the shelf in any computer shop. She introduced squibs, or potted summaries, of articles on the Contents page, put the writer's byline under the title of each story, included a great many photographs and many color drawings, and published short pieces calculated to create a stir in the press. From week to week, she moved departments around, putting in the front of the magazine those with certain pieces deemed catchy, provocative, or controversial. She introduced new departments, with headings like "Showcase"—a term straight out of the entertainment industry. Even the feel of the paper stock gave the impression of a high-class fashion publication: the stock was heavier, showing the advertisements, photographs, and art work to advantage. She brought out theme issues, focussing on music, politics, blacks, women, fashion, movies. (The movie issue carried a tag line in the Table of Contents which read, *"The New Yorker* Goes to the Movies," as if it had never gone to the movies before.) In fact, Brown's *New Yorker* subverted all the editorial principles that Mr. Shawn had held inviolable: most obviously, the principle that nothing would ever be published in *The New Yorker* just to sell magazines, to create a sensation or a controversy, to be popular or fashionable—to be "successful." With Brown, however, being successful—courting special subject matter, topicality, and stylish trends—became the raison d'être of *The New Yorker.*

There were other departures. Issues were skipped, with the material combined in double issues, and old material and old covers were republished. But there were also covers whose sole aim was to create a sensation—one an incendiary Valentine's Day cover that showed a black woman and a Hasidic man embracing and kissing, and another an April cover that depicted an Easter bunny being crucified on a tax form. There were scandalous photographic essays. In an essay entitled "In Memory of the Late Mr. and Mrs. Comfort," one photograph showed a beautiful woman copulating with a skeleton. Similarly, all kinds of advertisements were courted and accepted, as if the policy of holding them to a certain standard of taste and decorum had never existed: one issue carried an offer for "sexual products," complete with a clip-out coupon requesting a catalogue from the advertiser and providing an assurance that the customer was over twenty-one years of age.

All these departures created what is called, in modern parlance, a "buzz." Certain pieces may have been read by more people than had ever read anything in *The New Yorker* before.

But the magazine continued to lose money, as it had done since Mr. Shawn's firing. (The losses were rumored by magazine cognoscenti to be huge, but their exact size remains unknown, since the magazine is part of a private company and does not have to make such disclosures public.)

While Brown got rid of most of the middle-aged writers from Mr. Shawn's day, she kept around a few writers who had come to the magazine in Ross's day, and she published occasional pieces by them. She also revived an ancient column called Shouts and Murmurs from his *New Yorker*. The subtle message seemed to be that she was burying the commercially inhibited *New Yorker* of Shawn and celebrating the rollicking, liberated *New Yorker* of Ross. Conveniently, since Ross's magazine was long gone, harking back to it posed no risk of contradiction. The harking back was merely a public-relations gesture: it was good business to provide a fig leaf of continuity for the revolutionary changes.

In fact, as was customary at other corporations preoccupied with image, public relations took center stage. Brown recruited Maurie Perl, whose expertise in public relations had been honed in television: for seven years she had worked at ABC for Barbara Walters. In February, 1993, she was made a vice-president of the magazine and its director of public relations. She developed a "hot list" of politicians, business leaders, journalists, writers, and television people in New York, Washington, and Los Angeles, and saw to it that they received advance copies of *The New Yorker* by special courier each week, along with a press release highlighting one particular piece, or more than one. The list was regularly modified, depending on what piece or pieces she wanted to draw attention to. Even a memorial service for Joe Mitchell, held by the magazine in 1996, was handled as a special project of the p.r. department, and many of Joe's friends and colleagues were excluded, no doubt because they—or, rather, we—were not considered worthy of inclusion.

Under Brown, corporate culture flourished in the office.

Brown herself acted as if she were part of the business office, breakfasting and lunching as a matter of course with prospective advertisers. There was a constant turnover in the staff, heralded by a stream of memos asking everybody to welcome this one or bid farewell to that one, or informing us of a new title for this one or a change of position for that one. The new people and new titles proliferated until it seemed that the job Mr. Shawn had done alone and Gottlieb had done with the help of Kaplan and Chip now required a score of workers or more. There was, however, no gain in elegance or in efficiency: many staff writers—including this one, in 1994—were "terminated," and subsequently, when I got a letter from Brown's *New Yorker* rejecting a pending project, my name was misspelled.

I am, for obvious reasons, no expert on Brown's *New Yorker*. I have never worked for her, nor have I had any direct professional dealings with her. At the time Gottlieb left, two of my three Oxford pieces that he had accepted were waiting to run. She sent word to me through Chip that she was killing one. The other, Chip reported, she was publishing because she had known one of the people who figured in it—Alasdair Clayre. That piece was then in the final proof stage, but I never received any queries from her or had any conversation with her about it. In fact, I have talked to her only once. During her first several months at *The New Yorker*, people kept asking me what she was like. I told them that I hadn't met her yet—that these were early days for her and she was probably too busy to drop by and say hello. Finally, after all that needling, I became so curious that I got an appointment with her by calling her secretary, and stopped by her office at the arranged time. We exchanged one or two amenities, then neither of us could think of anything more to say. Actually, most of our meeting, which couldn't have lasted more than five minutes, was taken up with an embarrassing confusion over which chair she should sit in and which chair I should sit in. Oddly, I ended up sitting in her chair.

EPILOGUE

T HE LAST FIVE YEARS OF MR. SHAWN'S LIFE WERE TOR-
mented. His departure from *The New Yorker* had come so
suddenly that he had had no chance to plan for his new
life. In fact, after he left he never seemed to get his bear-
ings. Roger Straus, the president of the book publishers
Farrar, Straus & Giroux, made much in the press of the
fact that Mr. Shawn had agreed to be an editor at his company,
but Mr. Shawn actually had very little work to do there, and, in
any event, the job was honorary and unpaid. True, he could have
had an office there, but that was never a real possibility, since he
would have had trouble coping with the automatic elevators in
the publishers' offices, on Union Square.

Still, Mr. Shawn did need to get out of the apartment and
have a daily routine, so all of us were delighted when we heard
that he had got the use of an office in the Brill Building,
thanks to Lorne Michaels, who was the executive producer of the
television program "Saturday Night Live" and the founder of
Broadway Video, a production company that leased several floors
in the building. I had heard Mr. Shawn say more than once that

he enjoyed watching "Saturday Night Live"—that it followed *The New Yorker's* tradition of humor and satire. The Brill Building spanned half a block on Broadway at Forty-ninth Street, and was thus only a short distance away from *The New Yorker,* but we were so respectful of Mr Shawn's privacy that none of us went near it. We had a good sense of the lore that had grown up around it, however, for under the fictitious name of the Jollity Building it had been the subject of a well-remembered three-part Profile by Joe Liebling. In 1941, when the Profile was published, the building quartered bandleaders, theatrical agents, bookmakers, and sundry fly-by-night "promoters," along with a dance hall and a poolroom. Most of the "heels," as the renting agent called the individual tenants, were so nearly down and out that they were required to pay in advance the monthly rent of ten or twelve dollars for their cramped, cubicle-like offices. When tenants couldn't come up with any rent money, they worked out of eight telephone booths in the lobby, living the life of a band of roving gypsies. In the forty-six years since Liebling's Profile, the building had undoubtedly undergone some renovations and changes in ambiance, yet it was shocking to think of Mr. Shawn ending up there, even if it was also cheering to know that his office was housed in a building that his magazine had made something of a landmark. In any event, we liked to imagine that he was surrounded by eccentrics there, much as he had been in our office.

❧

ONCE IN A WHILE, Mr Shawn and I met for lunch at the Algonquin, at his old corner table in the Rose Room. In the beginning, he was still reading every word of *The New Yorker* and scrutinizing every drawing in it—in fact, mentally reëditing it. He wished that he had been able to stay around long enough to teach Chip exactly what made a good Talk story; Chip had begun editing the Talk department, and, possibly because as a fiction editor he had had little experience with it, Mr. Shawn felt that it had fallen off even more than other departments. He bemoaned the fact that Gottlieb seemed not to realize what made a good article or a good drawing, but he added charitably, "Of course, Gottlieb has no experience running a magazine," and he never said an unkind word about Gottlieb as a person. In all the years I knew Mr. Shawn, although it was clear in discussions with him that he had taken the intellectual measure of everybody, he never breathed a negative word about anybody. He always seemed to be more interested in discerning the springs of people's actions than in judging them. In both literary and economic terms, the magazine was on the skids, and I asked him more than once whether he thought that its decline could somehow be arrested and reversed.

In the early days, he did think so; in fact, he thought that he should be ready in case Newhouse called him and asked for his help. Months went by, and the call never came. When I brought up the subject at one of our later lunches, in January or February of 1988, he said he had stopped thinking that Newhouse would ever turn to him.

"Why?" I asked.

"I don't know," he said. "He's a very proud man." Then he said, "That's just my guess. I don't know why he hasn't. I don't know him very well." He remarked that the magazine's decline had gone so far now that there was no way of reversing it, but he refused to be drawn into a direct discussion about the future of *The New Yorker*. Instead, he ruminated aloud about what had happened to *The Saturday Review* in the early seventies, when its new owners changed its character, and what had happened to Coca-Cola when its owners changed its formula, and, indeed, what happened to "Saturday Night Live" when Lorne Michaels left the show for four years, earlier in the decade.

Several times, we talked about the possibility of his starting a new magazine—a much smaller and more modest one than the old *New Yorker.* He had been following the birth and success of the *Independent* in Britain with great interest, he said, but he didn't think that the kind of magazine he had in mind could succeed in the current publishing climate here, even if money could somehow be raised for it. I had the feeling, though, that if he had been ten or twenty years younger he might have had a different view.

❧

Mr. Shawn had left *The New Yorker* in the middle of working on my book "The Stolen Light," and when I asked him how we should proceed he had immediately said that we should continue as we always had. I therefore kept sending him drafts, proofs, pictures, and catalogue copy, as I always had, except that now I sent them to his apartment. He edited the book and its sequel, "Up at Oxford," chapter by chapter, much as he had edited all my books except "Face to Face"—the only one that had not originally appeared in his *New Yorker.* I remember we spent one long afternoon going over his queries at his Algonquin table after the restaurant had emptied. Though eerie, it was like being back in his office.

Generally, before we got down to work in the Algonquin we chatted over our meal. But I kept being struck by how many of our usual subjects of conversation had suddenly become painful to him—and, by extension, to me. Those were the Reagan-Bush years, and he was much disheartened at what their Administrations had done and were doing, at what was happening in the country at large, and at how little political comment of any consequence there was to be found: he was depressed by the lack of serious journalism. He told me that every day he woke up and had an idea for a Comment, a long fact piece, or a drawing that might go into *The New Yorker.* But now there was no one at the magazine whom he could suggest it to and who could help to get it into print. Even the subject of his sons' futures made him uneasy. Both Wallace and Allen had chosen professions—theatre and music, respectively—that were full of hazards and threatened financial insecurity.

After each of our lunch meetings, Mr. Shawn insisted on walking back to the office with me, as he had always done, and once we reached the entrance to the building we would stand on the sidewalk in front of it and finish our conversation. He would never enter it, even just to walk through to the Forty-third Street exit, but instead would turn away, as if part of his injunction at the accession of Gottlieb had been that he couldn't cross the threshold of *The New Yorker's* building.

❧

AFTER A YEAR or two, Mr. Shawn stopped coming to the Algonquin, and to Forty-fourth Street, altogether. He also stopped reading the magazine. I had the impression that, except for separating himself from the office, giving up reading *The New Yorker* was the most painful thing he had ever done. But doing so had a calming effect on his spirits, for he was no longer constantly disheartened by what he read. Now we started having lunch at a quiet corner table in the Oak Room of the Plaza. We would usually meet at one-thirty, and would sit and talk and work until three-thirty or four.

At one point, I said to him that his old colleagues at the office hoped he would write his memoirs. He said that that wouldn't happen. He couldn't write about anybody he had known at *The New Yorker,* because he was still governed by the same rules of discretion that he had been governed by while he was at the magazine. I asked if he was writing anything. He said he had started something but he didn't know whether anything would come of it. He was as reluctant to talk about his writing as most of my colleagues were to talk about theirs, so I didn't even know whether it was fiction or fact until after he died. Then it turned out that it was a short novel about a solitary old man who was a pianist living in a single room in an old hotel. It was as if Mr. Shawn had been writing about a life that he might have ended up with if he hadn't got married, come to *The New Yorker,* and had a family.

As time went on, I noticed that his voice was becoming softer and softer until, finally, it was little more than a whisper. There wasn't much energy in it. In addition, his legs were unsteady, and he walked slowly.

The last time I saw him, perhaps four or five months before he died, he seemed to be in lower spirits than ever: he spoke haltingly, with long silences. Still, even when I heard from Cecille that he was sick, I kept sending him pieces of my writing for his comments, recalling how he had always wanted to help all of us when he was in bed with a fever—he had wanted us to feel that we could always reach him. However frail his body, his mind seemed always alert and his energies engaged.

I now wonder whether it was a burden to him in his last years to be dealing with my writings when he was undergoing what amounted to extreme deprivation—whether I was treating him as if he were the Mr. Shawn inside my head, the man I had met when he was fifty-two years old, rather than the man of our Oak Room meetings, who wore two hearing aids and whose voice was fast fading away. Even when he had just had a cataract operation, in October, 1987, and now, during the months that were clearly leading up to his death, I often approached him as if nothing had changed. Yet I know that he would have been distressed if I had ceased to do so. However infirm, he always liked being wanted.

Mr. Shawn died on December 8, 1992, at the age of eighty-five—strangely, forty-one years to the day after Ross died. It had been Mr. Shawn's expressed wish that he be cremated and that there would be no funeral or memorial service of any kind. Years later, Allen told me that, although he knew that his father wouldn't have wanted it, he hadn't been able to resist reading a poem at the time of the cremation.

I asked him what it was.

He hesitated. The cremation had been private, with only Cecille, Wallace, Allen, and Jamaica present. But then he told me that it was John Donne's "A Valediction: Forbidding Mourning," which begins:

> As virtuous men pass mildly away,
> And whisper to their souls, to go,
> Whilst some of their sad friends do say,
> The breath goes now, and some say, no:
>
> So let us melt, and make no noise,
> No tear-floods, nor sigh-tempests move,
> 'Twere profanation of our joys
> To tell the laity our love.

AS LONG AS people know how to read, they can always turn to any of the issues of the magazine that came out under Mr. Shawn's editorship—these issues have attained the status of archives—and they will sense the care with which he saw to it that every word was properly written and every line correctly drawn. Even the precise color of *The New Yorker* logo every week was looked at and pondered over. Nothing was done for any reason other than that of striving for excellence. As Mr Shawn had said, "falling short of perfection is a process that just never stops."

An evening or two after he died, people spontaneously gathered at the Century club for a drink. But the occasion struck me as jarring and incongruous, a little like the advertisements surrounding his magazine's text. Even the magazine did not know how to bid him farewell. It devoted a whole feature to eulogizing him, and many of us contributed to it. But E. B. White, in his hastily composed obituary of Ross for Comment, in 1951, captured more of Ross than all of us, working together, could capture of Mr. Shawn. Indeed, William Shawn remained as elusive in death as he had been in life. Sometimes I wonder whether I knew him at all. He hardly ever talked about himself, always turning the conversation to the interests and concerns of the other person. But it is Mr. Shawn, whether the aging Mr. Shawn or the Mr. Shawn inside my head, who forms and animates my memory—and, indeed, this book.